Ireland Through the Looking-Glass

Flann O'Brien, Myles na gCopaleen and
Irish cultural debate

Ireland Through the Looking-Glass

Flann O'Brien, Myles na gCopaleen
and Irish cultural debate

CAROL TAAFFE

CORK UNIVERSITY PRESS

First published in 2008 by
Cork University Press
Youngline Industrial Estate
Pouladuff Road, Togher
Cork, Ireland

British Library Cataloguing in Publication Data.
A CIP catalogue record for this book is available from the British Library

ISBN-13: 978-1-85918-442-4

The author has asserted her moral rights in this work.

Typeset by Tower Books, Ballincollig, Co. Cork
Printed by Gutenberg Press, Malta

www.corkuniversitypress.com

Contents

Acknowledgements

Firstly, I must thank John Nash who supervised the PhD thesis on which this book is based. His excellent guidance over the years was indispensable, as was his sharp eye for nonsense. All later additions in that vein are my own. I am very grateful too for the comments of Declan Kiberd and the help of Terence Brown at a later stage. The research for this book was made possible by a postgraduate scholarship and a post-doctoral fellowship granted by the Irish Research Council for the Humanities and Social Sciences.

All extracts from Brian O'Nolan's work and correspondence are reproduced with the kind permission of the Brian O'Nolan Estate. Quotations from Brian O'Nolan's papers are courtesy of the John J. Burns Library, Boston College, the Special Collections Research Center, Morris Library, Southern Illinois University Carbondale, and the Harry Ransom Humanities Research Center, the University of Texas at Austin. Material from the papers of Timothy O'Keeffe and Niall Montgomery is reproduced with the permission of Mrs Mimi O'Keeffe and the McFarlin Library, University of Tulsa, and courtesy of the Montgomery family and the National Library of Ireland. I would like to thank the staff of these libraries for their help and efficiency, and especially the staff of the Library in Trinity College Dublin. Sections of chapters two and four were first published in an earlier form in the *Irish University Review*, vol. 34, no. 2 (Autumn/Winter 2004), 247–260 and the *Canadian Journal of Irish Studies*, vol. 32, no. 2 (Autumn 2006), 27–33.

Many people have helped this long project, usually in ways they cannot suspect. I am grateful for the work of Tom Dunne, Sarah Watson and Catherine Coughlan in Cork University Press, and to Cork's anonymous readers for their suggestions. Thanks also to Anthony Cronin, Mary English and Dave McHugh for generously giving their time on Flann O'Brien-related business. I am indebted to Ronan Crowley and Christine O'Neill for drawing my attention to the Niall Montgomery Collection.

Thanks especially to my brother, Francis and to Amanda Webb for putting up with all the last-minute demands I kept making of them from strange parts of the globe. The mob in and around Wilton Place also helped in their own inimitable way, mostly by refusing to listen to any talk of Flann O'Brien after the second year or so. And thanks to my colleagues in TCD and elsewhere, particularly Elizabeth Hsinyin Lee, for listening to it for far longer.

My greatest debts are to my parents, Frank and Breege Taaffe, to whom this book is dedicated. It was in the Taaffe household that someone first demanded to know why I had never heard of *Cruiskeen Lawn* and that Flann O'Brien, or did I ever open a book at all? The result is partly their fault.

Textual Note

The following abbreviations are used throughout:

ASTB Flann O'Brien. *At Swim-Two-Birds*. London: Penguin, 1939, 2000.

TP   Flann O'Brien. *The Third Policeman*. London: Flamingo, 1967, 1993.

CL   Myles na gCopaleen, 'Cruiskeen Lawn', *The Irish Times*.

ABB   Myles na gCopaleen. *An Béal Bocht*. Cork: Mercier, 1941, 1999.

HL   Flann O'Brien. *The Hard Life*. London: Scribner, 1961, 2003.

DA   Flann O'Brien. *The Dalkey Archive*. London: Flamingo, 1964, 1993.

BM   Myles na Gopaleen (Flann O'Brien). *The Best of Myles*, Kevin O'Nolan (ed.) London: Picador, 1968, 1977.

PM   Flann O'Brien. *The Poor Mouth*, Patrick C. Power (trans.). Illinois: Dalkey Archive Press, 1973, 1996.

SP   Flann O'Brien. *Stories and Plays*. London: Hart-Davis, MacGibbon, 1973.

FC   Flann O'Brien. *Further Cuttings from Cruiskeen Lawn*, Kevin O'Nolan (ed.). Illinois: Dalkey Archive Press, 1976, 2000.

HD   Flann O'Brien (Myles na Gopaleen). *The Hair of the Dogma*, Kevin O'Nolan (ed.). London: Paladin, 1977, 1989.

MBM   Flann O'Brien (Myles na Gopaleen). *Myles Before Myles*, John Wyse Jackson (ed.). London: Grafton, 1988.

IP   Flann O'Brien (Myles na gCopaleen). *Rhapsody in Stephen's Green: The Insect Play*, Robert Tracy (ed.). Dublin: Lilliput, 1994.

FW   Flann O'Brien. *Flann O'Brien at War: Myles na gCopaleen 1940-1945*, John Wyse Jackson (ed.). London: Duckworth, 1999.

Introduction

> We are merely carrying out, with footnotes and unnecessary
> additions, the whim or fancy or creative vision of a great novelist.[1]

Such topsy-turveydom seems properly to belong to the world of Flann
O'Brien but the phrase is Oscar Wilde's. Ironically, his argument in 'The
Decay of Lying' that it is life which imitates art (and not the other way
round) incongruously gave Stephen Dedalus the mimetic image of Irish
art as the 'cracked lookingglass of a servant'.[2] But the comic fiction and
journalism which Joyce's unwilling successor, Brian O'Nolan, wrote at his
peak in the 1930s and 1940s carefully evades the post-colonial obsession
with reflecting a nation back to itself. Instead, it presents its reader with
a much stranger country on the other side of the looking-glass – a comic
vision of an independent Ireland which has become estranged to itself,
and yet which has all the uncanny familiarity of Lewis Carroll's
Wonderland. Where contemporary Irish fiction writers tended to imitate
the Joyce they found in *Dubliners*, who chastised his readers with faithful
glimpses of themselves in 'my nicely polished looking-glass',[3] O'Nolan's
work was more characteristically based on the principle of the 'self-
evident sham' (ASTB, 25) which in his eyes encompassed much of the
culture of the young state. Though in the post-independence years many
were still engaged in the long business of inventing Ireland, the country
which emerges from his alienated comic vision, like the Gaeltacht of *An
Béal Bocht*, betrays his astute awareness of the prescriptive nature of such
enterprises. His long-running *Irish Times* column, *Cruiskeen Lawn*, may
have circled well-worn ground – satirising the language revival, the
scandal of censorship and perennial worries about national identity – but
it also attended to the very nature of cultural debate itself, to its rhetoric,
its repetitiveness and its endless capacity for self-caricature. Wilde
asserted that to 'pass from the art of a time to the time itself is the great
mistake that all historians make',[4] but while O'Nolan's artful comedy
partly developed in opposition to its time (as Wilde would recommend) it

1

was also constantly in creative friction with it. The comic world of Flann O'Brien and Myles na gCopaleen exposes a nonsensical country that is only on the other side of the looking-glass, and this book argues that O'Nolan's self-reflexive preoccupation with the nature of art and the persona of the artist betrays a crisis of identity ultimately rooted in the cultural dynamics of post-independence Ireland.

The basic premise of this study of O'Nolan's fiction, drama and journalism is to explore how his comic writing shaped, and was shaped by, contemporary Irish cultural politics. While his experimental fiction has in the past attracted most critical attention, here the distinction between the humorous columnist and the experimental novelist is narrowed. Attending to the various comic modes O'Nolan exploited as well as the effect of his bilingualism (his work being informed as much by the Gaelic Revival as it was by Joycean modernism) reveals a writer whose idiosyncratic humour was at once in conflict with, and wholly indebted to, the charged cultural debates of the Irish Free State and its successor. O'Nolan was essentially a reactive writer, and the nuances of his humour invite close attention both to the intellectual environment which informed it and to the ambivalent relationship between the humorist and his readership. Unmooring his work from its historical context obscures the degree to which his uneasy dissatisfaction with the status quo was complicated by a lingering sympathy for many of the tenets of the new State. The experimental comic was also a senior civil servant, and O'Nolan had much invested in the new Ireland which many of his contemporaries excoriated – indeed in some senses he embodied the very values that he mocked. With analysis of comic genres and modes, as well as the conflicting literary and cultural contexts informing his humour, this book does not assume an inherent subversiveness in his comic writing. Rather, it maintains that his brash literary experiments have often masked the degree to which his humour was complicit with the social and cultural values of contemporary Ireland.

In doing so, it focuses predominantly on the most successful and productive period of O'Nolan's career, from his earliest (Irish-language) publications in *The Irish Press* to the first months of the post-war *Cruiskeen Lawn*, and ending with a retrospective on his late novels. Yet he began and ended his career as a comic journalist, and what remains as true of the novels as of the journalism is the importance of a sense of audience throughout his work. Where *At Swim-Two-Birds* was devised as an in-joke for a literary coterie in 1930s UCD, *Cruiskeen Lawn* conducted a similarly intimate dialogue with the readers of *The Irish Times*. O'Nolan's gradual progression from writing exclusively in Irish, to a period of bilingualism and then abandonment of the language is an underestimated shift in his career that itself underscores the importance of reception to the humorist. His recurrent preoccupation with the persona and role of the author was as much shaped by the difficult position of the Irish writer in the 1930s and 1940s as it was by literary modernism. The draconian censorship legislation instituted in 1929 effectively marginalised the writer as a dubious, presumably subversive, character. Yet the lingering ethos of cultural nationalism implied that writers (and other artists) could or should occupy an instrumental role in social and political life. The dissident, political character of *The Bell* might be seen as the natural consequence of this contradiction, but O'Nolan depicted its contributors as precious characters in paranoiac retreat from the Plain People of Ireland. Similarly, his ambivalent response to Joyce – though usually caricatured as a debilitating anxiety of influence – interestingly seems to hinge on the chasm which Joyce exposed between the modernist artist and the 'plain reader' (a complaint particularly obvious in Mylesian attacks on the Joyce industry). Such criticism exposes the extent to which he was unwittingly influenced by the orthodoxies of his day; disdainful of modernism's elitism, he was also nevertheless ambivalent in his attitude to the populism extolled by Gaelic Revivalists and other cultural nationalists. Curiously, like Seán O'Faoláin's ambition that *The Bell* should move in the common stream of life, Myles na gCopaleen's sneer at the 'keltured idiocated'[5] Dublin which he entertained in *The Irish Times* carries a confused echo of their common nemesis, Daniel Corkery. O'Nolan's ambiguous relationship to the Plain People of Ireland, his status as experimental novelist and newspaper columnist, Irish-language writer and anti-revivalist, as well as his literary collaborations (recognised and otherwise) reveal him to be a writer who uniquely illuminates the conflicting loyalties of his generation in the new State.

Each of the following chapters focuses on a different aspect of O'Nolan's multi-faceted career, broadly encompassing his development from an eccentric humorist to a more dour cultural critic. In his early self-invention as Flann and Myles (and his collaborative literary enterprises), O'Nolan was already playing the literary game at one remove, exploiting and undermining the cult of personality in a post-revival and post-Joycean culture. Yet while *At Swim-Two-Birds* is in part a brilliant fantasia on contemporary literary debates, its debts to the intellectual and cultural ethos of UCD in the early 1930s also expose his dependence on a receptive local audience, and its attending constraints. *The Third Policeman*, on the other hand, famously found no readership at all in his lifetime. Ironically, its bleak form of nonsense (obviously less culturally specific than *At Swim*'s) ultimately had a liberating effect on O'Nolan's later reputation. Yet this was at the cost, perhaps, of a recognition of the cultural underpinnings of its wartime humour and the implications of its estranged vision of Ireland. The novel's surreal take on faith and physics is strangely balanced by an orthodox deference to unfathomable mysteries, and this conflicted irony is again visible in O'Nolan's response to the Gaelic revival in *An Béal Bocht* and the early *Cruiskeen Lawn*. The first decade of the celebrated *Irish Times* column brought more consistency as he gradually adopted the role of a cultural critic, but with it also came the slow calcification of his comic persona. This book finishes at two endpoints in his career: his unsuccessful experiments with drama in 1943 and his return to the novel form in the 1960s with *The Hard Life* and *The Dalkey Archive*. As the later work most starkly demonstrates, comedy may have the capacity to be subversive, but it is also adept at expressing and enforcing conformity. Exploring the links between comedy and culture – what O'Nolan's blend of parody, satire and surreal humour owed to the peculiar climate of mid-twentieth-century Ireland – reveals the humorist's curiously ambivalent response to post-independence Irish culture, and particularly to the position of the writer within it.

1

The cult of the author:
Brian, Flann and Myles

'I considered it desirable that he should know nothing about me but it was even better if he knew several things which were quite wrong' (*TP*, 59).

Critics have produced many versions of Flann O'Brien, but only long after Brian O'Nolan himself had started the business of multiplying his literary identities. Now, alongside Brian Ó Nualláin, Flann O'Brien, Myles na gCopaleen, George Knowall, John James Doe, Matt Duffy, Count O'Blather, Brother Barnabas, and possibly Seán Ó Longáin, a host of new personalities has developed.[1] Since his death on April Fool's Day 1966, Brian O'Nolan has been reincarnated as a cult author, as the writer's writer whose characters migrate to other fictions, as a surreal humorist who inspired the writers of the ABC television drama, *Lost*, and – in final imitation of Joyce – as the quintessential Dubliner, with a city-wide project urging its citizens to read *At Swim-Two-Birds* in summer 2006. But chief among his many incarnations have remained the irascible Myles of Dublin lore and his more academic counterpart, the post-modernist Flann O'Brien. Keith Hopper's study, which has been the most influential in casting O'Nolan in this image, provocatively argued in 1995 that the critical reception of his work had been largely split between an indigenous school of criticism, 'invariably folksy and anecdotal, and often lacking in critical acumen'[2] and that of international post-structuralists who 'locate O'Brien's work within an experimental tradition of avant-garde fiction, [and] their critiques are invariably (and deliberately) decontextualised'.[3] While the division was slightly opportunistic – in the absence of many book-length studies, Hopper cited brief references in overviews of post-modernist fiction, rather than more varied journal articles on his work – the stark contrast he drew between Irish and international criticism was instructive.[4] For the Irish reader, the Mylesian legend is still as unavoidable as it is for the Dublin pub-goer, who literally encounters Myles (or his image) in most of O'Nolan's past haunts. It is unsurprising that this lingering presence should have left its mark on the earliest Irish critical publications, which Hopper criticised for mystifying 'the cult of the author'.[5] However, these came from friends and colleagues whose reminiscences were evidently intended to facilitate O'Nolan's growing reputation, rather than provide critical responses in themselves (and in doing so, they interestingly followed a precedent set by Joyce criticism).[6] A more fruitful aspect of Irish criticism in this period was the burgeoning interest in O'Nolan's relationship to the Irish language and Gaelic literature, subjects which were first explored in the 1980s.[7] Tending to focus on the more topical and satirical aspects of his writing, these brought critical debate on his work into the arena of Irish cultural politics, where it has largely remained since the late 1990s. As with Hopper's 'tribal retrieval'[8] of O'Nolan as a post-modernist in 1995, the most recent tendency in criticism (originating in Ireland or otherwise) has been to consciously merge formalist and cultural approaches to his fiction. Now, more than ten years on from Hopper's seminal study, the critical landscape can no longer be broadly split between folksy anecdotes and a deracinated post-structuralism. In the first years of the twenty-first century, Brian O'Nolan has been most commonly reinvented as a post-modernist, post-colonial, Menippean satirist.[9]

This study adopts a more historical approach, examining what O'Nolan's varying blend of parody, satire and surreal humour owed to the peculiar cultural climate of mid-twentieth-century Ireland. In doing so, it combines cultural and historical analysis of his work with attention to its various comic genres and modes. While his innovative fiction has deservedly earned him an international reputation, it is less often seriously considered that this was accompanied – and outspanned – by a unique career as a humorous columnist, one which owed a great deal of its character to the claustrophobia of Emergency Dublin. It is no accident that in the early 1940s Myles na gCopaleen was busily undermining all absurd authority (including his own) in *Cruiskeen Lawn*, just as Seán O'Faoláin and *The Bell* writers were reviving the idea of the writer as a public intellectual. And the metafictional involutions of his early fiction were matched, if not surpassed, by his similarly unconventional exploits in *The Irish Times*. This was a career poised between the work of an experimental novelist and a popular newspaper columnist, between the aggressive formalism of literary modernism and the provincialism of Irish cultural debate, between English- and Irish-language literary traditions, but which trespassed all such categories. Hopper's depiction of a critical terrain divided between cosy appreciations of the legendary Myles and an impeccably academic post-structuralism could easily have been inspired by O'Nolan's work itself. Such a contradiction is latent in *At Swim-Two-Birds*, a novel whose semi-autobiographical passages formed an extended in-joke for O'Nolan's cohorts in UCD, and which derides literary self-indulgence, particularly that of modernist writers. At the same time, its student narrator's pedantry liberates himself (and his readers) from literary convention and everyday tedium, reinventing the novel as a 'self-evident sham' (*ASTB*, 25) and releasing himself and his friends into a literary fantasy. While on one level, the novel might be cosy, insular and anti-intellectual, it nevertheless delights in its own cleverness and in the intoxication of turning fiction loose on fiction. *Cruiskeen Lawn* displays similar characteristics: its humour exploited an intimate relationship with its *Irish Times* readership, but the column also betrayed an entirely introverted preoccupation with language and logic. Throughout O'Nolan's fiction and journalism, the showman and the scholar exist side-by-side. The contradiction is writ large in *Cruiskeen Lawn* and has probably contributed to the fact that only one extended study of the column, Keith Donohue's *The Irish Anatomist*, has been published over the last forty years. Admittedly, the neglect is also a matter of expediency – few would care to plough through its twenty-six year run, much of it highly variable in quality. But its reputation has also suffered from the suspicion that a daily newspaper column is of dubious literary value, as if the garrulous showmanship of Myles na gCopaleen were responsible for the demise of the more discriminating Flann O'Brien. Hugh Kenner's lament for a lost brilliance has sounded the characteristic note: 'Was it the drink was his ruin, or was it the column? For ruin is the word'.[10] Yet the strange course of O'Nolan's career reflects – even more than his acclaimed parodic novels – the challenge his work presents to customary notions of authorship, to the integrity of the work of art and to ideas of what constitutes 'literature' itself.

As Stephen Young points out, *Cruiskeen Lawn* exploits the same strengths as the fiction, 'systems of competing voices, or styles, in patterns of maximum digressiveness',[11] and arguably its ephemeral and episodic nature was more congenial to O'Nolan's talent for improvisation than the extended effort needed to produce novels. While critics have referred to the demands of his newspaper work and the temptation to play up to readers with a measure of distaste, O'Nolan was a writer who evidently benefited from a responsive readership, as can be seen from his reaction to the commercial failure of *At Swim* and the rejection of *The Third Policeman*.[12] Jack White, a colleague in *The Irish Times*, contended that Myles productively exploited a relationship with his readers which was far more intimate than that available to any novelist: 'In effect he was able to keep up a dialogue with his audience, absorbing the reactions into the next work to be produced.'[13] However, Anthony Cronin presents this as a disabling influence:

> ... [Myles] gradually came to represent, even for his most fervent admirers, the quintessential Dublin intellectual, combining the wit and brilliance which they liked to think of as characteristic with the acerbic, denigratory outlook which was also common ... The fate of many licensed jesters had overtaken Myles. He had become his admirers and they him, so that it was sometimes difficult to distinguish one from the other.[14]

Admittedly, *Cruiskeen Lawn* probably exacerbated O'Nolan's showman tendencies, encouraging him to exploit the posture of the plain man ensconced in *The Irish Times* who scorned artists, 'corduroys' and all their narcissistic affairs (such as the campaign against literary censorship). But long before O'Nolan became the 'licensed jester' of *The Irish Times* reading intelligentsia, *At Swim* and *The Third Policeman* betrayed similar preoccupations. Both novels challenge casual distinctions between high and low culture; *At Swim*'s indiscriminate parodies contrive to reinvent the experimental modernist novel as a 'belly-laugh',[15] while *The Third Policeman* is a murder mystery re-written as an epistemological thriller. They may be auto-critical metafictions, but they are also highly sceptical of scholarship and similarly earnest intellectual pursuits. An American reviewer of the 1951 edition of *At Swim* identified an unusual difficulty which the book presents to its critics:

> ... "At Swim-Two-Birds" is neither a profound dissection of the human enigma nor a sophomoric attempt to impress through obscurity. It is simply a tremendously effective satire on Irish literature, a very funny book at a high literate level ...
> Don't take it too seriously, and "At Swim-Two-Birds" really is a masterpiece, but a masterpiece of comedy, not of Joycean depth.[16]

The difficulty is to divine *how* to read *At Swim* as 'a masterpiece of comedy'. As a highly literate comedy it invites a literate response, but the text so thoroughly usurps and travesties the work of the critic that to offer this response seems to miss the point. (In one sense, it should have been entirely predictable that the author of *At Swim-Two-Birds* and *The Third Policeman* would, in later years, become obsessed with the evils of the growing Joyce industry.) Any reader familiar with *Cruiskeen Lawn*'s diatribes against scholars and exegetes might well baulk at the incorporation of Myles into an academic framework.[17] Ironically, the preoccupations of his counterpart, Flann O'Brien, reveal a writer as enamoured of the nuts and bolts of fiction as any of the Harvard scholars he derided. In Brian

O'Nolan, the plain man meets the literary narcissist, and criticism of his work is forced to come to terms with this paradox.

As much as O'Nolan's fiction and journalism challenge a high modernist concept of literature for a cultural elite, his magpie literary personalities undermine the accompanying image of the lone genius. Myles often presented himself as a refined man of letters, but in his private correspondence O'Nolan just as often imagined himself as a commercial writer, a newspaper hack. While Joyce was a recurrent obsession throughout his career, so too was the fortune earned by the author of *Gone With the Wind*. And indeed the two images of the writer were not mutually exclusive; O'Nolan's reading of modernism was prescient in bypassing the image of a disinterested artistry free from the world of commerce, particularly in his scorn for the 'limited edition ramp'.[18] Though Hopper notes that *At Swim* heralded the death of the 'author-god' long before Roland Barthes conceived the notion,[19] O'Nolan also nurtured a kind of personal celebrity in the guise of Myles na gCopaleen. Long before Bord Fáilte, the Irish tourist board, posthumously elevated him into the pantheon of Dublin literary characters, he was happily commodifying his alter ego, even allowing Myles to appear in advertisements for Odearest mattresses.[20] The self-reflexive nature of his fiction undeniably extended to his presentation of himself as author (the multivalent Myles being the authorial persona on stilts), yet arguably the way in which O'Nolan fetishised the idea of the author betrays how indebted his outlook was to 1930s literary Dublin. Conscious manipulation of the author's persona was hardly unusual in a culture which had already played host to Yeats, Joyce, Moore and Gogarty, and O'Nolan's self-reflexive habits produced a myriad of authorial personae in place of the personality cults accompanying most successful Irish writers. Despite the credence given to his assertion in 1964 that 'the compartmentation of personality for the purpose of literary utterance ensures that the fundamental individual will not be credited with a certain way of thinking, fixed attitudes, irreversable [sic] technique of expression',[21] the distinction between Flann, Myles and plain Brian O'Nolan was his least successful literary illusion. The brilliant polymath that provided O'Nolan with a stock comic character all through his writing career, from Brother Barnabas to Myles na gCopaleen, eventually migrated to fuel the legend of Brian O'Nolan himself, and lost most of its irony in the process.

It is curious that posthumous biographical sketches of Myles/O'Nolan quickly began to read like cliché, given his own campaign against the form. In literary memoirs of the 1950s, the standard unholy trinity in Irish literature, Joyce, Beckett and Flann O'Brien, acquires a less sober counterpart in Kavanagh, Behan and Myles na gCopaleen.

John Ryan, editor of *Envoy* and proprietor of the Bailey, fixed the standard thumbnail portrait of O'Nolan as a frustrated, hard-drinking civil servant in his reminiscences: 'Myles had reached the zenith of his powers while still a student of University College. His life, thereafter, was a diminuendo.'[22] His life thereafter, of course, comprised his entire literary career. The image was not contradicted in *Dead As Doornails*, in which Anthony Cronin presented a more nuanced picture of brilliance stultified (and even policed) by its environment, an assessment repeated in his later biography:

> Brian became somehow fixed at a time of brilliant promise and pyrotechnical display . . . transplanted from the hothouse confines of UCD to the equally pernicious atmosphere of intimately acquainted Dublin. His humour became the currency of its denizens, the mode of his column their manner of response . . . He existed in and through the response and understanding of his audience.[23]

Ironically, in setting the scene for what is represented as a frustrated literary career, these reminiscences inadvertently employ the kind of shorthand characterisation that would be exploited satirically in *Cruiskeen Lawn*. Their Dublin is a grim city, populated by pious hysterics and state functionaries, one that is wholly insulated from European culture and over-endowed with frustrated artists furiously drowning their sorrows. *Dubliners* might echo through such representations of intellectual life in the city, but O'Nolan was highly aware of the interplay between fiction and life that produces the necessary half-truth, and he wisely recognised the usefulness of the well-placed cliché. 'Myles na gCopaleen' himself rested on a wealth of literary convention, being a strangely erudite stage-Irishman descended from Gerald Griffin's *The Collegians* by way of a more sentimental namesake in Boucicault's *The Colleen Bawn*. By the time the first biography of O'Nolan was published in 1987, this stereotyping had lost all its playfulness. Brian O'Nolan seemed to have acquired the flimsy proportions of a *Cruiskeen Lawn* 'Bore' or 'the Brother'; its first chapter announced him as 'A Dublin Character'.[24]

To some degree, in popular terms (as far as this can be gauged), he has remained 'the Dublin Character'. In the early 1960s *Cruiskeen Lawn* ran a short series on 'The True Biography of Myles na Gopaleen', a fantastic account of a life of myriad achievements that followed the polymathic pattern set by *Comhthrom Féinne*'s Brother Barnabas thirty years earlier.[25] An equally fanciful Mylesian character still resurfaces in *The Irish Times*, though now the tall tales have turned into anecdotes, and art masquerades as life. The stories which have proliferated about Brian O'Nolan over the last forty years, generally equipped with a punning punchline, echo the scurrilous activities of Sir Myles na gCopaleen (the da) or the contrived adventures of Keats and Chapman. A typical tale concerns a parliamentary secretary, Brendan Corish, returning from lunch one day to find an individual spilled across the steps of the Customs House. He found himself helping up a drunken O'Nolan, who yet had the wit to mutter 'Corish Iompar Éireann'.[26] The other guise in which Myles finds himself resurrected is as a guardian of standards in public life, the pose he adopted in the later years of *Cruiskeen Lawn*. In 2001, one of the many controversies attending the Flood Tribunal in Dublin prompted one political correspondent to find a contemporary equivalent to Myles's nickname for the Dáil, a 'magisterium of chancers' (the answer was provided by one individual's remark that the politicians who had solicited money from him 'made the Mafia look like a crowd of monks').[27] Though the artful wit captured in the anecdotes was a characteristic of the Mylesian persona from its very beginning, the reputation for political baiting and drunken mishaps was really only acquired in the 1950s and 1960s.[28] In the early 1940s, Myles na gCopaleen had a somewhat more eccentric image, one deriving entirely from the writing itself.

It is a measure of the success that O'Nolan had accrued in the first years of *Cruiskeen Lawn* that the first profiles of Myles na gCopaleen were published in 1943; all looked back over O'Nolan's entire career to date. It was, in fact, the year in which he was most in the public eye. *At Swim-Two-Birds* and *An Béal Bocht* were behind him; he had two plays produced in Dublin that spring, one of which was subsequently published by Cahill, along with an anthology of *Cruiskeen Lawn*. Neither of the plays was well received and they performed relatively poorly at the box office, compounding the failure of *The Third Policeman*. In the spring and summer he served as secretary to a tribunal on a fire in a Poor Clares' orphanage in Cavan; the report it published in September exonerated the order from responsibility for the deaths of thirty-five children unable to escape the building. As his wife attested:

> In later years . . . [he] would aver to the subject of the Cavan fire, and his memories of the event never faded. In its combination of indifference, pettiness and lack of charity, the disaster encapsulated much of what he felt was wrong in the Ireland of his day.[29]

Keith Donohue argues that all these events combined to create a significant change in *Cruiskeen Lawn* in 1943, the year when the Irish language columns dropped out of sight and its character became increasingly polemical and satirical.[30] Whether it is a matter of coincidence or not, around the same time O'Nolan was first publicly identified with Myles na gCopaleen. At that stage, Myles's celebrity was well established; there was no question of 'Flann O'Brien' being revived to sell the plays O'Nolan was producing in the Abbey and the Gaiety that year. Myles even made a unique guest appearance at the first night of *Faustus Kelly*:

> ... there were many enthusiastic calls for the author at the final curtain. These were answered by a gentleman, dressed as the traditional stage Irishman with pipe, caubeen and cutaway coat who did a little bit of a jig and then silently vanished.[31]

Tempting as it is to imagine O'Nolan aping the stage Irishman on the boards of the Abbey itself, the appearance was by a company actor. The stunt was evidently a means of protecting O'Nolan's identity, or at least of not rubbing his superiors' noses in the fact that a civil servant in the Department of Local Government and Public Health was satirising local councillors on the stage of the national theatre. However, his flimsy cover was blown three months later in a profile written by the American journalist, Richard Watts, for the *New York Herald Tribune*. A press attaché in Dublin, Watts had reviewed *Faustus Kelly* for *The Bell* and reported back to the American public that a young civil servant, Brian O'Nolan, was the 'most interesting new writing talent' he had encountered in Dublin.[32] Little harm to O'Nolan to have his fame spread far and wide in New York, but *The Irish Times* marked the recognition given to their columnist by replicating a large portion of Watts's article, including the identification of O'Nolan with Flann and Myles.[33] Perhaps the public confirmation of this badly-kept secret (he had already been identified with Flann on the dust-jacket of *At Swim-Two-Birds*) encouraged O'Nolan belatedly to assume some measure of the authorial responsibility he had avoided in *At Swim* and replace his trademark nonsense with the tones of the outraged citizen. At any rate, Myles's earlier Abbey appearance as a farcical stage Irishman, a postscript to a political satire closely related to his day-job, brought into dramatic relief diverging aspects of the Mylesian persona.

However, it is interesting that Watts's sketch of *Cruiskeen Lawn* shows that at the time, the column was primarily regarded as an erudite, literary endeavour, rather than a cutting satire. It also presents the column's author in a manner quite distinct from the posthumous Mylesian legend:

> His is a column devoted to magnificently laborious literary puns, remarkable parodies of De Quincey and others, fanciful literary anecdotes, an erudite study of clichés that sounds like the result of a collaboration between Frank Sullivan and the faculties of Trinity College and the National University, scornful dissection of the literal meaning of high-flown literary phraseology and a general air of shameless irony and high spirits.[34]

Watts's article captures the peculiar intellectual dignity that was as important to the Mylesian comic persona as the tailcoat and cigar were to
Groucho Marx. A slightly different picture emerges from an interview
that O'Nolan gave to Stanford Lee Cooper of *Time* magazine the following summer, when his 'shameless irony and high spirits' were
evidently in full force. Though the article was not published until August,
perhaps the prospect of his immortalisation was the inspiration for Myles
to comment in May that:

> It only occurred to me the other day that I will have biographers.
> Probably Hone will do me first and then there will be all sorts of
> English persons writing books 'interpreting' me, describing the beau-
> tiful women who influenced my 'life', trying to put my work in its
> true and prominent place against the general background of
> mankind, and no doubt seeking to romanticise what is essentially an
> austere and chastened character, saddened as it has been by the con-
> templation of human folly.[35]

When the *Time* profile appeared, it came complete with the mysterious
beautiful woman (O'Nolan's obscure and deceased wife of 1933, Clara
Ungerland, 'blond, violin-playing daughter of a Cologne basket weaver')[36]
and a tale of a dramatic attack on the author in a German beer-cellar for
disparaging the name of Hitler. Otherwise, the image which O'Nolan (or
Cooper) presented was deliberately humdrum. The author was a 'consci-
entious, hard-working civil servant . . . busy with matters of state', who
avoided 'the metropolitan arty crowd' in favour of 'the talk at the tough
bars and quayside pubs' (perhaps a slight exaggeration on someone's part,
the Scotch House being a favourite of many civil servants). O'Nolan, a
prodigious chess player, 'writes so easily that he grows bored with it',
which explains the abrupt conclusion of *At Swim-Two-Birds*.[37] As the presence of Clara Ungerland testifies, it is dangerous to take any of this too
seriously, but it is an interesting portrait of O'Nolan as a self-professed
plain man, a deliberate outsider in literary Dublin.

The first domestic profile of Myles, published in *The Bell* in 1946,
came to quite the opposite conclusion. Whatever bravura O'Nolan had
displayed to his American interviewer, his *Bell* profiler Thomas Hogan
(aka Thomas Woods, a fellow civil servant) was not convinced by the
broadsides against 'corduroys' and their ilk in *Cruiskeen Lawn*, or any
other swagger of intellectual independence. Presciently, in 1946 he was
already writing that Myles na gCopaleen's best days were behind him,
unconsciously setting the tone for the critical work that would follow:

> . . . [Myles] shows clearly the influence of his environment – the den-
> igratory atmosphere of certain back-rooms inhabited by the native

'highbrows' is found in his work . . . His growth is thwarted by the debility characteristic of the kind of post-coitum depression of a city that did once produce something. Myles is our type – he is the active embodiment of Dublin's, and Ireland's, destructive element. His best work, *At Swim-Two-Birds*, is far behind him, and the line of his present work [*Cruiskeen Lawn*] is brilliant but futile.[38]

Far from O'Nolan's self-portrait as the caustic outsider, he was damned as a typical example of the Dublin intellectual, and of the species at its worst. Hogan's judgement, harsh as it was, would be echoed over forty years later in Anthony Cronin's biography. The post-Joycean environment (this 'post-coitum depression') certainly left its mark on O'Nolan's writing, but arguably he exploited a more nuanced relationship with his audience than these readings allow. Hogan may have been correct to observe that 'Myles is our type', but given the ironies of the Mylesian persona, this is not necessarily a reliable diagnosis. It is telling that O'Nolan's interview for *Time* resulted in a crafty compilation of the biographical clichés such profiles used to 'explain' an author's work (the mysterious beautiful woman, for one), along with nods to the effortless and eccentric brilliance that was part of the Mylesian mystique. Such a self-conscious dialogue with form – in this case the critical biography – was as much a part of *Cruiskeen Lawn* as it was of the novels. One of the products of this self-reflexiveness in *At Swim* is a sense of authorship as a collaborative effort, between the storyteller and his audience, between the author and the other authors he is merrily plagiarising. Myles na gCopaleen was created in the same fashion. It is telling that he once queried regarding Joyce: 'Did he seek to evolve for himself, chiefly by talking in strict confidence to stooges, mostly American, a mythical personality? Did . . . (*pardon me while I swallow this yellow capsule!*) . . . did . . . James Joyce ever exist?'[39] While he regularly accused Joyce of encouraging a cultish reputation, he was no innocent in the matter himself; Myles was Brian O'Nolan's mythic personality, albeit one who eventually became indistinguishable from his author.

A portrait of the artist as a young Joycean

Of course, in most matters of literary creation (of mythic alter egos or otherwise) O'Nolan bashfully followed the example of James Joyce. At least, such is his critical reputation. If the association with Joyce was an irritant in his lifetime, it has since become a dominating (and sometimes domineering) theme of his critical reception.[40] The irony is that on emerging as a writer in the late 1930s, O'Nolan confronted the problem of Joyce as deliberately as most of his Irish contemporaries avoided it, and in doing so he found a powerful foil against which to define his own priorities as a writer. Yet the sub-Joycean label stuck, partly bolstered by Myles's increasingly caustic comments on that other writer in later years. But in this case, the Mylesian mystique is a little misleading. Brian O'Nolan was not the only contributor to *Cruiskeen Lawn*; like any long-running columnist he had his stand-ins, chiefly Niall Montgomery, whose contribution to *The Irish Times* column was much greater than has been acknowledged. Of all the *Cruiskeen Lawn* columns on the subject of James Joyce, it is likely that the majority were written by him: a professional architect, part-time Joyce scholar and sometime scourge of a burgeoning critical industry.[41] His contribution to the column is dealt with more fully in chapter five, yet if the Mylesian preoccupation with Joyce was not wholly – or even mainly – O'Nolan's, the confusion was entirely plausible. His debut novel, *At Swim-Two-Birds*, of course selectively parodies both *A Portrait of the Artist as a Young Man* and *Ulysses*, though he was already protesting in 1939 that the novel had 'nothing in the world to do with James Joyce'.[42] Whether or not he was to be believed, reviewers were understandably predisposed to think otherwise. Seán O'Faoláin's complaint that the whole thing reeked of 'spilt Joyce' was typical of the critical responses both on its first British publication in 1939 and its re-issue in 1960.[43] All this 'spilt Joyce' had an ironic intent, however. In a 1938 review of new Irish fiction entitled 'The Joyce Country', O'Nolan's friend Niall Sheridan complained that the dominance of Joyce was now so complete that Dublin itself was beginning to look like 'an inferior plagiarism from *Ulysses*'.[44] If there were no means for the Irish novelist of the 1930s to escape the Joycean shadow, then parading the influence on stilts – as *At Swim* does – might at least knowingly preclude comparisons with the more famous writer. Naturally, if that was the strategy, it did not work. But neither did it do the young writer any harm to invite identification with his notorious predecessor. As early as 1935, O'Nolan published parodies of 'Work in Progress' in the UCD student magazine, *Comhthrom Féinne* (one of which was reproduced in *Ireland Today* in 1938).[45] Though he often chided Joyce for an aesthetic ambition far beyond the reach of the plain people of Ireland, an acquaintance with his work undoubtedly lent a sheen of sophistication to the bearer, even (or especially) in a censorious climate like that of Ireland in the 1930s and 1940s. Tellingly, on Myles's Irish days in the early *Cruiskeen Lawn*, tirades against the folk bias of the language revival often ended with Joyce being wheeled out as the case for the opposition. At the time, O'Nolan was still clearly recognised as a Joycean acolyte, albeit an unpredictably critical one. Throughout the 1940s, he generally added his own gloss to *Irish*

Times reviews of the latest Joyce criticism, and the connection between the two writers was sealed when John Ryan invited O'Nolan to edit the special Joyce issue of *Envoy* in 1951. The contributors whom he gathered for that issue – including Denis Johnston, 'Andrew Cass' (his civil service boss, John Garvin), Montgomery and Patrick Kavanagh – produced a rather ambivalent portrait of Joyce as a brilliant crank, one whose identity was firmly rooted in Irish Catholicism, whatever his protests of *non serviam*.[46] In a firm gesture of repatriation that followed a couple of decades of American scholarship, the consensus seemed to be that Joyce could only be properly understood by an Irishman. The double movement to ostracise Joyce's achievement while insisting upon his credentials as a repressed Irish Catholic (just like any other, notably themselves)[47] is revealing. What is intriguing about the much-discussed relationship between O'Nolan and Joyce, notoriously culminating with the latter darning Jesuits' socks in *The Dalkey Archive*, is not so much Joyce's influence on O'Nolan, or even Myles's occasional vituperation of him. A more curious aspect of the relationship is the various ways in which he exploited Joyce – the personality, as well as the work – as a means of illustrating his own identity as a writer.

To a certain extent, O'Nolan invented Joyce in his own image; according to his introduction to the *Envoy* issue, Joyce was 'a truly fear-shaken Irish Catholic' who 'spent a lifetime establishing himself as a character in fiction' – substitute 'Myles na gCopaleen' there and the effect is much the same.[48] Not only that, but Myles asserted on more than one occasion that 'his true felicity . . . was in writing comic stuff', as well as an 'almost supernatural skill in conveying Dublin dialogue'.[49] The view might be O'Nolan's or Montgomery's, or both. From the Dedalean student of *At Swim-Two-Birds* to the resurrected Joyce of *The Dalkey Archive*, the writer and his work served as a fairground mirror for O'Nolan's aesthetic preoccupations. *At Swim* and *Cruiskeen Lawn* bear out José Lanters's contention that while Irish satire of the 1920s had focused on the turbulent political scene 'by the 1930s this focus has shifted to a concern with the increasingly precarious position of the individual, especially the artist himself, in a conservative, even repressive society'.[50] O'Nolan's fiction, which typically places a passive protagonist in a merry-go-round structure, is a good example of the kind of writing Lanters describes, but it was Joyce who had set the agenda for it. For the generation who followed him, the rebellious Stephen Dedalus was the archetype of the Irish artist, albeit an archetype who could not be imitated. By 1951, the portrait of the Irish artist which O'Nolan presented in his *Envoy* essay, 'A Bash in the Tunnel', had become a rather more curious concoction. It provides the punchline to a tall tale about a man ('that oddity, an unauthorized person')[51] who manages to lock himself into the dining car of a train in order to consume illicitly vast amounts of CIE whiskey. Locked in the car, which shunters move into a tunnel, he is unwittingly left to conduct a night-long bash that lasts for three days,

'I was in bed for a week. Did you ever in your life hear of a greater crowd of bastards?':

> Funny? But surely there you have the Irish artist? Sitting fully dressed, innerly locked in the toilet of a locked coach where he has no right to be, resentfully drinking somebody else's whiskey, being whisked hither and thither by anonymous shunters, keeping fastidiously the while on the outer face of his door the simple word ENGAGED![52]

The image fits Joyce, O'Nolan contends, who, like our friend here, manifests 'a most Irish characteristic – the transgressor's resentment with the nongressor'. It fits O'Nolan even better, who (using a characteristically regressive image) locks his man in a box within a box, another one of his passive creatures who is shunted about while maintaining an illusion of studied preoccupation. While he draws attention to the mischievous transgression of this 'unauthorized person', the man's disgruntled submissiveness is slightly more telling.

It is revealing that O'Nolan conflates Joyce with a portrait of the Irish artist (albeit the Irish artist as Brian O'Nolan), as if he were the very embodiment of the species. Arguably, the association was rife as early as the 1930s, when he was just setting out on his career. With *Ulysses* hailed as a masterpiece, if a notorious one, and the even more notorious 'Work in Progress' appearing piecemeal over the 1920s and 1930s, Joyce's position was already overbearing. O'Nolan's contradictory impulses to identify with Joyce at one moment, and dissociate from him the next, are curiously suggestive of the ambivalent regard in which literary Dublin held Joyce in the 1930s and 1940s. In 1934, Samuel Beckett starkly sketched the Irish literary scene in a review of recent Irish poetry, which divided contemporary Irish poets between 'antiquarians and others, the former in the majority'.[53] With the battlelines so plainly drawn, Joyce was becoming an important piece of cultural currency. Whatever the reservations O'Nolan later professed towards modernist writers, it was surely a more attractive prospect to be identified with the sophisticated, 'modern' successors to the revival generation, than with faded imitators of past glories. As Niall Sheridan recalled of his fellow students in 1930s UCD: 'We felt that the Anglo-Irish Renaissance was already a spent force . . . [Beckett] had opened new horizons with *Murphy*. Joyce, of course, was in the very air we breathed'.[54] And as Cronin argues, Joyce served an almost symbolic function for their university circle – in marked contrast to the realist novelists coming to prominence in Ireland, who seemed to studiously ignore his presence. The Catholic literati of the National University were inevitably following in his footsteps, but the Joycean legacy was a difficult one:

> Joyce and his challenge would be defused by making him a mere logo-machic wordsmith, a great but demented genius who finally went mad in his ivory tower . . . On the other hand Joyce and a view of mod-ernism as a predominantly aesthetic philosophy could still provide a sort of absolution and a sort of charm against infection for those who despised the new Ireland . . .[55]

Cronin suggests that while many of these students were critical of the nationalist and religious pieties of 1930s Ireland, an outright rejection of such sacred cows (in the Joycean manner) would be felt as a betrayal of a newly-won Irish identity. Joyce could, however, be assimilated as a deranged aesthete who could nevertheless be invoked to castigate the philistine ten-dencies of de Valera's Ireland. But O'Nolan himself ridiculed the implication that a familiarity with Joyce might guard against contamination by the plain people of Ireland. The reviewers who dismissed *At Swim-Two-Birds* for being derivatively Joycean ignored the criticism implicit in his reduction of the experimental modernist novel to a more populist farce. And while Montgomery's critical work on Joyce often favoured a bewilder-ingly rococo style, when writing as Myles he too pitched in against the perceived snobbery of the Joyce school. In 1948, one Joyce critic com-mented with displeasure that while the 'Philistines' had merely stagnated in Joyce's Dublin, at present the new Catholic middle class was 'rampant and aggressive' with 'only Peadar O'Donnell's *The Bell* and (to a lesser degree) *The Irish Times* to raise their voice in protest, as Matthew Arnold used to do'.[56] Montgomery/Myles seized on the implicit condescension towards the lumpen-Catholics, protesting that he had already warned Costello, Dev and Cosgrove to 'Watch that Romish crowd. Keep a sharp eye on your men. Those fellows would form a middle class as quick as they'd look at you! And then? Well, you know what it was like being the laughing-stock of Europe . . . How would you like to be the laughing-stock of the New York publishing houses?'. He played up the hint of Anglo-Irish prejudice towards a philistine Catholic Ireland, while laying claim to Joyce as one of the tribe:

> . . . Nobody can say Joyce hadn't courage – I'd no more dream of trusting meself outside the door of a taxi – some of those middle-class Catholic croppies might knife you in the neck with a pike or some-thing. You'd take your blooming life in your hands and that's the truth. There's some kind of a secret about Joyce though – I think he had a class of an understanding with that crowd. Couldn't be up to them. Live where you and I would starve. . .[57]

O'Nolan echoed the theme in an *Envoy* article in 1950. The point at issue was the sneering condescension of intellectuals for 'the herd', particularly in the virulence often expressed towards popular newspapers and those who contributed to them. Denouncing 'the herd' was a legitimate exercise, he conceded, but not in the hope of reforming them. And again, he neatly appropriated Joyce – more commonly the weapon of such cultural elitists – to argue the case for the opposition:

> If everybody in Dublin wrote books and plays and wallowed in the political and literary preciosities of the *New Statesman* and defunct *Horizon*, the town would be the despair of Joyce if he were still in it and would in any event be generally uninhabitable.[58]

Though hardly a cultural leveller himself, O'Nolan disdained the manner in which Joyce could be exploited to scold the unenlightened mob. The virtues O'Nolan praised in his writing were quite distinct from those valued by many of his early critics; the praise for Joyce expressed in *Cruiskeen Lawn* is succinctly echoed by *The Dalkey Archive*'s Mick Shaughnessy, who admires him for 'his dexterity and resource in handling language, for his precision, for his subtlety in conveying the image of Dublin and her people, for his accuracy in setting down speech authentically, and for his enormous humour' (*DA*, 96).

At the same time, while *At Swim* shows that O'Nolan was obviously one of the more appreciative readers of Joyce among Irish novelists, the novel also betrays a certain adherence to the values of contemporary Ireland (aesthetic and otherwise) which worked to exclude him. As the following chapter demonstrates, to some degree *At Swim* echoed the contemporary consensus on Joyce in literary Dublin, a place still infused with revival ideals on the uses of a national culture and quite prepared to believe that *Finnegans Wake* was 'the ultimate fantasy in cod'.[59] As Joyce's rising status was consolidated in the 1940s and 1950s with an increasing number of imposingly academic studies of his work, a straw man was created which enabled Myles na gCopaleen to be cast as the bard of common sense. By 1954, he was deploring the fact that by including so many 'salacities' in *Ulysses*, Joyce had needlessly alienated a great number of his potential Irish readers: 'I ask – though no Bowdler I – is it not a great pity that an expurgated edition of 'Ulysses' is not published, *virginibus puerisque*?'.[60] On the other hand, ten years earlier Myles (or one of them) was quite prepared to defend Joyce's 'obscenities' on aesthetic grounds:

> . . . Rouault uses qualities of violence and crudity to establish awe, reverence and stillness, while Joyce, in stating his arid and cold view

of life, uses what would be discerned for obscenities if isolated . . .
art is not necessarily 'beautiful', nor has it necessarily any evangelical
function . . . art may also displease, disturb, frighten or disgust.[61]

Joyce inadvertently exposed the mass of contradictions in the Mylesian
persona. On occasion he needed to be defended from the mob, or rather,
from the rather narrow values of contemporary Ireland; at other times he
had to be seized from the clutches of those who high-handedly berated
the philistinism of the plain Irish. His obscenities or obscurities could be
defended on the grounds of artistic merit, but his aesthetic preoccupations could also be declared to be farcically self-indulgent.[62] The
inconsistency was of course partly the product of Myles's mixed
parentage, but it was also a reflection of a real ambivalence that was not
peculiar to either O'Nolan or Montgomery. A Mylesian image of Joyce as
an egotistic, self-obsessed figure turns up even in John Garvin's *James
Joyce's Disunited Kingdom and the Irish Dimension*, a book peppered with
asides on O'Nolan's comic appropriation of Joyceana and which sometimes reads as though Garvin had in turn acquired Myles's wry
perspective on his subject.[63] For example, discussing how the eny-
clopaedic mode of the 'Ithaca' episode of *Ulysses* anticipates the
(dis)organisation of *Finnegans Wake*, Garvin remarks that:

> There is a logical progression in his mind from his name endorsed on
> a schoolbook as of Clongowes Wood, Sallins, Co. Kildare, Ireland . . .
> the Universe, to the artistic representation of all human history as a
> universalisation of the solipsistic projection of the imago of James
> Joyce.[64]

The judgement could have come from *Cruiskeen Lawn*. It would be curious
to know which way the influence ran and whether, as Thomas Hogan
argued in his *Bell* profile, the many-headed Myles was simply a typical
product of the embittered Dublin intelligentsia. (No doubt this bitterness
was due not only to the uncongenial atmosphere of contemporary Ireland,
but to these intellectuals' position – in the wake of Yeats and Joyce – as a
particularly belated addition to 'the most belated race in Europe'.)[65] The
article which Garvin had earlier contributed to the *Envoy* issue was in
parts even more caustic than his comment above, yet he himself was no
sour Dublin know-all, but a committed Joyce scholar. Bearing this in
mind, the reason behind the largely uneasy response to Joyce from Irish
writers, even from declared admirers such as Garvin, Montgomery and
O'Nolan, arguably bears more consideration than that offered by Hogan.
Indeed, examining how Joyce's texts were mediated by Irish writers and
critics, including O'Nolan, and how they were acculturated to 1930s and

1940s Ireland (as much as they could be), throws into relief the dominating literary values of the post-revival period. To follow the trajectory of the domestic response to 'Work in Progress', or the changing attitudes to *Ulysses* over this time, is to see a clash of cultures developing comparable to that dramatised in *At Swim*'s dissonant comedy. The Irish response to Joyce can be construed, like *At Swim* itself, as a debate over the proper condition of Irish literature, one which was all the more interesting for the little sustenance it drew from the texts which it purportedly addressed.

The differing responses to Joyce in surveys of Irish literature published by John Eglinton, Stephen Gwynn, and Aodh de Blácam in the mid-1930s starkly illustrate the social and political faultlines in Irish literary criticism. The Joyce whom the revivalist Eglinton evokes in *Irish Literary Portraits* is 'Roman in mind and soul',[66] who by forcing the English language to unaccustomed tasks, shows himself to be an enemy of 'the whole of the English tradition'.[67] In *Irish Literature and Drama*, Gwynn's Joyce is instead the dispossessed Catholic failed by his country, *A Portrait* being a post-Parnellite study of 'a diseased soul in a diseased country'.[68] Only a glancing, apologetic reference is made to the difficulty of *Ulysses*, Gwynn's focus being 'the poignant cry of the disinherited [which] runs all through Joyce's writing'.[69] However for de Blácam, a rather puritan exponent of Irish Ireland, not even such a clearly political appropriation was desirable. *A First Book of Irish Literature*, a literary handbook ranging from the mistiest reaches of Gaelic epic to Corkery's recent *The Hidden Ireland*, simply omits any reference to him at all. Instead, it is Canon Sheehan who is said to rival William Carleton as 'the greatest Irish novelist',[70] a rather peculiar response (or non-response) to Joyce's difficulties which was in fact only an extreme example of a fairly widespread condition. De Blácam's assurance that 'the Ireland of the people'[71] was the ultimate court of address for a work of literature echoed Corkery's placement of the truly Irish writer among the crowd at a hurling match in Thurles. The realist novelists of the 1930s, whom O'Nolan implicitly mocked in the anti-realist *At Swim-Two-Birds* (and quite openly abused in *Cruiskeen Lawn*) made similar assumptions. Among Joyce's earliest Irish admirers was Frank O'Connor, whose more virulent criticism of his later work seems partly inspired by a hangover of revivalist ideas about the instrumental role of culture and art in the life of the nation (or 'the people').[72] A Joycean aesthetic, deemed by *popular* consensus to be remote and inaccessible – as well as indecent – could hardly fulfill such a role.

However, initially there were plenty prepared to welcome *A Portrait* and *Ulysses* as the work of an urban Catholic writer qualified to speak for the rising Catholic middle class, though the direction signalled by 'Work in Progress' made such an interpretation difficult to sustain.[73] For Joseph

Hone, writing in 1923, *A Portrait* had announced 'the passing of that literary Ireland in which everyone was well-bred except a few politicians',[74] but the literary Ireland which succeeded it charged Joyce with complicity in a new aesthetic aristocracy. Seán O'Faoláin's dismissal of *Anna Livia Plurabelle* sounded a characteristic note. The piece, he wrote:

> . . . comes from nowhere, goes nowhere, is not part of life at all. It has one reality only, the reality of the round and round of children's scrawls in their first copybooks, many circles of nothing . . .[75]

Given that O'Faoláin's manifesto for *The Bell* in 1940 would declare it to be 'not so much a magazine as a bit of Life itself',[76] this was criticism indeed. By the time *Finnegans Wake* was published in 1939, Joyce had solidified for O'Faoláin and O'Connor into the monomaniacal parody of himself which would become familiar in many *Cruiskeen Lawn* columns. Perhaps disillusioned by his later work, another theme of his Irish critics was now his unjust treatment of Ireland, a criticism reiterated even by the contributors to the 1951 *Envoy* issue, whose indignation might reasonably have been cooled by the passing of time. In the late 1930s, O'Connor argued that though *A Portrait* had created a protagonist whose 'despair is the despair of Ireland', it was 'an extreme and fantastic book'[77] replete with an ugly hostility towards Ireland. By 1943, this disquiet had developed into a 'strong sense' of Joyce's artistic failure: 'Joyce's virtuosity seems to me to belong to a second rate brain'.[78] The trace of bravado chimes with Myles's facetious remark that Joyce was, in fact, 'illiterate': 'He had a fabulously developed jackdaw talent of picking up bits and pieces, but it seems his net was too wide to justify getting a few kids' schoolbooks and learning the rudiments of a new language correctly. Every foreign-language quotation in any of his works known to me is wrong'.[79] To his compatriots (as to himself), Joyce was simply another Icarus who had flown too close to the sun. However, there was no Joycean irony to temper their judgements.

Effectively, O'Nolan's wry comments on Joyce and his critics were of a piece with the dominant critical consensus in Ireland. Despite the complication of *Finnegans Wake*, the reinvention of Stephen/Joyce in the image of a Catholic nationalist lingered long after the late Revival period. O'Nolan, who more often emphasised his work's technical virtuosity and monumental humour, nevertheless shared the common reaction to Joyce's self-invention as an artist – not in his response to the Joyce who created *Ulysses* or *Finnegans Wake*, but to the mythic personality of *A Portrait* and the only slightly less mythic impresario who directed the reception of the later works ('James Joyce was an artist. He has said so himself').[80] The insults produced by the Myles syndicate worsened in proportion to the growth of Joyce's critical reputation; by 1957, he was calling Joyce 'a complete prig, a snob, and a person possessed of endowment unique in the archives of conceit. Nearly all the commentators he attracted must be classified as literary scruff . . . Nobody but a Dubliner could appraise its subtlety'.[81] And nobody but these particular Dubliners could be quite so unforgiving of the fact that Joyce's work strained beyond the 'comic stuff'. Joyce's self-conscious artistry, though genially parodied in *At Swim-Two-Birds*, met with similar antagonism elsewhere – O'Faoláin, for example, juxtaposing Liam O'Flaherty (as a critical realist who would do service to the 'new Ireland') with the aloof introspection of Stephen Dedalus.[82] Though the duo behind Myles hardly shared O'Faoláin's intellectual bias towards the functional uses of literature, the same caricature of Joyce sometimes crept out in *Cruiskeen Lawn*. In March 1944, an *Irish Times* review of Harry Levin's *James Joyce: A Critical Introduction* initially set the pedant in Myles railing against the stray apostrophes that bedevilled the title of *Finnegans Wake*. With growing debate on the flurry of modernist art to hit Dublin, it also inspired a wry disquisition on modern artists. These Myles compared unfavourably with their medieval counterparts, who were 'decent workmen' and modest church-goers:

> Nowadays your 'artist' is a neurotic imbecile; he has the cheek to discern in his own dementia the pattern of a universal chaos and it is no coincidence that most of his books are dirty and have to be banned. Beware of 'culture', reader; of 'art' and 'artists' be careful and apprehensive. Such things were very fine when they came out first, they were part of the commonplace shape of life and nobody could possibly take exception to them. But when isolated in our own day to become merely a self-conscious social cult . . . know then that words like 'culture' and 'art' do not mean what they meant . . . [That] is not an attitude that should be encouraged, however much it may float our poor country out into the main stream of European culture.[83]

The latter phrase was Herbert Read's, who in a recent piece on Dublin's modernist Exhibition of Subjective Art had assured his audience that he had not expected to find a showcase of 'provincial art' in Dublin, nor did he. It was all reassuringly European: 'And that, I venture to say, is something new in the modern history of this country'.[84] The colonial condescension was refracted back into Myles's reading of international Joyce criticism, which had developed a habit of liberating the writer from his own benighted society. Though the column never expressed the revivalist nostalgia for a popular national culture which afflicted some of Joyce's earliest Irish critics, traces of the ethos remain in Myles's ironic irritation at the degeneration of culture to 'cult'.[85]

If fault was found with Joyce and the cultish aura of the modernist writer, the corollary might be that the pose of the plain man was felt to be more congenial. Certainly, *Cruiskeen Lawn* exploited all the comic incongruity in reintegrating 'James Aquinas Joyce' (as it habitually called him) back into the mainstream of plain Dublin life. But in doing so, not only could Joyce's vanities be set off to their best advantage, but also the narrowness of contemporary Dublin. On one occasion, an encounter with a street orator calling for the revival of the Irish language – a topic usually close to O'Nolan's spleen – drew Myles into a curious digression:

> On many sides I hear it said that English 'must go'. Very well. But . . . are we absolutely sure . . . that . . . we . . . *have* English . . . Poor Jimmy Joyce was the boy that made English 'go' – I knew the father well, many a ball had with his hat inside the back room in Corless's fine figure of a man always wore a frock coat grey derby never struck a woman in his life. I hear there's not two consecutive words of English in that book *Flanagan's Awake* matteradamn what anybody says. Could we . . . make that the national language?[86]

The cosy and claustrophobic city that Joyce had satirised in *Ulysses* was resurrected by Myles in all the Joycean hangers-on who had ever claimed to shake his father's hand. The shrill language revivalist whom this column mocked simply represented another aspect of this insular culture, for which there could have been no better punishment than *Finnegans Wake*, a text so inscrutably aloof (as well as international) that it outraged all the homely virtues of mid-century Dublin. Yet for all the criticism of Joyce which peppered the later years, at a time when Myles was referring to his contemporaries as 'an eruption of literary scabies' he reserved praise for Joyce and Yeats as the only two Irish writers of genius in the last century.[87] Even in 1956, when ridicule of Joycean critics (generally American) was standard in the column, *Ulysses* was defended from charges of difficulty and obscurity, Myles arguing that its 'mental ingestion in full calls for intelligence, maturity, and some knowledge of life as well as letters'.[88] So while the criticism of Joyce in *Cruiskeen Lawn* often chimed with the contemporary consensus in Irish literary circles, he was also usefully exploited in negotiations with the Plain People of Ireland – one day being cast as a villain of the literary elite, and the next as the intellectual scapegoat of Ireland's cultural guardians. Whether or not O'Nolan and Montgomery were always in agreement on the matter of Joyce, the elliptical Mylesian manner created its own kind of consistency. The conclusion of that 1944 article on the modern artist is illuminating in its way:

... People who call to my lodgings for advice often ask me whether being Irish is itself an art-form. I am not so sure that the answer can be yes. One asks oneself whether the state of being Irish is characterised by the three essential requisites of James Aquinas Joyce – *integritas, consonantia, claritas* ... It would save so much trouble if we could all answer in the affirmative. "Paudrig Crohoore, R.H.A.", would be a grand way out; that each citizen would be an artist would save us all a lot of trouble and embarrassment.[89]

'Paudrig Crohoore, RHA' might be read as a swipe at professional Irishness, particularly the vogue for folk culture in the age of de Valera, but by removing the temptation for artistic posturing (in order to distinguish one from the common herd), it also reminded the promoters of art as a 'self-conscious social cult' that each artist was a citizen as well. While Joyce might have been a 'charm against infection for those who despised the new Ireland',[90] his apparent detachment jarred with the taste for controversy and provocation expressed in *Cruiskeen Lawn*, which from the late 1940s onwards led to Myles increasingly developing the part of the outraged citizen, or plain person. If the resurrection of Joyce in *The Dalkey Archive* mirrored the inclusion of a Dedalean narrator in *At Swim-Two-Birds*, O'Nolan's portrait of the artist had soured in the intervening years. J.C.C. Mays argues that 'the image of Joyce that Brian O'Nolan sees is an image of himself as artist'[91] and that his treatment in *The Dalkey Archive* is effectively an expression of 'embittered self-hatred'.[92] It was, at the very least, a fairly blunt means of literary revenge, making the writer comically subservient to the Catholic Church and its guardians of literary morals, the Catholic Truth Society. But O'Nolan did an even stranger thing in this novel by twinning Joyce with the evil genius, de Selby, the eccentric inventor of a substance with the power to destroy the world. His narrator, Mick, imagines having the two collaborate on a 'monstrous earthquake of a new book, something claiming to supplant the Bible' (*DA*, 131) – placing the conservative supporter of the status quo in collaboration with a destructive and subversive personality. Though the final portrait of the artist in O'Nolan's fiction was again of Joyce (or Joyce/de Selby), it unwittingly dramatised the contradictory facets of his own literary personality more starkly than ever before.

The invention of Flann and Myles: the letter controversies

It was in October 1938 that this idiosyncratic personality first came to the attention of the Irish reading public, though O'Nolan had been contributing piecemeal to newspapers and magazines for a number of years. Six months before the publication of At Swim-Two-Birds, the triumvirate of Brian, Flann and Myles made its first appearance when 'Flann O'Brien' invaded the letters page of The Irish Times. His contributions sparked off a farcical correspondence which, conducted under many pseudonyms, would run on and off in the paper over the following two years, finally leading to the commissioning of Cruiskeen Lawn. The preoccupations of Flann and his siblings (Oscar Love, Lir O'Connor, his sister Luna, and others) were already very much those of Myles na gCopaleen: the self-importance of Dublin's writers and the subversive potential of the plain man. Since the letters make the most of O'Nolan's facility for erudite ingenuity and endlessly digressive nonsense, they form an obvious bridge between At Swim and the newspaper column. But the letters also show him jostling for his own space in literary Dublin, heralding the arrival of a new character on the scene. Flann O'Brien first emerged in the midst of a quarrel between Seán O'Faoláin and Frank O'Connor over the state of the Abbey Theatre. The (very public) private argument they had been conducting between themselves for a fortnight in The Irish Times was exploded – and summarily ended – by O'Nolan's irreverent contribution. His alter ego, soon to be revealed as a novelist in his own right, signalled a very different attitude to the idea of the public intellectual. The rather earnest sense of cultural responsibility assumed by O'Faoláin and O'Connor (then still a director of the Abbey) was ridiculed by an adversary whose playful inscrutability owed something to Joyce, but with added sting.

Flann O'Brien's intervention in 'Ideals for an Irish Theatre' struck immediately at what he detected to be its underlying snobbery. O'Faoláin had complained that the Abbey was without direction or identity – too fascinated with 'Peasant Quality' and in need of a transfusion of contemporary European drama. He challenged O'Connor to establish an agenda for the theatre, as Yeats and Lady Gregory had done. A testy correspondence ran over the next fortnight, O'Connor defending his 'P.Q.' actresses on the grounds that those from 'good schools' were often educated 'out of knowledge of their own people', while O'Faoláin replied that realist drama did not require such an attachment to 'bog-field actuality'.[93] Changing tack, the defendant claimed that whatever faults the theatre had, they were also the faults of Irish life, Irish authors and Irish audiences, particularly of the kind of Irish audiences who guffawed at moments of high tragedy on the stage.[94] O'Faoláin in turn sorrowfully lamented the loss of a once stellar reputation: 'Whatever one might say of the so-called "Anglo-Irish" they had taste . . .'[95] Enter Flann O'Brien:

I do not know whether the petulant bickering which is going on in your columns, between Mr O Faoláin and Mr O'Connor is a private affair or whether any puling highbrow gentleman of refined tastes may take a part . . .

The issue between these two items is plain and quite unimportant. Mr O'Connor wants plays about peasants acted by peasants, who know not the muck that passes for education at "good schools", and presented, preferably, before an audience of – peasants, I think; people, at all events, who would be too bucolically shy to laugh uproariously when diverted by something which Mr O'Connor considers desperately tragic . . . But none of this nonsense for Mr O Faoláin. He asks the Abbey directors to give some idea of what they want and what they do be about in their dim boardroom. He then tells them what they want in a few well-deserved, well-chosen words . . .[96]

His solution was simple: since Abbey audiences had degenerated in recent years from 'an esoteric coterie' to those who came looking for a good laugh and got it ('notwithstanding the fury of a 1,000 red-faced art-stuffed boyos in the wings'), he advised the Board to invest in five hundred extras (peasants) who could occupy the stalls and laugh only when directed. Yeats's vision of an audience for an Irish national theatre was easily fulfilled, even if its patrician undertones happened to be exposed along the way. A Yeatsian sense of cultural importance seemed to have shrunk to self-importance in 1930s Dublin, or at least it was being read as such. O'Brien suggested that O'Faoláin and O'Connor gather the city's wealth of artists and critics in a mammoth Art Jamboree: 'The City Manager would welcome the project because he could use the place for a rubbish dump, and nobody would mind or notice or know the difference'. The time for ideals was past, theatrical or otherwise.

One of the striking features of this correspondence is how Mylesian it had become long before the intervention of O'Nolan. With all the strutting and posturing, it is easy to see where he learned the tricks of his trade. O'Connor and O'Faoláin's impatience with the plain people of Ireland (whether those who smirked at Abbey tragedies or clung to what O'Faoláin considered a 'vulgar' drama) would be parodied at length in *Cruiskeen Lawn*. So too would the inverse snobbery expressed in a fear that artists might be educated 'out of knowledge of their own people'. But the primary target of Flann O'Brien's letter was the declamatory tone that both writers quite naturally employed in the pages of *The Irish Times*. Whatever O'Nolan owed to Joyce (in reacting against his example as much as in following it), the playful postures of Flann O'Brien and Myles na gCopaleen were as much a reaction against those closer to home. To read the column at length is to encounter a frequent irritation

with Ireland's self-anointed critics and cultural guardians. At the beginning this mostly manifested itself in O'Nolan's skill, as he put it, as a
'Faoláinthropist'.[97] He was next set loose by a speech O'Faoláin made to
the Dublin Literary Society, which deplored the fact that Irish novelists
wasted 'half their spirit' in battling a native provincialism:

> I see that tremendous cerebrite, Mr Sean O Faoláin, has been at it
> again. He announces that Irish novelists are in a bad way, thanks to
> the "venom of provincialism and nationalist and religious obscuran-
> tism". What other way would they be, or what can Mr O Faoláin
> expect from a nation that associates the name of Marx with a day at
> the races or a night at the opera?[98]

Lest this might seem a backhanded insult to the plain people, he suggested that before O'Faoláin left for more civilised shores he might
establish a branch of the Dublin Literary Society or PEN in every town
and village in Ireland: 'The branch could be occupied with decontami-
nating provincialism, dispersing obscurantism and promoting the ballet,
verse-speaking and *Weltanschauung* . . .' O'Faoláin himself maintained a
careful silence, but for the first time a suspicious pseudonymous syndicate sprang into action, 'Hazel Ellis Warren' praising Mr O'Brien for
'pouring cold water on the pseudo-intellectuals of our city' who were
forever proclaiming their lives to be in danger from 'the barbarous,
priest-ridden Irish people'.[99] Soon afterwards, the march of the plain
people resumed when Flann O'Brien responded to O'Faoláin's anger
over an *Irish Times* review of a lacklustre play from Frank O'Connor:
'*Time's Pocket* has justified itself ten times over if it serves to draw from
Mr Sean O'Faoláin one of those amusing letters in which he protests
once again that he is "an artist".'[100] O'Nolan had finally hit his mark –
this time O'Connor condemned his letters as 'personal abuse' and
called on the editor to identify their author and distance *The Irish Times*
from 'the methods of literary gangsters and hooligans'.[101] Smyllie
smoothly replied that the identity of the author was known to him and
the next day he closed the correspondence.

From the very outset of these letter controversies O'Nolan was developing a distinct position of his own, not quite within or without the
literary fraternity. The vanity and self-importance of the Irish writer (or
at least, of the writer as represented by the unlucky Seán O'Faoláin) was
a main point of attack, and in particular, the Irish writer's very loud
protests at his persecution by the plain people. Noting that the attacks
on O'Faoláin did not prevent him from contributing to *The Bell*,
Donohue argues that there was no real animosity behind these letters:
'Beneath O'Nolan's writings as Flann O'Brien or Myles na gCopaleen

lies a deep irony about meaning, truth and whether language was an adequate tool for logic and reason . . . The artifice of the debate takes precedence over the character of the debater'.[102] There is some truth in this, but the persistent baiting also had an edge. As Montgomery, one of his fellow perpetrators, recorded it: '[Brian] compares himself to a man at a rathole with an ashplant, waiting for the rats to come out'.[103] The recurrent themes of these letters would sound through his early fiction, and it is no coincidence that when *Cruiskeen Lawn* made its first regular appearances in English in September 1941 it was WAAMA – the artists' association headed by O'Faoláin – which was its first object of derision. Yet if *The Irish Times* provided O'Nolan with the perfect opportunity to bait the Dublin intellectual on home ground, given the venues from which he mounted his attacks (an experimental novel and a broadsheet largely ignored by the plain people of Ireland) he was really only playing the prodigal son. The letters also helped 'Flann O'Brien' to gain some useful notoriety before the publication of *At Swim-Two-Birds* in March 1939.[104] Ironically, startled by the irascible responses he finally elicited from O'Faoláin and O'Connor, O'Nolan swiftly wrote to his publishers proposing to abandon the pseudonym 'Flann O'Brien'.[105] (His fears were unsubstantiated since O'Faoláin eventually gave *At Swim* a fairly positive review.)[106] Nevertheless, any self-interest he had in generating these literary free-for-alls was at least consistent with his criticism of the two. In contrast to their high-mindedness, Flann O'Brien declined to take the business of literature as anything other than plain business.

Partly as a result of that workmanlike attitude, O'Nolan presented his readers with a conundrum which would remain a motif throughout his career: the problem of literary attribution. Running parallel to the *Time's Pocket* farrago was a more sober debate in the letters page over Franco's Spain. This involved a character called Oscar Love who played a more facetious part in later Flann O'Brien-generated controversies, also contributing to the flurry of letters that greeted the arrival of *Cruiskeen Lawn* in 1940. In the midst of the discussion of Spain, Oscar Love challenged a glowing account of life under Franco:

> . . . how many travellers in Spain resemble Alice –
> "The dream-child moving through a land
>   Of wonders wild and new,
> In friendly chat with bird and beast –
>   And half believe it true."[107]

In his next letter, he cited another piece of nonsense from G.K. Chesterton; he also claimed to have been in Spain in 1934.[108] If this was O'Nolan, then he was participating in two very different debates concurrently (and in very different ways), sometimes contributing letters under different names on the same day. Yet it was a long way from Flann O'Brien's playful provocation of O'Connor and O'Faoláin, even if Oscar Love signed his letters from Blackrock where O'Nolan was living at the time. The riddle of Oscar Love's identity is only one of many; the collection of pseudonymous letters which bombarded *The Irish Times* in 1939– 40 has generally been attributed to a group consisting of O'Nolan and friends such as Niall Montgomery and Niall Sheridan (though the latter's account does not mention his own contribution).[109] Yet if Flann O'Brien and Oscar Love were one and the same, then O'Nolan was already compartmentalising his authorial personality, using one pseudonym for facetious literary frays and another for more serious matters. Certainly, Brian, Flann and Myles were shadowed by a host of minor characters – apart from the Mylesian Brother Barnabas and Count O'Blather, O'Nolan also worked in the guise of some less idiosyncratic authors: Lir O'Connor (possibly), Jimmy Cunning, George Knowall, John James Doe, and perhaps more.[110] And of course to add to the confusion, the by-line of Myles na gCopaleen masked work by many hands. For many years O'Nolan's claim that *Cruiskeen Lawn* was not all his own work was his standard defence against material which offended his superiors in the civil service. Yet this may be true of more than the column: as early as 1943 he was noting acerbically that Montgomery's contribution to his adaptation of *The Insect Play* had not passed muster with the directors of the Gate.[111] O'Nolan's various masks obscured more than simple evasiveness. And quite besides the problem of attribution, in assuming so many literary identities he risked acquiring none at all. At this stage of his career it was a literary fate that seemed probable to some, given the relentlessly mannered styles of *At Swim-Two-Birds*.

The final outing of O'Nolan and friends in *The Irish Times* inadvertently raised that very point.[112] It was provoked by a review of Maurice Walsh's *The Hill is Mine* by Patrick Kavanagh, who unwisely raised a question close to Flann O'Brien's heart: 'What is an artist? Can a writer of bestsellers, like Maurice Walsh, be an artist?'. The answer was yes, given that 'nearly all the prose and verse innovators of the past twenty-five years or so' (including Eliot, Yeats and Joyce) had nothing in particular to say, achieving only a kind of empty virtuosity.[113] The letter-writers largely ignored Kavanagh's red flag (perhaps seeing no point to disagree), instead careering into a debate on boy scouts and the Hitler *Jugend*. Flann O'Brien made his appearance when Kavanagh's 'Spraying the Potatoes' was published in the midst of the debacle: 'Perhaps *The Irish Times*, timeless champion of our peasantry, will oblige us with a series in this strain covering such rural complexities as inflamed goat-udders, warble-pocked shorthorn, contagious abortion, non-ovoid oviducts and nervous disorders among the gentlemen who pay the rent'.[114] There was little else in this vast correspondence which bore any relation to its headline: 'Literary Criticism'. When Kavanagh was eventually allowed the final word he seized on just this point. Returning to his original review, he asserted that these 'disciples of Joyce and Eliot' were 'expert in the art of saying nothing':

> There is tragedy here . . . Too soon they will know the misery of literary men without themes, poets without burdens, ploughmen without land. Such grief has Higher Education brought to simple-minded, decent fellows, who might have developed in happiness as Corporation workers in actual sewers . . .[115]

This might have been a little galling for O'Nolan, given that recent reviews of At Swim-Two-Birds had also criticised its fluency in saying nothing.[116] Ironically, the correspondence he had conducted on and off in *The Irish Times* over the previous two years had been relatively consistent in its themes. While by the summer of 1940 the whole thing had developed into unadulterated nonsense (at which point other *Irish Times* readers, including its editor, were in on the act), Flann O'Brien's contributions were usually marked by an impatience with all forms of literary pomposity. Interestingly, O'Nolan did not take issue with Kavanagh's harsh opinion of the literary greats of the previous quarter century: At Swim's reviewers may have complained that it had nothing to say, but it could be argued that this modernist parody was making the very same point. Certainly, O'Nolan was a more self-conscious – or more sophisticated – writer than many of his contemporaries; one as inclined to question the parameters of critical debate as to engage with his opponents. The letter controversies which ran from October 1938 until *Cruiskeen Lawn* began in October 1940 are an interesting yet slightly cartoonish illustration of his humour at work. Cumulatively, they form a grand, shaggy dialogue, much like the endless dialectic in At Swim-Two-Birds, The Third Policeman and the dialogues of Cruiskeen Lawn, or even the debates between Collopy and Fr Kurt Fahrt in The Hard Life, or de Selby and St Augustine in The Dalkey Archive. Individually, they are also models of intellectual agility, mimicry, and evasion, but for all their nonsense, they do not simply provide argument for argument's sake. It is a curious paradox of At Swim-Two-Birds that O'Nolan firmly contained the various fantastical levels of the text within the student's realistic, semi-autobiographical frame narrative; the image could be used for his humour in general, which never wholly works free of its cultural moorings. It is no accident that Flann O'Brien first appeared (in 'Ideals for an Irish Theatre') in the midst of a debate between two prominent writers, the subtext of which was the role of the Irish writer in public life. While O'Faoláin complained because O'Connor did not appropriate the public and declamatory position which Yeats had occupied at the helm of the national theatre, O'Nolan made the very debate itself ridiculous. When, again, O'Faoláin complained of the obstacles which censorship and obscurantism presented to the Irish writer, O'Nolan made his reasonable grumble appear precious and patronising. Since the late 1930s saw the passing of the revivalist generation that had had such an impact on Irish culture and politics, it was natural that O'Faoláin should have resisted the impulse to return Irish writers to the sidelines (though worse was promised by the Censorship of Publications Act). It was equally natural, given that it was this cross-infection of culture and politics which produced the most reactionary elements of the Gaelic revival, that O'Nolan should have derided any attempts by his fellow writers to mount the rostrum again.

Given his antipathy to the very public and vocal roles assumed by writers such as O'Connor and O'Faoláin, as well as to the more remote mythos already accumulating around Joyce, it is easy to see why he has been cast as a peculiarly diffident individual skirting behind the masks of Flann, Myles, and their various associates. But this image is arguably more a creation of his readers than of his work – now forming part of the myth of Brian O'Nolan himself. While the playful, hyper-literary Flann O'Brien almost monopolises academic criticism, and the acidic Myles (shielding the elusive civil servant) arguably dominates his popular reputation, it is nevertheless questionable how important these individual identities are in themselves. The distinction between Flann and Myles is extremely precarious, though admittedly one of the many things they have in common is a body of writing whose ironies, exaggerations and mannered styles allowed O'Nolan a certain evasiveness. But he did not really hide himself behind these various masks – as Bernard Benstock points out, in *At Swim* 'the author himself began the process of confusing himself with his literary creations'.[117] In his very first novel, he placed himself (or a creature confusingly like himself) in the starring role, and as Joyce did, resolutely blended fiction and life throughout. Indeed, apart from *The Dalkey Archive*, all of his fiction assumes a wavering, sometimes self-referential, first-person narrative, though these are coupled with a distancing style. If O'Nolan was hiding behind the masks of Flann and Myles, he at least ensured that the illusion was fairly transparent. While his early comedy can seem to negate any authorial standpoint (charged with a seemingly endemic irony, it is also full of interior contradictions) this hardly contrived the death of the author – indeed, he created an endless array of extravagant and imposing authorial personalities in Brother Barnabas, Flann O'Brien, Myles na gCopaleen, and others. The intellectual slapstick of *Cruiskeen Lawn*, the adoption of polemical positions which can be adjusted, abandoned, attacked, and adopted again, reveal a comic writer in creative friction with his environment. While O'Nolan was not quite the empty vessel that Kavanagh implied him to be, the dominance of parody in his fiction is perhaps one indication that he was an essentially *reactive* writer. The irascible Myles of legend may be a muddle of academic criticism, popular notoriety, and endless anecdotes, but the more mischievous and irresponsible personae which O'Nolan fashioned in the late 1930s and early 1940s were partly crafted in response to the literary personalities around him: an inscrutable and playful Joyce, or an earnest and slightly didactic O'Faoláin. Interestingly, while images of the writer and concepts of his (and it was predominantly 'his') social role were polarising in the 1930s, O'Nolan side-stepped – by choice or circumstance – the precarious career of the aesthetic modernist or the public intellectual for a civil service job. It is hard not to hear envy in Mick's response to Joyce in *The Dalkey Archive*, as he observes that de Selby is fortunate to be wealthy, gifted, and free to follow his fancy: 'I had always thought of yourself, he said earnestly, as belonging to that sort of company. Your work seems to lack a sense of hurry' (*DA*, 126). But O'Nolan's often stated ambition to be a truly commercial writer itself reveals a lingering attachment to the mores of the Irish middle class and its ideas of social value.[118] There may have been a poet in the Senate, but in Ireland the cult of the author was still not a popular concept. Quite apart from his stylistic brilliance, it is also O'Nolan's peculiar brand of radical conformity which makes him one of the most interesting figures of this period, and the following chapter investigates how the conflicted intellectual environment of 1930s Dublin shaped the strangely ambivalent comedy of *At Swim-Two-Birds*.

2

The genesis of
At Swim-Two-Birds

Reviewing *At Swim-Two-Birds* on its publication in 1939, Jorge Luis Borges aptly described it as an exploration of 'the many ways to conceive of the Irish novel'.[1] But while *At Swim* might be read as a novel about writing a novel, it is more specifically a novel about writing an Irish novel of the 1930s. Its student narrator – a latter-day Stephen Dedalus[2] – presents his reader with a work in progress which blends parodies of medieval Irish literature, Joycean modernism and contemporary popular fiction, from the cowboy western to the Catholic moral fable. These parodies, combined with the seedy realism of the student's frame narrative, have bolstered O'Nolan's reputation as a representative figure of a disillusioned, post-independence generation – a subversive satirist who was wholly frustrated by the dour monotony of the Irish Free State.[3] However, *At Swim*'s humour betrays a curiously ambivalent outlook on contemporary Irish culture, one that is explicable in terms of the intellectual environment which informed its double-edged comedy. This novel is not simply a collage of literary styles; it dramatises the process of composition, demolishes the notion of original genius and allows its characters to oscillate between the roles of writer and reader, storyteller and audience. Above all, it indicates that collaboration is an inevitable component of literary production, whether this is suggested in the student's literary parodies or explicitly dramatised in the critical debates between his characters. Dialogue is made an essential element of the text, and O'Nolan acknowledges Dublin's oral culture as much as its literary heritage. By structuring his novel as a work in progress, he could draw attention both to his contemporary intellectual environment and the influence of his literary precursors. The result is an intertextual work which also emphasises the actual context of the act of writing (and reading). This makes *At Swim* interesting not only as a metafiction – which is how much criticism approaches the text[4] – but also as a novel highly aware of its own cultural context, one which supplies a moving shot of Irish culture at a significant point of transition. While *At Swim*'s student narrator may imitate the avant-garde literature popular among his contemporaries, he also shows a suspicion of its pretensions that is more congenial to the Ireland of his day.

Since the novel's central conceit is to expose itself in the process of being written, the critical battles between storytellers and audience are intrinsic to its development. True to the convention of the Fianna tales, Finn only tells his stories when prompted by Conán, but his modern-day successors are similarly reliant on a responsive audience. *At Swim* presents the process of composition as a communal effort – effectively it is a text designed in committee. The torture of Trellis is passed from hand to hand, the student is criticised and goaded by his friends; when Brinsley complains that Furriskey, Shanahan and Lamont are indistinguishable, he is prompted to include a memorandum (in true civil service mode) of their '*respective diacritical traits or qualities*' (*ASTB*, 161). There are also more subtle influences at work. Though Lamont expresses impatience with 'Sir Storybook' (*ASTB*, 78), or Finn MacCool, his account of Sweeny's leaps from tree to tree nevertheless inspires a contemporary equivalent, the yarn about Jumping Craddock. No new storyteller entirely sheds the other's style, and the account Orlick gives of Trellis's torture, for example, passes from the quaint coinages of Finn MacCool to the student's starched prose, to the slang of the Dublin cowboys (*ASTB*, 175). The romantic notion of the author as an original genius is thoroughly demolished; each new digression embarked on in the novel is as a response to something else, and each new storyteller betrays the influence of his predecessors. Yet admittedly, each character recounts his tale primarily in the style suitable to his own genre, so *At Swim* often reads not only as a novel produced by committee, but as an experiment in assembly-line fiction – albeit with all the pieces inserted in the wrong order. There was a precedent for this: while O'Nolan was in UCD, he colluded with the poets Denis Devlin, Donagh MacDonagh and other friends in composing what Niall Sheridan called 'the Great Irish Novel.' This was to be a parody of a generic best-seller, which would apply the principles of the industrial revolution to literature. Each contributor would write a chapter, and the book – with the working title, *Children of Destiny* – was to be constructed from a series of 'ready-made' fictional clichés.[5] If *At Swim* owes something to this project, it is also the student magazine writ large; a model of chaotic composition. The only structure this novel really has is that of a work in progress, and both O'Nolan's playful intertextuality and the student's self-reflexive frame narrative suggest that the process of writing is a collaborative effort.[6] His model of the writer at work is not the bard alone in his cell, but the raconteur at large in the pub.

Yet when the student presents readers with a choice of three beginnings 'entirely dissimilar and inter-related only in the prescience of the author' (*ASTB*, 9) it is of course a feat of narrative counterpoint impossible for the storyteller but not for the printed page. For all the tall stories that are swapped in *At Swim*, its reader is never allowed to ignore the mechanics of modern literary production. Littered with sub-headings, encyclopaedic lists, and at one point a direction to turn back forty-three pages (*ASTB*, 103), it is all the paraphernalia of print culture which makes this novel possible. Like Joyce's transformation of Homer's *Odyssey*, it too reinvents the storyteller's tale unfolded in time as a text organised in 'technological space'. However, the experience is not quite that of the Joycean text, as Hugh Kenner describes it:

> The reader explores its discontinuous surface at whatever pace he likes; he makes marginal notes; he turns back whenever he chooses to an earlier page . . . He is manoeuvred, in fact, precisely into the role of the scholiasts whose marginalia encumbered the Alexandrian manuscripts of Homeric texts; only here is a text designed, as Homer's was not, precisely for this sort of study.[7]

At Swim might as well be designed to resist this kind of study. Where Kenner's *Ulysses* manoeuvres its readers into careful scholarship, in *At Swim* O'Nolan transformed his own scholarly work (on the Middle Irish epic, *Buile Suibhne*, for example) into a piece of creative abandon. He would fully exploit the disruptive potential of footnotes and marginalia in devising the blasted time frame of *The Third Policeman*, but in this novel such devices still compete with the sheer entertainment of its narratives. The complexity of its three-fold structure (a book within a book within a book), as well as the neat parallelism between its characters, is comically undermined by the student's willingness to allow the manuscript to develop as much by chance as by design: providing summaries for lost pages and a choice of three openings. The reader of *At Swim* is never entirely on solid ground, never sure what to take seriously or not, its ironies complicated by what O'Nolan considered to be its general air of 'erudite irresponsibility'.[8] The novel teeters between the worlds of storyteller and scholar, between the temptation of instant gratification and the satisfactions of chewing over the literary cud.

In doing so, it reflects the populist streak in contemporary Irish writing as much as the hieratic character of international modernism. Even if *At Swim*'s cowboys are unreliable judges of literary merit (as Trellis's trial literally demonstrates), it is telling that their response to Sweeny's poetry – a recital of Jem Casey's 'A Pint of Plain' – has passed into Dublin parlance far quicker than the tale of the mad king. O'Nolan knew his mark. For some, Shanahan's judgement of a sophisticated Gaelic literature simply reflects the debased tastes of the modern reading public: 'you can get too much of that stuff. Feed yourself up with that tack once and you won't want more for a long time' (*ASTB*, 75). However, an earlier draft had another of the Dubliners defending the complexity of Bach's counterpoint:

> ... there's great crack in that when you get in on it ... understand it once and you'll never have anything else. You have to get used to it, you know, take it easy. You can't swallow it like a drink. It has to be chewed by the teeth. Look at it like this crust, say.[9]

Or like the hard crust the student chews on while devising the bizarre opening of *At Swim*. This novel may satirise the plain Dubliners' philistinism, but the student's literary pretensions are equally sardonic. It is this relentlessly ironic vision in *At Swim* which many critics have found hardest to digest, as if the novel's contradictions ultimately betrayed a vacant core; as one reviewer put it: 'I did not notice that he had a single original idea to express; and I should reluctantly put him among the bores'.[10] Perhaps in order to stave off this danger, Sweeny has sometimes been cast as *At Swim*'s lone authentic voice, as the lyrical heart of a corrosively self-reflexive text. Since the Sweeny poetry largely escapes parody, Declan Kiberd argues that this Gaelic voice strikes 'a single, pure note amidst a cacophony of false sounds and broken intervals'.[11] But the student's constant textual interference arguably tells a different story: in *At Swim*, it implies, there is no unadulterated base note, no underlying seriousness. It is notable that where a contemporary like Frank O'Connor sought to recapture the storyteller's 'lonely voice' in his short stories, O'Nolan's *An Béal Bocht* – which parodied the lonely voices that emanated from the Gaeltacht in the 1920s and 1930s – wryly drew attention to their literary craft, to the mediating influences of editor, genre and audience. If O'Connor's imaginative response to the realist trend of the 1930s was coloured by a lyrical romanticism, O'Nolan's impersonal version of modernism is practically medieval.

The significance of *Buile Suibhne* for this unending work in progress may be as much textual as thematic, since it originated in a manuscript culture which knew nothing of the deadening finality of the printed book. While the textual self-consciousness of *At Swim* undoubtedly owes a great deal to Joycean modernism,[12] its peculiarities also betray O'Nolan's familiarity with a literary tradition far removed from nineteenth-century concepts of authorship, original genius, or the notional coherence of the novel form. Where Joyce's parodies played on the manner in which revivalist translators mediated Gaelic literature to a contemporary audience, O'Nolan's knowledge of it was firsthand, founded on his work as a student of Irish in UCD. Like *At Swim*, *Buile Suibhne* is something of a patchwork creation, a compilation of prose narratives from various sources which were used to link existing poems.[13] The text O'Nolan used was itself a composite version of this tale, its editor, J.G. O'Keeffe, arguing that two interwoven but differing versions effectively competed within its pages.[14] The Fianna material in *At Swim* is similarly rooted in unstable, polyphonic texts – *Acallamh na Senórach*, a founding collection of Fianna tales, has been described as the work of a gifted literary magpie: 'a reservoir into which a brilliant late-twelfth century innovator had diverted several streams of tradition which previously had normally flowed in separate channels', culminating in 'a new untraditional creation'.[15] The description might be as well suited to the evolution of *At Swim* itself, its fractured form (like both the Irish texts) alternating between prose and poetry, and the student playing the roles of editor and compiler as much as that of sole creator.[16] When doodling on the title page of his own manuscript, O'Nolan wryly signed himself not as author, but as 'Chief Controller' of *At Swim-Two-Birds*. The 'Controller' of *At Swim*'s wayward strands is in large part an orchestrator, an arranger of found material, just like the lazy Dermot Trellis who filches his characters from existing works, or the medieval scribes who collated various strands of oral and literary tradition. Little wonder that shortly before the novel's publication Niall Montgomery was gleefully anticipating 'seeing Frank Swinnerton and the other English critics in the soup properly.'[17] *At Swim*'s precocious student exploits all the novelties of the Gaelic tradition in modernist dress, and the result for contemporary readers was a novel which landed somewhere on the border between chaos and coherence.

Along with *Ulysses*, *Buile Suibhne* offered a useful model of creative disharmony. O'Keeffe's introduction laments 'a certain lack of unity' in the text, a failure to achieve artistic coherence: 'It is possible that this may be due to an incomplete text, or it may be the author's way of representing the incoherent mind of the madman'.[18] O'Nolan plays with both possibilities throughout *At Swim-Two-Birds* – with the student misplacing pages and hints of Trellis's madness – though it is soon clear that cohesion will not be regarded as a major virtue. (As the conclusion makes clear, the mania for order is a questionable thing in itself.) Indeed, his attempt to police his disordered text with sub-headings and other textual markers distract as much as they clarify. The appearance of 'Chapter 1' on the first page, for instance, only advertises its own redundancy as it gradually becomes apparent that there will be never be any sign of a chapter two. But this is not only a text which thrives on contradiction, with each story or style calling forth its opposite. As implied in the textual combination of *Ulysses* with medieval Irish manuscripts, the novel carries within it a competing set of contexts in which to read it. When the student explains his work to Brinsley, his rationalism carries all the weight of 1930s literary fashions:

> The novel, in the hands of an unscrupulous writer, could be despotic . . . a satisfactory novel should be a self-evident sham to which the reader could regulate at will the degree of his credulity. It was undemocratic to compel characters to be uniformly good or bad or poor or rich. Each should be allowed a private life, self-determination and a decent standard of living . . . The modern novel should be largely a work of reference . . . A wealth of references to existing works would acquaint the reader instantaneously with the nature of each character, would obviate tiresome explanations, and would effectively preclude mountebanks, upstarts, thimbleriggers and persons of inferior education from an understanding of contemporary literature . . . (*ASTB*, 25).

If a novel could be assembled like a Ford motor car, then the student's manual might be a good place to start. Exploiting all the building-blocks readily available to the modern intellectual, his literary manifesto is impeccably modernist, not least for providing a conceptual key to the work in progress. At the same time, it also manages to travesty the agit-prop literature of the 1930s, substituting political theory for aesthetics. The joke was already implicit in *Children of Destiny* (as Sheridan describes it), at once a cynical piece of assembly-line popular fiction and a thoroughly modern experiment in collectivist art – much like a novel heralded by the journal *New Masses* in 1936, which was to be composed by the Committee of King's Norton Proletarians. Like the possibly apocryphal *Children of Destiny*, this literary experiment quickly ground to a halt, only a quarter written.[19] Yet the principle of the collaborative, 'ready-made' novel, constructed out of bits and pieces of everyday material, might also bring to mind the practices of the modernist avant-garde as much as the Ford assembly-line or the proletarian collective.[20] Like the newspaper column which would later dominate O'Nolan's career, *At Swim* – in all its unpredictable chaos – reads as a brilliantly creative response to the cultural flux of the 1930s. For the city of London, the contradictions of the decade might be illustrated in the involvement of Humphrey Jennings, pioneer of Mass Observation and British documentary film, in organising the 1936 Surrealist Exhibition.[21] The cultural confusion of 1930s Dublin similarly underscores the crowded pages of *At Swim-Two-Birds*.

This novel's jarring storylines are a fitting response to a decade in which Joyce's *Work in Progress* punctuated literary debate on the threat of mass culture, when European literature was becoming more politicised just as many Irish writers were disengaging from their own revolutionary past, and when the fervent promotion of an authentic, Gaelic Ireland was appearing ever more hollow to O'Nolan's determinedly cosmopolitan generation.[22] There is none of the revivalist ambition for a unifying national literature in *At Swim*; instead, its combination of incongruous styles presents an image of a fractured literary culture. Yet this rag-bag of a novel does incorporate one framing context in which to read its multiple ironies: the context of its own composition. Its competing strands are presented as a product of the student's perspective on Irish literature and it is a student who is an undergraduate in 1930s UCD, as was O'Nolan himself. The form of *At Swim* (parodies followed by parodies) might owe more to *Ulysses* than to *A Portrait*, but it is *At Swim*'s framing portrait of the artist which most clearly exposes the contrast between Joyce's Dublin and post-independence Ireland. Where the Royal University's students in *A Portrait* hang about the steps of the National Library discussing Aquinas or the grand future of Irish nationalism, their successors in *At Swim*, now students of the National University, give the impression that an unrelenting cynicism is the prevailing feature of intellectual life in 1930s Ireland. And as O'Nolan's friends later testified, the student's narrative in *At Swim-Two-Birds* cuts peculiarly close to the bone, much of it faithfully reproducing conversations which O'Nolan had with his friends while writing the novel. Niall Sheridan quickly recognised his own contribution to the work:

> ... he began to show me sections of the book as it progressed, explaining the rationale behind each episode and its place in the overall design. Very soon, these sessions began to form part of the text, and I found myself (under the name of Brinsley) living a sort of double life at the autobiographical core of a work which was in the process of creation.[23]

The frame narrative of *At Swim* suggests that its cynical perspective on Dublin's post-revival, post-independence and post-Joycean literary environment was fairly representative of O'Nolan's university circle. In any case, it is a novel firmly rooted in his experience of UCD in the 1930s, a place still soaked in nationalist sentiment, yet which appreciated the contrary ambitions of its prodigal son, James Joyce.

The student: *Comhthrom Féinne* and 'the National'

O'Nolan graduated from UCD with a BA in English, German and Irish in 1932, and returned from 1933 to 1935 to write an MA thesis on Irish nature poetry. It was in UCD's student magazine, *Comhthrom Féinne*, that 'Scenes from a Novel' (the kernel of *At Swim-Two-Birds*) was first published in May 1934. This story, which tracks the revolt of a set of characters against their author, was designed to effect the demise of Brother Barnabas, the persona O'Nolan had used for his frequent contributions to the magazine. It is likely that he began writing *At Swim* in mid-1935, around the time he finally graduated from UCD and joined the civil service.[24] That his academic environment remained a presence in the novel is visible on one level simply from the texts which O'Nolan chose to parody: the Finn MacCool sections are based on Standish Hayes O'Grady's collection of Fianna tales, *Silva Gadelica*, which, along with *Buile Suibhne*, was cited in the bibliography of his MA thesis.[25] Similarly, Brinsley's dry observation on the student's manuscript, that 'the plot has him well in hand' (*ASTB*, 99), originated in Niall Sheridan's description in *Comhthrom Féinne* of O'Nolan's work in progress.[26] A translation of Catullus which Sheridan had published made a brief appearance in *At Swim*;[27] he also claimed to have owned the original of the tipster's letter replicated in the text.[28] Even their graduation night celebrations provided the appearance of the hapless man covered in 'buff-coloured puke' (*ASTB*, 39).[29] It is clear on one level how much *At Swim-Two-Birds* was designed as an in-joke, casting O'Nolan's friends in a cod-Joycean epic. These real-life incursions also built on Joyce's practice of undercutting a revivalist appeal to a mythological past with a touch of dingy realism. Eimar O'Duffy employed the same trick in *King Goshawk and the Birds*, as did Samuel Beckett, desecrating Cuchulain in pantomime fashion in *Murphy*. What is peculiar about how this strategy is adapted in *At Swim-Two-Birds* is that by staging a work in progress, O'Nolan also dramatises the dynamics of an intellectual environment.

The intellectual ethos of UCD in the 1930s reflected its position as the direct descendant of Newman's Catholic University, founded in 1854 as a rival institution to Trinity College, Dublin and the new Queen's Colleges in Belfast, Cork and Galway. At the inception of the National University of Ireland in 1908, which incorporated the former Queen's colleges, UCD was expected by many to be the bridgehead of the Catholic, nationalist ethos, which some took as shorthand for the national culture. An official history of the NUI published in 1932 echoed the contemporary tendency to identify the national culture exclusively in those terms:

> The Catholic University, originating in the face of a long-established Protestant University, and of new Colleges maintained under Government control which took no count of the weight of religious belief or of national history, represented truly the currents of ancestral Catholic and Irish culture. Its existence asserted and fixed the principle that the future outlook and organisation of Higher Education should be in conformity with the national tradition.[30]

As a UCD honours student in Modern Irish, O'Nolan attended courses conducted by the Gaelic scholars Douglas Hyde and Osborn Bergin, neither of whom was in much doubt about the character of 'the national tradition'.[31] It was Hyde who famously declared to the Robertson Commission in 1902 that 'the only hope of a new university doing good to Ireland will be to have it frankly and robustly national, in a spiritual and intellectual sense, from the very outset . . . We want an intellectual headquarters for Irish Ireland'.[32] UCD's identification with Irish Ireland was underlined by its distinguished Faculty of Celtic Studies and its links to the Irish Folklore Commission. Nevertheless, there was a certain irony in UCD's loaded nickname, 'the National,' as in its reputation as a flagship of Catholic equality, since the numbers benefiting from higher education in the 1930s were miniscule. In the academic year 1930 to 1931, for example, there were a total of 1,684 students registered in UCD.[33] As a privileged minority, UCD's students could be confident of their future success in the Free State and signs of disaffection with the status quo were often quite cosmetic.[34] It is telling that the NUI constituency returned mostly conservative Cumann na nGaedheal deputies to the Dáil, until university representation in parliament was abolished in 1934.[35] The student body largely maintained the university's Catholic and nationalist ethos, indeed, many battles were waged with the university senate during the 1930s in order to ensure 'the National' lived up to its name – one such being the students' pressure to have a monument erected to the republican hero, Kevin Barry.[36] A 1934 *Comhthrom Féinne* editorial complained that the university remained officially non-denominational (more specifically, non-Catholic), despite fourteen years of self-government. Guerrilla action was taken one night in March 1936, when students erected crucifixes on classroom walls. Forced by the college to withdraw them, they retaliated with a highly critical article in *The National Student*, requiring a further apology to college authorities.[37] From its establishment, the non-denominational NUI had been unsatisfactory to the most Catholic (and nationalist) reaches of Irish society, but all made the best of the opportunity presented. It was UCD which pressed for the establishment of Irish as a compulsory matriculation subject in 1909, and the first issue of *The National Student* in 1910 declared that the

NUI's mission was no less than the regeneration of the country: 'where else is Ireland to seek her future leaders except in that University?'[38] UCD responded to that clarion call by keeping the Censorship Board well-stocked with its academics for the next few decades.[39]

However, one student's review of At Swim-Two-Birds for *The Irish Times* presents an alternative interpretation of the character of UCD:

> It has been the custom for some time now to refer to the "National University tradition", a thing which most would find much difficulty in defining. It is clearly consoling to be able to proffer as evidence for it something which it is suggested has been produced by it . . . all who have stood (or swayed) and shouted at the Literary and Historical, or who have read and blushed as they read the *National Student* (or its predecessor, *Comhthrom Féinne*, so foully done to death in an anti-Gaelic moment) will recognise the inspiration of Mr Flann O'Brien's new book, "At Swim-Two-Birds", and will glory in it . . .[40]

The 'National University tradition' was something which Niall Sheridan had attempted to define for the jubilee issue of *Comhthrom Féinne*, if only by concluding that it did not exist. Or at least, he decided that its writers were characterised by their idiosyncracy: 'There is no well-marked trail on our particular slope of Parnassus, only a number of individual goat-paths'.[41] One thing that *is* striking about most of the names which Sheridan cites in his article – such as Eimar O'Duffy, Austin Clarke and James Joyce – is their uniformly critical attitude towards contemporary Ireland. As an institution, UCD could hardly be noted for a culture of dissent. So perhaps the literary heritage which 'the National' was developing was evidence of an institution at odds with its own identity. O'Nolan certainly belonged to a self-consciously irreverent sect within the college; as the author of the *Times* piece above obliquely acknowledged, for a number of years he assumed leadership of the 'Mob' which heckled the debates of the famed Literary & Historical society.[42] *Comhthrom Féinne*, at the time predominantly parodic and satirical in tone, was largely controlled by O'Nolan and his circle – what Niall Sheridan called 'a sort of intellectual Mafia'.[43] Between 1931 and 1935, O'Nolan was its most popular and most prolific contributor, with his polymathic alter ego, Brother Barnabas, foreshadowing the eccentric Myles na gCopaleen. The magazine's appetite for caricature and parody was well served by O'Nolan's swooning Yeatsian poet, Lionel Prune, and a Syngean playwright, Samuel Hall, who was fascinated by the poetry of life on the bog.[44] And as in At Swim-Two-Birds, many of O'Nolan's skits reflected the contemporary preoccupation with the Celtic past; a report on 'The "L & H" from the Earliest Times',[45] produced ancient minutes recorded in Ogham script (as well as simian auditors with tails intact). To complete O'Nolan's satire of all branches of the Irish literary scene, Brother Barnabas's return in *Comhthrom Féinne*'s Jubilee issue was made in a Wakean muddle of Middle Irish and Latin: 'In Brathair Barnapas cct. Tri Filid in Domain Homer O Grecaip, Fergil O Latinnip ocus Paranabas O Gaedelaip'.[46] But the derisive nature of *Comhthrom Féinne* in O'Nolan's time was not appreciated by all. Though his intermittent absences were bemoaned by some editors, in May 1935 another complained of the magazine's low standard of comedy, caused by contributors mistaking personality for humour and facetiousness for wit.[47] When the magazine finally reverted to the title of *The National Student* in October 1935 – by which stage Barnabas had finally retired – its editor vowed to maintain a 'more serious note' than had been evident in recent years.[48]

Even in its most facetious incarnation, *Comhthrom Féinne* is interesting not only for the extent to which its humour prefigures *At Swim-Two-Birds*, but also for exposing the various intellectual (and as O'Nolan's contributions imply, pseudo-intellectual) trends competing for dominance in 1930s UCD. In 1934, he was mocking fellow students who alternated between playing the Gaelic revivalist and flaunting their cosmopolitan modernism:

> As soon as I arrived in town, I instantly joined the Gaelic League . . . And just as I had, at an earlier day, publicly thumbed Jolas' *transition* in London's fogs to show those cads that the apparent paradox implied in the juxtaposition of the Horizontal Worldview and a bus-ride to Brixton could be reconciled, united, adjusted and dissolved in the micro-universe of my mind . . . so also I felt bound to mutter Gaelic obscurities on tram-tops to Donnybrook on a wet Thursday to bridge the disparity between a shoddy foreign machined suiting and a Gaelic Ireland, free and united.[49]

The shabby reality of Gaelic Ireland, free if not united, had tarnished its appeal for his generation, who matured as the country struggled with the transition from nationalist idealism to the reality of life in a small, economically vulnerable state. Conformity with the Irish Free State's insular conservatism was unattractive to many, but so too was Joyce's melodramatic path of rebellion and exile. Joyce might have been a talismanic figure for O'Nolan's circle in UCD, but the admiration which they expressed for him was decidedly ambivalent. Barely a decade after political independence, a more populist aesthetic was proving attractive – perhaps in imitation of the political trend of British literature in the 1930s, but perhaps also because it was more easily assimilated to a nationalist outlook. O'Nolan's fairly indiscriminate satire of literary fashions in

Comhthrom Féinne arguably betrayed a certain evasiveness (if not indeci-
siveness) about such matters on his part. But an article by his
contemporary, Charlie Donnelly – a committed socialist who would be
killed in the Spanish Civil War – shows that even he was warily negoti-
ating a path between an insular nationalism and a vacant
internationalism. As he put it, the 'modern, young Irishman' tended to
be familiar with 'extra-Irish' contemporary thought, which had the effect
of cutting him off from his 'emotional environment'. This presented an
aesthetic (and emotional) difficulty:

> The modern Irish artist cannot throw over modern thought. Neither
> can he agree to throw over Ireland. In his consciousness, the two must
> fuse. Modern Irish art must be in touch with the people . . . [but] to
> be of any importance it must be in touch with more than the people.[50]

It seems curious to hear an echo of Daniel Corkery from such unex-
pected quarters, even if Donnelly qualifies the assertion in *Synge and
Anglo-Irish Literature* that the Irish writer 'sprung from the people' simply
needed 'a mental equipment fitted to shape the emotional content that is
theirs, as well as the nation's, into chaste and enduring form'.[51]
Donnelly's reference to an 'emotional environment' which the young
Irishman would find incompatible with modern thought is telling, artic-
ulating a cultural uneasiness felt perhaps by many of his fellow students.
The article appeared in an issue which is likely to have been edited by
O'Nolan, and this predicament is tellingly echoed in the comic drama
between the student and his uncle in *At Swim*, which finally ends with
the student's acknowledgement that this plain Dubliner is 'Simple, well-
intentioned' (though he does add with characteristic superiority, 'pathetic
in humility' (*ASTB*, 215)).[52] Despite expressing scorn for the 'Celtic
Twilight people', Donnelly ends with a dire warning against intellectual
seduction by newer trends, by 'the clever and the facile and the semi-edu-
cated, and political and literary charlatanry'.[53] He was not alone in his
criticism; the literary charlatans were again in the frame a few months
later when a *Comhthrom Féinne* editorial complained of the indolence into
which the Gaelic League had fallen, leaving students to trail after fashionable European movements.[54] Considering the climate of the early
1930s, perhaps this suspicion of contemporary European thought was
inspired as much by political movements as by literary fashions. (At the
time, barely a decade after the civil war, it was understandably free of
explicit political commentary.) But whether or not this wariness was
partly inspired by contemporary European politics, it indicates that even
the irreverent literary caste who compiled the magazine were not entirely
unsympathetic to the biases of the plain people.

It is one of these UCD undergraduates whom O'Nolan sets at the centre of *At Swim*, and the novel which he produces is a glorious jumble of revivalist parodies, modernist aesthetics, popular fiction and the turgid prose excerpts to be found in school readers. Considering the aesthetic challenges which Donnelly foresaw for the 'modern, young Irishman'[55] – now in possession of an intellectual equipment unsuited to express his own experience – the muddled result is hardly surprising. Flaunting all these disparate elements, *At Swim-Two-Birds* travesties the image of the national tradition which was being institutionalised in UCD; even O'Nolan's MA thesis on Irish nature poetry made an explicit attack on the critical values of Irish Ireland. Where Corkery's *The Hidden Ireland* located the endpoint of Gaelic civilisation in the *aisling* poetry of the eighteenth century, O'Nolan took this poetry's political bent (and its nationalist keening) as a sign of the final demise of the genre.[56] (Admittedly, he also argued that Irish nature poetry had already reached its peak by the twelfth century.) Aodh de Blácam's *Gaelic Literature Surveyed* – one of the texts cited in his MA bibliography and also a set text for UCD's BA course in Modern Irish – neatly illustrates the brand of cultural polemics which provoked O'Nolan's satire.[57] De Blácam was a favourite target of his from the early days of *Blather* to *Cruiskeen Lawn*, and *At Swim*'s gleefully anachronistic mayhem pointedly contrasts with fanciful notions of the unchanging Gael like that he presents in *Gaelic Literature Surveyed*.[58] His sense of Gaelic literature is that it dealt with 'a continuous historic present', the peculiarly static Gael showing the same mode of thought in the eighth and the eighteenth centuries: 'the Gael found a way of life long ago, and a religious faith, that satisified him then and forever, and seemed to offer all that a man can wring from the world'.[59] The irritation of Shanahan and friends at the long-winded talk of Finn MacCool would seem to tell a different story. *At Swim* debunks the notion of an unchanging (or even continuous) Irish tradition, presenting a moving shot of contemporary Irish writing that jarringly juxtaposes its past, present and future. On the other hand, the nostalgic hankering after tradition that issued from some modernist quarters fared no better. *At Swim* irreverently fulfills T.S. Eliot's dictum that:

> ... the historical sense compels a man to write not merely with his own generation in his bones, but with a feeling that the whole of the literature of his own country has a simultaneous existence and composes a simultaneous order.[60]

The novel adheres to the letter, if not the spirit, of Eliot's theory – this 'historical sense' is relegated to farce in the Red Swan Inn where Dermot Trellis houses his characters: 'There is a cowboy in Room 13 and Mr

McCool, a hero of old Ireland, is on the floor above. The cellar is full of leprechauns' (*ASTB*, 35). But it is in the manner of a rather different modernist, James Joyce, that *At Swim* desecrates the idea of cultural purity which was the hobbyhorse of exclusivist nationalists. It faithfully depicts the multicultural muddle in any reader's (or writer's) mind, combining tricks learned from Heinrich Heine and Joyce with excerpts from *Buile Suibhne* and eighteenth-century English prose.[61] Despite the best efforts of the propounders of clean literature, the Censorship Board, and various other fans of isolationism, O'Nolan's Ringsend cowboys demonstrate that a national culture is a peculiarly hybrid thing; they may be merely 'a gang of corner-boys whose horse-play in the streets was the curse of the Ringsend district' (*ASTB*, 59), but they are imagined as the cattle-rustling heroes of *Táin Bó Cuailgne*, or of the American frontier, or as the dare-devils of imperial Africa.[62] The Ringsend cowboys are, indeed, 'the product of a mind which fed upon adventure books of small boys' (*TP*, 196) – of that or a mind fed upon the 'Cyclops' episode in *Ulysses*. While Trellis's fear of moral and intellectual corruption goes so far that he decides to read only green books (which are, by implication, all reassuringly Irish books), *At Swim* itself is a model of glorious contagion.

But if O'Nolan's model for the combination and juxtaposition of many different literary styles is *Ulysses*, the effect of the technique in *At Swim-Two-Birds* is far different. Since the novel is structured as a work in progress, and the characters on every plane of the text (from the student's friends to the Good Fairy) can interrupt and comment on each other's stories, *At Swim* does not simply present a clash of literary styles. It also dramatises a battle of wills between some very different branches of the reading public. Stephen Dedalus looked to Aquinas in shaping his own aesthetic theories, but this student gives voice to the demands of the contemporary literary marketplace. So it is not only the rather catholic range of literary influences which *At Swim* acknowledges that undermines fantasies of a univocal Gaelic culture; O'Nolan's jarring combination of critical voices, reflecting diverse readerships, implicitly challenges the sense of community so important to the idea of a *national* culture. As Declan Kiberd sees it, the author of *At Swim*'s fragmented narratives may be 'scandalized by the splitting of modern readership into so many discrepant constituencies. His work might be read as an attempt to restore a lost unity or at least to glue all the shattered pieces together as best he can'.[63] But arguably, the student's juxtaposition of discordant styles and genres (themselves punctuated by headings and spaces in the text) only emphasises and exaggerates these divisions. The various authors and storytellers in *At Swim* might espouse the didactic function of literature, like Trellis, or view it as an aesthetic object, like Orlick, or they might simply aim to entertain their audience, like Shanahan. But as the combination shows, for the author of *At Swim*, literary value is relative; these different authors have little purchase outside their own constituency. And this has repercussions for the student narrator himself – the semi-autobiographical character who functions as O'Nolan's literary alter ego, in the manner of Stephen Dedalus.[64] *At Swim*'s range of reference might indicate that its ideal reader is the UCD Arts undergraduate circa 1931 (a little specific, in market terms), but O'Nolan's semi-autobiographical frame narrative relieves the novel of the consequent claustrophobia. In one ironic gesture, he both acknowledges the limits of his intellectual independence, and asserts the critical detachment which makes it possible. Just as Trellis is the fall-guy for the propagators of 'clean' literature, and Shanahan's bloodthirsty tastes impugn the connoisseur of pulp fiction, the student gives O'Nolan ample scope for self-mockery. Tellingly, around the time he began writing *At Swim-Two-Birds* another student virulently attacked *Comhthrom Féinne*'s small band of modernist poets, Joycean imitators, and self-consciously erudite humorists – in other words, the vein of writing brilliantly cultivated by O'Nolan in the magazine over the previous years.[65] *At Swim*'s student is the very image of the literary type who was under attack; the novel displays all the literary characteristics which a more friendly critic, Donagh MacDonagh (reportedly a collaborator on *Children of Destiny*) had derided in an earlier issue. MacDonagh had blamed the sterility of contemporary literature (as he saw it) on the baneful influence of modernism. The problem was a 'facile cleverness which is killing all originality . . . the more brilliant of my contemporaries . . . write rather to show their culture and cleverness than to convey any new idea to their reader'.[66] The description fitted O'Nolan well; it fits his fictional alter ego even better. The student's literary manifesto, which advises that the modern novel should be largely a work of reference to preclude 'persons of inferior education from an understanding of contemporary literature' (*ASTB*, 25), knowingly plays on this cultish literary snobbery. In fact the novel he proposes to assemble from ready-made parts owes as much to Henry Ford as it does to the modernist collage. His fragmented text might have a modernist façade, but its eclecticism is deliberately superficial. Showing no literary discrimination (dropping a betting letter or a snatch of eighteenth-century prose into his text as easily as a Middle Irish lay), he produces a text which is as confused as *Ulysses* – at least as it appears to the unwary reader – but without its underlying structure. With his studied nonchalance, he implies that his disjointed narrative owes as much to accident as design, or indeed as much to the conventions of the popular serial as to Joyce (supplying '. . . *a summary of what has gone before*, FOR THE BENEFIT OF NEW READERS'

(*ASTB*, 60)). The text this latter-day Stephen Dedalus produces might be *Ulysses* as re-written by the plain reader.

'Tell me this, do you ever open a book at all?': *At Swim-Two-Birds* and the Plain People of Ireland

The conflict of literary values dramatised by *At Swim*'s querulous readers and storytellers – a conflict between a notion of fiction as a popular, marketable commodity, and as something available only to the educated few – betrays the critical context of this 1930s metafiction. As argued in chapter one, the disparity between the plain man and a self-professed cultural elite is a recurrent theme in O'Nolan's comedy. Comic dialogues between the two would become a staple of *Cruiskeen Lawn*, whether involving Myles and the Plain People of Ireland, or other erudite and urbane characters forced to tolerate the garrulous 'Dubbalin man' (such as the voice who endures stories of the Brother at a myriad of Dublin bus-stops). The same dynamic can be seen in embryo in *At Swim* – in the dialogues between the uncle and the student, or in the contrast between the cowboys' blunt attempts at fiction and the student's hyper-literary efforts. In these scenarios the humour cuts both ways, the Mylesian character typically being too exaggerated to serve merely as a straight man. The student's intellectual swagger serves the same purpose in *At Swim*, and his characters' unwitting ripostes to the author of their crazy tale ensure that any scorn is evenly distributed: 'I like to meet a man that can take in hand to tell a story and not make a balls of it . . . I like to know where I am, do you know' (*ASTB*, 63). On the other hand, his intellectual snobbery (however ironically delivered) is perversely justified by the narrow-mindedness of Shanahan and friends. The latter's criticism of Orlick's literary efforts could just as easily come from the hostile reader of *At Swim*: 'this tack of yours is too high up in the blooming clouds. It's all right for you, you know, but the rest of us will want a ladder' (*ASTB*, 168).[67]

Shanahan is a caricature of the modern mass reader, the harried everyman who regularly cropped up in the critical literature of the period, and who in Ireland became the particular focus of the censorship campaigns against British newspapers and other 'evil literature'.[68] But although he betrays more sympathy for Jem Casey's doggerel than for the poetry of *Buile Suibhne*, when subjected to Finn MacCool's long-winded tales he maintains a (qualified) respect for 'the real old stuff of the native land':

> . . . stuff that brought scholars to our shore when your men on the other side were on the flat of their bellies before the calf of gold with

> a sheepskin around their man. It's the stuff that put our country where she stands today, Mr Furriskey, and I'd have my tongue out of my head by the bloody roots before I'd be heard saying a word against it. But the man in the street, where does he come in? By God he doesn't come in at all as far as I can see. (*ASTB*, 75)

Though the 'man in the street' in 1930s Ireland hypocritically praises the Gaelic culture in which he has little interest, the student's uncle and Mr Corcoran (whose committee debates the propriety of jazz music and the foreign waltz) indicate that the revival is very much a middle-class activity. Further up the social scale, the snobbish Good Fairy expresses an equally hollow appreciation of modernist literature: 'I always make a point of following the works of Mr Eliot and Mr Lewis and Mr Devlin. A good pome is a tonic' (*ASTB*, 120). O'Nolan's derision of the reading public – and its cultural class divisions – seems fairly equally distributed. Where an F.R. Leavis could imagine the advent of mass culture as a matter of crisis, *At Swim* implies that it is the public who need protection from these overweening authors.[69] Myles na gCopaleen later expressed a similar ambivalence towards *Ulysses* (whose innovations *At Swim* emulates and rejects all at once) – not concerning Joyce's literary skill, but rather the unreasonable demands he made of the reader:

> Joyce has been reported as saying that he asked of his readers nothing but that they should devote their lives to reading his works. Such a method of spending a lifetime would be likely to endow the party concerned with quite a unique psychic apparatus of his own. I cannot recommend it.[70]

A contemporary handbook on Joyce literally anticipated Shanahan's complaint on behalf of the man in the street: 'the plain reader may ask, "But where do *I* come in? . . . why should I risk cramps in the cranium by worrying about Joyce?'.[71] The contemporary trend to target 'the plain reader' with books offering to decipher modernist literature is turned on its head by *At Swim*; O'Nolan lays bare the construction of his own text and gives the plain reader (embodied in Shanahan, Furriskey, and company) the power to re-write the story as he sees fit. He reverses the question which esoteric modernist texts implicitly pose to the reader – here it is the plain man who interrogates the author: 'Tell me this, do you ever open a book at all?' (*ASTB*, 10).

The derisive voice off-stage – as exemplified by *At Swim*'s unruly characters – was a congenial form to O'Nolan; he had honed his talents in this line when leading the mob of hecklers at UCD's L&H debates. His comic incursions earned him the society's silver medal in the 1931–32 session, but they were not uniformly appreciated, and when James Fitzpatrick called for the extermination of these obstructive 'pests' in *Comhthrom Féinne*, O'Nolan made a revealing defence:

> Let me enlighten Mr. Fitzpatrick as to the first principle of public speaking. It is to compel the attention of your audience. Regard the "sane" 10 per cent as superfluous pests. They will listen in any case. The 90 per cent is your audience. Do not address dock labourers on Canon Law, and if you must, speak to them in their own language . . . the successful speaker must know and understand his audience of plain people.[72]

Perhaps, he might have added, the successful writer must do the same. Anthony Cronin argues that O'Nolan nursed an ambition to produce a best-seller, one which he hoped that *At Swim-Two-Birds* would fulfill.[73] As it was, the public's initial indifference to the novel was sealed when Longman's remaining stock was destroyed in an air-raid just over a year after publication.[74] Given the nature of *At Swim*, his ambition was a little unrealistic. But if he conceived himself primarily as an entertainer, perhaps such a goal should not be so surprising; after all, the literary skills he practised in *Comhthrom Féinne* were those of a performer (as he developed the talent for extemporising which would serve him well in *The Irish Times*). While a complimentary copy of *At Swim* found its way to Joyce, via Niall Sheridan, O'Nolan also dispatched a copy to the popular novelist, Ethel Mannin. In the accompanying letter, he described the novel as 'a belly-laugh or high-class literary pretentious slush, depending on how you look at it'.[75] She chose the latter option, which prompted the following reply:

> It is not a pale-faced sincere attempt to hold the mirror up and has nothing in the world to do with James Joyce. It is supposed to be a lot of belching, thumb-nosing and belly-laughing and I honestly believe that it is funny in parts. It is also by way of being a sneer at all the slush which has been unloaded from this country on the credulous English . . . I'm negotiating at present for a contract to write 6 Sexton Blake stories (25 to 30,000 words for £25 a time, so please do not send me any more sneers at my art). Sorry, Art.[76]

It is strange to think what O'Nolan actually expected from Mannin, aside from sneers at his 'Art'. Perhaps he really did believe that *At Swim* could attract a popular readership, and that such a well-connected personality (who was also a familiar and trusted figure to the 'plain reader') was well-placed to help it on its way.[77] But Mannin had recently turned up as something of a literary villain in Q.D. Leavis's *Fiction and the Reading*

Public in her capacity as a promoter of the Book Guild. Founded in 1930, it promised to guide its subscribers through the morass of contemporary fiction and 'pernicious' literary criticism to find an entertaining read. Mannin asserted that their selections catered *'for the ordinary intelligent reader*, not for the highbrows':

> One of its chief aims is to avoid indulging in the deplorable affectation of recommending as a work of 'genius' the sort of thing which is dubbed clever simply because it is mainly unintelligible and written in an obscure manner . . .[78]

At Swim exploits the very kind of facile cleverness that Mannin found so objectionable, displaying all the window-dressing of the 'unintelligible' modernist novel. Whether or not there was a mischievous element in O'Nolan's decision to send Mannin a copy, it may have been in the belief that *At Swim*'s fairly domesticated brand of modernism made his novel palatable to the 'ordinary intelligent reader', who was these days beginning to feel a little disenfranchised. Certainly, his emphatic denial of having any ambition to produce 'Art' is curious, as if she could hardly have issued a greater insult.

However, this is not to imply that *At Swim* itself betrays an inherent sympathy for the plight of the plain man, whatever O'Nolan's posturing.[79] The critical debate had its own peculiar connotations in Ireland. At the turn of the century, Lionel Johnson had condemned the influence which the populist, political ethos of Young Ireland exerted on Irish writing, and his complaint could hold true for the critical mood of the 1930s:

> Against any living Irish poet, who writes in any style uncultivated then, is brought the dreadful charge of being artistic: and sometimes, if it be a very flagrant case, the unspeakable accusation of being English.[80]

Daniel Corkery was by now playing spokesman for this outlook, admitting the brilliance of many Anglo-Irish writers only to argue that their writing showed a 'disparity between intellect and emotion', making them far inferior to the Irish writer of the people, who required simply 'a mental equipment fitted to shape the emotional content that is theirs, as well as the nation's, into chaste and enduring form'.[81] In *Gaelic Literature Surveyed*, de Blácam had similarly praised the Irish people's simplicity: 'Ireland still is little troubled by the complexities of the study'.[82] At *Swim*'s brand of cynical erudition is surely a response to this stultifying climate, but the text does betray a suspiciously 'plain' resistance to the notion that a novel should have any aesthetic pretensions. The student accommodates his cleverness to his environment – being careless of his literary ambition in an acceptably ironic manner – and O'Nolan effectively does the same. In *At Swim*, aesthetic pretensions seem allied to social pretensions, Orlick's literary gifts being discovered by the appearance of 'some pages of manuscript of a high-class story in which the names of painters and French wines are used with knowledge and authority' (*ASTB*, 164). And for all its irreverent comedy, O'Nolan himself was very careful to ensure that his novel did not openly offend public taste. Prior to publication, an editor's judgement that particular sections of the novel showed an unnecessary 'coarseness' produced an immediate and unqualified undertaking to remove anything of the kind.[83] When his responsibility for the book was indicated in 'a London literary paper' shortly before publication, he unsuccessfully requested Longman's to change the title: 'I am really very anxious for reasons that have nothing to do with modesty, to have nothing that is not thoroughly orthodox in literature attributed to me'.[84] O'Nolan's position in the civil service might have been the source of his anxiety, but no matter how concerned he was not to be associated with literary 'filth', he just as deliberately avoided any association with literary pretensions. It is almost as if one could be substituted for the other.

The sensation caused by *Ulysses* certainly implied that the two were indistinguishable, and it is indicative of the consensus on these matters that there was effectively no need to ban Joyce's work in Ireland. Though O'Nolan stocked his student's bookcase with works by Joyce and Huxley (whose *Point Counter Point* was the first book banned under the 1929 Censorship Act), in later years even Myles would criticise the 'salacities' of *Ulysses*.[85] As Lanters perceptively notes, Shanahan spells out 'bee-double-o-kay-ess' (*ASTB*, 168) as if it were a dirty word – only 'pee-eye-ell-ee-ess' (*ASTB*, 160) is granted the same distinction.[86] Since practically all contemporary literary fiction had to be obtained under the counter in 1930s Ireland, perhaps any literature could not escape seeming faintly scurrilous. O'Nolan himself wryly suggested as much when reflecting on *At Swim* in 1959: 'It had been widely put about that the book was "very dirty" . . . maybe it was, but the point is scarcely material: having the reputation of being a pornographer, literary pimp and muck-raker is what matters in Dublin, let one's wares be as clean as the blue sky'.[87] Given the comically broad intepretation of the 1929 Censorship Act, originally designed to block only pornography and material on birth control or abortion, Irish culture seemed to be suffering from a peculiar kind of intellectual puritanism. As Flann O'Brien remarked in a 1940 letter to *The Irish Press*, 'our notorious national rule of thumb . . . identifies obscurity with obscenity. If he [an outraged correspondent] was told that incunabula had been discovered in his cellar, he would probably give orders for the place to be fumigated'.[88] Sexual modesty was being blurred with its intellectual counterpart. No wonder O'Nolan denied Mannin's charge of aesthetic ambition in *At Swim*; what respectable Irishman of the 1930s would be caught writing 'bee-double-o-kay-ess', especially of the brazenly literary variety? Perhaps only an eccentric, an outcast or even a madman, and Sweeny is readily on hand in *At Swim* to illustrate that the writer's lot is a curse.

Many a writer in 1930s Ireland may have had sympathy for his sufferings, driven to distraction for offending a cleric. Back in the days of *Comhthrom Féinne*, another of O'Nolan's alter egos was already complaining that government censorship was hampering his latest enterprise, University College Ballybrack. UCB's curriculum posed some difficulty for its students:

> All the books prescribed are banned in the Irish Free State. Students are advised to spend a fortnight in France reading up the course. We regret to announce that Dr Kahn's Treatise on Advanced Algebra, prescribed for the degree of B.Sc. is also banned, strong exception having been taken to some of the Surds in Part ll of the work . . .[89]

If obscurity was often enough to rouse suspicion, in the case of *At Swim-Two-Birds* it would have been justified. While the novel underwent a degree of self-censorship before publication, it is nevertheless laced with proscribed material. This ranges from Finn MacCool's praise of birdsong, which elaborates on variations of the 'pilibeen', or plover (a word which Dinneen also translates as 'pedant' and 'penis'),[90] to allusions to rape, abortion, and a teasing reference to the main target of the Censorship Act: 'Some [student societies] were devoted to English letters, some to Irish letters and some to the study and advancement of the French language' (*ASTB*, 48).[91] While O'Nolan's clever use of language frustrates the censorship, at the same time, as Hopper argues, it 'tacitly affirms it by that very cleverness'.[92] Yet the success of a censorship culture ultimately depends on its invisibility, and *At Swim* also wryly draws attention to the unmentionable act. As the uncle arrives home unexpectedly, for example, the student hastily covers 'such sheets as contained reference to the forbidden question of the sexual relations' (*ASTB*, 91–92). In a more subtle fashion, the two surviving drafts of *At Swim* expose how O'Nolan effectively recorded his own self-censorship in the final text. Some of its traces are quite clearly preserved: a riddle Kerrigan originally posed about the definition of a 'blunderbuss' ('a taxicab full of pregnant prostitutes') survives into the published version as an 'obscene conundrum', mysteriously unexplained.[93] The cowboys' rich Dublinese was another casualty of

O'Nolan's 'decarbonising process',[94] and left its own rueful echoes. In the earlier draft, Shanahan condemns (with innocent irony) 'a scutter of dirty filthy language'[95] from the cowboy Red Kiersay. Gentrified into a *'stream of dirty filthy language'* in the published version, his remark now elicits a prim reaction from his audience: 'Well dirty language is a thing I don't like. He deserved all he got' (*ASTB*, 57–58, my italics). The cowboys' remarks may, as Samuel Anderson argues, be simply 'a preemptive concession to the censors',[96] but they also inscribe into the text the very prudery which necessitated these revisions. If the cowboys are happy to listen to tales of citizens being violently fired off a tram during a shootout, so long as there's no 'dirty language' involved, their skewed priorities tellingly mirror those of the censors themselves.

Yet one act of censorship which has remained well-hidden was the dilution of *At Swim*'s religious irreverence, its last disappearing traces visible in O'Nolan's re-naming of the 'Good Spirit' as the 'Good Fairy': 'I think this change is desirable because "Fairy" corresponds more closely to "Pooka", removes any suggestion of the mock-religious and establishes the thing on a mythological plane.'[97] The 'mock-religious' was indeed more central to the earlier version, with the Pooka and Good Fairy originating as a Devil and an Angel, and their struggle over Orlick's soul firmly belonging to a Christian universe of good and evil rather than to a strange corner of folk Irishry. Of course, the Catholic element still pervades the published text – 'aestho-autogamy', a peculiarly sexless form of procreation that conveniently produces fully-formed civil servants, does not need to be explicitly identified as 'immaculate conception' to be read as such.[98] (Furriskey, Shanahan and Lamont were originally dubbed the 'three Magi' at Orlick's birth.)[99] But what is far clearer in the earlier draft is the negative impact of the 'Lent-gaunt cleric' (*ASTB*, 20) on Ireland, clerical persecution being a common factor not only to Trellis and Sweeny (whose story provides the model for Trellis's torments), but also to Finn MacCool. He wryly recalls the debates between Oisín and St Patrick in *Acallamh na Senórach*, a clash between pagan and Christian Ireland:

> What makes me mad . . . is a bookful of history. It is the most dishonourable storybook of them all . . . Patrick that came from far away to badger Oisín of the Fian of Finn, Lent-boned Patrick of the acolytes and the generous nuns, the hero with the crooked spear. Where was cornyellow Finn that he had not a restraining thumb on every shore of the eight shores of Erin against the coming of the sanctified stranger? Where but hog-tied in the house of a book-poet.[100]

This Finn, who could 'burst God with the power of a breath whistled from his tooth-gap',[101] is no more a friend of the cleric than Sweeny himself. His badgered Oisín seems to stem from the more caricatured ballad forms of the *Acallamh* in which Patrick is 'a bigoted cleric, pronouncing the doom of hell upon the Fenians, and Cailte or Oisin the defiant pagan'.[102] So it is defiant paganism which underscores Finn's scorn for 'book-poets', perhaps the very same writers who introduced a Christian element to the old tale of mad Sweeny, originally the story of a king driven mad by the scene of battle.[103] It undermines too the twinning of Gaelic and Catholic in the modern Irish identity, a notion then being popularised by Daniel Corkery, among others. Of course, the composition of *At Swim* belonged to a decade which saw the ever closer association of Church and State, from the celebration of the Eucharistic Congress in Dublin in 1932 to the recognition of the 'special position' of the Catholic Church in the 1937 Constitution. Other discarded passages mischievously reminded this openly pious society of its hidden negative. Trellis, himself a vocal saint and private sinner (with a larger role in this draft), casually interrupts Finn's complaining to muse on problems of sin and sanctity:

> Supposing, said Trellis with a long chuckle, that a streetwalker makes £20,000 from her trade, saves it up over a period of fifty years, repents in her old age and builds a church with the money? Is it a church within the meaning of the act or what is it? Is it a brothel? Tainted money, I mean. Is it tainted subjectively or is it only unclean to those who know the commodity that was traded for it?[104]

The point, for all his characteristic prurience, is the interdependence of good and evil:

> You cannot have one without the other. Each gets its force by reason of the other and would be meaningless without the other. There was no good in the Garden till the serpent came, only negation and bathos. Therefore the devil created good.[105]

The Pooka and the Good Fairy, or the Devil and Angel, are on hand to bear out his thesis, their preposterously balanced disputation giving his idea dramatic shape. But as the Good Fairy's peevish behaviour implies, in *At Swim* there is little glory in being on the side of the angels. Where he tends to voice the respectable pruderies of de Valera's Ireland, the battle between good and evil is also clearly bounded by the sexual morality of contemporary Irish Catholicism. The Good Fairy's discovery of the Pooka in bed with his 'shank of a wife' (*ASTB*, 103) sets up the opposing principles of body and spirit, underscored by the Pooka's simultaneous awakening of all the 'evil creeping things' (*ASTB*, 103) in the forest who were 'slumbering under great stones after the godless rigours of the night'.[106] It is true to form that this pious spirit would demur from hearing the adulterous story of 'Dermot and Granya' ('If it is dirty, of course, etiquette prevents me from listening to it at all' (*ASTB*, 140)), and his protest against playing cards for a woman betrays the misogynistic assumption that their only use is for sex, which is – for an angel – immaterial: 'How many times have I got to repeat that I have no body?'.[107] Yet his public piety is ironically undermined by the fact that of all the card-players in the Pooka's game, he is the only one to deal in the diabolical even numbers. Trellis's comparable obsession with 'the terrible cancer of sin' (*ASTB*, 36), particularly as reported in tabloid newspapers of the kind which inspired the Irish censorship campaign, has a similar correlative in the fact that *he* is the character who actually commits sexual assault. (The conduct of the elderly Finn MacCool towards Peggy similarly subverts fantasies about the purity of Gaelic Ireland and its literature.) An excised description of Peggy and Furriskey parting as lovers, 'having first lain together in a suggestive attitude in a ditch for fear that Trellis would be awake and watching them',[108] not only hints at the unhealthy interest he takes in such activities, but casts it in the image of those self-appointed policemen who roamed the highways and byways of rural Ireland for the discovery of courting couples.

As a despotic author, Trellis effectively divests his characters of free will, just as a paternalist censorship culture impinges on the freedom of its citizens. Given the strict edicts of the time, O'Nolan could not entirely let his characters misbehave as he saw fit. But nevertheless, as many critics have recognised, the Sweeny story points to how the conflict between pagan Ireland and a punitive Church might resonate in 1930s Dublin. In *Buile Suibhne*, when Sweeny hears the vespers bell peal out at Snámh-Dá-Én, he utters a repentant lay which is pointedly omitted from the novel which bears its name: 'O Christ, O Christ, hear me!/O Christ, O Christ, without sin!/O Christ, O Christ, love me!/sever me not from thy sweetness!'.[109] (Swim-Two-Birds is also the place where the *Acallamh* records that Finn was converted to Christianity.)[110] The earlier version of the novel's conclusion has the contrite student similarly hearing 'the Angelus pealing out from far away, perhaps from the Church at Snamh da En or Swim-Two-Birds'.[111] But by the time the revised text was being prepared for publication, not only had O'Nolan obscured the allusion but he was readily agreeing with Longman's that his title was too 'difficult', while offering equally bizarre alternatives.[112] His personal dislike for 'At Swim-Two-Birds' perhaps stemmed from the fact that much of the religious satire had already been stripped from the novel and that alerting the Irish reading public to what remained was not the wisest tactic. As *At Swim* recognises, the plain people would be all too ready to police its humour –

'no disrespect', the uncle warns Mr Connors as he wheels out an innocuous joke about the clergy (*ASTB*, 136); 'You won't get very far by attacking the church,' Furriskey cautions Orlick (*ASTB*, 172). O'Nolan ultimately took their advice. Gone is the moment when Moling enters Trellis's bedroom and mistakes his chamber-pot for a font, happily imagining its 'whiteness, its star-twinkle face' in his new church.[113] Gone too is Orlick's response to the cowboys' demand for swifter punishment of Trellis. 'You can kill a man with a slasher or powder the walls of his stomach with fine glass . . .':

> — The aesthete will favour the crucible.
> — By God that's the man! said Furriskey, eye-quick and hand-quick. Crucifixion! By God we'll crucify him! We'll nail him up. Eh, Mr Lamont? We'll nail him up to the mast!
> — You certainly hit the nail on the head when you said crucifixion, Mr Orlick, said Shanahan in admiration.
> — I said nothing of the kind, Orlick answered.[114]

Nevertheless, in the opening paragraphs which follow, Trellis is repeatedly discovered in bed with 'one foot crossing the other in the manner of a slothful crucifixion'.[115] O'Nolan was pragmatic in recognising that such passages would never pass the censor, though ironically their comedy is testament to a culture deeply suffused with religious imagery. What they do reveal is the fairly shallow nature of his self-censorship, despite his outward orthodoxy. In this respect, what is notable about his later work (at least until the appearance of Fr Kurt Fahrt in *The Hard Life*) is how deliberately it avoids any hint of religious impropriety. If the populist values of the Plain People of Ireland contributed to the student's parody of modernism in *At Swim*, the popular religious ethos of 1930s Ireland muffled another aspect of O'Nolan's comedy.[116] At one point in the earlier draft, having described the supernatural appearance of Trellis to the virgin-born Furriskey in the form of a cloud, the student worriedly asks Brinsley whether he 'might be open to a charge of blasphemy'.[117] By the time the final version was prepared, his question about the 'propriety' (*ASTB*, 50) of these matters had clearly been answered. In both drafts, the doubtful pages are meekly 'lost'.

Perhaps then it is fitting that by the end of *At Swim* this irreverent student has made a dubious reconciliation with his uncle, abandoned his spare-time literary activities and condemned all the rebellious exponents of *non serviam* to the fire. Yet the convenient tidiness of this conclusion undermines the conventional *Bildungsroman* ending. With a similarly brash disregard for plausible resolution, it is suggested that Trellis's unusual experiences are the symptom of a mania:

The eyes of the mad king upon the branch are upturned, whiter eye-balls in a white face, upturned in fear and supplication. His mind is but a shell. Was Hamlet mad? Was Trellis mad? It is extremely hard to say. Was he a victim of hard-to-explain hallucinations? Nobody knows . . . It is of importance the most inestimable . . . that for mental health there should be walking and not overmuch of the bedchamber. (*ASTB*, 217)

If that were the case, the student's mental health cannot be much more robust than that of Trellis. Originally the madness theme stemmed from a much longer parallel between the writers in *At Swim*, still reflected in Trellis's punishment by Moling and Jem Casey's arrival in Sweeny-fashion from the depths of a tree (*ASTB*, 118).[118] The likelihood is that it was downplayed since it made a little *too* much sense of its structure, as in the following conversation between Brinsley and the student:

— There are too many planes and dimensions in this work of yours. This author invents people who in turn invent other people, and so on ad infinitum. The half of the characters are writing books. Nobody could be expected to follow that sort of thing.
— There is no necessity for them to follow it, I answered. The man that starts all the trouble is Trellis, who is stated to be eccentric. It is quite possible for a man who is half-crazy to be obsessed with and bullied by his characters.[119]

The original ending, 'Mail from M. Byrne', similarly explained away the novel's peculiarities by having Byrne instruct the student to hint that 'Trellis is neurotic and may be imagining all the queer grotesque stuff' that was going on (*MBM*, 184). *At Swim* may have had more coherence in its manuscript draft, but O'Nolan's revisions steadily contributed to the novel's pattern of estrangement, preserving it from the trite neatness which sometimes marrs his short stories.[120] The ultimate conclusion instead is nothing of the kind, echoing the novel's triadic patterns but otherwise allowing him to neglect tying up any of his loose ends. The work in progress finally preserves its air of incompleteness, its ironic possibilities, conceding only the literal conclusion that in the world of the book, 'death is a full stop' (*ASTB*, 216).

Luigi Pirandello, whose *Six Characters in Search of an Author* provides a precursor to *At Swim*, identified a similar resistance to closure, a contradictory doubleness as being central to 'the humoristic disposition'.[121] He contended that humour arose out of a state of mind, a psychological process, in which the humorist was engaged in perpetual self-parody. According to Pirandello, a habitual self-consciousness meant that every feeling, accompanied by reflection, was shadowed by its opposite: 'Every genuine humorist is not only a poet, he is a critic as well'.[122] It is a theory which could have been designed with the self-reflexive narrator of *At Swim* in mind. The double-edged nature of its comedy can be seen in the student's attitude to authorship – while his manuscript purports to strip the despotic author of all his power, and allows the reader to 'regulate at will the degree of his credulity' (*ASTB*, 25), his interruptions and directions also emphasise his ultimate control over the text. But on the other hand, irony and parody are so pervasive in *At Swim* that the author's position is effectively undermined because the text has no anchoring point of authority. The ubiquity of parody in the novel is telling; a sense of conflict or ambivalence is inseparable from such a technique, which both subverts and reinforces the authority of its target text.[123] While *At Swim* may exaggerate the alliterative runs and gigantism of Fianna stories gleaned from *Silva Gadelica*, for example, O'Nolan's lively parodies are themselves a form of tribute – not least to O'Grady's idiosyncratic translations. On the twenty-fifth anniversary of his death, O'Nolan clearly expressed his admiration for the latter's 'profound learning . . . humour and imagination' in an *Irish Times* article. These translations, he wrote, devised a 'curious and charming English . . . in an effort to render to the student the last glint of colour in any Irish word'.[124] The sincerity of the tribute is indicated by his own prose, which fully exploits the curious and idiosyncratic turn of phrase. As with *At Swim*'s use of Joyce, its parody of O'Grady betrays as much a desire to emulate his work as to scorn it.[125] Such ambivalence in the novel ensures that O'Nolan remains 'a malevolent subverter of any secure authorial authority'.[126] While *At Swim*'s various authors and storytellers are voluble and intrusive, its pervasive comic ambiguity ironically allows its actual author to remain scrupulously enigmatic. Tellingly, in his MA thesis, O'Nolan praised Old Irish nature poetry primarily for its impersonal quality and *At Swim* effectively maintains this impersonality, though ostensibly turning the notion on its head.[127] Though the student is everywhere visible in his novel, his ironic posturing creates a certain elusiveness. The double-edged comedy of *At Swim*, built on paradox and contradiction, is similarly tricky to pin down on any point. It is typical of O'Nolan that he casts an ironic eye on the student's supposed carelessness; there is more of a structure to *At Swim* than there should be, given the student's boasts about his disregard for his manuscript. In a similarly ambivalent move, his discreet mention of unmentionable matters – and partial elision of others – wavers somewhere between criticism of the Free State's censorship culture and a certain complicity with it. *At Swim* even contradicts itself as a metafiction, safely containing the characters' insurrection within a realist frame narrative. Such contradictions have led some critics to read the novel as an indeterminate Menippean satire.[128] While Lanters presents Mervyn Wall's *The Unfortunate Fursey* in the same vein (as a carnivalised allegory of Emergency Ireland), in 1982 Wall himself denied any critical or satirical intent in his novel, expressing a cavalier attitude to its composition:

> When the reviews came out, I was astonished to read that I had employed irony and that I wrote sardonically. That hadn't been my intention. I just wrote it for fun. The thing just flowed out.[129]

If this seems peculiarly at odds with *Fursey*'s satire of a puritan, almost theocratic state, Wall's only concession was to admit that 'one writes instinctively. . . [and] one writes first for oneself'.[130] Given this claim, it is interesting that he turned to comedy, like so many of his Irish contemporaries – all the more so, because the comic text allows for this kind of doublethink, a means of assertion and retraction all at once. At a time when realist writers like Seán O'Faoláin were beginning to define the role of the Irish writer as a dissident voice in a conservative society, the comic mode offered a more ambiguous way of expressing dissatisfaction with the status quo.

The nonsense techniques of *The Third Policeman* take this one step further; though purportedly set in hell it presents a curiously estranged version of Ireland. One thing *At Swim* certainly has in common with nonsense texts (which typically promise meaning but never quite deliver it) is its lack of resolution. Though the novel ends with the incineration of Trellis's characters and a kind of reconciliation between the student and his uncle, its ultimate 'conclusion' is nothing of the sort. In its bizarre ending, *At Swim* stays true to its episodic nature, anticipating *The Third Policeman*'s dictum that a question is always better than an answer: 'Answers do not matter so much as questions . . . There is no answer at all to a very good question' (*ASTB*, 201). The novel's lack of resolution reinforces the air of provisionality that marks this whole work in progress. It is ultimately the form of *At Swim-Two-Birds* which frustrates its satire of cultural nationalists, high-handed modernists and the plain reader alike. As a metafiction which habitually turns back on itself, *At Swim* continually demolishes its own intellectual premises. This is also the nature of its comedy; the satiric elements of *At Swim* are generally undermined at one point or another by the novel's contradictory nature. The result is that amidst all the novel's layers of parody and all its competing voices, it is difficult to identify the voice of O'Nolan himself. But since *At Swim*'s semi-autobiographical frame narrative firmly roots this work in progress in 1930s UCD, it suggests a tantalising correspondence between O'Nolan's ambivalent, non-committal comedy and the paradoxes of the college's intellectual life at the time. By the 1930s, an institution whose history cast it as the intellectual headquarters of Catholic, nationalist Ireland, was developing a *literary* history that was beginning to tell a different story. In the years after independence, the national culture may have been conceived in very absolute terms, but with time it was becoming only too obvious that it was founded on a series of false antitheses – between an Irish, Catholic nation and its suspect minorities, between the merits of folklore and the dangers of modern popular culture, or indeed, between the purity of Irish culture and the depravity of European modernism. For those who now had to negotiate a period of transition in cultural nationalism, *At Swim*'s erudite comedy was conveniently ambiguous – not only mocking earnest cultural nationalists (the puritan plain people), but also their self-consciously intellectual antagonists. *At Swim-Two-Birds* is not simply a text that marked a period of change, casting a cold eye on nationalist politics, revivalist aesthetics, the literary marketplace, and the experimental modernist novel; it is also a paradoxical comedy caught up in that point of transition.

3

'Nonsense is a new sense':
The Third Policeman in 1939

Although first published in 1967, *The Third Policeman* had been composed in the shadow of war. O'Nolan began work on the novel less than six months after the publication of *At Swim-Two-Birds*. In October 1939, he informed his agents that 'I started another story (very different indeed) about August last but gave it up owing to the threatened disintegration of the universe. I cannot see any use in this writing at the moment'.[1] Their response was drily encouraging, assuring him that literary London was proceeding as normal, and the hiatus was short-lived.[2] By January 1940, the completed manuscript had embarked on a round of rejections from British and American publishers. Embarrassed by his failure to find a publisher, O'Nolan notoriously spread fanciful stories about losing the manuscript – one had it blowing out of the boot of his car on a drive through Donegal.[3] After this disappointment, his literary activities were confined to the letters page of *The Irish Times* until Smyllie commissioned the *Cruiskeen Lawn* column, which first appeared in October 1940. The manuscript of *The Third Policeman* did not resurface until his death in 1966, and there is no evidence that he had made any further attempts to have it published.[4] After he lost his civil service post in 1953, during which time he was producing syndicated columns for regional newspapers as well as *Cruiskeen Lawn*, writing scripts for RTÉ television, and working on Sweepstake and Guinness advertisements, *The Third Policeman* was not offered to any publisher. Instead, the manuscript was plundered for *The Dalkey Archive*, published in 1964, in which another de Selby has possession of Policeman Fox's omnium, now no longer a vague source of omnipotence, but an item with a destructive potential that rivals the post-war atomic bomb. (The original de Selby posed more esoteric dangers, Le Fournier arguing that the disturbing effect of his theories on the masses may have been responsible for the Great War (*TP*, 33).) Though the composition of *The Third Policeman* coincided with the outbreak of the Second World War, it is only *The Dalkey Archive* which shows any overt traces of that conflict. The use of atomic bombs on Hiroshima and Nagasaki had left its mark on *Cruiskeen Lawn* in 1945:

> What shall I say of the atomic grenade lately perfected in America and subsequently exported to Japan, duty free? It is an astonishing achievement, not so much in physics as in the more familiar sphere of human folly. I am aware that for humans there has been a long-standing arrangement whereby they can be absolutely sure of one thing, each for himself, i.e. death. There is no case on record of the pledge given to man that he will die having been broken. Yet scientists and governments are very worried about the possibility that people may not die, or may not expire in sufficiently gigantic numbers, and, in order to make sure, have devoted much thought and treasure to research on this subject . . . I do not find that the quest for it is an adult performance.[5]

Myles's distrust of politicians who offered safe guardianship of the bomb is echoed in the depiction of *The Dalkey Archive*'s Mick Shaughnessy, whose original plans to save the world by stealing de Selby's omnium lead to delusions of becoming a new Messiah. However, in adapting the earlier novel, O'Nolan belatedly heeded Longman's injunction in 1940 that he should have made his new book 'less fantastic'[6] than *At Swim-Two-Birds*. For all its colloquys under the sea, *The Dalkey Archive* is certainly the less 'fantastic' book, both in style and substance. Its realist narrative defuses the metaphysical threat of de Selby's experiments with life and death,[7] its humour mainly relying on the incongruity of the resurrected St Augustine and the jibes at the Jesuit order which O'Nolan continued from *The Hard Life*. In comparison, *The Third Policeman* is more of a fable, a parable of a soul in purgatory. Though it shares something of the later novel's episodic structure, it is essentially a story with a single brilliant trick at its core. While there is little obvious satire in its eerily estranged vision of rural Ireland, the novel's sense of bleak confusion was strangely appropriate for the winter of 1939. *The Third Policeman*'s humour depends for its effect on the narrator's pained reasonableness in the face of an incomprehensible world. It invites the reader's identification with the confusion of an innocent man, but one who is 'a heel and a killer'[8] too, a murderer like so many of the novel's characters. If *The Third Policeman* is a parable, it was a curiously timely one.

A few months after finishing the novel, while it was still travelling from publisher to publisher, O'Nolan was back in the letters page of *The Irish Times*. On this occasion, he was defending his new Irish-language *Cruiskeen Lawn* column from outraged patriots (some of his alter egos among them), and the following was contributed to the debate by Oscar Love:

The decay of humour in Eire is largely due to the spread of patriotism, for the patriot cannot appreciate his neighbours, but he worships himself.

Ireland cannot produce a Lear, a Lewis Carroll, or a W.S. Gilbert, because the Irish have not discovered that nonsense is a new sense. This sense is unknown to dictators. If present-day dictators possessed a sense of nonsense the world might be rocked with laughter instead of shocked with bombs.[9]

As a resolutely apolitical piece of nonsense, *The Third Policeman* might be precisely what this writer recommended. The whimsical element in this novel has much in common with the *Cruiskeen Lawn* of the early war years – or at least with that aspect of the column characterised by the Keats and Chapman stories, the farcical Myles na gCopaleen Research Bureau and the absurdities of the Cruiskeen Court of Voluntary Jurisdiction. However if, as Oscar Love remarked, 'nonsense is a new sense',[10] then O'Nolan's nonsense writing is much more than whimsical escapism. For one thing, the creation of the farcical and ambivalent Myles na gCopaleen persona was a deliberate move at a time when, as Myles complained, there were self-appointed pedagogues on every Dublin street corner, a 'vast number of individuals and organisations who are profoundly dissatisfied with the people here and who issue instructions to them as to how they should behave'.[11] Making nonsense of such shrill demagogues was the business of Charlie Chaplin's *The Great Dictator*, released in 1940, and though Chaplin's General Hynkel punctured Hitler's arrogance in just the manner Oscar Love had prescribed, Myles complained that his closing speech to camera was 'the end of what is possible in the sphere of human degradation. I remember blushing.'[12] Chaplin, the archetypal comic, was now apparently taking himself far too seriously, a dupe of the same sycophantic critics who had flattered Walt Disney into producing the recent *Fantasia*, in which 'Mr Michael Mouse . . . becomes, as *The Bell* would say, something taut, alert, an intimate thing in aesthetic experience. And his father, poor Mr Disney, begins to neglect his dress, try to look a bit wild-eyed and go for long walks in the rain.'[13] As Myles had it, both entertainers were casualties of precious critics who failed to take comedy on its own terms. Topsy-turveydom had surrendered itself to the world it should parody: Disney's 'Silly Symphonies' were now abandoned in favour of their respectable counterparts and Chaplin's slapstick had given way to political rhetoric. Whether or not Myles's criticism was wholly deserved, it explains a little why *The Third Policeman* is apparently less topical – or rather, less rooted in contemporary Ireland – than any of his other novels.[14] If nonsense was an *alternative* mode of making sense, a 'new sense' insofar as it was a self-reflexive and self-critical style of writing, then it was better protection against the arrogance of the patriot or the demagogue than any earnest satire or polemic. It also served as a defence against any charge of serious aesthetic ambition, while still allowing for full display of literary pyrotechnics. As O'Nolan assured his agents, *The Third Policeman* was simply 'a funny murder or mystery story and cannot be said to be a lot of highbrow guff like the last book'.[15]

The day before the first *Cruiskeen Lawn* was published in *The Irish Times* in October 1940, Oscar Love attacked a virulent critic of a recent *Times* editorial which had questioned the merits of the Irish language revival: 'Science may soon produce a serum to kill prejudice and provinciality. An advance order for the serum would not come amiss'.[16] This antidote to Irish provincialism and self-conceit was to be provided in the irreverent nonsense of *Cruiskeen Lawn*, which undercut the rhetoric of the newspaper columnist as much as it mocked the foibles of the Plain People of Ireland. Yet the same provincialism would find a very different reflection in *The Third Policeman*. In the autumn and winter of 1939, as neutral Ireland deliberately turned away from 'the threatened disintegration of the universe',[17] O'Nolan created something oddly similar to Ireland's 'self-contained otherworld'[18] in which to stage a disintegration of the known world. For Anthony Cronin, the novel's unsettlingly familiar depiction of hell (which looks something like Tullamore) is the product of a Manichaean perspective, the idea that 'the balance of good and evil in the universe as we know it had been disturbed in favour of evil. This world was perhaps hell, or part of its empire'.[19] And yet the narrator continually fails to see it for what it is, locked into a simple rationalism and preoccupied by his greed for the black box. By always trying to deny the peculiarities around him, he misses their true implication: that his old world has (literally) been exploded apart. The solipsistic nightmare which follows is a fitting punishment for the intellectual vanity that led him to kill Mathers in order to publish the definitive 'De Selby Index'. Yet all the characters of *The Third Policeman* exist in a similarly lop-sided private universe, a fact which the narrator is forced to recognise when he collides with the logic of the policemen. Like de Selby, they are equal to any perplexity; in Pluck's jurisdiction, the question 'Is it about a bicycle?' (*TP*, 57) has only one answer. Within its limits, everything is knowable and nothing makes sense – if a sentence can be logically executed then so can a prisoner. If the claustrophobia of this self-contained world anticipated the dominant mood of wartime Ireland, it is less than flattering that what passes for common sense in this parish is only a raving logic shared by a whole community. By February 1940, O'Nolan was already complaining of the tedium of neutral Dublin, a city which (with pragmatic logic) had apparently forgotten that there was a war on.[20] It seems his nameless everyman was not alone in his obtuse attitude to his own situation; a momentous change had happened in the world, but in Ireland for a while it seemed as if no one had noticed.

And yet *The Third Policeman* obviously resists such a contextual reading. Lacking the narrative pyrotechnics of *At Swim*, it may be, as Kenner says, 'nearly naturalistic'[21] but it is that 'nearly' which is the most unsettling thing about it. Like *At Swim* this is fiction on stilts, somehow approximating to an image of the real world and yet always slightly askew. Quite apart from the uncanny weather which follows the narrator's moods (as if in a ha'penny murder mystery), there are very literal reminders of the distortions of individual perspective, most often in the landscape he moves through: 'the trees and the tall hills and the fine views of bogland had been arranged by wise hands for the pleasing picture they made when looked at from the road' (*TP*, 39). In this novel, there is nothing natural under the sun and everything bears the prints of artifical design – where the earth is 'agog with invisible industry' and trees are described as being 'active where they stood', giving 'uncompromising evidence of their strength' (*TP*, 129) the clanking machinery off-stage is impossible to ignore. This topsy-turvey universe, where what is most natural is also most artificial, might be simply the product of Policeman Fox's meddling. Yet its artificiality is also that of an unnaturally circumscribed world, one that is dominated by a police barracks where true investigations are outnumbered by easy explanations. When faced with a character who has no name, Pluck looks for the answer in a finite range of possibilities – Mick Barry or Charlemagne O'Keeffe, Kimberley or Joseph Poe or Nolan (*TP*, 104–5) – in the latter case getting close to the mark. The narrator's own trust that everything in the world is knowable (he begins by questioning Martin Finnucane in a similar manner (*TP*, 46–7)) is constantly undermined throughout, only to be horribly reinforced at the end. The journey he takes is, of course, 'the fresh-forgetting of the unremembered',[22] a cycle which he has presumably gone through many times before. His intimation that this universe has an overriding structure betrays his place in a mystery novel – organised around a key or code which must be deciphered – yet *The Third Policeman* turns the genre inside out. Not only does it reveal the identity of the killer in the very first sentence: 'Not everybody knows how I killed old Phillip Mathers', it also reveals the murder weapon: 'smashing his jaw in with my spade' (*TP*, 7). (It is typical of O'Nolan that he obeys the conventions only literally by never *naming* his killer.) As Keith Hopper has argued, this artificial universe may be read as a metafictional counterpart to *At Swim-Two-Birds*, casting the narrator as interpreter of its mysteries and scattering clues that he is, if not a character in a novel, then at least a pawn in someone else's play.[23] The protagonist of *The Third Policeman* suggestively inhabits the condition of the book: frozen in time yet trapped in a cycle of eternal recurrence. Each new reading is a 'fresh forgetting', the same story played over and over again.

Yet the imponderables repeatedly posed in the novel – whether in de Selby's idiosyncratic theories, MacCruiskeen's unconscionable inventions or the properties of eternity which defy all definition – also suggest a resistance to such coherent explanations. Of course, quite literally speaking, the state of death is beyond human comprehension: 'I cannot hope to describe what it was but it had frightened me very much long before I had understood it even slightly. It was some change which came upon me or upon the room, indescribably subtle, yet momentous, ineffable . . . all my senses were bewildered at once and could give me no explanation' (*TP*, 24). *The Third Policeman* itself can have the same effect. Even its sober academic footnotes establish that little can be confidently established, either on the work of de Selby himself or on the true existence of his elusive commentators. Comically undermining all authority, the novel presents most acts of interpretation as bogus enterprises. Replete with the unknowable, the inexpressible and the indescribable, it 'asks us to think the unthinkable',[24] deliberately playing on the borders of understanding. Otherwise unorthodox in its depiction of an afterlife, in this much it bows to the notion of imponderable mysteries, so strong a feature of Catholicism. Hugh Kenner, who makes great play with O'Nolan's unholy trinity of policemen, nevertheless concludes that this is a novel 'far from deliberate enough to bear any great weight of interpretation'.[25] *The Third Policeman* parodies wild de Selbian schemas while apparently never troubling itself to be in any way schematic. Even its final revelation, which underpins its own structural logic, is undermined by the narrator's inexplicable recollection of events before his cataclysmic encounter with the black box. In that sense Pluck's logic is typical of the novel as a whole, adept at giving the appearance of explanation while explaining nothing at all. The result is nonsense, a comic arbitrariness which Lanters identifies in the narrative from the moment Mathers has been murdered in the most coldly calculated fashion: 'I heard him say something softly in a conversational tone – something like "I do not care for celery" or "I left my glasses in the scullery"' (*TP*, 16).[26] These strange banalities echo across the text to the indecipherable shouts MacCruiskeen mangles from the light – '*Change for Tinahely and Shillelagh!*' – which, however 'foolish and trivial', disturb the guilty narrator 'in a way that could only be done by something momentous and diabolical' (*TP*, 111). As befits a scholar's hell, this is a novel which teasingly plays on the very edge of meaning, its cyclical enigmas wryly reflected in the 'brain-destroying bicycle' (*TP*, 171) created by MacCruiskeen. That playfulness is a feature that *The Third Policeman* shares with nonsense writing, which suggestively has a self-reflexive bent similar to that of metafiction.[27] Wim Tigges's definition of the genre, based on the work of Lewis Carroll and Edward Lear, identifies four basic elements: 'an unresolved tension between presence and absence of meaning, lack of emotional involvement, playlike presentation, and an emphasis, stronger than in any other type of literature, upon its verbal nature'.[28] The false syllogisms and absurd logic of *The Third Policeman*, its narrative arbitrariness, fondness for lists, repetition and circularity, and its rearrangements of time and space are all classic nonsense devices.[29] As a comic mode nonsense is obsessed with logic, though it never quite deigns to make sense. Thriving on paradox, its subversion of authority is matched only by its whimsical authoritarianism. The advent of Myles na gCopaleen in late 1940, just when the manuscript of *The Third Policeman* was being consigned to a drawer, was not a bolt from the blue.[30] Myles's peculiar brand of pedantic chaos was already present in the abandoned manuscript.

Lost in Wonderland: nonsense features of *The Third Policeman*

Nonsense writing stretches logic to its illogical ends, exposing the irrationality of rational thinking. In *Philosophy of Nonsense*, Jean-Jacques Lecercle demonstrates how Victorian children's writers anticipated the insights of twentieth-century philosophy in their play with language and logic, but arguably what places *The Third Policeman* most firmly within the nonsense mode is its inherent resistance to being taken too seriously.[31] Like Lear and Carroll, O'Nolan exploited a marginal position in relation to canonical literature. The *Alice* books neatly fuse popular culture and high literature, with Carroll's caustic observations belying their status as mere children's books. Furnished with nursery rhymes as well as parodies of Tennyson and Wordsworth, they anticipate similar combinations in *At Swim* and *The Third Policeman*, where Standish O'Grady consorts with the cowboy western, and O'Nolan in a sense rewrites the murder mystery back-to-front.[32] Modernist texts such as *Ulysses* might have made similar combinations, but they did not risk confusion with marginal forms such as children's books or pulp fiction. In contrast, *At Swim-Two-Birds* blithely travesties the experimental modernist novel, subverting contemporary aesthetics to the point where it risks 'not really being "aesthetic" at all'.[33]

As in *At Swim*, there is a large element of chaos and redundancy in *The Third Policeman* that seems to resist too much structural coherence. Mathers's theory of the coloured winds, for one, seems blithely super-fluous. Its roots, if looked for, lead down many paths: to Des Esseintes's colour theory in J.K. Huysmans's *Against Nature*, to an old Irish epic, *Saltair na Rann*, or even Swift's *A Tale of a Tub*.[34] Yet arbitrary as Mathers's digression seems (in narrative terms), his story of the layers of coloured gowns which an individual accumulates during their lifetime clearly echoes the images of regression which multiply throughout the novel. In this sense, narrative arbitrariness is balanced by a structural parallelism reminiscent of *At Swim*, order and disorder competing within the cyclical frame of the novel. O'Nolan's final twist serves a function similar to the student's narrative in *At Swim*, both providing a rational frame for his wilder inventions, obeying an impulse to order (or simply make sense of) the nonsense narrative.

However, the flimsiness of these devices presents his critics with a double bind, never wholly fulfilling their function while still suggesting that his fantasies really do present some puzzle to be solved. It is telling that encyclopaedias and dictionaries – stubbornly open-ended forms – are constant shadow texts in *At Swim*, embodied in the Conspectus, the Athenian Oracle and the student's careful notation of rhetorical tropes. Its narrative (or anti-narrative) also echoes André Breton's observation in the first surrealist manifesto that the novel is 'pointlessly particular', a 'style of pure information': the student literally substitutes a list for char-acterisation in the '*Memorandum of the respective diacritical traits or qualities of Messrs Furriskey, Lamont and Shanahan*' (*ASTB*, 161).[35] Like the student's watch, the mechanics of this novel are seriously out of joint. Yet if 'the intractable mania that consists in reducing the unknown to the known, to the classifiable, lulls minds',[36] then *The Third Policeman* is a bracing alternative. And its pained narrator slowly comes to the realisation that, like the characters of *At Swim* (and as Breton argued, like all protagonists) the world he moves through allows him only the illusion of freedom. His narrative, instead of moving towards resolution, works nonsensically in the opposite direction. Enigma is at the heart of a novel in which a journey cannot lead anywhere, in which music is so refined that it cannot be heard and where, like *At Swim*, answers do not matter so much as questions. Of course, even the central figure is nameless, as unsure of his identity (which is none) as of anything else in the policemen's jurisdic-tion. Like Alice, who changes size, names and even species (accused at one point of being a serpent), the narrator's identity is constantly on the edge of dissolution. This is an eternally shape-shifting world, where Policeman Fox has the face of Mathers, men become bicycles and a soul is more easily identified than its bearer. The result has been a broad mix of allegorical interpretations of *The Third Policeman*, regarding it as anything from a deliberate metafiction to an involved commentary on Einsteinian physics, though readings have been offered with varying degrees of seriousness, the ingenuity of de Selby casting a long shadow.[37] The novel's slightly capricious quality may be partly due to its hasty composition, written in only five months while O'Nolan was working nearly six days a week at his civil service job.[38] But if *The Third Policeman* is to be believed, there is little that exegesis, classification, or any such scientific analysis can solve. Logic itself, as the novel shows, is circular, interminable and very nearly unbearable.[39]

At the same time, O'Nolan's pedantic brand of comedy is typical of nonsense precisely because of its self-reflexive fascination with its own procedures. *The Third Policeman*, with its sense of a hidden and inexplicable order, its satire of scholarly and legal pedantry, falls within a tradition of nonsense writing that is highly conscious (and highly suspicious) of procedure and ritual.[40] To a large extent, *The Third Policeman* replicates *At Swim*'s fascination with form, but here reality – not art – is recessive, and *life* is a matter of technique. The irony is that the narrator can obviously never master his situation, since this whole universe has been contrived to manipulate him. Though he reduces the social world to an intellectual problem, as his hero de Selby might do, it is not one that he is in any way equipped to solve. This is a reader embedded in the text who, like Alice in Wonderland, is held subject to its puzzles and riddles.[41] The omniscient voice promised at the opening ('Not everybody knows how I killed old Philip Mathers' (*TP*, 7)) is quickly lost, since the narrator is nothing more than a pawn in a perplexing mystery. In this latter-day Wonderland, most conversations are tricky games: finding a route around Mathers's 'no' means devising a way of thinking 'inside out' (*TP*, 29). But the narrator's own history implies that for him the world was always so perplexing. The estrangement began long before his search for the black box:

> . . . a certain year came about the Christmas-time and when the year was gone my father and mother were gone also . . . I was young and foolish at the time and did not know properly why these people had all left me, where they had gone and why they did not give explanations beforehand. My mother was the first to go . . . and as I thought the whole thing was very private and that she might be back on Wednesday, I did not ask him where. Later, when my father went, I thought he had gone to fetch her with an outside car but when neither of them came back on the next Wednesday, I felt sorry and disappointed. (*TP*, 8)

If his childish logic had already shown its inadequacies, as interpreter of the policemen's world he becomes an even less flattering image of the hapless reader, both a monomaniac and a murderer. The intellectual vanity which prompted him to kill is still in evidence when he eventually retrieves the black box from Policeman Fox:

> I could not help smiling at him, not, indeed, without some pity. It was clear that he was not the sort of person to be entrusted with the contents of the black box. His oafish underground invention was the product of a mind which fed upon adventure books of small boys, books in which every extravagance was mechanical and lethal and solely concerned with bringing about somebody's death in the most elaborate way imaginable . . . (TP, 196)

If the narrator had been a more assiduous reader of pulp fiction, he might have realised what kind of adventure he was in. It is his innocent assumption of superiority – and failure to recognise his own intellectual conditioning (given the echoes of de Selby throughout this otherworld) – which facilitates his punishment. Whether read in a theological or metafictional sense, if he suspected some design to the universe, then he would be some way to escaping his fate. After all, the very same humility paradoxically enables the characters' revolt in *At Swim-Two-Birds*. Tellingly, when the nameless narrator muses over the corporeality of his soul (known as Joe), his train of thought turns upon a motif familiar to readers of *At Swim*:

> What if he *had* a body? A body with another body inside it in turn, thousands of such bodies within each other like the skins of an onion, receding to some unimaginable ultimum? Was I in turn merely a link in a vast sequence of imponderable beings, the world I knew merely the interior of the being whose inner voice I myself was? (TP, 123)

This image of infinite regression appears throughout the novel – in de Selby's experiment with mirrors which allowed him to observe a younger self in 'an infinity of reflections' (TP, 67), in MacCruiskeen's nested boxes, or in the police station secreted in the walls of Mathers's house.[42] The conceit of the book within a book within a book in *At Swim* is replayed here as an inner signature of the narrator's circular and interminable hell. In the description of Mathers's 'mechanical' eyes, the layered personae of Brian O'Nolan also have an eerie counterpart:

> I got the feeling that they were not genuine eyes at all but mechanical dummies animated by electricity or the like, with a tiny pinhole in the centre of the 'pupil' through which the real eye gazed out secretively

and with great coldness . . . possibly behind thousands of these absurd
disguises, gazed out through a barrel of serried peep-holes. (*TP*, 26)

The serialism may be drawn from J.W. Dunne's *The Serial Universe*, giving
O'Nolan appropriately hokey scientific grounds for his tale of scholarly
crime and punishment, but the image of a 'genuine' personality lost
within layers of disguise, ritual and artifice reverberates through his work.
In another sense, Hopper argues that the Chinese-box pattern in the
image of a serial observer or a self-conscious narrator 'is an image for
determinism',[43] one which he identifies in the work of de Selby, who
'likens the position of a human on the earth to that of a man on a tight-
wire who must continue walking along the wire or perish, being, however,
free in all other respects. Movement in this restricted orbit results in the
permanent hallucination known conventionally as "life" . . .' (*TP*, 98).
There is a hint of this paranoid sense of entrapment in *At Swim*, its self-
reflexivity serving as a comic reaction against the forces of cultural
determinism. However, the theme is replayed in a darker guise in *The
Third Policeman*, where the nonsense fascination with order and disorder,
rules and procedures, is inflected with a strange foreboding.

In a place where losing an argument can mean hanging, the intellectual games typical of nonsense literature are hardly inconsequential and
an ability to conform to arbitrary rules (however bizarre) is invaluable. Yet
the eccentricity of *The Third Policeman* is that of the familiar world gone
only slightly awry – as Seamus Deane suggests, the civil service question-
naire haunts the narrator's interrogation of Martin Finnucane, and
Pluck's garbled officialese could easily be ascribed to the same source.[44]
In that respect, it is telling that the operative difference between the two
characters is the relative power of their positions; in these kinds of games,
the house always wins. Sergeant Pluck can satisfy himself that the narrator is not nameless and unidentifiable, an unknown quantity in his
jurisdiction, but must be related to the last nameless man (the narrator
himself?) who passed through his police station. His capacity for logic
unhindered by common sense far outstrips the narrator's, to the point
where he can justify stringing the other up on the scaffold. Like Carroll's
Alice, he is adrift in a world whose rules he cannot fathom, but which
retain a relentless logic. Alice is permanently frustrated in decoding the
conventions of her dream-world; no matter how cleverly she conducts her
verbal battles with disgruntled Wonderland characters, the cards are
stacked in their favour. Both novels employ a style of comedy which is as
much marked by the proper observance of convention as it is by a willful
absurdity; it is only unfortunate for their protagonists that no one
informed them of the rules of the game. The sense of inhabiting a

bizarre, and slightly sinister, system is common in Victorian nonsense literature; such systems might be legal, social, bureaucratic, or even linguistic – the one constant is their tendency to force the protagonists into a bewildered passivity. In 1931, Louis Aragon seized upon this aspect of nonsense writing in order to adopt Lewis Carroll as a proto-surrealist writer. Pointing out that Carroll was also writing in an age dominated by scientific rationalism, he contrived to draw political conclusions from the estrangement of Victorian society in *Alice*'s childlike distortions:

> . . . in those shameful days of massacre in Ireland, of nameless oppression in the mills – where was now established the ironic accountancy of pain and pleasure recommended by Bentham – when, from Manchester there rose like a challenge the theory of '*Free Trade*' ('when I use a word,' said Humpty Dumpty, 'it means exactly what I want it to mean, neither more nor less') human liberty lay wholly in the frail hands of Alice . . . [showing] the absurdity of a world which is only the other side of the looking-glass.[45]

Michael Holquist, on the other hand, rejects such cultural readings in portraying Victorian nonsense as a kind of 'immaculate fiction' which could be perceived 'only as what it was, and not some other thing' – in essence, only as fiction about fiction.[46] Arguably, *The Third Policeman* does not belong easily to either camp.[47] Its tale of an individual trapped in an inscrutable wonderland desperately trying to learn the rules of the game may have satiric undertones, but this is also a text enamoured of its own self-reflexive playfulness, of the expressive limits of language, and one that is ultimately centred on a pun (as it turns out, everything *is* about a (bi)cycle). The contradictory critical approaches might be attributed to a central paradox of nonsense: it is inescapably bound up with what it seeks to avoid, it has the anarchist's obsession with the law. Just as parody inadvertently reinforces the authority of its target texts, nonsense reinforces the supremacy of common sense and the material world, its escapist impulse being continually frustrated by what it apparently subverts.

It is interesting, given Oscar Love's proposal of nonsense ('a new sense') as a means of countering the absurdities of contemporary politics, that Roger Henkle characterises it as a strangely evasive, yet simultaneously engaged, mode of writing:

> . . . ambivalence and indirect attack, *angst* and muted self-assertion are beautifully accommodated in nonsense. The virtue of nonsense is its obliqueness; it is ideally suited to criticism from the 'inside' of a class or society by one too wracked by self-doubt to engage in open assault.[48]

If the contradictory postures of Myles na gCopaleen come to mind, the Irish wonderland in *The Third Policeman* (or rather, this peculiarly Irish corner of hell) may not be as remote as it appears. Preoccupied with verbal and social rituals – like *Cruiskeen Lawn*'s Catechism of Cliché – nonsense presents an estranged version of the everyday world; the politely bizarre conversations between Carroll's Alice and sundry Wonderland characters are only distorted reflections of the bizarrely polite encounters of the Victorian middle class. The easy familiarity of the policemen in O'Nolan's novel, maintained even when they decide to hang the narrator as a matter of personal convenience, bears similar comparison to the social mores of contemporary Ireland. However, any satiric potential must be fairly qualified, couched as it is in a form which begs not to be taken too seriously. As Tigges presents it, the Romantic individualism suppressed in the Victorian era broke out in its nonsense literature, but not in an overtly challenging fashion:

> ... the incompatibility of certain individuals from the intelligentsia with the type of society they had to live in could no longer be expressed in a manner which was strongly antagonistic to that society; such a policy would have led to social ostracism ... Nonsense ... perfectly expresses this emotional dissatisfaction, as well as endearing the authors to children and adults alike in a way that would be impossible to the satirical or social rebel.[49]

O'Nolan's commercial ambitions and his easy seduction by the success of *The Irish Times* column betray his own concern for public acceptance, and neither did he ever clearly outrage the sensibilities of 1930s Ireland. As noted earlier, for all its playful humour *At Swim* cautiously remained on the right side of the censors; indeed throughout his career O'Nolan easily agreed to requests from editors or publishers to omit any questionable material from his work. He never did rail unambiguously against the evils of nationality, language and religion, instead he cynically dismissed the Romantic arrogance of Stephen Dedalus's ambitions (conflating the character with Joyce). His combination of civil service duties with more eccentric 'spare-time literary activities' (*ASTB*, 9) was more in the line of the comparably conventional, if decidedly more eccentric, Charles Dodgson. It is telling that the Victorian nonsense writers similarly arrived in the aftermath of a Romantic (and even revolutionary) era – the pragmatic preoccupations of contemporary Britain framing their weird inventions, just as the solid character of the Irish Free State framed O'Nolan's.

This is the 'little world' depicted by Seamus Deane in *Strange Country*, one which succeeded the wild rhetoric of the revival and the subsequent

years of political upheaval: 'a world that has lost faith in the heroic consciousness of the heroic individual and has replaced it by the unheroic
consciousness of the ordinary, of the Plain People of Ireland'.[50] The revolutionary rhetoric was swapped, he implies, for 'ready-made language,
cliché, consensus', and the revival's fantasy and escapism for a more
rational disenchantment – one which had its attractions for O'Nolan.
The deadpan manner of *The Third Policeman*'s anti-hero is certainly of a
piece with this world, as is the garbled officialese of the eccentric
policemen. Indeed, *The Third Policeman* is suffused with this rationalism;
nonsense itself is logic run riot, as in Pluck's celebrated Atomic Theory. It
is no accident that parody, a deeply ambivalent mode, is a dominant
feature of *At Swim*, and through its nonsense manoeuvres *The Third
Policeman* is itself implicated in the 'little world' which the novel turns on
its head. As Lecercle argues, the predominance of 'clichés, *idées reçues*,
preconstructed thoughts' in Victorian nonsense makes it a vector of
Victorian ideology, though not itself being overtly ideological.[51] A similar
ventriloquism is visible in *At Swim-Two-Birds*, or in the Myles na
gCopaleen Catechism of Cliché, the Cruiskeen Court of Voluntary
Jurisdiction or Myles's catalogue of Bores, and it carries similar implications. But Lecercle presses his point even further, describing Victorian
nonsense as a 'conservative-revolutionary genre . . . deeply respectful of
authority in all its forms: rules of grammar, maxims of conversation and
of politeness, the authority of the canonical author of the parodied
text'.[52] Hence it might be said that nonsense texts combine a fantasy of
creativity with a self-conscious awareness of the power of convention;
ironically, their fantasies only emphasise the limits (and perhaps the
impossibility) of originality. This gives them the paradoxical quality of
Carroll's 'Jabberwocky' song, whose nonsense coinages obey the rules of
English grammar.[53] The result is a precarious balance between sense and
nonsense, an interdependence of conservative and subversive elements.
This kind of balance is maintained in *At Swim*, and not simply in its
incessant parody of various literary styles. Not only does O'Nolan prevent
his metafiction from imploding on itself by containing it within a realist
frame narrative, but the contradictory nature of the novel renders his
satire (of contemporary literature, or even contemporary Dublin) peculiarly ambiguous. Tellingly, in *The Third Policeman*, *At Swim*'s equation of
the artist with the madman is continued in the eccentric characters of de
Selby and MacCruiskeen, but the novel also replicates *At Swim*'s ambivalence on a more fundamental level. While *The Third Policeman*'s pattern
of estrangement exposes the disturbing nature of the 'ordinary' world,
the text's eccentricities also exploit a powerful sense of convention.
Hopper identifies a buried 'metonymic discourse'[54] about sexuality in *At*

Swim and *The Third Policeman*, decoding this as 'a reflection of the transitional Irish Free State and the tragedy of Irish male attitudes to sexuality'[55] (in other words, misogynistic and homophobic, as well as sexually ambivalent). Yet in O'Nolan's double-edged comedy there is also a precarious balance maintained between subversive and conformist impulses. In *The Third Policeman*, it is generally Joe who voices the orthodox line, fulfilling a function similar to the aggravating Good Fairy in *At Swim*. When Mathers makes enigmatic allusions to the sins of his youth (a weakness for 'Number One' and involvement in an artificial manure-ring), Joe is quick to intervene: '*No need to ask him what Number One is, we do not want lurid descriptions of vice or anything at all in that line. Use your imagination . . .*' (TP, 30). A more Catholic sophistry emerges in response to Pluck's story about the female teacher riding around on a 'male' bicycle: '*Of course the teacher was blameless, she did not take pleasure and did not know . . .*' (TP, 92). O'Nolan's sexual pun is blatant enough in itself, but it is dragged to a nonsensical conclusion in the dalliance with Pluck's bicycle. The result is an odd couple worthy of Edward Lear and wholly reminiscent of nonsense literature, which generally only accommodates love and sex in peculiar Owl-and-Pussycat combinations. As Hopper recognises, this boy-meets-bicycle affair is conducted in 'the language of male domination and female submission',[56] but the nonsensical coupling also subverts this discourse. O'Nolan's ambiguous comedy is reminiscent of Lecercle's argument that Victorian nonsense is 'one of the vectors of Victorian ideology' while still having a non-committal, politically indeterminate quality. The confluence of Joyce, Beckett and Brian O'Nolan in early twentieth-century Ireland (a trio as fond of riddles as Policeman MacCruiskeen and friends) is a curiosity comparable to the appearance of nonsense writing in Victorian England. In O'Nolan's case, the social and psychological profile of the Victorian nonsense writer fits curiously well (as far as these things do); the more pertinent question is whether his own form of nonsense bears an analogous relationship to Irish culture.

The Irish circle of hell

In October 1939, the physicist Erwin Schrödinger moved to Dublin at the invitation of Éamon de Valera to escape the Nazi regime. Over the next two decades, this most intellectually conservative of world capitals was to play host to the Nobel prize-winning scientist. Somewhere in the Institute for Advanced Studies on Merrion Square, the Plain People's confidence in the visible reality of the world around them was gradually being exploded by the founder of wave mechanics. O'Nolan may or may not have taken account of the new arrival when devising de Selby's incredible theories, but there were certainly stranger things happening in this remote corner of Europe than its calmly neutral exterior implied. The most common analogy made between *The Third Policeman* and contemporary Ireland centres on a 'feeling of confinement'[57] and stagnation, but both were also host to a series of increasing improbabilities, not least among them the prospect of Ireland successfully maintaining its neutrality throughout the new war. That fantastic circumstance provided the rationale for Arthur Riordan's wartime musical, *Improbable Frequency*, in which Schrödinger and Myles na gCopaleen collaborate on a machine (the Probability Adjustment Tank, or PAT) whose waves manipulate the laws of probability in order to keep Ireland neutral.[58] In the hands of Riordan, Emergency Dublin is decidedly Mylesian, a place where – in the style of a Keats and Chapman story – unsuspecting citizens find their actions following the dictates of a bad pun. Art and life are in deep confusion, but then in Ireland they had been for a long time.

The country *The Third Policeman*'s narrator describes on his doomed journey is uncanny but familiar (to a degree which a student of German like O'Nolan might have considered *unheimlich*), gradually developing an estranged and slightly surreal version of Ireland. Yet if its landscape is recognisably Irish, it is also a parody of Irishness, unchangingly dotted with lonely fields, bogs and turfcutters:

> Brown bogs and black bogs were arranged neatly on each side of the road with rectangular boxes carved out of them here and there, each with a filling of yellow-brown brown-yellow water. Far away near the sky tiny people were stooped at their turfwork, cutting out precisely-shaped sods with their patent spades and building them into a tall memorial twice the height of a horse and cart . . . a house stood attended by three trees . . . quiet in itself and silent but a canopy of lazy smoke had been erected over the chimney to indicate that people were within. (*TP*, 88)

The peculiarly contrived nature of these scenes is dulled by their familiarity, though everything is 'almost too pleasant, too perfect, too finely made' (*TP*, 41). It is a 'strange country' (*TP*, 41), a sort of perverse pastoral, though Pluck's Atomic Theory moves the narrator to remark that though it appears 'real and incontrovertible and at variance with the talk of the Sergeant . . . it was possible that I would have to forego the reality of all the simple things my eyes were looking at' (*TP*, 89). Whatever it is, the oddly stilted scene is hardly 'real and incontrovertible', a fact clear to the reader if not to the devotee of de Selby (who would remind him that

life is merely a hallucination). As it turns out, this is a landscape perco-
lated by the Atomic Theory, where mountains keep 'a respectful distance'
and sheep are self-consciously 'attired in fine overcoats' (*TP*, 80). Many
critics have noted how such passages operate metafictionally, both
hinting at the novel's supernatural dénouement and nodding at their
own textuality.[59] The former is not to be discounted, given that the
description of turf-cutting reads more like grave-digging, with sods being
stacked into 'a tall memorial'. However, these descriptions also anticipate
the artificiality and predictability of the landscape in *An Béal Bocht*, where
an unseen hand is responsible for the unhappy situation of the Gaels:

> We lived in a small, lime-white, unhealthy house, situated in a corner
> of the glen on the right-hand side as you go eastwards along the road.
> Doubtless, neither my father nor any of his people before him built
> the house and placed it there . . . If there were a hundred corners in
> all that glen, there was a small lime-white cabin nestling in each one
> and no one knows who built any of them either. It has always been
> the destiny of the true Gaels (if the books be credible) to live in a
> small, lime-white house in the corner of the glen as you go eastwards
> along the road and that must be the explanation . . . (*PM*, 16–18)

In parodying Tomás Ó Criomhthainn's *An t-Oileánach* and other tales of
the Gaeltacht marketed for their authenticity, O'Nolan wrote a book
which presents Irishness cut to a literary pattern. Bónapárt Ó Cúnasa is
the wholly artificial product of the 'good Gaelic books' (*PM*, 16) of Irish
life, which themselves had become formulaic. *The Third Policeman* inches
towards the technique of *An Béal Bocht*, presenting an Ireland which has
already become estranged to itself. This never develops into a consistently
satirical or parodic mode – the digressive and aimless nature of its narrative ensures that much – but it is a significant force behind O'Nolan's
self-reflexive nonsense. The self-consciousness of *At Swim-Two-Birds* can be
largely attributed to a revivalist literary culture which had spent too long
deliberating over the premises of Irish literature (so that writing an Irish
novel now meant writing an 'Irish' novel). *The Third Policeman* does not
engage with the question to the same degree, but it carefully inserts those
quotation marks.

Yet perhaps what is least remarked about the novel is how suddenly it
presents an eerily fantastic Ireland with no traces of the revivalist baggage
of fairies and ancient heroes, no delicate mists or whimsy. The fantastic is
reclaimed from a debased tradition and sternly re-injected with a touch of
doom. Compared to much contemporary Irish fiction, such as the stories
of rural life which were being published by O'Faoláin and O'Connor, *The
Third Policeman*'s 'Irishness' is relatively low key, almost incidental. There

are no comic rural dialects; instead, conventional stage-Irishness is replaced with the clockwork diction of a Free State civil servant, though that clockwork has gone wildly astray: '"A constituent man," said the Sergeant, "largely instrumental but volubly fervous"' (*TP*, 84). Pluck's admiration for MacCruiskeen can find no higher expression than to describe him as 'a walking emporium, you'd think he was on wires and worked with steam' (*TP*, 78). Certainly, both policemen embody Bergson's theory that speech and actions are comical to the degree that they are mechanical and automatic, but they are also state functionaries gone haywire.[60] This is Chaplin's *Modern Times* transplanted to a rural Irish parish, where an abstract concept like eternity is really a contraption worked by a machine. (The narrator's deadly meeting with Mathers is suitably shot through with creaking mechanics: 'Words spilled out of me as if they were produced by machinery . . .' (*TP*, 27).) In *The Third Policeman*, it is the 'ordinary', habitual world which is made strange, to the point where it has become alienating (and was perhaps always so); the eeriness of the policemen's station depends on a sense that we have not strayed very far from home.[61] Like *At Swim*, it exploits the incongruity between the fantasies of a well-stocked mind and day-to-day banality. The imaginative world of Folkestone, Paris and Hamburg is far from the reality of a sequestered life out the back of an Irish country pub; it seems the two worlds can only intersect in a literary nightmare punctuated by the doomed 'de Selby Index'. What better punishment for a distracted philosopher than an eternity conceived in the utmost banality, as a device operated by levers and pulleys, where the omnipotent 'essential inherent interior essence' (*TP*, 113) of everything is entrusted to a country policeman who uses it for getting muck off his leggings.

The nearest predecessor to O'Nolan's fantasy was James Stephens's *The Crock of Gold*, which so impressed him that in late 1938 he had lobbied the author for permission to translate the novel into Irish.[62] If it had gone ahead, this would have been his next project after *At Swim-Two-Birds*. Instead, while both *At Swim* and *The Third Policeman* show traces of Stephens's influence – in the erudite dialogues of the Pooka and the Good Fairy, deluded philosophers and hapless policemen – a significant difference between them is the pressure of normality in O'Nolan's novels. The sexually mischievous Pan arrives into Stephens's Ireland with the wry remark that he has been away some time, but the overwhelmingly male rural world of *The Third Policeman* tells its own story: some elements of Irish life were fantastic enough to render leprechauns and fairies super-fluous. What becomes most terrifying in this novel is not the murder which sets the plot into action (Mathers's demise is coldly and grotesquely comic), but the surreal ordinariness of what follows. Hugh

Maxton hears the chilling terseness of Daniil Kharms's sketches echoed in *The Third Policeman*'s impersonal prose: 'In terms of grammar, the passive voice can rarely if ever have been used to such a violent effect, sublimated into a coerced "normalcy" though that effect might be'.[63] It is the deadpan narrator – rather than the policemen – who wholly destabilises any concept of normality; faced with MacCruiskeen's brain-staggering inventions, he attempts to cling to the illusion that 'everybody was an ordinary person like myself' (*TP*, 77). But this would imply that our measure of the ordinary is an individual who can 'mechanically' smash a spade into an old man's chin, indeed smashes it to the extent that he feels 'the fabric of his skull crumple up crisply like an eggshell' (*TP*, 17). Nonsense is adept at evoking a sense of coercion in normality, as if its derangement was a side-effect of the psychological violence in making sense. But like Swift's *A Modest Proposal*, *The Third Policeman* also exposes the insidious nature of the rational voice – quite beside its obvious limitations. Pushed to express suitable concern at the lavish destruction wreaked by the Atomic Theory, the narrator's response is nicely judged: 'Would it be advisable . . . that it should be taken in hand by the Dispensary Doctor or by the National Teachers or do you think it is a matter for the head of the family?' (*TP*, 85).[64] The pained civility in the face of a delicate matter only exposes more clearly the common absurdity in the deference to local hierarchies. Just as in the *Alice* books, *The Third Policeman* turns the rational world upside down, but in a way that only exposes its logic all the more. As Joe observes, '*Anything can be said in this place and it will be true and will have to be believed*' (*TP*, 88), but it is the narrator's own plausibility which is the most ominous.

The boredom and stagnation of the Free State years, now an image bordering on cliché, might itself be read as a deadpan response to once remarkable affairs, as revolution was dulled into respectability. At the turn of the century, a large amount of print was being devoted to the improbability of Ireland, whether as an independent nation-state or as the mystical invention of the Celtic Twilight. By the time *The Third Policeman* was written, the improbable had long since become a reality, both in political and literary terms. Its strange country may not be quite identifiable as Ireland, but it is not quite unfamiliar enough to be anything else. The vague tone of the opening chapter echoes a sheaf of *faux naïf* literary accounts of Irish childhoods, from the Blasket autobiographies to Joyce's *A Portrait*. (One of the narrator's few observations about his father is that 'on Saturdays . . . he would mention Parnell with the customers and say that Ireland was a queer country' (*TP*, 7); Simon Dedalus might readily agree with the disturbing peculiarity of a country that so disgraced Parnell.) Time and space are displaced in a realm where none of the earthly laws hold good, so this is admittedly a strangely amorphous Ireland: post-Parnell it seems, but probably pre-independence. As Kenner notes, this is a country inhabited by *policemen*, not 'guards' or gardaí.[65] There is no Dáil in existence (O'Corky refers only to an 'Act of Parliament' (*TP*, 80)), though the story of Quigley, the explorer who arrives home to be interrogated with pokers and shotguns, is regarded as 'a terrific indictment of democratic self-government, a beautiful commentary on Home Rule' (*TP*, 165). The anglicisms may simply be pre-emptive concessions to O'Nolan's London publishers (*The Third Garda* would surely have been an obscurity too far), but the historical vagueness is appropriately disorientating, exaggerating the sense that wherever we are, it is not quite home. Yet there is a good deal of dislocated normality about: aside from the metaphoric function of bicycles in the text, their social importance in rural Ireland of the 1930s might well account for Pluck's unfortunate obsession, quite apart from his eternal frustration with the county council. It is the balance of strangeness and familiarity that is so disquieting, the more so since *The Third Policeman* implies that something approximating rural Ireland is in itself sufficient punishment for all eternity. (Admittedly, since the narrator's crime was committed in the name of intellectual inquiry, he is also stranded in a hell stuffed with imponderables.) In 1950, Myles's contribution to existentialist thought, 'Mylesistentialism', wryly underlined the point in its refusal of all utopian philosophies: 'I want to upset once for all this luciferian aberration and state boldly that we are all in hell, or in something so near it as makes no matter'.[66]

Considering the achievements of the previous decade, including the mechanical perfection of genocide in the atom bomb and Hitler's final solution, Myles's observation might seem reasonable enough. But back in the Irish (Catholic) circle of hell, diabolical threats were generally imagined to take a more esoteric spiritual form. Yet there is a strange parallel between the timing of *The Third Policeman* and Beckett's *Watt*, composed in wartime France but also set at some indistinct period, in some place near Dublin. The following could easily have been written of O'Nolan's novel:

> . . . this is a country and a capital seen from a long way off, and seen both as existing a long time ago, long before this war with its terrors and violent upheavals, and yet also belonging to a set of conditions which can be said to belong to no particular time or place at all . . . the world of the mind confronted with an irrational universe, a world of horror as disturbing in its way as the real world in which the writer was living.[67]

Admittedly, the irrational universe depicted in *The Third Policeman* is hardly 'a world of horror' to rival the tortures Beckett concocts for characters and readers alike. Indeed, Joyce declared *Murphy* and *At Swim-Two-Birds*, which were published within a year of each other, to be as alike as 'the devil and holy water'.[68] In another bout of antithetical neatness, he characterised them as '*Jean qui pleure*' and '*Jean qui rit*',[69] but there is nevertheless a certain kinship between Beckett and O'Nolan. The correspondences between nonsense and the absurd have been noted by various critics; the distinction Tigges draws between the two is that in nonsense 'language *creates* a reality, in the absurd, language *represents* a senseless reality'.[70] (Then perhaps the 'Emergency', that strange linguistic parallel to the Second World War, was a piece of nonsense in itself.) In his words, the absurd conveys meaninglessness, where nonsense avoids a total absence of meaning; it admits anguish, where nonsense is resolutely unemotional.[71] Despite the common metafictional aspects in *Watt* and *The Third Policeman*, their 'shared concepts of relativity and language',[72] the cyclical futility played out in *Watt* and *Waiting for Godot* is only anticipated in a more comic form in *The Third Policeman* and *An Béal Bocht* (where Bónapárt Ó Cúnasa, who miserably fulfills the literary destiny of the Gael, ends up replacing his father in prison). A self-reflexive attention to language and logic, a preoccupation with inertia and indecision is common to both writers, who repeatedly produced texts that turned back on themselves. Contrasting Beckett with a fellow comic modernist, Wyndham Lewis, Kenner suggested that 'the great Irish writers . . . have always been able to regard a human dilemma as essentially an epistemological, not an ethical, comedy'.[73] It is debatable whether this is even true of *Ulysses*, but nevertheless it has a certain validity for *The Third Policeman* – its ordering principle not the bitter ethical laugh, but perhaps the hollow intellectual laugh, the kind which 'laughs at that which is not true'.[74] However, O'Nolan's intellectual comedies were more carefully circumscribed than Beckett's, whether consciously or not. Niall Montgomery identified the only common features of their work as being a Joycean talent for accurate Dublinese, closely followed by 'bicycles, scatology, and plenary literary powers'.[75] The broader parallels between the two are perhaps indebted to the strange conglomeration of modernism, philosophical pessimism, the 'new physics' and the looming presence of war which were all part of the intellectual currency of the 1930s. Among the most debated publications in Dublin while Beckett was in Trinity College were those on the new science of relativity.[76] While O'Nolan makes hay with contemporary intellectual hypotheses about the nature of space and time, spurious and otherwise, unlike Beckett, he ultimately closes off such disturbing speculation. In its self-contained moral structure, these are diabolical threats *The Third Policeman* is all too neatly poised to defuse.

It is telling that *The Dalkey Archive* twins the evil genius, de Selby with James Joyce; in his 1951 *Envoy* essay on Joyce, O'Nolan had drawn a comparison between his literary predecessor and another ambitious over-reacher:

> Both had other names, the one Stephen Dedalus, the other Lucifer . . . Both started off very well under unfaultable teachers, both had a fall. But they differed on one big, critical issue. Satan never denied the existence of the Almighty; indeed he acknowledged it by challenging merely His primacy. Joyce said there was no God, proving this by uttering various blasphemies and obscenities and not being instantly struck dead.[77]

To the contemporary Catholic, like O'Nolan himself, the modern physicist arguably did nothing less. But in his eyes, Joyce was still a Catholic writer (albeit with the Jesuit strain injected the wrong way), one who used humour 'to attenuate the fear of those who have belief and who genuinely think that they will be in hell or in heaven shortly, and possibly very shortly. With laughs he palliates the sense of doom that is the heritage of the Irish Catholic'.[78] This same deterministic doom is at the heart of *The Third Policeman*'s satire of the follies of scientists and philosophers. Anthony Cronin describes O'Nolan, like most contemporary Irish Catholics, as being 'a medieval Thomist in his attitude to many things, including scientific speculation and discovery':

> For the Thomist all the great questions have been settled and the purpose of existence is clear. There is only one good, the salvation of the individual soul; and only one final catastrophe, damnation . . . Thus, all secular knowledge is largely a joke. And science and philosophy are even more of a joke inasmuch as they pretend to hold out a hope that the end result of their enquiries will be to reveal something about the mystery of existence or to affect the balance of good and evil. All scientists are, to some extent, mad scientists . . .[79]

Arguably, the popular image of the (mad) scientist as a wild-haired Einstein shows that such reservations were not peculiar to the mid-century Irish Catholic. Yet O'Nolan inflects modern science in *The Third Policeman* in a manner that ultimately re-establishes the traditional universe. As Myles was later to assert: 'The "science of theoretical physics" is not a science but a department of speculation . . . Insofar as it purports to be concerned with investigating the causation of life according to rational criteria, it is sinful' (FC, 98). Whether Myles is to be taken seriously or not, it is telling that O'Nolan's library – now in Boston College – contained the curiously titled God and the Atom, a book that sought to reconcile contemporary science with Christianity.[80] The new physics in fact made its way into The Third Policeman by means of J.W. Dunne's popular books, The Serial Universe and An Experiment With Time.[81] In the former (which, for example, describes atoms as 'little round things like billiard balls'),[82] Dunne manages a scientific explanation for nothing less than eternal life. The key, he indicates, is to admit that a rational science must factor the observer into the phenomena observed. The regression then implied by a self-conscious observer means that 'we are faced with what is, for all empirical purposes, a serial world.'[83] Viewing experience through time allows a suitably regressive mode of description, but:

> All talk about 'death' or 'immortality' has reference to time, and is meaningless in any other connection. But a time-system is a regressive system, and it is only in the lop-sided first term of that regress that death makes its appearance . . . in second-term time (which gives the key to the whole series) we individuals have curious – very curious – beginnings, but no ends.[84]

For Dunne, immortality exists in 'second-term time' since it is only in the second term of a simple series in which the series itself is revealed. And this infinite time regression exists in a fourth dimension, which is presumably where souls and places like Pluck's police station are given a home. In this way, Dunne neutralises contemporary science for the Christian believer, appropriating it to prove the existence of a God and an afterlife. These contortions are replicated in The Third Policeman – though littered with images of serialism and regression, and generally adopting the amoral and inconsequential progression of the nonsense text, it also adapts Dunne's fairly dubious science to a Christian morality tale.

In this fallen world, the absurd is a given – all that is left, as the novel's epigraph has it, is to 'reason with the worst that may befall'.[85] As a nonsense novel, The Third Policeman is as far from a conventional murder mystery as it is from a mystery play, but the narrator is in one sense the unenlightened everyman, his worldly greed distracting him from his true spiritual condition. Indeed, the novel combines the Catholic purgatory with a Dantesque hell, a place where the 'dead and the damned are doomed to go round and round, never remembering precisely who they are and why they are there.'[86] But it is also a paranoiac's dream, its protagonist the victim of hidden maleficent forces, a cog in a pitiless machine. While this brand of modernist pessimism might sit a little uneasily with the Christian undertow of The Third Policeman, the novel also carries traces of Celtic tales of the otherworld.[87] O'Nolan's own pithy summary, 'Hell goes round and round',[88] is closer to the cycles of death and rebirth in the Celtic tradition (its art laden with spirals and cycles as images of eternity) than it is to Catholic doctrine. In the otherworld stories which he studied in UCD, a journey is commonly used to symbolise the life of the soul and it is in line with this tradition that the entrance to eternity should be down a country lane, accessible to any traveller.[89] It is equally typical of his incongruous combinations – in this case, of pagan and Christian concepts of the afterlife – that the *actual* entrance seems to be through a church:

> The structure looked exactly like the porch of a small country church. The darkness and the confusion of the branches made it hard for me to see whether there was a larger building at the rear . . . The door was an old brown door with ecclesiastical hinges and ornamental ironwork . . . This was the entrance to eternity. (*TP*, 132)

And just to confuse matters, once the narrator enters eternity (through a kind of elevator) it is revealed to be no more than a mechanical device – a physicist's fantasy worthy of de Selby, perhaps even the apocryphal machine of perpetual motion.[90] In effect, O'Nolan's characteristic eclecticism allows three worlds to collide in *The Third Policeman*: Celtic paganism, Christianity, and their latest rival, secular science. Nevertheless, like *At Swim-Two-Birds*, this novel exposes an omnipotent character behind the scenes pulling the strings (so perhaps this is a theocratic universe). But *At Swim*'s student is as hollow a creator as his protegé, Dermot Trellis, assembling his novel from odds and ends of other works. Individuality is rendered as questionable a notion as originality in a novel where 'aestho-autogamy' (the efficient reproductive process which immediately results in 'finished breadwinners' (*ASTB*, 41)) anticipates the assembly-line fate of the student and his friends. *The Third Policeman* treads over the same ground, although here the narrator (also without a name, the distinguishing mark of individuality) is confronted with an unintelligible universe in which he is easily disposable. If it is no compliment to observe that Irish art is the 'cracked lookingglass of a servant' (*U* 1.146) it is worse to then add, as *At Swim*'s Brinsley did, that 'Slaveys . . . were the Ford cars of humanity; they were created to a standard pattern by the hundred thousand' (*ASTB*, 32). Just to press the point home, the sight of the servant's mass-produced corset which inspired this reflection causes Trellis to pun at the close of the novel that 'Ars est celare artem' (*ASTB*, 216), advice which the student has, of course, sedulously ignored. The undercurrent of mechanical reproduction in *At Swim* (which has its linguistic equivalent in the cliché, so abused in *Cruiskeen Lawn*), is carried through to the weirdly mechanical universe of *The Third Policeman*, where as the Atom Theory proves, men are mostly half machine.

The Irish circle of hell is a peculiar brew: part Catholic, part pagan, its outdated vision of the age of technology leavened by a pessimistic streak that is wholly modern. Like *At Swim*, O'Nolan's second novel is partly assembled out of literary scraps and borrowings but it escapes the simple confines of metafiction, its 'perceptual games'[91] having more unsettling implications. Its interplay of reality and illusion would take on an uncanny relevance in a country that would spend the next five years dutifully ignoring the neighbouring war, its strict programme of press censorship inviting citizens to discount the visible evidence around them. The language of such times has a certain affinity with nonsense, creating an alternative reality (however improbable) that can only be sustained on its own terms. Such internally coherent worlds crop up throughout *The Third Policeman*, and their survival depends on the tricksiness of language. There is the god-like satisfaction of the clerk in Pluck's voice when he demolishes the narrator's defence against a charge of murder; the latter protests that he cannot be prosecuted since he does not have a name:

> 'For that reason alone,' said the Sergeant, 'we can take you and hang the life out of you and you are not hanged at all and there is no entry to be made in the death papers. The particular death you die is not even a death (which is an inferior phenomenon at the best) only an insanitary abstraction in the backyard, a piece of negative nullity neutralized and rendered void by asphyxiation and the fracture of the spinal string . . .' (*TP*, 105)

The novel's central truth is mischievously hidden in Pluck's sophistry – since the narrator *is* literally 'a piece of negative nullity', he's not worth hanging. Legal fictions are allowed a literal reality: his lack of a legal personality betrays the fact that he doesn't exist at all and like the characters of *At Swim-Two-Birds*, he can easily be written out of existence: 'If you have no name you possess nothing and you do not exist and even your trousers are not on you although they look as if they were from where I am sitting . . .' (*TP*, 64). So speaks the bureaucrat, a species which of course long included O'Nolan himself. But it is the footnotes on de Selby's life and works which make greatest play with the illusions (and delusions) of the text. The conventional footnote points beyond the narrative to a body of evidence, if usually only to a web of other books; here there is no illusion of escaping from the text into a world of hard facts. Their very presence in the novel undermines any naturalistic illusion, pointedly beginning their intrusion in chapter two as the narrator recalls his visit to Mathers's house (which, according to de Selby's theories, may as well be considered 'a large coffin' (*TP*, 22)). By the time they have usurped the main narrative in chapters eight, nine and eleven, a minor distraction has become a major textual disruption. The underlying story (literally speaking) is one of forgery and impersonation, of unverifiable experiments and inscrutable texts – in the world of de Selbian textual scholarship, it seems anything you say will be true and will have to be believed. The sage himself is the victim of his own ingenuity; according to Le Fournier, he is his own first misinterpreter, retrospectively reading his own absent-minded doodles as intricate plans for 'roofless "houses" and "houses" without walls' (*TP*, 22). If de Selby's canon is wholly unreliable – Hatchjaw building a career on the assertion that most of the works are forged – the two thousand illegible pages of the Codex are its apotheosis: 'of which four copies at least, all equally meaningless, exist in the name of being the genuine original' (*TP*, 151). One commentator reads it as 'a penetrating treatise on old age', another divines in the same passage 'a not unbeautiful description of lambing operations on an unspecified farm' (*TP*, 150), and yet another dismisses the lot as 'a repository of obscene conundrums, accounts of amorous adventures and erotic speculation' (*TP*, 151). The parody of Joycean texts and their critics is unavoidable (particularly, as Lanters suggests, of *Finnegans Wake*),[92] but the armed warfare which develops between critics who doubt that their adversaries really exist belongs more properly to the canon of Flann and Myles. The instability of literary personality might be some consolation to a narrator who remains throughout irresolutely nameless, since Kraus is suspected by Bassett to be an invention of the more splenetic du Garbandier (*TP*, 122), while Hatchjaw believes 'du Garbandier' to be a pseudonym for the 'shadowy' Kraus (*TP*, 174). Like the letter controversies O'Nolan and friends were conducting in *The Irish Times*, the de Selby industry follows a self-propelling logic: Le Clerque publishes an article on the Codex, which he has never seen, later asking Hatchjaw to denounce the embarrassment as a forgery (*TP*, 151), and Hatchjaw – unmasker of all forgeries – is finally arrested for impersonating himself, with du Garbandier implying that he 'was not Hatchjaw at all but another person of the same name or an impostor who had successfully maintained the pretence, in writing and otherwise, for forty years' (*TP*, 176).[93] At the head of it all sits the illusory Flann O'Brien, a person no more substantial than the de Selbian critics themselves. And at the end of it all, it turns out that O'Nolan has manipulated his own critics into a very uncomfortable position.

In its literary sub-plot, *The Third Policeman* implies that the very authority of authorship is dependent on a confidence trick. Who would take the illegible Codex seriously (or, O'Nolan may have felt, the illegible *Finnegans Wake*) if the name of de Selby were not attached to it? In its unreadability, there can – very profitably – be no end to the 'brand of nonsense' (*TP*, 150) that is created in attempting to decode it. In its own way, his novel is another kind of confidence trick, a second reading usually being devoted to working out just how it was done. But for a novel which subtly exposes the machinery of literature, *The Third Policeman* is also strangely dismissive of explanations and interpretations. This is a mystery novel in the broader sense, a thriller of the uncanny in which the de Selbys of this world (and their critics) have little to commend them. Any orthodox Catholic would not wonder that the narrator's descriptive powers fail him at the threshold of eternity – when faced with the effect of the black box, or with MacCruiskeen's unfathomable inventions. In the nonsense world of *The Third Policeman*, it is clear that understanding has its limits, though as the narrator excitedly envisions the uses of omnium (*TP*, 195), it seems that imagination does not. The novel's conundrums are worthy of MacCruiskeen himself who, like O'Nolan, is 'a comical man . . . a menace to the mind' (*TP*, 78). His bizarre inventions imitate the qualities of time and eternity – and the quixotic inventions of fiction – insofar as they dazzle the brain: 'you could spend half an hour trying to think about it and you could put no thought around it in the end' (*TP*, 71). In the 1950s, Myles na gCopaleen would portray Joyce as the literary heresiarch of miscommunication, 'whose original simple and pure aim had been, not to be understood, certainly not to be misunderstood, but to be un-understood. The James Joyce Society is now engaged in this complicated negative evangelism and hopes soon to free Joyce's mind from the contamination of the Joyce books'.[94] It may repeat the cycle of scholarly crime to argue that, up to a point, *The Third Policeman* may be read as a displaced satire that presents an estranged version of Ireland, an oddly monotonous hell where authority is wielded in a capricious fashion. But the evidence for this is nevertheless oblique and suggestive; given the conundrums at the heart of the text, to look for an over-arching coherence in it seems ironically to ignore some of its point. Whatever may be inferred from the characteristically eclectic elements that go to make up *The Third Policeman* – Einstein, Dunne and Bergson; Manichaean Catholicism and Charlie Chaplin, war and the atom – the unravelling power of the novel's nonsense ultimately protects it from too deliberate an interpretation. Sense is presented as merely the stage prop of nonsense; as the narrator approaches the police station, the familiar world seems 'to have no purpose at all save to frame it and give it some magnitude and position so that I could find it with my simple senses and pretend to myself that I understood it' (*TP*, 56). Perhaps the attraction for O'Nolan in creating de Selby was that the sage always proved an enigma to his critics and it is telling that *The Third Policeman* has attracted a comparable variety of criticism. Nonsense, after all, is an impeccably evasive form, one which must be anathema to satirists, demagogues, and soap-box orators of all types. As Pluck advises the bewildered traveller in his jurisdiction – an unperceiving sinner as well as a hapless reader – 'The first beginnings of wisdom . . . is to ask questions but never to answer any' (*TP*, 62).

4

Irish Myles:

Cruiskeen Lawn and *An Béal Bocht*

The idea that nonsense, or at least a finely-honed sense of absurdity, was the best protection against all kinds of demagoguery and shrill polemics was put to the test in *Cruiskeen Lawn*. O'Nolan's *Irish Times* column was published exclusively in Irish for its first year and thereafter English and Irish columns alternated until 1943. In this Irish period of *Cruiskeen Lawn* – as in the novel it inspired, *An Béal Bocht* (*The Poor Mouth*) – O'Nolan astutely intervened in contemporary debates within the language movement while defying a revivalist tradition which cast the writer of Irish primarily as a 'language worker': as educator, ideologue, linguist, but rarely simply as a *writer*. His idiosyncrasy was further assured by his unusual position as the first Irish-language columnist in a traditionally Anglo-Irish newspaper, one which he exploited to satirise the language movement and its opponents alike. Yet the popularity of *Cruiskeen Lawn* among Irish enthusiasts was partly due to a general sense of disillusionment by the early 1940s, when the ailing Gaelic League was superseded by a number of new (and more stridently political) revivalist organisations. O'Nolan echoed many of his generation in his attacks on the ossified image of the Gael and in his attempts to dissociate Irish from its popular reputation as the dead or dying repository of a rural folk culture. Perhaps less common was his antipathy to the ideological freight of the Irish language, and his increasing identification of revivalist ideals with a xenophobic nationalism was arguably a significant factor in his move away from Irish after 1943. The course of O'Nolan's commentary on Irish language politics is a peculiarly revealing one, developing from the playful mockery of the early *Cruiskeen Lawn* to his last significant contribution on the subject, a more analytical manuscript on the language revival dating from the late 1940s. This development would be broadly representative of the changes in *Cruiskeen Lawn* over the war years, which was increasingly inspired less by the anarchic spirit of Groucho Marx than by the frustrations of a beleaguered civil servant.

At *Swim-Two-Birds* secured O'Nolan a place in Vivian Mercier's ground-breaking comparative study *The Irish Comic Tradition*, but his comic journalism more intriguingly captures the neurotic relationship between Ireland's official languages in the early 1940s.[1] Despite having the bilingual ease which many of his contemporaries lacked, it would be misleading to cast him as a writer who effortlessly moved between two languages and two literatures. Reading through the Irish period of *Cruiskeen Lawn* highlights his frustration with contemporary Irish writing and with attitudes to the Irish language (both on the part of committed revivalists and their detractors) which were wholly incompatible with his own conception of it as a modern European language. By the early 1940s, the image of the Irish language had already hardened into caricature – resented as something the state forced on its citizens, indelibly associated with nationalism, and forever on the point of dying out. Given that so much of O'Nolan's comedy played with parody and pastiche, mocking stereotypes and caricatures, it is curious that he has also been accused of perpetuating such a negative image of the language. In 1989, Michael Cronin wrote that the 'totemic image of the imaginary Gaeilgeoir' which still haunted Irish speakers, one born of 'critiques of the unholy triad of nationalism, ruralism and Catholicism' had found its most trenchant expression in *An Béal Bocht*.[2] In 1991, Myles na gCopaleen was again dragged into the fray when Éamon Ó Ciosáin challenged Reg Hindley's argument in *The Death of the Irish Language* that the principle factors in the decline of Irish in the nineteenth century were economic rather than political, drawing attention to the cynicism that a largely middle-class language revival generated in deprived Gaeltacht communities.[3] Ó Ciosáin accused him of reiterating a 'conservative consensus' which presented colonial oppression as liberal economics, casting the (doomed) language as a natural casualty of modernisation:

> Hindley can . . . be classified in another conservative consensus – that of stereotyped versions of the Irish language movement itself. He casts the movement as it has traditionally been depicted by Myles na Gopaleen, laying stress on nationality, spirituality, folklore and other considerations which were and are far from feeding the people of the Gaeltacht.[4]

So, far from liberating Irish from its association with the 'baby-brained dawnburst brigade',[5] as O'Nolan periodically claimed to have done, in some eyes his satire contributed to the woolly-jumpered caricature of the language. However, as numerous correspondents to *The Irish Times* pointed out in the 1940s, the attractions of O'Nolan's writing provided a natural incentive for learning Irish which the state-sponsored revival never achieved. Perhaps it should be no surprise that his writing produced such contradictory effects, casting him both as a progressive champion of the language and as its conservative foe. It is worth remembering that while O'Nolan deplored the appropriation of Irish for a nationalist agenda, he was equally scathing about those who dismissed the language on the grounds of its political or cultural associations:

> It is common knowledge that certain categories of Irish speakers are boors. They (being men) have nun's faces, wear bicycle clips continuously, talk in Irish only about *ceist na teangan* and have undue confidence in Irish dancing as a general national prophylactic . . . Hence, some self-consciously intellectual citizens are anxious to avoid being suspected of knowing Irish owing to the danger of being lumped with the boors. There is, however, a *non-sequitur* there. A knowledge of Irish does not necessarily connote adherence to the social, cultural or political philosophies of any other Irish speaker.[6]

O'Nolan did not single-handedly create this caricature of the Irish speaker, albeit being one of its more successful proponents, but *Cruiskeen Lawn* also maintained that 'the Irish speaker' was not a species unto itself. His satire may have brilliantly encapsulated the conservative, ruralist bias of the language revival, but *Cruiskeen Lawn* and *An Béal Bocht* also proved that the Irish language movement had an alternative future.

O'Nolan was in a curiously privileged position to judge the revival's success. Though Irish was his first language, he was not quite the 'native speaker' – that lodestar of the revival movement – but in fact a first-generation Gael, whose upbringing was wholly shaped by the ideology of the language revival. His father, Michael Nolan, was a part-time teacher for the Gaelic League whose brother, Fr Gearóid Ó Nualláin, was Professor of Irish in Maynooth. The family moved frequently throughout O'Nolan's childhood, though never living in a Gaeltacht area, and yet Irish was maintained as the language of the household. Although family holidays were spent in the Donegal Gaeltacht, it is curious that though O'Nolan and his siblings were fluent in Irish, this fluency had its provenance in a *learned* language, not largely supported by contact with native speakers. Nevertheless, when recalling his days as a student in UCD, he claimed to have been surprised at the generally low standard of Irish spoken in the university, particularly by Douglas Hyde.[7] Some reviewers of *An Béal Bocht* levied similar criticisms at Myles na gCopaleen himself,[8] though admittedly it was practically impossible at the time to produce a book in Irish without provoking one or another faction of the revival's self-appointed grammarians. Ironically, the pedantry with which Myles na gCopaleen upbraided the English language and its abusers in *Cruiskeen*

Lawn unconsciously echoed the rebarbative habits of the language revival's literary critics. His multilingual wordplay, his attention to the perils of translation and his diatribes on the proper and precise use of language might be the preoccupations of a writer conscious of his craft. However, it is telling that the qualities which O'Nolan praised in Irish – its precision, flexibility and elegance – are noticeably aesthetic, serving to counterpoint the political or cultural virtues which were more usually associated with the language.

Interestingly, when he began his literary career in 1931 he did so as a bilingual writer. In the same year that he made his first (English) contributions to *Comhthrom Féinne*, he also produced the first of twenty Irish sketches which would appear intermittently in *The Irish Press* and its evening paper until the end of 1932.[9] Some of these sketches parody the style of the Fianna tales, as *At Swim-Two-Birds* would do, or create a non-sensical, topsy-turvey world where Irish is the common language of the country and English is in danger of extinction.[10] However, overall they lack the satirical bite of *Cruiskeen Lawn* – perhaps when writing for Fianna Fáil's *Irish Press*, O'Nolan was less inclined to attack the language revival than when he was with *The Irish Times*. On the other hand, these pieces are unusual among his work since they are not written in the guise of any dramatic persona; no Myles assumes responsibility for them, or even a Brother Barnabas, but plain Brian Ó Nualláin.[11] But already O'Nolan was playing with the form of the newspaper, as in 'Mion-Tuairimí ár Sinnsir', which is a report of ancient manuscripts found in the National Library during re-building, and comprising a series of polite but petty letters sent by outraged citizens (such as 'Fionn Mac Cumhaill Mac A. Isl.') to an ancient Gaelic newspaper.[12] In 'Teacht agus Imtheacht Sheáin Bhuidhe', a parody of a Fianna story is given a personal twist.[13] As the Gaels attempt to prove the excellence of their literature to a Saxon visitor, they list masterpieces which sound as if they might have come from a student's copybook: 'Yesterday and Today', 'Old and New', 'Night and Day'. The second of those titles, *Sean agus Nua*, was a bilingual short story collection produced by O'Nolan's uncles.[14] Apart from these articles, he also intermittently published Irish pieces in *Comhthrom Féinne* in the early 1930s.[15] But in this period, the story which most obviously anticipates the later work is 'Aistear Pheadair Dhuibh', published in March 1933 in *Inisfáil*, a short-lived London publication aimed at Irish emigrants.[16] The story is a succinct parody of Gaeltacht autobiographies, almost a copy of *An Béal Bocht* in miniature. But in this version, the hero becomes so frustrated with his life on the bog that he asks his priest who created 'an tir ocrach seo' (this hungry land). Not God, the priest replies, but two Dublin writers. After Peadar dispatches the two with his double-barrelled shotgun, life on the bog becomes much more pleasant: '*tá siopaí ar an phortach anois, agus tá* bus-ticket *agus* cigarette *agus* daily mail *le fagháil ann*' ('now there are shops on the bog, where you can get bus tickets, and cigarettes, and the daily mail').[17] As the tale shows, in the early 1930s many of O'Nolan's comic staples were already in place, though this particular story also neatly dovetails with the frustrations of its emigrant readership.[18] When he next returned to Irish with *Cruiskeen Lawn*, his satire of the revival and its literature would also gain point from the context in which it was published – in a newspaper traditionally associated with an Anglo-Irish ethos.

In 1940, when O'Nolan began writing his irreverent Irish column, the language movement was on the brink of a minor renaissance that reflected a new attitude among his generation. This decade was marked by a number of initiatives among Irish speakers to modernise attitudes to the Irish language and to distance it from the conservatism represented by the Gaelic League. Breandán Ó Conaire argues that his cynicism towards the old guard of the revival movement was quite representative of the time, pointing to a surge of new Irish associations and periodicals in the 1940s which wrested dominance from the moribund Gaelic League.[19] New journals such as *Comhar*, *Feasta*, *Éire*, *Inniu*, and *An Glór* matched publishing initiatives like Sairséal agus Dill and An Club Leabhar, and organisations like Glún na Buaidhe and Ailtirí na hAiséirí. The movers behind these projects, like the new generation of writers such as Seán Ó Ríordáin and Máirtín Ó Díreáin, were 'urban, intellectual to a degree and dissatisfied with what many of them regarded as a generation which was out-of-touch with the reality of modern Ireland'.[20] However this new generation continued the internecine fighting which characterised the older Gaelic League, and O'Nolan made his own contribution by turning his pen on some of the above. Nevertheless, these revivalists largely recognised that the language revival had engendered an unhealthy amount of navel-gazing among Irish speakers. As Myles na gCopaleen, O'Nolan did more than any other Irish writer to demonstrate that Irish speakers might indeed extend their remit beyond the Irish language (death and revival of), even if they were '*dairíribh i dtaobh na teanga*'.[21] He refused to be confined in his first language to a ghetto of revivalism and nationalism, and in effect, acted as if the Irish language belonged to the mainstream of Irish life. His critics among revivalists showed more awareness of its vulnerability, but in the face of the regular keening for the language, his attitude showed an encouraging assumption of its vitality.

The first *Cruiskeen Lawn* column, published on 4 October 1940, plunged Myles into the midst of Irish language politics, though of course, he immediately proved that he would not be serious about the language at all. The column was responding to a leader in *The Irish Times* which had questioned the state (and the desirability) of the language revival. Bertie Smyllie had queried the wisdom of the £2 grant, or *deontas*, which was awarded for each Irish-speaking child in a household since, he claimed, the Irish language was not adequately equipped to deal with modern life. An Irish speaker could not explain the current war to his child; a dinner-table discussion in the Irish language would be reduced to 'requests for food or drink and other expressions of the elementary wants of life'.[22] Before Myles replied, the *Times* readers had their say on this provocation. One, taking 'the patriotic view', argued that the language was a necessity and to ensure the success of the revival, it should be made *truly* compulsory in all areas of Irish life.[23] As noted, Oscar Love appeared the following day, and showed a more acute understanding of what this position implied:

> I would remind him that patriotism is destroying Europe, and it may yet destroy Ireland . . . We cannot have faith in the strength and good-ness of our own people if we possess no respect for the virtues of our neighbours.[24]

The letter anticipated an attitude which O'Nolan maintained throughout *Cruiskeen Lawn*: the Irish language was a good and necessary thing for Irish people; the political purposes it was often encouraged to serve, on the other hand, were dangerous and destructive. The first *Cruiskeen Lawn* column took a more light-hearted approach to the issue. Myles took it upon himself to supply his Irish readers with a glossary of warfare (sug-gested interpretations of 'Molotoff bread-basket' were '*Manna Rúiseach*', '*Rúiskeen Lawn*', '*Féirín ó Stailín*'), but he also parodied the revival's limited image of the language:

> If on and after tomorrow the entire *Irish Times* should be printed in Irish, there would not be a word about anything but food and drink. Those who find that they cannot do without 'incendiary bombs', 'decontamination', and the like, would have to get some other paper to accompany their ghoul's breakfast. The Irish would be full of *caint na ndaoine* . . . *sean-fhocla* and *dánta díreacha*, and would embody exam-ples of *béarla féinne* and even *én-béarla* or bird dialect . . .[25]

The revivalist argument that the Irish language was a bastion of purity and nationhood which would protect the Irish people from the depravity of modern European or American culture had always been farcical. Now that Ireland's isolation really had been achieved, not by linguistic fiat but by political machinations in wartime, the aspiration was doubly ironic. After all, the revivalist ambition itself was a product of European romanticism, and as Oscar Love pointed out, there was an ominous similarity between the arguments of exclusivist nationalists and the tenor of contemporary European politics.

As can be seen from *At Swim-Two-Birds*, O'Nolan's instincts ran counter to this exclusivist trend. *At Swim* pointedly integrates not only aspects of European modernism and American popular culture, but also Irish-language classics while recognising that the official respect afforded the Irish language ('the real old stuff of the native land' (*ASTB*, 75)) ironically only betrayed its marginal position in Irish life and Irish culture. From the outset, O'Nolan distinguished himself from the public face of the language revival movement and for some, his controversial position was exacerbated by the fact that his column appeared in *The Irish Times*. Barely a month into *Cruiskeen Lawn*'s run, the conservative *Standard* published the following ditty:

> The Soupers and the Jumpers
>   Had done their loathy best,
> With their Lutheran ersatz-bible
>   Their Smyllie Homes and the rest,
> Ere a native anti-Irish chick
>   Was bred in their Bird's Nest . . .
> . . . A ridiculous little rodenticule,
>   A wingless Irish bat,
> A cuckoo-mouse emerged, arrayed
>   In Jimmy Agate's hat
> Squeaking neo-Gaelic through
>   The back of its head and that . . .[26]

This antagonism is remarkable since *Cruiskeen Lawn* was the first regular Irish column in the paper, at a time when Irish writing in any of the national dailies was relatively rare.[27] Admittedly, the mixed reception that greeted *Cruiskeen Lawn* was aggravated by O'Nolan's surreptitious attempts to whip up a controversy over the column. He contributed under pseudonyms to a battle in the letters page which ran for the whole of October. Oscar Love re-appeared, as did Lir O'Connor, who noted that 'your little horseman . . . appears to take for granted the assumption that Irish is neither dying nor dead, but is, in fact, a vigorous, contemporary European language'.[28] Another supporter went by the curious name of 'Cóilín Ó Cuanaigh', giving his address as 36 Parnell Square; the name belonged to one of Pádraic Ó Conaire's characters and the address was that of the Gaelic League's headquarters.[29] *Cruiskeen Lawn*'s critics tended to be sensitive to the vulnerability of the language and its revival; one wrote that an Irish column would be of interest if it 'were on sensible topics and written by someone obviously not embittered . . . Fun and humour are to be welcomed in such a column, but there is no fun in hitting below the belt.'[30] The most vociferous complaint came from a self-styled 'West-Briton-Nationalist': 'I have heard many adverse comments on Irish. But you are spewing on it.'[31] However, the reception was mostly positive; UCD's Cumann Liteardha na Gaedhilge congratulated the paper on its venture on 30 October, and another correspondent welcomed it as a respite from the stuff of contemporary Irish literature:

> Soon, perhaps, the bovine public will revolt, and shovel the coffins and the cabins, the 'bad times' and the 'throubles', the culture-market and the (accidentally-irreverent) quasi-devotional claptrap into a huge pile, set on top the tinkers and the maundering crones, holding aloft the weather-forecasts, meteorological inquests, and botanical, geological and astronomical studies which today masquerade as Irish poetry . . . [32]

Myles, he remarked, injected badly-needed humour into an Irish literary scene where success was determined by a coterie. (If only for the latter comment alone, the letter is suspiciously reminiscent of O'Nolan.) However, *Cruiskeen Lawn* would not only provide a unique contribution to modern Irish writing, it would also exploit the national language itself as a means of undermining the Irish patriot's propensity for self-worship. While topical news rarely infiltrated the column, its nonsense was less purely *nonsensical* than that of *The Third Policeman*, which O'Nolan had completed about ten months earlier. *Cruiskeen Lawn* maintained a more satirical edge, if only (as Myles might argue) because there was more nonsense surrounding the Irish language than any he could devise.

Initially, *Cruiskeen Lawn* was published three times a week in Irish, with a smattering of English and whichever other languages took O'Nolan's fancy on the day. The cultural and social conservatism of the Gaelic League, squabbles over the niceties of grammar and dialect, the lingering cult of the native speaker, and the rural bias of contemporary Irish literature formed the staple fare of the column's satire over its first year – along with nonsense stories and multilingual wordplay. The characters who peppered the early *Cruiskeen Lawn* included Taidhgín Slánabhaile, a pedant who corrected Myles's expressions in pidgin Irish, and berated him for lapses into English (as Donohue notes, a precursor of the Plain People);[33] Pangur Bán, the scribe's cat (inspired by the medieval lay, '*Mise agus Pangúr Bán*'), and Seán a' Díomais, his pig, who became a member of Muintir na Tíre and aspired to a seat in the Dáil.[34] September 1941 saw the advent of Díoghruagach Ó Maol Blagaide, an eighteenth-century bard who could have stepped from Corkery's *The Hidden Ireland*:

> . . . *file náisiúnta na hÉireann agus laoch liteardha a fuair gorta agus greadadh mar chúiteamh ar a ndearna sé ar son a thíre agus a theangadh* . . .

> . . . the national poet of Ireland and a literary hero who was rewarded for his service to his country and his language with starvation and beating . . .[35]

A typical swipe at the Gaelic League was O'Nolan's assertion that '*fáinne*' derived from 'phoney', attributing the word's curious etymology to a story about destitute Gaelic Leaguers selling the gilded rings to London pawn-brokers in the 1900s.[36] The inventiveness of Dinneen's dictionary was also a regular theme, inspiring Myles to devise some lexicons of his own:

> An t-Iarthar – the West of Ireland
> Iarthóir – a West of Ireland man, an applicant for a grant, a chancer
> An Tuaisceart – the North of Ireland
> Túismightheóir – A North of Ireland man, a father of a large family, a
>   populator . . .[37]

However, his linguistic playfulness was often more pointed. *Cruiskeen Lawn* may have been replete with nonsense etymologies, exploiting comic slippages between one language and another, but Myles could also locate a telling cultural neurosis in the most arcane of linguistic matters. Perusing the forms for the 1943 census, he landed on a strange creation, '*gnéas*' (sex, or gender), a word that was unaccountably absent from the dictionary of 'Fra Dinninnico':

> Can it be that the 'idea' is . . . *neamh-Ghaedhealach*, un-Irish, like Rowan Hamilton's quaternions? Can it be that this interesting verbum has been coined under the authority of an Emergency Powers Order and minted beyond in Foster Place as a concession to the mad modern world?'[38]

Cruiskeen Lawn also eagerly waded into the oldest of battles over the revival of Irish. An early disagreement over the form of Irish that should be pre-served – whether a literary, archaic language, or the more idiomatic version which remained in common use ('*caint na ndaoine*'/common speech) – had been resolved in favour of the latter. O'Nolan was not impressed with the consequent folk bias of the revival, nor with those who kept an eye on the authenticity of each other's dialect. In an early *Cruiskeen Lawn*, a by-passer addresses a bull in Irish, mistaking his nose-ring for a *fáinne*. The bull responds genially, but with typical pedantry: '*Ní dóigh liom go bhfuil an focal san ag an athair Peadar. . .*' ('I don't think Father Peadar uses that word . . .').[39] Fr Peadar Ó Laoghaire, the loudest

spokesperson for the victorious supporters of *caint na ndaoine*, proud exponent of the Munster dialect, and author of the first Irish novel, *Séadna*,
would become a regular fall-guy in *Cruiskeen Lawn* (indeed, the very per-
sonification of the unctuous character 'who spoke Irish at a time when it
was neither profitable nor popular').[40] Ó Laoghaire's prolific writing
career, more devoted to linguistic than to literary concerns – and to the
preservation of what O'Nolan termed 'peasant patois'[41] – is repeatedly
cited in *Cruiskeen Lawn* as a singularly corrupting influence on Irish
literature:

> An té nach bhfuil ró-láidir 'san intinn, síleann sé nach bhfuil de dhíoghbháil
> air le mór-saothar litríochta Gaedhilge do chumadh acht eolas ar gramadaigh
> na teangadh agus bfhéidir na corra deasa cainnte atá le fagháil i "Séadna".
> Tuigeann sé gramadach an Bhéarla freisin acht ní scríobhann sé a chuid
> litríochta sa teangaidh sin . . .

> The man who is not too strong in the head believes that all that is
> needed to write a great work of Gaelic literature is to know the
> grammar of the language and maybe the odd nice phrase like those
> found in *Séadna*. He also understands English grammar but he
> doesn't write his literature in that language . . .[42]

But O'Nolan's criticism was not based merely on aesthetic grounds,
any more than was the advice Ó Laoghaire issued to aspiring Irish writers.
At the turn of the century, Ó Laoghaire had declared that 'real literary
intelligence does not exist in the mind of your average English reader',[43]
and warned Irish writers against imitating the English novel, since the
astute Irish speaker would dismiss the result as *ráiméis*, or nonsense.
Ironically, his comparison of folk Irish to modern English owed much to
the Victorian preoccupation with physical and mental degeneration. If
the Irish language were used to translate an English novel, it 'would be
like a great, strong-minded, vigorous, muscular man, suddenly become an
idiot. The Irish language is essentially strong. The English of the present
age is essentially weak'.[44] In comparison to 'frothy' English, Ó Laoghaire
argued, Irish was an unusually precise language, its lack of abstraction
due to the illiteracy of most Irish speakers. The Irish speaker:

> . . . has an exact notion of the meaning of every one of the words in
> his vocabulary. To him all the words represent *Things*, not a certain
> number of letters representing sounds. His words are the names of his
> ideas, not of certain black marks on white paper.[45]

This vaunted simplicity was thoroughly decimated in the hyper-literary
concoction, *Cruiskeen Lawn*, and its linguistic naïvety wholly subverted in

An Béal Bocht.[46] In the novel, O'Nolan did not simply expose how formulaic and clichéd the style of writing fostered by Ó Laoghaire had become. Parodying the new genre of the Gaeltacht autobiography, *An Béal Bocht* exaggerated its literary conventions and undermined the very notion of authenticity and artlessness which Ó Laoghaire fetishised. In O'Nolan's hands, Tomás Ó Criomhthainn's noble islandman is demoted to a 'whinelandman',[47] a patchwork of Yeatsian, de Valerian, and Victorian images of the Gael. The 'authentic' Gaelic Ireland, *An Béal Bocht* implies, is a chimera; Corca Dorcha's grotesquely comic poverty, on the other hand, illustrates one consequence of presenting the Irish language as a bulwark against the modern world.

An *Béal Bocht* was published in December 1941, but it had long been anticipated by the parodies of folklore and Gaeltacht literature in *Cruiskeen Lawn*. Over the previous decade, the drive to collect folklore had received institutional sanction: the Institute of Irish Folklore was established in 1930, and 1935 saw the foundation of the Irish Folklore Commission and its journal, *Béaloideas* (the latter mutated into 'Béal-IDIOCY' in *Cruiskeen Lawn*). The 'school's project' of 1937–38 had engaged children throughout the country in recording local traditions and stories, producing a huge volume of material. Myles, ever the urbane littérateur, drily satirised the cultural value attributed to these tales,[48] and his folktale parodies – the 'Tales from Corkadorky' – began to appear in February 1941. These stories were the precursor to *An Béal Bocht*, and they celebrated the true misery, stupidity and cupidity of the Gaels. 'Corkadorky' recalled Corca Dhuibhne, the region of Kerry which incorporates the Blasket Islands, which in the previous two decades had produced the autobiographies of Tomás Ó Criomhthain, Peig Sayers and Muiris Ó Suilleabháin.[49] While *Cruiskeen Lawn* was generally published in Gaelic type (apart from the clumsy interruptions of Taidhghín Slánabhaile), the Corkadorky tales aggravated their awkward flavour by appearing in Roman type.[50] None of the inhabitants of Corca Dorcha were any more fortunate than *An Béal Bocht*'s Bónapart Ó Cúnasa: 'Téig na Gorta' was so hungry that he tried to sleep all the time; Éamon a' Chnuic was so miserable with the wet and rain that he swapped houses with the devil and went to live in hell.[51] The fifth tale from Corkadorky is a senseless, rambling story; an authentic piece of folklore from one of its elderly inhabitants. Many folktale ingredients are jumbled together – an ancient king's three sons, a journey to America, a bargain with the devil, and so on – until there is an interruption from an impatient Taidhgín Slánabhaile:

> . . . neel bun naw bawr lesh an skayl. Nee higim kad taw ar shool sa
> skayl i naykur . . . kunahayv an gkirun tú skayl sa pawpeyr naw fwil
> ayn bree lesh awgus naw tigin tú fayn?

> . . . there's no top nor bottom to the story. I don't understand what's
> happening in it at all . . . why are you putting a story in the paper that
> has no sense in it and which you don't understand yourself?[52]

Myles's excuse is that he might get a folklore prize from the *oireachtas*.
Though the festival was revived only in 1939, O'Nolan did not greet its
return with any enthusiasm. In fact, he detected a strange similarity
between the word 'oireachtas' and the word 'eructation', which he obligingly defined for his Irish readers as 'a belching forth'.[53] The inhabitants
of Corca Dorcha were Frankenstein's monsters, the progeny of the
anthropological spirit crossed with romantic nationalism. But there was
another element informing these Gaelic grotesques – the colonial image
of the Irishman. The catastrophe-ridden landscape of Corca Dorcha is
home to a simple but untrustworthy peasantry, perpetually putting on the
poor mouth. One of *Cruiskeen Lawn*'s illustrations depicts a top-hatted
gentleman circled by beggars; it is the visit of John Bull to Corca Dorcha:

> "Aigh am só soraigh, maigh gúd píopal," arsa Seán Buidhe, "but Aigh thábh
> nó téins. Aigh thábh notuing smólar dan a cramh."
> "Má's seadh," arsa na Gaoidhil d'aon-ghuth go cíocrach, "tabhair dúinn a
> dhuine uasail, fiú radharc ar an gcoróin!"
> "Maigh gúdnas," arsa Seán, "thamh freightfilligh Aighris iú ól ár. Thiar, fíost
> iúr aighs on dis cóin."
> "Gurameelamahagutaginna-oosal."

> "I am so sorry, my good people," said John Bull, "but I have no
> change. I have nothing smaller than a crown."
> "If that's so,' the Gaels said hungrily, in one voice, "give it to us, sir, to
> have a look at."
> "My goodness," said John, "how frightfully Irish you all are. Here,
> feast your eyes on this coin."
> "Thankyouverymuchsir."[54]

Spelling English as Irish, and vice versa, was a favourite trick of
O'Nolan's, in this case illustrating the Victorian Englishman seen
through Irish eyes, so it is no surprise that the Gaels' servility is presented
as a mask for their chicanery. O'Nolan's tableau depicts the Gael, as seen
by the visiting Victorian, but as played by the Corkadorkians, and
recorded by Myles na gCopaleen. And to complicate matters further, the
latter is himself derived from a notoriously 'Oirish' product of the
Victorian stage – which was devised by an Irishman.[55] Tracing the sources

of the cultural phenomenon that is Corca Dorcha is not an easy task. Fifteen months into the run of *Cruiskeen Lawn*, *An Béal Bocht* would arrive to further muddy the question.

An Béal Bocht and the *fíor-Ghael*

Although *An Béal Bocht* is evidently founded on parodies of the Gaeltacht autobiographies published in the 1920s and 1930s, its satirical perspective is less straightforward than this might suggest. As O'Nolan's comedy recognises, these autobiographies marked a point of contact between two cultures. Whether directly inspired by a visiting folklorist, or by the writer's own recognition that a way of life was disappearing from the modern world, they cater for the stranger, and much of *An Béal Bocht*'s humour depends on the perils of this encounter.[56] The Corkadorkians not only play roles for the visiting *gaeilgeoirí*, but for their urban readers. The architects of Corca Dorcha are more plentiful than a handful of Gaeltacht writers, and it is home to Yeats's noble savage, Irish Ireland's historically oppressed but moral Gael and the urban Irishman's bogtrotter. In O'Nolan's hands, the conventional tale of hard times on the western seaboard becomes a piece of cultural shorthand for all that was most farcical in the Irish self-image. *An Béal Bocht*'s peasant is not as Ó Laoghaire might have seen him, the natural embodiment of authentic Irishness, but a hybrid creation of literary tradition and social prejudice.

While *An Béal Bocht* most famously parodies Ó Criomhthain's *An tOileánach*, O'Nolan's respect for his target text is equally well acknowledged.[57] It might be more accurate to say that his novel targets imitations by less able writers, but its satire is more generally directed at the very fashion for the genre itself. Arguably, the significance which Gaeltacht literature acquired in contemporary Ireland was little derived from its literary value, or even from its anthropological interest; the figure of the peasant had become so central to Irish cultural discourse that, as Edward Hirsch has argued: 'to define an idea of the Irish peasant was to define an idea of Ireland itself'.[58] Since this was a preoccupation of the Anglo-Irish literary revival and Irish Ireland alike, Bónapárt Ó Cúnasa has an unusually mixed ancestry. Authentic Irishness (that of the *fíor-Ghael*) was arguably conceived as a foreign quality in twentieth-century Ireland, an unattainable thing exiled to the most remote corners of the country. The difference between O'Nolan's peasant and most of its other literary manifestations (even Kavanagh's counter-revivalist image of Patrick Maguire) is that he alone stood outside the discourse of authenticity. He is transparently unnatural, a straw man made to damn every other straw man that embodied the Irish national spirit. Synge might not have strained too much for authenticity in his depiction of a west of Ireland peasantry, but as O'Nolan saw it, even the 'amusing clowns' which Synge produced were nevertheless accepted as the true article:

> . . . when the counterfeit bauble began to be admired outside Ireland by reason of its oddity and 'charm' . . . [we], who knew the whole inside-outs of it, preferred to accept the ignorant valuations of out-siders on things Irish. And now the curse has come upon us, because I have personally met in the streets of Ireland persons who are clearly out of Synge's plays.[59]

Hence, the Irishman becomes a parody of himself, the caricature inter-nalised and reproduced – Bónapárt Ó Cúnasa is another of these literary Frankensteins, a walking cliché. He soon learns that the 'good books' of the Gaels are a near infallible guide to the misfortunes of his own life, from the beating he receives on his first day at school, to his adventures courting in the Rosses and his eventual incarceration.[60] Literary turns of phrase are to be taken as literal precedents in Corca Dorcha. Bónapárt's mother dirties her hearth in order to ensure that his upbringing is impec-cably Gaelic, so that he can truly be (as Séamus Ó Grianna puts it in *Caisleáin Óir*) 'i mo thachrán ag imeacht faoin ngríosaigh' (ABB, 14)/'a child among the ashes'. But it is not simply the people of the Gaeltacht who are responsible for the image of the Gael; the misery, poverty and *strange-ness* of Corca Dorcha is refracted through visitors' perspectives. There is the visiting government inspector who recoils from the stench of Bónapárt's hovel and is happy to take a pig's grunting for English;[61] the scholar who equates the most difficult and inaccessible Irish with the most authentic, and wins university degrees with his exegeses of another pig's grunts; and the gentlemen from Dublin who break Sitric Ó Sánasa's water bottle since it mars the almost perfect picture of abject poverty which he presents. From these men's point of view, *gaelachas* is charac-terised by meanness, ignorance, a primitive way of life, and most of all, by its irredeemably *foreign* nature.

An *Béal Bocht* plays in a number of ways on projected images of the Gaelic peasant, the latter being defined (whether in a positive or negative fashion) as everything antithetical to the modern citizen. The Irish Ireland version, as described by Aodh de Blácam in 1935, was nothing short of the saviour of civilisation:

> Small wonder that the children of such homes are they from whom priests and nuns, scholars, poets and brave soldiers come, all that is most choice in the human race. . . .

> We see the European urban civilisation going down to-day in cor-
> ruption of body and mind, in merciless warfare, and in unbelief . . .
> Only "green" Europe, the peasant lands behind the big cities, prom-
> ises to live on after the ruin . . . [62]

Like Ó Laoghaire before him, de Blácam was an adept in the language of
corruption and degeneration. In contrast, O'Nolan's Seanduine Liath (or
Old Grey Fellow) shows the canny nature of the Victorian stage-
Irishman.[63] His is the strain of Gaeldom which prides itself on shrewd
dealings; as he advises Bónapárt: 'If pennies are falling . . . see to it that
they fall into your own pocket; you won't sin by covetousness if you have
all the money in your own possession' (*PM*, 51). But the Seanduine Liath
aside, it is more often the virtuous and simple Gael beloved of conservative revivalists who is parodied in *An Béal Bocht*. It is little wonder that
Bónapárt queries whether the Gaels are really human (*PM*, 100), since
they are apparently presumed to have an inhuman fortitude:

> . . . it had always been said that accuracy of Gaelic (as well as holiness
> of spirit) grew in proportion to one's lack of worldly goods and since
> we had the choicest poverty and calamity, we did not understand why
> the scholars were interested in any half-awkward, perverse Gaelic
> which was audible in other parts . . . (*PM*, 49)

The plaint anticipates de Valera's notorious 1943 St Patrick's Day speech,
which similarly trusted in the nation's lack of interest in the material
things of life and envisioned a happy countryside of frugal homesteads.[64]
O'Nolan targeted both this idealism and the even louder complaints of
misery and hardship which answered it. (It is a habit of Corkadorkians to
sit about lamenting the evil fate of the Gaels.) Interestingly his own
uncle, Fr Gearóid Ó Nualláin, lauded Irish above the more mercantile
languages of Latin, French and (above all) English:

> . . . *é lán de bhastúntacht an nouveau riche agus d'adhradh an airgid. An
> Ghaoluinn amháin, is í is Críostamhla agus is spioradáltha agus is
> Catoilicighe ortha go léir* . . .

> . . . [English] is full of the loutishness of the nouveau riche and the
> adoration of money. Irish alone is the most Christian, spiritual and
> Catholic of them all . . . [65]

However, de Valera's St Patrick's Day speech was partly making a virtue
out of necessity and the mythology of the spiritually-minded Gael had a
similar origin. Undoubtedly, it was continuing poverty and isolation
which did most to preserve the Gaeltacht areas into the twentieth

century.[66] In the intervening years, there was a dramatic reversal in all that their harsh life was taken to signify. The qualities which served as negative indices of Irishness in the nineteenth century, became fetishised by nationalists in the twentieth. In both periods, the true Irishman, or *fíor-Ghael*, arguably remained something alien to the majority of Irish people.

As one critic of *An Béal Bocht* has put it, the *gaeilgeoirí*'s efforts to maintain monolingualism in depressed economic areas left the people of the Gaeltacht stranded as 'exotic linguistic artifacts'.[67] The choice of words is telling: the 'exotic' Gaels being strangers in their own country. Many early language revivalists encouraged this sense of estrangement, proposing Irish as a bulwark against the modern world and the Gaels as a people apart. Cardinal Logue emphasised their unworldliness at the 1899 *Oireachtas*:

> We never had in Irish that broad and fetid stream of corruption which is flooding the country at the present day through English literature. Wherever the Irish language is spoken, the people are pure and innocent . . . [68]

This purity and innocence is certainly true of the Gaels of *An Béal Bocht*; not only does Bónapárt not understand the provenance of his son, he is even innocent of the workings of alcohol (though this doesn't stop him stealing a dead man's drink at the Corca Dorcha *feis*). This exaggerated simplicity parodies the coyness of the Gaelic autobiographies, though it is coupled with a certain precociousness reminiscent of *An tOileánach*:

> 'There's an awful lot of heat in that fire truly . . . but look, sir, you called me son for the first time. It may be that you're my father and that I'm your child, God bless us and save us and far from us be the evil thing! . . . '
> . . . At that time I was only about in the tenth month of my life . . .
> (PM, 15)

However, neither the sexual innocence of *An tOileánach* nor *An Béal Bocht* was wholly the work of its author. Both books attracted a degree of censorship prior to publication which in each case was influenced by the received image of the Gael. Ó Criomhthain's 1929 Irish text was cut by his English translator, Robin Flower. In O'Nolan's case, it was his prospective publishers, Browne & Nolan, who raised concern over certain episodes in the novel; in April 1941 he wrote assuring them that he had excluded all references to 'sexual matter' from the book (apparently including an episode where Bónapárt follows a woman on the road and incurs the wrath of her husband).[69] They also feared causing offence by the implication that families in the Gaeltacht housed pigs in their kitchens and stole freely from their neighbours. One of the passages excised from Flower's translation of *An tOileánach* also dealt with the pig in the house,[70] which suggests that the comic Irishman was as significant a taboo as 'sexual matter'. Given that editors meddled with both *An tOileánach* and *An Béal Bocht*, it is ironic that the latter itself draws attention to such mediation between the author and the reader. Indeed, *An Béal Bocht* echoes O'Nolan's other self-reflexive texts in this respect, with Myles's editorial function recalling the student narrator of *At Swim*, or the scholar-murderer of *The Third Policeman*; however, as editor of Bónapárt's memoirs he is obviously following a precedent set by the Gaeltacht autobiographies. Myles draws attention to the editorial mediation of the outsider, and in the standard fashion, states in his preface that this book is as much a linguistic project and an act of cultural reclamation as anything else. Of course, it is made immediately clear that for all Myles's assertions to the contrary, the faithfulness and authenticity of Bónapárt's account might not be wholly trusted: 'This document is exactly as I received it from the author's hand except that much of the original matter has been omitted due to [pressure of space and to] the fact that improper subjects were included in it'.[71] Indeed, Myles's first act as editor is to gloss some of Bónapárt's muddled anglicisms with their correct Irish equivalent.[72] Already the true Gael is being revised into a more Gaelic version of himself. O'Nolan's mischievous exposure of such acts of editing means that from the outset, *An Béal Bocht* signals that it is targeting not merely the literary merits of such texts or their linguistic politics (such as old battles over the status of dialects and the victory of *caint na ndaoine*). It also cynically exposes how texts like *An tOileánach* were quietly tailored to serve a particular cultural agenda. While *An Béal Bocht*, like *At Swim*, is a virtuoso exercise in parody, both novels also match their self-reflexive literary styles with a self-reflexive attention to their intellectual and cultural contexts. *An Béal Bocht* highlights a point of mediation between the writer and the reader, though here the mediation is obviously not just on a textual, but on a cultural level – the encounters between the hapless inhabitants of Corca Dorcha and the urban *gaeilgeoirí* mirror that between the (edited and revised) Gaeltacht authors and their readership.

As it transpired, in drawing attention to the offensive nature of Ambrós the pig, O'Nolan's publishers were not being over-cautious. *An Béal Bocht*'s reviewers were reasonably sanguine about his attacks on the *gaeilgeoirí* and the absurdities of revivalism, but the combination of Ambrós and the questionable moral standards of the Corkadorkians caused trouble in some quarters.[73] When the Seanduine Liath goes 'hunting', as becomes the Gael, it is to rob his neighbours' houses. Many reviewers who otherwise lauded the book acknowledged that such passages were likely to cause offence:

> The implications of general dishonesty on the part of Seanduine and others in Corca Dorcha are very far-fetched . . . [and] are tinged with bitterness. They spoil the many cases of justifiable satire, ridicule, exposure of clichés and aspects of pseudo Gaelicism that make the book very readable and enjoyable . . . [74]

The Bell's reviewer was even less forgiving: 'Whatever may be said about the Gaeltacht, it was never merely cheap'.[75] *The Leader* instead accepted the smelly Ambrós as 'a jibe at the Anglo-Irish humourists and uplifters of an earlier generation'.[76] Certainly, O'Nolan would later echo the judgement that Carleton alone provided a faithful portrait of the Irish peasantry, subsequent nineteenth-century novelists producing only 'a canon of amiable cawboguery' and things worsening with the likes of Synge, Gregory and Yeats, who 'persisted in the belief that poverty and savage existence on remote rocks was a most poetical way for people to be, provided they were other people'.[77] However, the greater part of *An Béal Bocht* depicts both the Gaels and their observers as being culpable for the misery of Corca Dorcha. Though the Corkadorkians are bound by the precepts of the 'good Gaelic books' (PM, 100) to accept the harsh life which is fated for them, they are wilfully fascinated by their own ill-luck. The *gaeilgeoirí* might wish to preserve Corca Dorcha in its primitive state, but the only sign of native industry in the place stems from the Seanduine Liath's dishonesty. In this much, O'Nolan parts company with Ó Criomhthainn and other writers, ascribing the Corkadorkians a stage-Irish temperament which is distinguished by dishonesty, laziness and chronic helplessness.[78]

The Corca Dorcha *feis* is the closest O'Nolan comes to implying that the *reality* of life in the Gaeltacht is ignored by language revivalists.[79] His intertextuality tends to indicate instead that realism is nothing of the sort, but is only a naïve accumulation of clichés. As *An Béal Bocht* progresses, his parodic references to Ó Criomhthain and Ó Grianna give way to a more ominous sense of being confined by literary fate; one that rivals the claustrophobia of *At Swim-Two-Birds* or the nonsense universe of *The Third Policeman*. Bónapárt's incarceration following a trial he can't understand is the final, most Gaelic and most miserable product of the encounter between the Gael and English speaking society. In one sense, it is the pre-determined end of the generic Gael, Jams O'Donnell,[80] but it also gives literal expression to Bónapárt's literary entrapment. It is no accident that this child among the ashes, the scribe of a community whose like will never be seen again, is taught by a schoolmaster called Aimeirgean Ó Lúnasa, who recalls the founding-figure of Gaelic litera-ture and completes the literary circle.[81] This literary paralysis is underlined in Bónapárt's journey to *Cruach an Ocrais/* Hunger-stack mountain in search of its legendary treasure. He finds the treasure, but also its ancient owner, Maoldún Ó Pónasa.[82] Maoldún addresses Bónapárt in middle Irish – as might have been anticipated – but more eerily, he is otherwise no different from the storytellers whom Bónapárt has already met in the Rosses:

> I saw the dead person – if he were dead or only soaked with spirits-weariness – endeavouring to settle himself on his stony seat, to shove his hooves in the direction of the fire and to clear his throat for story-telling . . .
>
> – *It is unknown wherefore the yellow-haired, small, unenergetic man was named the Captain – he whose place and habitation and steadfast home was a little lime-white house in the corner of the valley* . . . (PM, 109).

The stories of the Gaels are as interminably repetitive as the plot of *The Third Policeman*. Bónapárt cannot escape his literary fate any more than the women of the Rosses who gather on the shore every evening crying for their fishermen. Life in the Rosses is even more predictable than that in Corca Dorcha[83] so it is fitting that there Bónapárt encounters the greatest menace of all to *An Béal Bocht*'s Gaels: the Sea-cat. Bónapárt's drawing of the creature looks very like a prostrate Ireland, 'the pleasant little land which is our own', as Myles helpfully notes:

> Many things in life are unintelligible to us but it is not without impor-tance that the Sea-cat and Ireland bear the same shape and that both have all the same bad destiny, hard times and ill-luck attending on them which have come upon us. (PM, 77)

This creature is dreaded for bringing bad luck; in effect, it gluts itself on the misfortune of the Gaels. It is a suggestive image – Irish nationalism had long justified itself by drawing attention to the miserable state of Irish subjects under British rule, but somehow cultural nationalists had revised an abject image of the poverty-stricken (yet spiritual) Gael into a marker of authentic Irishness. Bónapárt Ó Cúnasa may finally be interred by a foreign legal system, in the classic colonial manner, but it is a stultified Irish tradition that maintains his miserable condition.

Despite some reviewers' objections to Ambrós and the moral state of the Corkadorkians, *An Béal Bocht* was enthusiastically welcomed, even in the Irish-language press. Barely two months after publication, an *Irish*

Times advertisement reported that the first edition was sold out: 'an event without precedent in the history of the publication of books in Irish'.[84] A review published in *The Standard* early in January 1942 corroborates this claim, telling how a bookseller had to sell his own copy to an importunate customer before he had finished reading it, and calling it 'one of the daftest, bitterest, most hardhitting and outrageous books ever written in modern Irish; it is also one of the best'.[85] *The Leader* pointed out that it was 'the first purely humorous work of any dimensions to be written in the language in modern times'.[86] Strangely enough, it was not this stalwart of Irish Ireland, but *The Irish Library Bulletin* which took offence at O'Nolan's temerity in mocking the literary works of native Irish speakers, and it launched the ultimate insult:

> *Níl amhras ná gur bhaist ughdar an leabhair seo thuas a leabhar féin maith go leor . . . acht d'fhág sé aon nidh amháin gan luadh-do b'é ba chóir do a rádh "droch-sgéal ar an droch-shaoghal, breacaithe i ndroch-Ghaedhilg!"*
>
> There's no doubt but that this author christened his book well . . . but he left out one thing he should have mentioned; it is: "a bad story about the bad life, scribbled in bad Irish!"[87]

But given the parodic style of *An Béal Bocht*, it is arguable that any linguistic awkwardness was in fact deliberate. Nevertheless, the criticism did strike home. A 1950 *Cruiskeen Lawn* column purported to reproduce Browne & Nolan's reader's report on *An Béal Bocht*, and did so in similar terms: 'I can safely assert that in an experience of sixty years this is quite the craziest piece of Irish I have ever met . . . What surprises me most is the self-assurance of the author . . . For want of knowledge he cannot begin, or continue or finish a sentence properly . . . spend none of the firm's money on this work.'[88] Browne & Nolan did reject the novel in May 1941,[89] but their actual reader's report only mentioned O'Nolan's Irish in praising his use (or abuse) of phrases from the 'Gaeltacht' books.[90] O'Nolan himself felt that his peculiar use of Irish was central to the book's humour, rejecting Timothy O'Keeffe's suggestion in 1960 that *An Béal Bocht* should be translated into English: 'The significance of most of it is verbal or linguistic or tied up with a pseudo-Gaelic mystique and this would be quite lost in translation . . . '.[91] Apart from obvious instances of wordplay in the text,[92] much of its humour comes from his satire of *caint na ndaoine*, which Ó Laoghaire recommended as the proper basis of all Irish prose. The Seanduine Liath can pick up 'a whisper in Galway, half a word in Gweedore and a phrase in Dunquin' (PM, 42) in a morning's walk, and O'Nolan's ambition to satirise the Gaeltacht as a whole is reflected in his prose, which 'blends their various dialects in a composite Irish literary style no other writer of Irish . . . succeeded in doing.'[93] *An Béal Bocht's* primary source text, *An tOileánach*, was a product of the Kerry Gaeltacht (though, as noted, some of the episodes parody the Ulster writer, Séamus Ó Grianna). The meeting with Maoldún Ó Pónasa, who speaks middle Irish, is a diversion to the scholastic tradition, while Bónapárt's journey to the Rosses introduces him to the idiom of the Ulster writers. On the road there, he meets another Jams O'Donnell:

> He stopped in front of us, recited the Lay of Victories, walked three steps of mercy with us, took a tongs from his pocket and threw it after us . . . It was evident that he was Ultonian according to the formula in the good books . . . (PM, 64).

As might be expected from 'the good books', this Jams asserts that he has 'no Gaelic, only Ulster Gaelic' (PM, 64), and proves it with his faithfully provincial turns of phrase. It is the Seanduine Liath who disingenuously enquires whether he has read Ó Laoghaire's *Séadna*, the template for the folk style he represents.

Throughout disputes over the standardisation of Irish, O'Nolan supported the drive to adapt the language to the needs of a modern, literate, centralised state.[94] He pronounced, for example, that it was 'monstrous' that schoolbooks were to be provided in the dialects of Ulster, Connacht and Munster:

> . . . Irish, we are agreed, cannot be revived because it is a babel rather than a language, a welter of shrill provincial jealousies. It requires to be attacked with a sledge-hammer, made simple, uniform and rational. Far from addressing this task, the present situation is to be perpetuated for at least another generation of distracted school-children.[95]

The backward look was hardly receptive to the needs of the urban Irish speaker, and certainly not to the demands made of a state language. Tellingly, when O'Nolan praised any Irish prose, it was on deliberately aesthetic grounds. His genuine regard for *An tOileánach*, for example, was based on the fact that 'every page is a lesson how to write, it is all moving and magnificent'.[96] (Flower's translation, on the other hand, was a 'parcel of bosh and bunk . . . it gives a wholly wrong impression, hiding inside its covers of opulent tweed' (HD, 180).) In a 1941 review of Eoghan Ó Domhnaill's *Scéal Hiúdaí Sheáinín*, O'Nolan acknowledged the harshness of the lives such writers recounted, but did not find that praiseworthy in itself; interestingly, he negatively compared the shapeless prose of the

Ulster writers to their counterparts in the Blaskets.[97] Deliberately judging such books in aesthetic terms might have been a way of evading the cultural baggage which they dragged in their wake, but it also demanded a *literary*, rather than a linguistic, standard. Comparing *An tOileánach* favourably to *Séadna*, O'Nolan asserted that:

> . . . ní an 'Chainnt na ndaoine" nó na 'cora deasa cainnte' atá ann a bhronnann uaisleacht litríocht air. Níl aon bhaint ag liteardhachas an leabhair leis an nGaedhilg. Tá an fíor-stuif darásach daonna ann, tá sé ealadhanta, bogann sé an léightheóir chun cumhtha nó áthais do réir mar is rogha leis an údar . . .

> . . . it is not the 'common speech' or 'nice idiom' in it which grants it the nobility of literature. The literary quality of the book has nothing to do with Irish. It has true humanity, it is skilful, it moves the reader to sorrow or joy as the author chooses . . .[98]

Arguably, O'Nolan made little allowance for the oral roots of this literature; *An Béal Bocht*'s satiric repetition of *seanfhocail* (proverbs) and the other linguistic props of the Gaeltacht books recalls *Cruiskeen Lawn*'s 'Catechism of Cliché' rather than the structure of an oral narrative.[99] What another writer might praise as authentic *caint na ndaoine* and folk wisdom, O'Nolan represents as automatic, inert and fatalistic responses to the vicissitudes of life. Some of these phrases are merely the verbal tics of the authors whom he was parodying, such as Ó Criomhthain's refrain, or the storyteller's chant: '*is scéal eile an scéal sin agus lá eile dom á innsint sa scríbhinn seo thíos*' (ABB, 10-11, 12, 32), or the habit of setting everything '*i dtóin an tí*' (which appears too often in *An Béal Bocht* to cite).[100] Along with respectful references to '*ár sean agus ár sinsear*' (ABB, 35, 41, 93), and the resigned reflection that '*ní mar a shíltear a bhítear*' (ABB, 16, 32, 84), the book is littered with formulaic (and superstitious) exhortations.[101] The most common is Bónapárt's reflection that: '*is iontach an saol atá inniu ann*', which is repeated in one form or another nine times.[102] Aside from these reflex responses, one word which is unfailingly reiterated throughout *An Béal Bocht* (apart from '*fearthainn*'/'rain') is '*cinniúint*'/'fate'. The repetition is wholly warranted since it was the sources of these hackneyed phrases, the Gaeltacht autobiographies, which fixed a certain image of Gaeltacht life in the popular consciousness. The linguistic circularity and predictability of *An Béal Bocht* provides a suitable correlative to the Corkadorkians' fatalism.

In a way, this itself reflects the stereotype of the Irish language which O'Nolan repeatedly countered in *Cruiskeen Lawn* – an image of a language frozen in a rural idiom and wholly unadaptable to contemporary

Ireland. One day Myles reported that he had been reading a book on music which was littered with French expressions:

> Lá éigin, b'fhéidir go mbeidh striapach pinn éigin ag iarradh snais a chur ar a bhaoth-Bhéarla le sciotacháin Gaedhilge – lá éigin nach fada uainn, nuair bhéas Éire arís ag Cáit Ní Dhuibhir.

> "There is a distinct *blas* of *fág-a-bhealach* about Stravinsky, a sort of mad *thaidhbhsiúil* ebullience mixed with a *beagáinín* of *mise is tusa is an bóthar go réidh faoi n-ár gcosa*. One might even say he is *dána* in the better sense of *dán*, a poem . . ."[103]

French was perhaps not guaranteed to raise the tone of any critical prose, but certainly indicated its pretensions. In its place, the Irish is comically subversive, its incongruity heightening the absurdity of this linguistic snobbery, but also betraying its own shortcomings. The language had not been integrated into urban life, it had not adapted to the modern world. Arguably, neither had Ireland, but opponents of the language revival glossed over that point. Perhaps, eventually, O'Nolan began to agree with them. But over the first couple of years of *Cruiskeen Lawn*, the column's satire targeted both those who piously deferred to the national language and those who condescendingly dismissed its revival. *An Béal Bocht*, which was of course descended from *Cruiskeen Lawn*'s 'Tales from Corkadorky', continued in the same vein. While comically indicting contemporary attitudes to the Gaeltacht, it also pilloried the state of contemporary writing in Irish. But O'Nolan's particularly literate brand of humour was itself a promising development, not least for appealing to an audience which was not otherwise well served by Irish publications. By the mid 1930s, of the 127 novels which An Gúm had published since its inception in 1926, eighty-four were translations of European novels.[104] Arguably there were simply not enough competent writers available to meet government ambitions to create a body of literature in modern Irish, but O'Nolan had little respect for An Gúm's policies and his frustration was echoed by other writers. Seán de Beaumont (the editor of *An tÉireannach*, a socialist news weekly which was produced in the Gaeltacht from 1934 to 1937)[105] complained in 1939 that An Gúm's policy was insulting to the people of the Gaeltacht, implying that they could not produce their own literature.[106] Seosamh Mac Grianna similarly interpreted such statistics as betraying a lack of faith in contemporary Irish writing:

> Níl litríocht ar bith sa Ghaeilge is fiú a léamh. Níl scríbhneoir ar bith Gaeilge againn ar fiú scríbhneoir a thabhairt air. Taobh thall den fharraige Ghaelaigh atá gach rud a bhfuil tairbhe ar bith ann.

> There is no literature in Irish worth reading. We have no Irish writer
> fit to be called a writer. Everything of merit is across the Irish sea.[107]

Surveying contemporary writing in 1935, Leon Ó Broin remarked that
Irish books in print were still a novelty, and that the impulse to experiment was dampened by the prospect of a limited readership.[108] At a time
when most still wrote for the student, and with priorities that were more
linguistic than literary, it is understandable that O'Nolan would incongruously compare Ó Laoghaire's attempt to transfer an oral folk tradition
to the page to another writer who masterfully blended the oral and the
textual, James Joyce. Remarking that Joyce's work was more Irish than
much of that written by people who knew no word of English, he con-
cluded that:

> Nuair bhéas ughdar ion-churtha leis ag scríobhadh i nGaedhilg, beidh an
> teanga mhathardha as baoghal agus ní bheidh go dtí sin. Ins an mheántráth,
> beidh an saothar cuanna mín-mheilte sin againn – "Séadna". Agus "Niamh,"
> "An Béal Beo," "An Mháthair," maraon le'na lán treachlasice eile atá comh
> bréagach mí-ghaedhealach is tá sí suarach.

> When we have an author writing in Irish to compare with him, then
> the mother tongue will be out of danger and not till then. In the
> meantime, we have such charming, foolish work as *Séadna*. And
> *Niamh*, *An Béal Beo*, *An Mháthair*, along with a lot of other rubbish
> that is as false and un-Irish as it is contemptible.[109]

An Béal Bocht is a corrective to this brand of literature; it is telling that,
like *At Swim-Two-Birds*, the book is a thoroughly intertextual concoction
and so steeped in modern Irish fiction that it sets a formidable challenge
to any reader less well versed in this tradition.[110] In contrast to much Irish
writing that had been published since the revival, *An Béal Bocht* was a conspicuously literate text. So too was the sophisticated *Cruiskeen Lawn*, and
given the critical and commercial success that greeted both enterprises, it
is doubly strange that after 1943 O'Nolan rarely wrote in Irish at all.

The demise of the Gaelic satirist

There is no obvious reason why O'Nolan did not build on the commercial and critical success of *An Béal Bocht* in December 1941 with another
work in Irish; more curiously, from late 1943 onwards, the number of
Irish *Cruiskeen Lawn* columns dwindled immensely. When the column
began to appear daily in September 1941, O'Nolan had alternated Irish
and English, but by October 1943 articles written wholly in Irish were

becoming rare and they effectively disappeared after 10 March 1944. Throughout the rest of the decade, only five columns were published in Irish.[111] (In December 1952, 'Myles na gCopaleen' mutated to 'na Gopaleen', finally deferring to a monolingual English readership.)[112] Perhaps this was a sign that Niall Montgomery was increasingly contributing to *Cruiskeen Lawn*, but interestingly as the Irish columns dwindled out during 1943, Myles became progressively more preoccupied with the activities of two new revivalist organisations, Glún na Buaidhe and Ailtirí na hAiséirí.[113] Formed in 1942 after a split within Craobh na hAiséirí (an energetic breakaway group from the Gaelic League that had included O'Nolan's brother, the journalist Ciarán Ó Nualláin), they shared an unhealthy brand of right-wing exclusivist nationalism, as well as a bitter rivalry.[114] Some of their activities merely added to the stock of revivalist absurdity which fuelled *Cruiskeen Lawn*, as when Myles noted with pleasure in November 1942 that Ailtirí na hAiséirí had just proposed rebuilding the royal palace in Tara.[115] But from early 1943 onwards, they began to be presented in a more sinister light, their vehement street orators inspiring regular complaints in *Cruiskeen Lawn*. In March, Myles wrote:

> I was recently held up at a Dublin street corner by a small crowd who were listening to a young man with a strong North of Ireland accent who was aloft on a little Irish scaffold.
>
> "Glún na Buaidhe" he roared, "has its own ideas about the banks, has its own ideas about amusements, has its own ideas about dancing. There is one sort of dancing that Glún na Buaidhe will not permit and that is jazz dancing. Because jazz dancing is the product of the dirty nigger culture of America . . ."
>
> Substitute jew for nigger there and you have something beautiful and modern.[116]

In time of war, the consequences of the racist and chauvinistic attitudes of some language revivalists were not easily ignored. Indeed, for all their defiant Irishness, it is ironic that the xenophobic leanings of these right-wing groups bore an uncomfortable similarity to contemporary European politics.[117] The connection was emphasised in *Cruiskeen Lawn*. Later that year, faced with another exhortation to the youth of Ireland to deal '*Bás do'n Bhéarla*', or 'Death to English', as the spoken language of the Irish people, Myles advised that it would be better to exhort all and sundry 'to read the papers and have a look at what goes on on the shrapnel-pocked crust of HM Mother Earth'.[118] Given that references to these groups cropped up in *Cruiskeen Lawn* throughout 1943, it is feasible that their more aggressive breed of language activism made O'Nolan increasingly less inclined to continue writing in Irish. From the beginning of *Cruiskeen Lawn* he had always been writing against the grain, whether satirising the language's nationalist associations, or playing up its sophistication and complexity as an antidote to the folk bias of the revival. And Myles cunningly reminded these language enthusiasts that their fond racial fantasies were in contradiction with the history of the revival itself:

> Wanders through the streets . . . a native person standing on a rather cute little Irish scaffold and talking loudly and hoarsely to himself. We want to see Ireland free he told himself and the most important plank in our platform is the revival of the Irish language. We want to see Ireland thoroughly Irish, he said.
>
> Now excuse me one moment. I think that it was in the 90's that some readers of this journal, bored with knitting and transplanting the silk worm, founded the Gaelic League for the long winter evenings. I mean our Protestant heritage . . . Almost immediately this club is 'discovered' by readers of the other journals in the country. And now, ever since the century turned (the way milk does) we have been haunted by hordes of tweed-bearing flat-nosed Paddies whose great agony, whose eternal anguish is that the (small) world will somehow fail to appreciate that they are . . . *Irish*men![119]

Late in 1944 came an interesting footnote to this intermittent diatribe against Glun na Buaidhe, Ailtirí na hAiséirí, and all their ilk. That December, O'Nolan wrote his only known drama in Irish, a short sketch called *An Scian* (*The Knife*).[120] The piece satirises the rivalry and bigotry of these groups, centring around a violent argument between a husband and wife who belong to the opposing associations. At the climax of the row (after many cries of '*Glún na Buaidhe abú!*') the husband stabs his wife in the back. The knife he uses is a wedding present, given to him on his retirement as secretary of his branch of the Gaelic League.[121] As a satire of the internecine warfare in the language movement (or to be more exact, the Gaelic League) *An Scian* is certainly pointed, if unremarkable. But given O'Nolan's targets, it is a little ironic that it was his own brother, Ciarán, who was co-founder and editor of Glún na Buaidhe's newspaper, *Inniu*.[122] The two brothers had followed very different paths; while Brian O'Nolan was writing *At Swim-Two-Birds* in their home in Blackrock, Ciarán was composing an Irish detective novel, *Oíche i nGleann na nGealt*, also published in 1939. He spent his entire career as an Irish-language journalist, while Brian O'Nolan, safely ensconced in *The Irish Times* and with the success of *An Béal Bocht* behind him, chose fairly quickly to return to English. It was a curious decision for a writer to stop working in his first language but perhaps one which was never consciously made. The aggravation he expressed at the political appropriation of the Irish language in the 1940s was undoubtedly a factor, but perhaps also was the lack of a supporting framework of modern Irish writing. While *At Swim-Two-Birds* had ingeniously exploited the Middle Irish texts which O'Nolan had encountered in UCD, *An Béal Bocht* had gutted the entire modern prose tradition. A new generation – such as Máirtín Ó Cadhain and Seán Ó Ríordáin – was coming to the fore, but perhaps too late to provide him with any sense of intellectual community. In the meantime, *Cruiskeen Lawn* sated itself on a diet of folk parodies and anti-revivalist bile.

By turning to English, O'Nolan might have secured himself a much wider readership, but he sacrificed a unique position as a fluent writer in Irish who was a scourge of both revivalists *and* their opponents. *Cruiskeen Lawn* and *An Béal Bocht* effortlessly shattered stereotypes about the Irish language and those who spoke it; after Myles na gCopaleen, there could be no easy assumptions about the character of the Irish speaker. As Bertie Smyllie recognised: 'Until Mr Myles na gCopaleen came along, all the Gaels had been refusing to admit that anyone knew anything about the language but themselves . . . I think he has done more than anyone else for the Irish language'.[123] O'Nolan's colleagues in *The Irish Times* have testified that Smyllie encouraged him to continue with the Irish columns, if only to irritate the scions of the Gaelic League. Unsurprisingly, the disappearance of Irish from *Cruiskeen Lawn* also prompted objections from many readers. Myles's intermittent response to these complaints was usually to assert that the language was simply too troublesome to handle, and that it was preserved in an anachronistic form that made it inadequate for his uses.[124] Curiously, just when the number of Irish columns was declining, *Cruiskeen Lawn* published one of its most eloquent defences of the language. Like many before, it was inspired by an *Irish Times* editorial which questioned the worth of the language revival. The folkery, bitterness and bigotry which had been satirised in the column over the previous three years did not prevent an assertion of the cultural value of the Irish language itself:

> There is probably no basis at all for the theory that a people cannot preserve a separate national entity without a distinct language but it is beyond dispute that Irish enshrines the national ethos and in a subtle way Irish persists very vigorously in English. In advocating the preservation of Irish culture, it is not to be inferred that *this culture* is superior to the English or any other but simply that certain Irish modes are *more comfortable and suitable* for Irish people; otherwise these modes simply would not exist. It is therefore dangerous to discourage the use of Irish because the revival movement, even if completely ineffective, is a valuable preservative of certain native virtues . . . [125]

Perhaps this fervour caused its writer some discomfort, the column continuing in a more characteristic tone that 'Even if Irish had no value at
all, the whole bustle of reviving it, the rows, the antagonisms, and the
clashes surrounding the revival are interesting and amusing . . . The lads
who believe that in slip-jigs we have a national prophylaxis make life less
stark.' If, at the time, O'Nolan had consciously decided to cut back on
the Irish columns, this was effectively their swansong. However, they still
appeared irregularly over the following months, and in December the
Gaelic Myles made a brief return to satisfy his readers' curiosity about the
disappearance of Irish from *Cruiskeen Lawn*. He imagined that they
worried that it had been made scarce by the war, like many of the pleasant
things of life, and they would suspect the involvement of the black
market. But he admitted (in Irish, ironically) that:

> Seachas Béarla, tá sí achrannach agus trioblóideach le ceapadh agus scríob-
> hadh mar is cóir. Acht rud abhfad níos measa, is deacra ar fad í do mhilleadh
> agus do bhascadh agus do thionntó bun-os-cionn dochum adhbhar siamsa do
> soláthar don lucht léighte. Tá an Béarla óg lúthmhar so-lúbtha; cailleach crap-
> chnámhach iseadh an Ghaoluing, céasta ag an aicíd ar a cruaidh craptha . . .
> Conathaobh í againn i n-aochor?
>
> Corr-uair is féidir rud do rá i nGaedhilg nach mbeadh ceaduithe i mBéarla,
> toisc aos a tuigsiona bheith tearc. Acht tá an buaidh céadna ag an láidir. Is
> trua gan mise i Sacsaibh, nó fuí ins na Sé Conndaethe dí-lionnmhar . . .

Compared to English, it is difficult and troublesome to write properly. But what is worse, is that it is even more difficult to mangle and
pummel and turn upside-down in order to supply something amusing
to the reader. English is young, agile and flexible; Irish is a withered
old hag, tormented with rheumatism . . . Why do we have it at all?

Sometimes it is possible to say something in Irish which would not
be allowed in English, because few understand it. But Latin has the
same advantage. It would be a pity to deny me to the Saxons, or to the
humourless Six Counties . . .[126]

The same theme returned the following June – the Irish language, he
claimed, was simply not up to the challenges he set it: 'The grammar was
subject to fungoid complaints, the syntax was old, patched and leaky,
some words completely unusable. Spending money on repairs was like
pouring money down a well . . .'[127] Given the fashion for modernisation
and post-war planning (of which Myles was also a fervent critic), he
implied that the language would soon become even more of an
anachronism in Irish life, and 'the day when standards *in anything* can be
dictated by peasant usage is gone forever. Paudrig Crohoore, with his
harp, his gnarled ash-plant and his smoke-stained wife is no longer the

accredited formulator of the Irish aesthetic'. This column neatly combined a characteristic swipe at the antiquated, 'peasant' bias of the revival
with a dig at the all too modern (and too European) perspective of
Ireland's social planners. Myles na gCopaleen had always demonstrated
that there were no safe assumptions about the allegiances of the Irish
speaker; now he was even surprising himself, and – however facetiously –
was echoing those who touted the Irish language as the ultimate defence
against the iniquities of a modern, urban society.

Aside from such responses to his readers' demands, a wholly neglected manuscript by O'Nolan on the Irish language revival (dating from
the late 1940s) offers an invaluable perspective on his attitude to the language shortly after he had effectively abandoned it in his literary
career.[128] The three extant chapters of the unfinished revival manuscript
provide a sober analysis of the condition of the Irish language and the
Gaeltachts, along with a polemic that deliberately unpicks the ideology
of revivalism. Though its preoccupations are familiar from *Cruiskeen
Lawn*, its tone – part cultural history and sober statistical analysis, part
anti-revivalist polemic – reveals O'Nolan's opinions with a clarity
unusual for a writer whose voice was more often masked by the ironies
of Myles na gCopaleen. Internal evidence suggests the manuscript was
most likely written in 1947 (or shortly thereafter), but there is no evidence that O'Nolan was commissioned to write a book on the language
revival. The recent fiftieth anniversary of the Gaelic League had also
prompted Myles to reflect wryly on the topic: 'Nothing was further from
my thoughts than a "gaelic revival" that connoted the atrophy of Irish
intellects nor did I dream that the publication of a few old tales should
become a base pathogenic influence on the minds of the young and the
innocent'.[129] The three chapters which remain are evidently preliminary
drafts, scribbled over with corrections and suggestions by Montgomery
but bearing no traces of his own revisions. Of these, 'Decline and
Revival' supplies a history of the language revival from the nineteenth
century to the 1940s; 'What is the position of the Gaeltacht?' provides a
statistical examination of the decline of Irish throughout the country, as
well as a discussion of government policy on the preservation of the language and the Gaeltachts; and the most entertaining chapter, 'The
Pathology of Revivalism', is a Mylesian broadside on revivalist polemics,
past and present.[130] Throughout, O'Nolan's account of the decline and
revival of the language is deliberately iconoclastic, writing against the
grain of a nationalist historiography and dourly questioning the very
possibility, and indeed *desirability*, of a language revival itself.

It is notable that in this work the hand of the civil servant weighs more
heavily than that of the creative writer, an approach which itself provided

a neat corrective to the cultural polemics which wielded such influence on government policies regarding the Irish language. This shift in style is most striking in 'What is the position of the Gaeltacht?', where the grimly analytic attitude which O'Nolan adopts might be the natural corollary of his anti-romantic satire in *An Béal Bocht*. Drawing on census figures and policy documents published since independence, the thrust of his analysis is economic rather than cultural, but he attributes government failure to devise suitable economic initiatives for the Gaeltachts to the inhibiting effects of their symbolism as the repositories of traditional Irish culture. This failure of political imagination, though preserving their traditional character, also preserved a devastating pattern of language decline. And crucially, as O'Nolan argues, the effect was that the people of the Gaeltacht continued to regard the Irish language as a sign of poverty and lack of education – what he later refers to as a 'prison of a language'.[131] The Gaeltacht Commission Report of 1926 formed his primary source of reference, its remit being to define the limits of the Gaeltacht, to suggest how administration and education in these areas could be provided through Irish and how their economic condition could be improved. Notoriously, as happened in later censuses, the statistics it gathered concerning the true extent of the Gaeltacht were a little too optimistic. But whatever its true limits, O'Nolan concludes that the report's findings unwittingly confirmed the 'status of the Irish language as the badge of poverty as well as of nationhood'.[132] The areas which the Commission identified as wholly or predominantly Irish-speaking tellingly coincided with those which had formerly come under the jurisdiction of the Congested Districts Board. Their preservation was due to the Board regarding them as 'hopeless', taking the view that no redistribution of land could make these areas economic (WG, 5-6). The legacy of this inaction was double-edged: the preservation of the original communities served to maintain the language to some degree, while on the other hand, this unrelieved poverty continued to fuel emigration. Ironically, while the Gaeltacht Commission recognised the negative effects of migration on the language, its solution was to recommend the re-settlement of large groups of Irish speakers in other counties. This proposal was expressed in revealing terms, effectively conceived as a means of redress for what the Commission termed 'the Evicted Tenants of the Race'.[133] O'Nolan's chapter makes no comment on this ideological indiscretion, nor on its quiet rebuttal in the government white paper which was published in response to the Commission's recommendations.[134] But observing that proposals for migration could only serve to undermine Gaeltacht communities, his conclusion is that an 'almost intractable anomaly arises in devising a plan to preserve Irish by economically rehabilitating people whose retention of Irish is to be ascribed to poverty . . . there is a distinction between helping Gaeltacht people and helping the Gaeltacht' (WG, 6–7). This was hardly a dilemma which could be admitted in either the Commission's Report or the government's white paper, though it later found satirical expression in the picturesque poverty of the Gaels in *An Béal Bocht*. The point had already been raised in evidence submitted to the Gaeltacht Commission during the public hearings of 1925:

> WHAT IS IT WE WANT? An impoverished seaboard on the north-west, west and south-west of this advancing State, with the Irish language alive and strong; or a seaboard advancing economically with the rest of the State as a bilingual territory? . . . The Gaeltacht is a valuable possession no doubt, but I fear we have been exploiting an impoverished people too much for the glory of having a Gaeltacht, without giving them something more than Irish to live for.[135]

The suspicion was harsh, given that the Gaeltacht Commission was instituted partly to respond to the continued impoverishment of the Gaeltacht. Nevertheless, its reluctance to entertain proposals for economic revival which might impinge on the traditional character of these communities showed it to be constrained by the role they played in the national imagination. O'Nolan criticises its overwhelming concern 'to patch up a pseudo-agricultural economy' (WG, 7), and proposed a radical shift from agriculture to state-supported industry, a move not made until the foundation of Gaeltarra Éireann in 1957. This reluctance to divert from traditional lifestyles betrayed a lack of reality which O'Nolan addresses in his conclusion to the chapter. Pragmatically, he points out that if the language was not even advancing in the Breac-Gaeltacht (partly Irish-speaking areas), then the revival could hardly be expected to succeed in the rest of the country. It was generally recognised that the disappearance of the Gaeltacht itself would make an attempt at general language revival entirely futile, and since many persisted with the notion that the language was 'the sole badge of Nationhood', the inference was that 'the existence of Ireland as a Nation hangs by the most tenuous of threads' (WG, 11).[136] It was a logical, if perverse, conclusion to an illogical line of thought.

'Decline and Revival' adopts a similarly iconoclastic approach in its account of the modern history of the Irish language. O'Nolan's diagnosis of the forces which contributed to the language's precipitous decline in the nineteenth century pointedly avoids repeating a tale of nationalist grievance. Where a 1937 Gaelic League pamphlet could calmly proceed from the premise that 'the propagation of English and the killing of Irish was a fixed state policy always persisted in as being necessary to the complete destruction of the historic Irish nation',[137] O'Nolan instead attributes the language's decay to social and economic factors rather than the deliberate machinations of a colonial government. Side-stepping the nostalgic polemic of *The Hidden Ireland*, he argues that while the Penal Laws stymied the development of the literary language, they in fact saved the spoken language by preventing the development of a Catholic middle class who would, out of their own self-interest, have abandoned the language much earlier than the nineteenth century. Indeed, he suggests that those in power most likely preferred to keep the Catholic population Irish-speaking as a means of securing against their economic advancement.[138] Indeed, O'Nolan emphasises the fairly recent association of the Irish language with nationalist politics, pointing out that academic study of the language was first instituted for the purposes of proselytism, while English was the language of nationalist agitation from the United Irishmen onwards. Sharply attentive to the complex topsy-turveydom of language politics in Ireland, his account of the decline of the Irish language challenges a cultural history popularly distorted through a post-revival perspective.

The crux of his argument is that from the days of the Penal Laws, 'English was the way which opened every door leading from rural squalor and poverty' (*DR*, 5). But if this was clearly the main factor in the decline of the language, he finds little reason for its revival. The central importance of the Irish language to cultural nationalism is barely adverted to in this chapter, with O'Nolan giving a bald account of the language revival that relies mainly on a litany of antiquarians and scholars, from George Petrie and Eugene O'Curry to Douglas Hyde and Osborn Bergin.[139] Although he glancingly admits the 'profound nation-wide re-awakening' which their work brought about, bringing 'the people back from apathy, servility and ignorance in cultural matters to take a keen pride in their ancient native institutions' (*DR*, 9), he incisively undermines the habit of legitimating the language revival through its association with separatist politics. If the revival movement filled the void created by the decline of parliamentary nationalism after the death of Parnell, then it represented nothing more than 'a completely fresh approach to an old problem which was purely political, fiscal and agrarian and not concerned with language or rival cultures' (*DR*, 9). And if the language revival was merely another expression of the sublimated 'separatist' tradition (itself an interesting choice of words, 'nationalism' is only once mentioned in this chapter), the implication, he argues, is that it has undoubtedly spent its force and 'there is no reality in it in an Ireland that is largely free':

> Those who believe that it was the Gaelic League which brought an
> independent Irish State into being should ponder the fact that the
> League's symbol was the Sword [of] Light and that one of the first offi-
> cial acts of the new State was to use the Sword of Light design for its
> lowest monetary token, the halfpenny stamp (*DR*, 9-10).

Seeking a justification for language revival in political nationalism might
be a self-defeating act (in a state that had now won its independence), but
nowhere in this chapter does O'Nolan enlarge on the legitimacy or value
of the revivalist impulse. His emphasis on the economic pressures which
contributed to language decline, while necessary in itself, arguably led to
an understatement of the more insidious effect of cultural influences –
the factors which conspired to cast Irish as a 'barbaric' and anachronistic
language. As the Gaeltacht Commission Report recognised, a language
not commonly used in public life by administrators, clergy or educators
suffered from a commensurate lack of status, even among its own
speakers. Tellingly, the 'refined popular culture' which the Commission
sought to preserve in the Gaeltacht, on the basis that its memories, folklore, songs and traditions contained 'the very soul of the Irish language',
was of course unmercifully satirised in *Cruiskeen Lawn*.[140]

The final chapter, 'The Pathology of Revivalism' not only subverts the
ideological premises of the language movement, but bluntly questions the
very possibility of language revival itself. The Gaels, as O'Nolan depicts
them, are peculiarly insulated from life in their Gaelic dream; as their
unrealistic aspirations indicate, they 'suffer mentally from the arrested
development of the Irish language itself'.[141] The epitome of this revivalist
delusion is expressed in the Gaelic League's aim to have Irish replace
English as the spoken language throughout the country:

> The Gaels see nothing absurd in ignoring the economic facts which
> killed Irish; instead they insist that the whole process must be
> reversed, that the Irish people must all be re-locked in the prison of a
> language they broke out from, and cut away from the civilisations to
> which English gives them access . . . (*PR*, 2-3).

There is some irony in the fact that such extremism has the effect of
making a language revival (itself a culturally enriching thing) into a tool
of cultural impoverishment. There is no stronger statement of O'Nolan's
antipathy towards the insularity of the revival movement, while also presenting it as a breed of cultural dilettantism wholly insensitive to the
reality of life in Gaeltacht areas. But a return to this 'prison of a language'
was hardly envisaged by any but the most deluded polemicists; the phrase
O'Nolan conjures up is itself more suggestive of his own attitude by the

late 1940s. Curiously, he does not take issue with state measures making Irish compulsory in education and other professions, ridiculing instead the more farcical expressions of the same principle, such as the Gaelic League pamphleteer who proposed that with sufficient state decrees, Irish could become the sole language of public life in 'at the outside, four years' (PR, 4). A similar fondness for assuming coercive powers over the public is identified in the activities of the Gaelic Athletic Association. Its ban on members attending or playing 'foreign' games is presented as an exemplary proponent of the broad assumption that 'things are either good (Irish) or bad (foreign)' (PR, 6). Noting the debt which the GAA owed to the development of organised spectator games in the urban centres of nineteenth-century Britain, O'Nolan cites the organisation as a prime example of the phenomenon whereby 'something either actually foreign or quite recent and synthetic is carried into the native Irish pantheon by the Gaels who solemnly swear that it is always there and bid everyone who calls himself "Irish" reverence it':

> . . . we have a body of men setting themselves up as an ultra-Irish organisation and existing on the basis that they are the genuine thing and that the majority of the inhabitants of this country (or *even*, a large minority) who have other ideas about sport are decadent and degenerate. This extraordinary impertinence is endemic in the whole Gaelic movement. It is the Irish people who are outlawed (PR, 6–7).

The exclusivists who frustrate the country's 'enormous natural power of assimilation' (PR, 7) are cast as the true suppressers of Irish culture – in thrall to a fake Gaelic tradition composed of European folk dances and other symbols of dubious descent. O'Nolan's polemic effectively implies that the Irish people have suffered a double act of colonisation and that their latest cultural overlords are the Gaels.

More satirist than analyst, O'Nolan's attention might be unfairly skewed towards the more ludicrous extremes of the language movement, but this manuscript is also marked by the experiences of the decade in which it was written. This chapter closes by repeating *Cruiskeen Lawn*'s intermittent wartime preoccupation with the unsettling similarities between the xenophobia of some language activists and contemporary European politics. A Gaelic cinema instituted on the back of a truck in O'Connell Street as an antidote to the foreign celluloid available elsewhere in Dublin's cinematic strip provided O'Nolan with his final image of the unhinged revivalist:

> The effect, whatever the intention, was to associate the Irish language (which is a fine and elegant thing) in the minds of passers-by with the

antics of "yawbs", with eccentricity, scenes in public, shrill extremism, childishness, even lunacy – everything abhorrent to the respectability and pretence to sophistication and culture which are the characteristics of city-dwellers everywhere (*PR*, 18).[142]

The aggressive provincialism of 1940s Ireland might account for O'Nolan's frustration in this manuscript, certainly as it was expressed by those activists who touted the language as a means of guarding a native Irish culture against all intruders. But for all his protests against metropolitan prejudices towards the language, by the mid-1940s he had effectively repeated the pattern set by earlier generations (those who associated Irish with 'degradation and servitude' (*DR*, 3)) by abandoning bilingualism to write solely in English. While the monolingual, Irish-speaking Ireland which he satirises might still have been the official goal of the Gaelic League, it can only have been seriously entertained by the most extreme (and delusional) language activists.[143] Few could have ever desired this prospect, and this 'prison of a language' perpetuates the fears of isolation and backwardness which inspired some of the revival's opponents. Ironically, his own writing in Irish had done much to counter such stereotypes of the language, creating in *Cruiskeen Lawn* a sophisticated, consciously *literary* brand of satire with an unmistakeably modern sensibility. In concentrating so much on the lunatic fringe of the revival, on the backward look of one branch of cultural nationalism, perhaps O'Nolan showed too little faith in the future. Máirtín Ó Cadhain's *Cré na Cille* was published in 1948, a novel credited with introducing European modernism to literature in the Irish language. Despite the inventiveness of *Cruiskeen Lawn*, and O'Nolan's peculiarly domesticated style of modernism in *At Swim-Two-Birds*, he never challenged Ó Cadhain's status as a founding-figure of a truly *modern* Irish literature. *An Béal Bocht* is a transitional book, but he never built on its success. While it acutely dissects the state of contemporary Irish writing, and the cant surrounding it (as did *At Swim*), its humour and linguistic inventiveness suggested a new vein in Irish-language writing which no one was more qualified than O'Nolan to develop, but he didn't.[144] Yet it is curious that in returning to the language he had virtually abandoned in his literary career, he momentarily slipped the mask of Myles na gCopaleen. The analyst and polemicist who emerges in the unfinished revival manuscript might not display the easy comic brilliance of *An Béal Bocht*, but he does provide it with a tantalising critical counterpart.

5

Newspaper wars:
Cruiskeen Lawn in the 1940s

On 1 April 1946, Myles na gCopaleen presented his readers with an unusually convoluted story, even by his own standards. 'Ran into myself down town the other evening', he reported, 'in rare form . . . and doesn't look my age at all.' He accompanies himself into a pub where he finds 'yours truly' standing at the counter. They all decide to head out to Sandyford; the driver of the cab, of course, being none other than 'the present writer': 'Begob is this what you're at now says my excellency to him no says he quick as a flash me real job is above in the Park receiving diginitiries and dhriving around in the landjue I oney do this in me spare time'. The Myleses, inseparable before 'the Split', grate on each other's nerves, one lecturing the other on careering round town 'acting the maggot as per usual': 'More I will not say at the moment but take it from me that the matter will not be permitted to rest at that but will be raised at another time and in another place'. On the road they meet 'Me, of all people', their drunken jaunt ending in a crash with 'the whole six of me up on the table in Vincent's . . . Laugh!!! I thought I'd die . . .'. The piece is oddly prophetic, given O'Nolan's later accident-prone tendencies when propelled by a full complement of 'intoxicated selves'. Yet its wry literalism also acknowledges the many different characters of Myles na gCopaleen, exploiting the variety of voices – from that of the plain Dubliner to the indignant rationalist – that could easily co-habit in any one column. The capricious and changeable character of Myles has become a staple of criticism on *Cruiskeen Lawn*, perhaps because it is one of the least contentious points that can be made about a newspaper column which sprawled over twenty-six years. But a degree of inconsistency was inevitable; as this story obliquely recognises, there was more than one Myles, and they did not always live in perfect harmony.

In a column that was published six days a week, the occasional ghostwriter is to be expected. O'Nolan not only admitted to having substitutes but advertised the fact, since it would allow him to deny responsibility for material that offended his political masters.[1] But where he pointed to a trio of writers behind Myles na gCopaleen, others have so far only confirmed the presence of two. On the 125th anniversary of *The Irish Times*, a tribute to Myles ended with a nod to O'Nolan's regular stand-in, Niall Montgomery, noting that it 'would be unjust if . . . he should not have a mention in the story'.[2] Yet besides hints and conjectures, such open recognition of his part in *Cruiskeen Lawn* is rare; Montgomery himself left no comment on his own contribution to the Mylesian myth.[3] What is clear is that his involvement was reasonably consistent from the earliest years, if always subordinate to O'Nolan's. His papers contain 159 surviving *Cruiskeen Lawn* columns dating from January 1947 to May 1958, averaging at forty-five columns a year in the late 1940s.[4] Nearly all of these were published and since *Cruiskeen Lawn* was appearing only three times a week after 1946, this comprised nearly a third of what eventually appeared in *The Irish Times*. (The first of these files, encompassing material from January to May 1947, is the fourteenth volume, which indicates that his contribution throughout the 1940s was greater than ever suspected.) Of course, O'Nolan himself wryly exposed all the shabby illusions of authorship to his readers, and given that he was a master of comic literalism it might, in the end, be worth taking this most misleading of writers most literally. The narratives hijacked by various characters in *At Swim*, the idea of compartmentation of personality for literary purposes, the emphasis on intertextuality and literary collaboration – all of this was not simply a reflection of modernist theory, but an image of his own writing practice. It is not just that *Cruiskeen Lawn* subsisted (in its leanest periods) on comic evisceration of the odds and ends of journalism: extracts filleted from newspapers, magazines, promotional booklets and other obscurities, filler material which banally echoed the more creative intertextuality of *At Swim* and *An Béal Bocht*. Myles himself was not so much a literary persona as a manner, if a brilliantly inconsistent one. And his inconsistency not only reflects the plain fact that his was not really a single (if a singular) voice, it also betrays Myles's position, as Anthony Cronin saw it, as the licensed jester of the Dublin intelligentsia.[5] The idea recalls O'Nolan's position at the head of the 'Mob' which haunted UCD's L&H debates, and certainly his texts are highly sceptical of the original genius, being guiltily laden with doubles and echoes, with hints of cultural predestination and the parodic doubling of texts and genres. The short story 'Two in One' provides the most grotesquely literal dramatisation of this obsession with the double; its narrator disguises himself in the skin of the man he has killed and is eventually hanged for his own murder.[6] For all Myles's aristocratic scorn for 'you Irish', *Cruiskeen Lawn*'s recursive parodies of Irish cultural rhetoric – whether in the aesthetic phraseology of *The Bell*, in the clichés of politicians and journalists, or in the tired paraphernalia of nationalist imagery – self-consciously points to his binds within a certain intellectual community. Whatever Myles's true debts to the intellectual disillusion of 1940s Dublin this was, at the very least, a community of two.

So quite apart from the posturing and irony which tended to preserve the inscrutability of the author of *Cruiskeen Lawn*, it is unsafe simply to conflate Myles na gCopaleen with Brian O'Nolan. This chapter, for the most part, takes 'Myles' as an entity in himself, though as Joseph Brooker argues, he is more accurately described as 'a function of style', a continuing improvisation, than as a character in any conventional sense.[7] He was, at least, an eternal member of the opposition – as many *Irish Times* readers first discovered on 12 August 1941 when, in response to a drive to promote Irish, Myles perversely announced that 'This is English Language Week'.[8] The column had often strayed into English before, most pointedly on St Patrick's Day when newspaper editors usually attempted to muster a patriotic smattering of Irish, but this was the first time that most readers could enjoy prolonged exposure to Myles. In deference to his new audience, the *fíor-Ghaels* he usually targeted were replaced by the cultural activities of the more anglicised middle-class Dubliner. Matters under discussion included the number of fakes in the National Gallery (to which Myles proposed to add his share), a project for sending ballet dancers to Leopardstown, and – in a typically oblique reference to the current war – the distinguished Russian general and Corkman, Tim O'Shenko ('Tom was the brother, of course'). From that September onwards *Cruiskeen Lawn* ran as a daily feature, alternating columns in English and Irish. Writing in English presupposed a much broader readership for Myles, and a very different context. On his Irish days, Myles could ridicule the quaintness of the language revival, safe in the presumption that while his audience would be proficient in the Irish language (and so hardly disdainful of it), as purchasers of the *Irish Times* they were unlikely to hail from the more extreme reaches of the revival movement. Converting to English opened up the more traditional base of the newspaper's readership, one perhaps less disposed to appreciate the subtlety of his criticism of the language revival.[9] And perhaps it was partly because of this that by the time the Irish columns finally ended in 1943, not only had Myles acquired a broader scope but also a more polemical character. Under the exigencies of the daily column, comic standbys such as the Brother were gradually retired and genial mockery of Dublin's middle-class culture (whether of language revivalists or *The Bell*) expanded to include satire of social and political affairs. Over those first five years, Myles gradually swapped the character of the eccentric man of letters for the more aggrieved air of the frustrated civil servant.

Though *Cruiskeen Lawn* appeared fairly consistently until O'Nolan's death in 1966,[10] it was in the earliest years that its most celebrated features made their appearance: Keats and Chapman, the Plain People of Ireland, the Brother, the Cruiskeen Court of Voluntary Jurisdiction, the long and varied history of Sir Myles na gCopaleen, the Research Bureau and the Catechism of Cliché, all of which were established by 1943.[11] *Cruiskeen Lawn*'s Bores arrived in 1944, but at this stage, the style of the column had already become more topical and discursive, having developed from haphazard collections of short items to addressing a single topic, often over a few days.[12] In the first months of the daily column, *Cruiskeen Lawn* ran an extended series on the Myles na gCopaleen WAAMA League and its troubled Escort Service but such sequences were rare, this sustained focus being more typical of Myles's later intervention in debates on social planning and post-war politics. These changes in the column over its first years – in its composition, its scope, and its delicate balance of nonsense and satire – are in part due to the circumstances of its publication during the war years (the conflict's official title in Ireland, 'the Emergency', managing a curious blend of a stereotypically British *sang-froid* and a stereotypically Irish insularity). Throughout the war, the draconian press censorship which was in place to protect Ireland's neutrality ensured a difficult period for *The Irish Times*, a paper long used to identifying with the Commonwealth and the British Army. At a time when Bertie Smyllie's editorials were regularly the subject of unwanted attention from the censorship authorities, Myles's wartime commentary was largely restricted to the inventions of the Myles na gCopaleen Research Bureau, a parodic twin to de Valera's Emergency Scientific Research Bureau. *Cruiskeen Lawn* became noticeably more topical after censorship was suspended in May 1945, as Myles commented on the atomic bomb, the Nuremberg trials, and the spat over the airwaves between Churchill and de Valera. Finally free to look beyond internal squabbles, the column swiftly responded to the consequences of war and this broader scope was sustained to the end of the decade. But by the late 1940s, the first signs of repetition and a sometimes self-indulgent crankiness were already evident. Ten years after Smyllie welcomed his 'Gaelic cuckoo' into *The Irish Times*, the nonsensical column which many had hailed as a welcome distraction from the gloom of wartime was juggling a mix of nonsense, satire, and tart political commentary.

But even when Myles was at his most arcane, perhaps the most unique aspect of this strange literary artefact was that it formed part of the daily life of contemporary Dublin. It was launched into the peculiar atmosphere of a wartime city, the pressures of the Emergency aggravating changes already underway in Ireland's social and cultural landscape. Predictably, emigration worsened during the war as many joined the Allied forces and others exploited employment shortages in Britain. The haemorrhage from rural Ireland in particular notoriously inspired the rural propaganda of de Valera's 1943 St Patrick's Day speech. As *The Bell* pointed out (and this speech tacitly admitted) emigration was not solely an economic problem; it was also an expression of dissatisfaction with the nature of Irish life.[13] The clash between Myles and the Plain People of Ireland is a comic symptom of these demographic changes. However, while the Plain People might appeal to the Dubliner who is disdainful of his country cousins invading the capital, they also satirised the cultural pretensions of a new breed of *Irish Times* reader typified by O'Nolan himself: the disenchanted, middle-class, Catholic civil servant. Much as the Emergency years forced the state to fall back on its own resources, they also forced a reconsideration of its cultural agenda, the very mixture of nationalist politics and revivalist aesthetics which these new *Irish Times* readers found increasingly questionable. As neutrality apparently cut Ireland off from Europe and America, while drawing it ever closer through emigration, military service and the occasional wayward bomb, this strangely contradictory experience exposed the true limitations of a '*sinn féin*' philosophy. Similarly, with British and American markets closing off throughout the war, Irish writers were finally forced to confront the practical consequences of literary censorship. The bitter Seanad debate over *The Tailor and Ansty* in 1943 might not have achieved any legislative changes (with an appeals board only being established in 1946), but it set on course a significant opposition to this cultural puritanism. Otherwise, the war years were not as stagnant culturally as might be supposed. The launch of *The Bell* in October 1940 was a significant act, even if the journal's liberal agenda still betrayed a bias towards defining culture in nationalist terms,[14] besides the minor renaissance in Irish-language publishing. In fact, the Emergency ushered in something of a boom for Irish writers, with increasing support from Irish theatres and more opportunities for publication at home (*The Irish Times*'s Saturday books page was a typical example, providing a forum for new poets).[15] It also necessarily reconfigured the tired parameters of Irish cultural debate; as Claire Wills argues, the point of contention was no longer between Irish and Anglo-Irish, but 'between self-sufficiency and a "Europeanly-minded" version of Irish society. It became for some an urgent battle over Ireland's European identity.'[16] In 1943, the Irish Exhibition of Living Art finally brought European modernism to Dublin, where both this landmark exhibition and its successors were chronicled with gleeful disdain in *Cruiskeen Lawn*.[17] Throughout this strange period of apparent stagnation and underlying change, the column stealthily developed, as Stephen Young put it, into 'a monstrous caricature of the whole of Ireland in the mid-twentieth century'.[18] Myles, a brilliant mimic of the multifarious Irish public, captured the confusions of an era when the consequences of cultural, political and economic isolation were beginning to undermine the state's nationalist ideology. While he inflated the stentorian voice to a farcical degree, criticising contemporaries such as O'Faoláin and O'Connor for their effrontery in pronouncing on the state of Irish society,[19] *Cruiskeen Lawn* itself gradually moved away from its comedic roots and became less of a variety act. Myles progressed over time from the nimble jester who mocked Dublin's intellectuals and Plain People alike to the censorious satirist disdainfully coming to grips with the post-war world.

But just as neutral Ireland's self-image partly depended on a sense of moral superiority to its neighbours (however inadequate this seemed when Nazi atrocities were finally revealed to Irish readers), the later moral satire of *Cruiskeen Lawn* could also ring a little hollow. The legality of the Nuremberg trials became a habitual bugbear of Myles in 1945 and 1946, as did the social welfare proposals first floated by 'H.M. Bolshevik Govt in the UK',[20] while both the horrors of wartime Europe and the poverty which inspired post-war social planning rarely penetrated what was, after all, a humorous newspaper column. Myles had his limitations, and by the post-war years it was becoming evident that the column had already reached its peak. The shift away from O'Nolan's inventive set-pieces to a looser style more responsive to the trivia of daily news slowly diluted its idiosyncratic character. Certain preoccupations remained: the dislike for artistic pretension, impatience with self-styled public men of letters, and pedantic parsing of *The Bell*'s prose. But along with patrolling Irish cultural debate, Myles not only turned his attention to the frequent strikes afflicting the country or the failings of CIE and the ESB, but also to the establishment of the United Nations and the shifting balance of international power. Towards the end of the 1940s, the column reflected a more uneasy awareness of Ireland's status in the wider world – either a curio for visiting reporters or, in Myles's imagination, in danger of becoming an outpost for American (military) tourists. The claustrophobia of the Emergency had opened out onto an even less comforting landscape. Nevertheless, *Cruiskeen Lawn* was increasingly prey to periods of sleepy automatism, one particularly dreary interlude being a long series of extracts from Lord Chesterfield's *Principles of Politeness* in 1948.[21] This method of composition, lazily relying on the secondhand bookstalls on Dublin's quays, might have been lifted directly from *At Swim*'s student.

For all of Myles's self-reflexive tendencies, it is at this point that the reader of *Cruiskeen Lawn* might become most conscious of the real business of the newspaper columnist – of piling words on words, parrying with readers and stirring up controversies. Concluding one particularly obfuscating column on the nature of thought, he expressed a 'sincere hope that no buffoon will write to me asking me what I am trying to say. Surely I have made it clear that I am not trying to say anything.' [22] His writing, as he claims, may be 'destitute of any functional quality', but his impact on mid-twentieth century Dublin was very different.

'the peasant jester': *Cruiskeen Lawn* and *The Irish Times*

From the very beginning, Myles na gCopaleen occupied a peculiar position in the Irish cultural scene. Thomas Hogan's 1946 profile for *The Bell* took a retrospective look at O'Nolan's career to date and drew particular attention to the delicate position of a satirist working in the Irish language who wrote for a paper popularly identified with Anglo-Ireland. As Hogan saw it, 'the great stupidity of the mind of the mass' was the proper material of the humorous columnist, but as a journal of the minority (of 'unionists and ex-unionists, intellectuals and mock-intellectuals'), *The Irish Times* could not safely exploit such condescension:

> . . . in writing for the *Irish Times*, there is the danger of appearing to be too much outside what Myles would call the national ethos. It is to be expected that the *Irish Times* will sneer at the Irish people (or so the Irish people are likely to think). On the other hand, by leaning too much the other way, Myles might seem the bridgehead of the Irish people in the *Irish Times* . . . In fact, Myles has skilfully evaded both traps . . . [but] the ambivalence of his position has left its trace in his work and has been responsible for a certain ambiguity in his approach.[23]

Myles, he argued, occupied an 'anomalous position' as the 'peasant jester in *The Irish Times*'.[24] It is difficult to gauge whether this anomaly was in fact felt by contemporary readers of *Cruiskeen Lawn*. Certainly, many of the initial responses to the column presented it as an Anglo-Irish plot, but many of these letters were probably attributable to O'Nolan and friends. The most vitriolic attack of this type, the *Standard*'s poem, says more about the biases of that paper than it does about typical attitudes to *The Irish Times*. But whether or not readers viewed Myles as a 'peasant jester' in an Anglo-Irish paper, the way in which the ambiguities of the Myles na gCopaleen persona were exploited betrays a certain self-consciousness about his position – sometimes playing the paternal aristocrat, sometimes the cunning peasant rogue. O'Nolan initially appeared to model his column on a humorist who wrote for a very different breed of newspaper, the *Daily Express*'s 'Beachcomber' (aka J.B. Morton).[25] The Plain People of Ireland were descendants of Beachcomber's dim-witted adversary, Prodnose, a reader who suffered repeated abuse for intercepting the writer's flights of fancy. Similarly, the inventions of the Myles na gCopaleen Research Bureau recalled those of Beachcomber's Dr Strabismus (Whom God Preserve) of Utrecht. The Cruiskeen Court of Voluntary Jurisdiction mirrored the absurd proceedings conducted under Beachcomber's Mr Justice Cocklecarrot, and Beachcomber's 'Dictionary for Today', itself borrowed from Flaubert's *Dictionnaire des idées reçues*, inspired an Irish-language equivalent in the first year of *Cruiskeen Lawn*. Many correspondents to *The Irish Times* pointed to the similarities between the two writers, but Hogan more interestingly set them apart. As Beachcomber (one of 'the Belloc-Chesterton school') was an outsider to English society by virtue of his Catholicism, he argued, the humorist was well placed to attack the values of the *Daily Express* reader. The position of Myles was quite another matter. Certainly, J.B. Morton was writing for one of the first newspapers to successfully target a mass readership; his editor constantly cited the *Daily Express* reader ('the man on the Rhyle promenade') as the ultimate consideration in his editorial decisions.[26] Along with the *Daily Mail*, the *Express* had a hand in creating the contemporary image of the man of the masses (or the plain man, perhaps), one reflected in the newly-minted law of torts whose yardstick of reasonable behaviour was the ubiquitous man on the Clapham omnibus. *The Irish Times*, on the other hand, was a good deal more antiquated. Long regarded as the newspaper of the ascendancy, the *Times* was left somewhat stranded after 1922. In a 1941 interview with *The Bell*, Smyllie admitted that its detractors still regarded his newspaper as being aimed at 'old ladies and colonels . . . "dug-outs" in the Kildare Street Club',[27] but he claimed to be targeting young readers fresh from school and university, the voters and leaders of the future. It was no harm to trumpet such a policy to *The Bell* – itself a declared champion of a new Ireland – but Smyllie's adoption of young writers from UCD such as Niall Sheridan (who introduced him to O'Nolan) bears out his claim.[28] Nevertheless, the *Times*'s lingering reputation placed Myles in a far different position to Beachcomber, whose erudite fancies ran against the grain of the *Daily Express*'s populism.

Despite Smyllie's rhetoric, in the early 1940s *The Irish Times* was still largely preoccupied with the activities of a certain class of Irishman. University notes maintained a conspicuous position in the paper, as did reports of horse shows and other society events. However, as the war progressed, changes in the format of *The Irish Times* made it more competitive in the marketplace, though its editorial stance retained its unique flavour. Early in the war it moved news to the front page – a significant change, if only in showing that it was now openly competing with its peers on the newsstand, rather than relying on the loyalties of its traditional readership.[29] As *The Bell* noted in 1945, 'it was a bad day for *The Independent* when *The Irish Times* quietly dropped the invidious "Roman" before "Catholic" . . .', even if its incursion into a middle-class Catholic readership stalled at Fianna Fáil's *Irish Press*, whose readers would hardly look favourably on Smyllie's vision of an independent Ireland with strong connections to the British Commonwealth.[30] In fact, the war years brought mixed fortunes for *The Irish Times*. Paper shortages and transport problems did reduce the circulation of British newspapers in Ireland (which had fallen by 60 per cent in September 1941),[31] allowing domestic newspapers to gain a stronger foothold. Yet paper shortages also took their toll, at one point reducing the *Times* to four pages. Disputes over press censorship disrupted normal production and led to a number of open attacks from senior government politicians (which Smyllie appeared to savour).[32] In one way, these constant skirmishes perfectly exemplified why *The Irish Times* was the natural home for the Gaelic oddity, *Cruiskeen Lawn*. While Thomas Hogan feared that O'Nolan's satire could be hampered by *The Irish Times*'s reputation as a rather patrician critic of the plain Irish, the paper's position during the Emergency was rather more embattled than this suggests. Smyllie, staunchly pro-Allied, appreciated a good battle with politicians and censors; as it turned out, his protégé thrived equally well in such an atmosphere.

On one occasion, a certain amount of Mylesiana even infected the 'Irishman's Diary' which Smyllie wrote as 'Nichevo'. References to Irish servicemen in the British forces were officially banned (ensuring that the *Times*'s obituaries slowly filled with fatalities from 'lead poisoning'), and this led to the curious incident of the Japanese soldiers:

> In his broadcast on Sunday night, Mr Winston Churchill, the British Prime Minister (NB Britain is an island to the east of Eire) mentioned by name nine military and naval commanders who had gained fame recently in North Africa and the Mediterranean. I append the names of the gallant nine:
>
> | | |
> |---|---|
> | General Wavell English | General Dill Japanese (North Island) |
> | General Mackie Australian | General Brooke Japanese (North Island) |
> | General Wilson Japanese (North Island) | Admiral Cunningham Japanese |

General O'Connor Japanese   Admiral Sommerville Japanese
General O'Moore Creagh Japanese

As the venerable member of the Samurai, San Tiok Eli might or might not have put it: 'Quae regio in terra non plena laboris?'[33]

The Tánaiste, Seán T. O'Kelly, might or might not have put it like that when he saw his paper that morning (providing it was not *The Irish Press* which he took with his breakfast), but – to hazard the obvious – it did not improve relations with the censor. Despite the conflicts which most newspapers had at some time or another with the censorship authorities, it was evidently *The Irish Times* which they regarded with most disdain. The Minster for Defence, Frank Aiken, dismissed the tiny anti-censorship lobby in the Oireachtas by growling that they 'represented in parliament what *The Irish Times* represented in the press'.[34] Senator Seán Campbell dispelled any doubts about the nature of this constituency:

> There is a little coterie in this country who affect to be devotees at the shrine of liberal thought and who do not like the censorship of books, nor the divorce laws nor many other things which the people of this country favour . . . [the anti-censorship is] the squealing of propagandists . . . the squealing of people who know they have no right to speak for the people of this country.[35]

Campbell's intemperance betrayed the beliefs (or prejudices) of 'the vast majority of ordinary people' whom he claimed to represent. (It is little wonder then that its most famous columnist often imagined himself beleaguered by the Plain People of Ireland.) To some extent, Smyllie's mischievous treatment of the press censors played into such prejudices. Wilful anomalies, such as his insistence on referring to Cobh and Dun Laoghaire as Queenstown and Kingstown, did not endear him to those who suspected that *The Irish Times* still yearned for a pre-lapsarian, pre-independence Ireland.

Aside from *The Irish Times*'s disregard for nationalist sensibilities, the paper was known as an opponent of literary censorship; its Saturday books page printed lists of banned books until the authorities divined that this was a subtle form of advertisement and restricted such notices to the obscure pages of *Iris Oifigiúil*. It was only fitting that this unorthodox environment, with its slight whiff of *belles-lettres*, should have played host to Myles na gCopaleen, but he nevertheless maintained a slightly embattled air within the *Times*. As the bridgehead of Ireland's liberal intellectuals, his editorial host was sometimes more foe than friend:

> The fuss that is made about the censorship in certain quarters makes me laugh. The rule is that you must make a scathing reference to the censorship at every possible opportunity in speaking or writing. Give the impression that it is a personal scourge, a thing that is destroying you, subjecting the "artist" in you to diabolical torment. Then you are made as an Irish intellectual and eligible for your first corduroys.[36]

Once *Cruiskeen Lawn* became fairly well entrenched in the paper, it was given a permanent home between the leading article and 'An Irishman's Diary', from which position Myles conducted intermittent campaigns against his own editor. As the persona became more defined, he was increasingly presented as a bemused (and grandly anglicised) visitor to these shores, a benign dispenser of advice to 'you Irish'. The grandiose tone had shades of Bertie Smyllie, as Mercier recognised: 'Does any other paper in the world allow its editorials to be parodied right on the editorial page?'[37] Of course, the very first column had attacked an editorial criticising the government's policy on the language revival and Myles continued in much the same vein.[38] Even in less satirical moods, the defiantly nonsensical character of *Cruiskeen Lawn* provided an antidote to Smyllie's dour leaders on the progress of the war. Myles fully exploited his position as the in-house clown; for him, a meeting with the editor was not only a sobering experience, but a lesson in journalistic cliché:

> . . . chatting away serious supplies position city its back to wall world cataclysm without precedent penalties of neutrality soft thinking no substitute for hard work things worse before get better outcome which no man can foresee and few would be so foolhardy as to predict. (The old relentless stuff that makes the reader every morning push away the Luke Waugham egg and light shaky cigarette halfway through breakfast.)[39]

Cruiskeen Lawn did not simply act as a counterpoint to the serious business being conducted across the page, but often subverted Smyllie's editorials with its own agenda. Myles had a habit of claiming responsibility for neighbouring articles, and when Smyllie complained in July 1945 that de Valera behaved as if the Irish were doing Britain a favour by remaining in the Commonwealth, he sorrowfully announced a few days later that he had had second thoughts about his editorial:

> I apologise . . . for insinuating that we have by brute force and strength of armour coerced H.M. Govt. into according us certain *ad limina* privileges vis-à-vis their consuls and pro-consuls. It's just sheer good nature on the part of your men, who are all decent fellows.

Permit me to say this for the British – they don't take half as high a
view of themselves as we decenter Irish do of them . . .[40]

Stephen Young has described *Cruiskeen Lawn* as a 'bizarre newspaper
inside the newspaper'[41] and it certainly had the air of an independent
republic within the *Times* – at least in its later, more polemical, incarnation. It remained in the leader page until the summer of 1945 when
Myles was moved to a less conspicuous position because, as Donohue
argues, of Smyllie's growing irritation at his attacks.[42] All this did not
deter him from one day providing his readers with a sample of his own
editorial style, in preparation for Smyllie's retirement. His 'parenthetical
technique' was to accompany his readers through every line of print,
thereby defusing any illusion of journalistic objectivity: 'tirelessly
explaining, interpreting, issuing warnings, conundrums and jokes . . . in
short, seasoning the news of the day, while disinfecting it, with all the
warm and comforting balm of his own delightful personality'.[43] Needless
to say, Myles and his meta-newspaper never escaped the confines of
Cruiskeen Lawn.

But it did in part illustrate the nature of the column itself: not so
much a newspaper within the newspaper as a kind of critical parasite,
with Myles acting the fastidious reader buried under acres of mediocre
print. On slow days, excerpts from all corners of the press (including *The
Irish Times* itself) underwent excruciatingly pedantic analysis in *Cruiskeen
Lawn*.[44] Though Myles had no compunction about padding out a column
with the odd windy paragraph from an ancient number of *An Claidheamh
Soluis*, many also provided launching-pads for his fertile imagination. His
praise for the clarity and precision of the Irish language was only matched
by his scorn for the slovenliness of modern English prose, particularly as
practised by journalists. The Myles na gCopaleen Catechism of Cliché,
the ultimate one-man campaign against the well-worn phrase, was introduced in March 1942 as a 'unique compendium of all that is nauseating
in contemporary writing':

> Is man ever hurt in a motor smash?
> No. He sustains an injury.
> Does such a man ever die from his injuries?
> No. He succumbs to them . . .[45]

Like *At Swim-Two-Birds*, the Catechism of Cliché was a distant descendant
of the 'ready-made' book which O'Nolan and his UCD friends had once
planned to write. However, *At Swim* is much more than a compendium of
hackneyed literary styles, and the Catechism similarly grew more nuanced
than the original concept might suggest. It might have owed something to

the 'Ithaca' episode of *Ulysses* (both deriving from the Catholic cate-chism), but as an anatomy of social conventions, it is more similar to Flaubert's *Dictionnaire des idées reçues*. Myles's generic obituary of the upstanding Irishman is a case in point; his mimicry of the form is exact, but more pointed is his satire of the tacit consensus concerning 'all that is best in Irish life':

> Of what was any deceased citizen you like to mention typical?
> Of all that is best in Irish life . . .
> What article of his was always at the disposal of the national
>   language?
> His purse . . .
> At what time did he speak Irish?
> At a time when it was neither profitable nor popular.
> With what cause did he never disguise the fact that his sympathies
>   lay?
> The cause of national independence.
> And at what time?
> At a time when lesser men were content with the rôle of time-server
>   and sycophant . . .[46]

As Myles later observed of the cliché, 'a sociological commentary could be compiled from these items of mortified language',[47] linguistic ruts reflect social ruts. The clichés attacked were not simply inelegant lumps of prose, but symptoms of thinking that had slipped into easy habits. The tortuously inverted catechism resorted to the simple solution of obstructing their convenience. Myles found the ludicrous in the most commonplace of phrases, generally the product of the parrot-like press:

> What does it behove us to proclaim?
> Our faith.
> In what does it behove us to proclaim our faith?
> Democracy.
> From what vertiginous eyrie does it behove us to proclaim our faith
>   in democracy?
> From the house-tops.[48]

The inventiveness – or inconsistency – of Myles's own prose style sub-verted common journalistic practice, defying any notion of a house style.[49] His voices not only outraged the bland uniformity of much jour-nalistic prose, but wryly hinted that even a byline was not a wholly reliable thing – which, in his case, evidently it was not. And like *At Swim-Two-Birds*, *Cruiskeen Lawn* drew attention to all the machinery of editing and printing that intervened between the writer and the reader, quite apart from the formal conventions which determined any writer's style. In the hands of Myles na gCopaleen, even the implied reader did not remain an unnoticed presence, being travestied instead in the form of the Plain People of Ireland. Neither was he coy about drawing attention to the position of *Cruiskeen Lawn* within the paper; when he wished to refer to what was going on in adjoining columns, he found that the easiest method of drawing attention was simply to point. On one occasion, he even led his readers across the page to 'The Irishman's Diary' for a change of air.[50]

This self-reflexive quality is partly what destabilises the persona of Myles himself; his habit of dissecting the journalese of *The Irish Times* or the jargon of *The Bell* shows an inescapable (if playful) self-consciousness about the very tools of his trade.[51] Indeed, *Cruiskeen Lawn*'s seemingly endless ironic regressions betray a dislocated centre of authority, as if the critic were forever overtaking the writer. Myles could betray some anxiety on this point, once despondently remarking that his 'sole contribution to the terrestrial literatures has been to refute each and every claim to originality on the part of other writers'.[52] But the manner developed for *Cruiskeen Lawn*, like the parodic *At Swim* and *An Béal Bocht*, also betrays O'Nolan's strengths as an essentially reactive and responsive writer. In a purely literary context, this can be seen in the way many of Beachcomber's comic devices were adapted for the very different environs of *The Irish Times*. And *Cruiskeen Lawn* was, at its root, a master ventriloquist's act – no matter who was pulling the strings – combining the interjections of the Plain People of Ireland with echoes of the pompous editor, Dublin pub talk, and every manner of hackneyed prose, from legal jargon to the meanderings of steam engine enthusiasts. It is because of this responsive quality in its comedy that Stephen Curran argues that *Cruiskeen Lawn* was ultimately beneficial to O'Nolan's career since it provided him with a ready-made (and much-needed) audience:

> . . . [In] *At Swim-Two-Birds*, audiences already figure as an indispensable structuring motif, and the presence of an alert, responsive readership proved a precondition for the satirical program initiated in his journalism.[53]

In *At Swim*, O'Nolan's parodies set up a dialogue with his predecessors (notably Joyce), one that is mirrored in the characters' comic debates on the stories in hand. The multi-faceted Myles, who berates and mimics his readers to varying degrees, is very much a descendant of *At Swim*. Even the conceit of presenting the novel as an unfinished work in progress – a long and rambling collage of different styles, its direction (if any) shifting in line with the interjections of its readers – strangely anticipates the actual form of *Cruiskeen Lawn*. Like *Comhthrom Féinne* in which O'Nolan and his deputies first honed their comic style, *Cruiskeen Lawn* gave Myles the opportunity to play off an actual readership, or as an *Irish Times* colleague, Jack White, put it: 'to keep up a dialogue with his audience, absorbing the reactions into the next work to be produced'.[54] It is telling that in its first English-language week *Cruiskeen Lawn* immediately sent up the cultural pursuits of the anglophone readership of *The Irish Times* (perhaps to provoke another skirmish in the letters page). As the column's remit broadened with time, Myles's relationship to his readership gradually changed, White arguing that 'he came to interpret this instant reaction as influence, or even power'.[55] But if a style of commentary eventually emerged that was at times more typical of newspaper columnists (comic or otherwise), his interventions in the cultural scene preserved Myles as something of the plain man's intellectual. His most frequent target in this line was *The Bell* and its editor, Seán O'Faoláin. Setting himself up against the most prominent writer and critic of the day certainly enabled O'Nolan to create an instantly distinctive critical identity for Myles. Ironically, he and O'Faoláin showed a good deal in common in their criticism, if not in their fiction. Both mocked the ideological fog surrounding the Irish language, both derided the pious attitude fostered towards rural Ireland in the 1940s and both queried the dominance of nationalism in Irish society. Nevertheless, as soon as *Cruiskeen Lawn* began to appear regularly in English, Myles made a fall-guy of the new literary establishment (such as there was). For three days a week, *The Bell*, the Abbey and others filled in for the old-guard Gaelic revivalists who fuelled his satire on his Irish days.

Myles on the Irish writer

In the first week of the bilingual column, O'Nolan introduced the Myles na gCopaleen WAAMA League, a parodic version of the artists' association which O'Faoláin had recently founded to improve conditions for those whose livelihoods were now dependent on the Irish market. Its comic antithesis, the Plain People of Ireland, appeared only a month later. The conjunction of the two neatly exemplifies the double-edged humour of *Cruiskeen Lawn*. While the Plain People flattered the prejudices of 'keltured idiocated'[56] Dublin whom the WAAMA League and its escort service mocked, like the uncle in *At Swim-Two-Birds* they served as a reminder to many new *Irish Times* readers of the rural Ireland they had just endeavoured to escape. Reports on the WAAMA League's book-handling and escort services remained a regular feature of *Cruiskeen Lawn* until early 1942. The breakaway organisation had been formed to solace Myles for losing the presidency of WAAMA to Seán O'Faoláin:

> One shrinks from gratuitous comparisons, but man for man, novels for novels, plays for plays, services to imperishable Irish nation for services to i. I.n., popularity as drawingroom raconteur for p. as d.r., which was the better choice? I leave the answer not only to my readers but also to a betrayed posterity who may yet decide that Dermot MacMurrough was not the worst . . .[57]

O'Nolan's WAAMA League operated as a kind of artist's mafia, whose members were adept in complaint and extortion. This was standard for his characterisation of Irish artists (and their followers), who ranged – in his eyes – only from genteel conmen to peasant conmen. The WAAMA League Escort Service was a good illustration of Myles's attitude to the species, providing ventriloquists for tongue-tied theatre-goers who conducted erudite conversations for all to hear. Of course, the ventriloquists went to the bad, ending by blackmailing their clients and letting loose 'a wilderness of false voices, unsaid remarks, anonymous insults, speakerless speeches and scandalous utterances'[58] in the city's theatres (not a bad description of *Cruiskeen Lawn* itself). The book-handling was a slightly more civilised affair, designed to accommodate the individual with a hefty purse and intellectual ambition, but little time to develop an impressively well-thumbed library. As with many commercial services, book-handling was offered in a variety of options, including the deluxe:

> Each volume to be mauled savagely . . . a passage in every volume to be underlined in red pencil with an exclamation mark or interrogation mark inserted in the margin opposite, an old Gate Theatre programme to be inserted in each volume as a forgotten book-mark (three per cent discount if old Abbey programmes are accepted) . . .[59]

Apart from the 'great cultural uprising of the Irish people'[60] which the book-handling and escort services were designed to enable, *Cruiskeen Lawn* was replete with caricatures of the Irish intellectual, or 'corduroy'. O'Faoláin was cast as the archetype of the species, as an arrogant and hectoring individual who constantly bemoaned the impossibility of dragging the plain people up by their bootstraps. Myles gave his adversary all the dimensions of a cartoon, presenting him as a precious intellectual haughtily defending his cronies from the vulgar attentions of the mob. Only in 1933, O'Faoláin had named his first novel *A Nest of Simple Folk*, and barely a decade later the Plain People of Ireland were treading all over this antiquated taste for the plain, simple and homespun. Writing in 1954, Myles banded O'Faoláin and O'Connor with a string of writers he classed as 'perverted Carletons': from Charles Lover to Somerville and Ross, J.M. Synge, Lady Gregory and Aodh de Blácam. The two were described as only the latest peddlers of the homegrown stage-Irishman, producing 'stories about wee Annie going to her first confession, stuff about country funerals, old men in chimney nooks after fifty years in America, will-making, match-making – just one long blush for many an innocent man like me, who never harmed them'.[61] The criticism is ironic given that their involvement in *The Bell* stemmed from a desire to represent Ireland faithfully to itself, with O'Faoláin's first editorial emphasising its critical and realist ethos. Its very title was a sign of the journal's attempt to shake off the legacies of romantic nationalism: 'All our symbols will have to be created afresh . . .'.[62] However, leaving behind the old symbols was no easy task. In one sense, it is telling that *The Bell* shares the same birthday as *Cruiskeen Lawn* – both were representative of a new phase of Irish writing which abandoned nationalist nostalgia and revivalist aspirations in favour of a more realistic assessment of life in independent Ireland. Nevertheless, as Terence Brown's account of this period would suggest, both were constrained by the unchanging boundaries of Irish intellectual discourse:

> For many, the years of the war were simply a continuation of pre-war experience, in economically straitened circumstances, with the language, national sovereignty, religion and the protection of Irish distinctiveness as the dominant topics of intellectual and cultural concern in a society still moulded by its essential conservatism . . .[63]

Any cursory reading of *Cruiskeen Lawn* proves that language and nationality (if not religion) still dominated Irish cultural discourse, but an alternative set of concerns slowly established itself during the Emergency. As travel to Britain became more difficult and Irish writers found their international market shrinking, they were forced to confront not only Ireland's censorship mentality, but also the basic conservatism of its intellectual culture. However, while the variety of contemporary European writing published in *The Bell* indicated a desire for a more cosmopolitan outlook,[64] ironically, its quest to discover the 'real' Ireland could appear suspiciously like the old revivalist project in new dress. O'Faoláin's parish-pump aesthetics inspired predictable scorn in Myles, the more so because to the author of *At Swim*, the former's quest for the authentic Ireland – if not authentic Irishness – showed a naïve faith in the sham perpetrated by realist fiction and undermined the premises of the cultural debates orchestrated in *The Bell*.

Whether *The Bell*'s goal to 'open a window on the world' was naïve or simply disingenuous, O'Faoláin's public persona was manna to *Cruiskeen Lawn*. Given that Myles fluctuated uneasily between bombastic self-aggrandisement and self-effacing absurdity, it is unsurprising that he parodied O'Faoláin's editorialising as mercilessly as that of Bertie Smyllie. However, Myles detected overweening authorial ego even when the artist remained 'within or behind or beyond or above his handi-work.'[65] He uncharitably diagnosed more egotism than realism in Frank O'Connor's 1947 travel book, *Irish Miles* (or *Irish Smiles*, as Myles dubbed it). O'Connor's pen portraits of the characters he passed along Irish roads met with a withering response:

> Mr O'Connor cycled about the country in shorts accompanied by ladies with French names, also on bicycles and clad in jodhpurs. It's one way of seeing the country, I suppose, though it seems to have more merit as an all-out plan *for being seen*. There's quite a point there, mind you. If you want to see really clearly, you must yourself be invis-ible, otherwise you are altering the sum of what you want to see by the addition of yourself.[66]

Myles, on the other hand, turns the notion of authorial invisibility on its head. He is the author writ larger than life, as farcically garrulous as Tristram Shandy. The flamboyant persona serves much the same func-tion as do the myriad authors in *At Swim-Two-Birds*; both draw attention to all the vagaries and contrivances of the authorial voice. But in this case, O'Connor's crime was not simply in seeking to draw a mask over the artificiality of his literary persona. While censorship was actively restricting the home market in the 1940s, there *was* money to be made in explaining the Irish enigma to an international audience and his post-war *Irish Miles* was typical of many books which provided tourist trips of inde-pendent Ireland as a slightly exotic theocratic state. Unlike the *Cruiskeen Lawn* syndicate, both O'Connor and O'Faoláin were full-time writers dependent on commissions; but in taking on such projects, they risked casting themselves as intermediaries between a sophisticated metropol-itan culture and a provincial backwater. Indeed, this was the image presented by O'Connor in his ill-fated article on 'The Future of Irish Literature' which was published in *Horizon*'s Irish issue of January 1942 – the issue itself being inspired by the embattled position of the Irish writer at home and abroad, aiming to balance the hostile press which neutral Ireland had been receiving in Britain. O'Connor assumed a strangely metropolitan perspective on Irish culture in his discussion of Seán O'Faoláin's latest novel, *Come Back to Erin*, which depicted a transatlantic love affair between 'a complex, cultured woman' (American) and 'a young provincial barbarian' (the Irish element). He contradicted most Irish critics of the novel by stating that he preferred O'Faoláin's American scenes to the sections of the novel based in Ireland:

> . . . the writer [O'Faoláin] has ceased to find what is most valuable to himself in Holy Ireland, and cannot translate back into its idiom what he has found outside it. Into that life a cultured Frenchwoman or American – and that means their creator – simply will not go.[67]

The implication was that he and O'Faoláin were not only intellectual outsiders in the Ireland of their day, but had also outgrown it. Though their Irish readership was restricted through censorship, O'Connor's attitude suggests that, in any case, there would not be a sufficiently sophisticated readership in Ireland for their work. Predictably, the article aroused antagonism in Ireland, no doubt aggravated by the fact that O'Connor's complaints were primarily intended for a British readership. Indeed, access to an audience outside Ireland was one of the greatest differences between Brian O'Nolan and his contemporaries. After the unsuccessful publication of At Swim-Two-Birds, he did not publish outside Ireland again until the 1960s,[68] unlike O'Faoláin, O'Connor, or Patrick Kavanagh, each of whom was represented in the Horizon issue. O'Faoláin's urbane tone in The Bell perhaps jarred on O'Nolan because he was so finely tuned to a local readership. For better or worse, Cruiskeen Lawn thrived on an unusual sense of intimacy with its audience. Despite O'Nolan's mockery of Ireland's theatrically plain people and self-conscious intellectuals, they may have been his saving grace – unlike his predecessors, this latter-day Myles na gCopaleen was deprived of the attraction of playing over the heads of the local crowd to a more cosmopolitan audience. Significantly, his own ridicule of Irish stereotypes, antique revivalism and the fíor-Ghael over the first years of Cruiskeen Lawn was unambiguously directed at a domestic audience. And strange though it may seem, because O'Nolan wrote solely for Irish readers, he was perhaps forced to be more realistic (in attitude, if not in style) than some of his contemporaries. While Myles may have appealed to a specific minority – a professional, urban middle-class – he chided them for the habit of looking abroad for approval. He was not impressed, for example, by complaints that a 1944 'March of Time' documentary on Ireland presented the place as a peasant backwater, the film-makers favouring shots of thatched cottages over new power stations: 'You flood the world with stamps to show that you have an unlimited lineage of great men dead . . . but you simultaneously require visitors to take note of the fact that your feet are no longer webbed.'[69] And while eschewing a flamboyantly outspoken stance (in the manner of O'Faoláin), Myles's strategy – like many others – was instead to adopt a cynical and derisive attitude to many of the culture's sacred cows. Tellingly, *Cruiskeen Lawn* never strayed too far into dangerous waters; religion, for example, is a topic noticeably absent from the column, although this may have more to do with the caution of *The Irish Times*. When Myles wryly remarked that the Institute of Advanced Studies had apparently discovered there were two St Patricks and no God, the newspaper was forced to settle a case for libel.[70]

This sympathy for native sensitivities was already in evidence when Myles joined in the general backlash against O'Connor's *Horizon* article. Roibéard Ó Faracháin's *Irish Times* review had savaged it on grounds which readers might have expected from *Cruiskeen Lawn*, launching an attack on:

> ... Mr. O'Connor's tantrums, eccentric literary judgements, and pathetic championship of great writers who are their own best champions. It is refreshing to find that Mr. O'Connor believes we need satire. We do, indeed. And one could name one gorgeous subject ...[71]

By the time Myles got around to the subject, O'Connor had already responded by querying Ó Faracháin's abilities as critic and poet.[72] Side-stepping the growing pettiness of the dispute, he instead took issue with the 'expensive upperbrow English monthly' itself: 'I am not too happy ... about a handful of the lads lining up self-consciously to be looked over by the visitor in the drawing-room'.[73] However, on this occasion his disregard for what the neighbours thought was perhaps a little disingenuous. Like Ó Faracháin, he detected a whiff of self-promotion in the article from which he had been sedulously excluded:

> We are told (so help me) that Irish literature began with Yeats and Synge and Lady Gregory. That's a quare one for you. As to the future of the thing, we have four pages on Mr. Sean O'Faolain (good man, Sean) and a half a page on Mr. Patrick Kavanagh. From the phrase "when O'Faolain and I began to write ..." one deduces that Mr. O'Connor is there too. This will help anybody writing an MA thesis. We now know where Irish literature began and the names of the three gentlemen responsible for sustaining it.[74]

For a Gaelic scholar like O'Nolan, the implicit dismissal of all pre-revival literature would be all too obvious, while O'Connor's casual sketch of the literary scene ('when O'Faolain and I began to write') unwittingly encapsulated the incestuousness of literary Dublin. Unfortunately, he soon wandered into another trap, concluding his criticism of the Abbey with a casual arrogance that was a gift to Myles: 'Small wonder that young men and women are fleeing the country in thousands. In the worst days of the blitz I used to meet them in the passport office . . . 'Oh, anything is better than Ireland,' they said hopelessly when I drew them into conversation'. As Myles interpreted it:

> This seems to mean that the present tide of emigration is due to the inferior fare that is being provided at the Abbey by Mr. Blythe.
> The brother is thinking of clearing out.
> *Is that so?*
> Thinking of beating it to the other side. Can't stand this country at all. Says we're all bunched.
> *Why is that, pray?*
> It's d'Abbey. Says the stuff they do be puttin' on at d'Abbey is more than flesh and blood can stand. Years since they had a Rooshian play or a pome by Yeets. All the crowd above in the digs are thinkin' of skippin' too. Th'oul place isn't the same since Yeets went. The brother is in a fierce temper about it.[75]

Myles's opportunism here was typical of his critical manoeuvres in *Cruiskeen Lawn* (and of his caricature of Irish writers as a peculiarly self-obsessed species with a persecution complex). At the time of writing, O'Nolan was serving as Private Secretary to the Minister for Local Government and Public Health, while his regular substitute was employed as an architect, both the day jobs being firmly anchored outside the literary world and its concerns. O'Nolan's tenure as a civil servant served as a forcible reminder of the banal but indispensable machine of actual (if slow) social reform. Implicit in Myles's attacks on the literary class in *Cruiskeen Lawn* is a sense that these characters had no authority to pronounce on the condition of Irish society, their criticism simply being self-aggrandising. Worse than that, it was condescending:

> Elsewhere in this essay we are informed about "the horror of Irish life," our "vulgarity," "provincialism" . . . We are all pretty low and bad and to tell you the truth, we ought to be thoroughly ashamed of ourselves. We are just ignorant bosthoons.
> *The Plain People of Ireland:* Is that so? Is that so, indeed?
> *Myself* – Shhh! Don't take it too seriously. You have me on your side, haven't you?
> *The Plain People of Ireland:* All the same, the cheek.[76]

It took a fellow writer to drive Myles on to the side of the Plain People of Ireland, a spot which he found increasingly congenial as the years passed.

But while both O'Connor and O'Faoláin were voluble personalities whose commentary on public affairs chimed with the social preoccupations of their fiction, the absurdist flavour of *Cruiskeen Lawn* and the polymath persona of Myles allowed him to play the didact while evading responsibility for the opinions he expressed. His bombast implicitly ridiculed the image of the Irish writer which had developed in *The Bell* under Seán O'Faoláin, and later Peadar O'Donnell – in other words, the writer as social commentator. As a showman and a stylist, Myles had little in common with those who followed the realist trend typified in *The Bell*; however, in fairness to his contemporaries, he diagnosed a condescending paternalism everywhere in Irish culture. The finger-wagging malaise ran all the way from the Friends of the National Collections to Glun na Buaidhe's hysterical street orators:

> Can we awful Irish louts (leaving aside for the moment our red faces, high cheek bones and gnarled hands) ever be made into little jintlemen? . . .
> . . . these 'Friends' tell us that we should be gracious. By what authority do they issue this impudent admonition? Who are *they* to talk? One passes by a street corner to hear oneself being told by a brat standing on a stool that one should be ashamed of oneself, that one has betrayed Emmet and Lord Edward and Tone, that an Ireland without Gaelic is not Ireland at all . . . Muintir na Tire takes a very poor view. The Monetary Reform Association takes a very poor view. *The Standard* takes a very poor view. *The Leader* is very unhappy. The GAA will not allow that one is Irish at all . . .[77]

The arch self-consciousness of Myles na gCopaleen was itself an antidote to demagoguery in all its forms. But by early 1944, when this column was published, he was in danger of becoming yet another self-appointed policeman of Irish public life. Yet the attitude that emerges from *Cruiskeen Lawn* is largely that of the lone ranger, asserting the individual's right to do as they see fit without suffering the admonitions of various parties – one distantly echoed in Myles's dialogues with the Plain People of Ireland, miniature dramas pitting his aristocratic character against the lumpen masses.

Still, in the *Cruiskeen Lawn* gallery of rogues, the arrogant demagogue was only as bad as the self-regarding artist who imagined himself to be something quite apart from the general run of people. (O'Faoláin and O'Connor could find themselves being attacked on both grounds.) Though the Joycean model of artistic indifference (and impenetrability) was abandoned by a generation of more openly political writers in the 1930s, Myles skirted both paths. When Patrick Kavanagh's review of the 1941 Royal Hibernian Academy exhibition was attacked by a number of disgruntled artists who snapped that he wasn't even an art critic, Flann O'Brien was exhumed for the defence. He pointed out that artists live by the patronage of the public, 'not by the praise of "qualified" and "intelligent" critics':

> What a world it would be if you could not complain about the quality of a pint unless you were a brewer, or complain about a play unless you were born and bred in the Abbey! . . .
> Incidentally, painters are the last people in the world to talk. They discuss and criticise everything without any shyness, and even write queer books about life. A well-known continental painter has found time in recent years to meddle in a lot of matters that have nothing to do with *Kunst*.[78]

Art for art's (or artists') sake didn't wash; neither did the idea that the artist or writer was in a privileged position to enlighten the plain people on their deficiencies. As *At Swim* suggests, O'Nolan for one conceived the relationship as a more equal dialogue. Tellingly, his only contributions to the *The Bell* were on the decidedly non-literary topics of pubs, dance halls and dog races.[79] It would be misleading to cast Myles simply as a champion of the plain man, but *Cruiskeen Lawn* demonised writers suspected of transforming literature into a private professional fiefdom to which only the initiated had access:

> Of all the arts the wind can blow, literature, as well as being the most objectionable, is the most inferior. Music, painting, sculpture, architecture, do not require to be transformed before an "uninitiated" man; a foreigner or a "barbarian" can appreciate them . . .[80]

Though the passages cited above show Myles in a democratic mood, as a critic he did not consistently identify himself with the public voice. The hieratic tone adopted in conversation with the Plain People of Ireland was no doubt a mockery of O'Faoláin's Arnoldian manner in *The Bell*. However, Myles's sympathy strayed between the Plain People (bewildered by 'corduroys') and the urbane Irishman who was frustrated by the conservative folksiness of Irish culture.[81] Indeed, the student's uncle in *At Swim-Two-Birds* haunts the Plain People, who inspire a similarly ambivalent affection. Whether they were accepted as self-caricatures by his readers or projected as the dim country cousins of the more astute Dubliner, they quickly gained common currency in 1940s Ireland. By 1943, the coinage had become so accepted that O'Faoláin was moved to query the provenance of these peculiarly plain individuals: 'Why, one asks, are the people suddenly become "plain"? Is this a previously unheard-of Irish love for the homely, the ordinary, the unaffected? Is there a desire abroad that we should be artless and simple-hearted, as guileless as children . . .?'[82] He answered his own question with reference to the comely maidens of de

Valera's recent speech, but the mythical plain people had long held a strange fascination in Ireland. It is tempting to consider that one of Myles's inspirations could have been a republican newspaper published under their name during the civil war; it unabashedly addressed its weekly editorial 'To The Plain People of Ireland'.[83] Ironically, one *Bell* editorial betrayed O'Faoláin's own fondness for appeals to the plain folk:

> In general . . . we keep on trying to project a picture of popular life, to live in tune with it, to move in its atmosphere, to feed on it, to get from it that assurance of normality, balance, health, which must be lost by those who live in cliques, great cities, salons, teashops, government offices.[84]

A lurking deference to the noble savage had haunted the literary revival, and as O'Faoláin's comments on de Valera recognised, it had also invaded the political culture of 1940s Ireland, which was characterised by a casual paternalism. However, while Myles's Plain People satirised the revivalist image of the simple and saintly Gael, as well as the anti-intellectual streak in contemporary Ireland, they were a curiously double-edged comic device. As *Cruiskeen Lawn*'s demonisation of Seán O'Faoláin shows, Myles was often used to play the plain man, and O'Faoláin was only one in a long litany of items deemed offensive to the plain and sensible Irishman: the anti-censorship campaign, *The Bell*, exhibitions of modern art, James Joyce (on a bad day), even the artistic aspirations of Charlie Chaplin. Though the Plain People were to some extent designed to flatter the urbane, post-revival intellectual of the 1940s, they were also employed in *Cruiskeen Lawn* to maintain a degree of sceptical philistinism concerning the Irish artist and all his endeavours, including his role as a social commentator.

Myles: the (un)civil servant

When the English columns first appeared regularly in 1941, their themes reflected the preoccupations of *At Swim* and the early letter controversies; the phasing out of the Irish columns late in 1943 coincided with Myles acquiring a broader and more topical range. Nationalism became a more frequent topic in the summer and autumn of 1943 (hardly surprising in the midst of a world war), with Myles pointedly affecting a rather urbane attitude to the matter:

> No decent person should consent to have himself called an Irishman, an Englishman, a Jew, a German, simply because of considerations of

> geography or because of a genealogical convention devised long before
> his time . . . If one prefers to have a nationality, it should be the one
> dictated solely by reason . . . Most of us, however, think it sufficient to
> enter a caveat when we hear ourselves described as Irishmen and for
> the rest are content to be uncommunicative and mysterious as to what
> other nation, if any, we conceive ourselves to belong . . .[85]

The solution he proposed on a number of occasions was simply to resign
from the Irish nation (and thereby from its attendant stereotypes).[86] Since
these columns began appearing in mid- to late 1943, at a time when Myles
was berating the revivalist groups Ailtirí na hAiséirí and Glun na Buaidhe,
and slowly abandoning the Irish-language columns, arguably they reveal a
growing tedium with the limited focus of intellectual debate in Ireland.
Admittedly, *Cruiskeen Lawn* was no innocent in the matter, its satire had
frequently orbited around issues concerning the Irish language and the
question of national identity – from the imagery of the Gael popularised
by language revivalists to *The Bell*'s anxiety over the shaping of a 'new
Ireland'. But it was also the summer of 1943 when a number of significant changes were introduced to the column, as Myles banished many of
its comic stalwarts and began to address a single subject over a number of
days.[87] Earlier in the year, O'Nolan had produced his first (and only)
anthology of *Cruiskeen Lawn*, and Curran argues that his selections showed
him to be refining the Mylesian persona: '. . . [it was] clearly intended not
simply as a representative volume but as a means of consolidating certain
features and of identifying the column as satirical'.[88] Whether or not
O'Nolan was deliberately pushing *Cruiskeen Lawn* in a more satirical direction in 1943, over the following couple of years the shift from comic
set-pieces to more sustained narratives certainly allowed Myles to develop
in a more consistent fashion. Ironically this meant that the guerrilla
satirist would gradually acquire the admonitory tone which he had criticised in O'Faoláin and others. In any case, with the phasing out of the
Irish columns in late 1943, Myles was treading a precarious path between
scorn for a fake, insular Irishness and what was presented as an equally
insecure faith in all things modern and European. His attack on a
Comhdháil na Gaeilge speech which had referred darkly to the international
'threat to Irish culture' was followed by the wry observation that:

> . . . this should appear in the same issue containing an Irish
> "Beveridge Plan," in the same year in which Pat has excelled himself
> in a disgusting aping of foreign technological and social catchwords
> . . . I do not find that there is anything discernible under the head of
> "Irish culture". If the speaker has in mind step-dancing, crubeens
> and potheen, I say that is not culture. If he means French pictures

made-in-Ireland, young architects blathering about prefabrication, plastics and "planning," I say that none of that is culture . . .[89]

The shifting identity of Myles na gCopaleen himself was mirrored in this perception of Irish culture, a phantasm suspended somewhere between the shibboleths of a national tradition and insecure imitation of European fashion. But as his impatience with Ireland's 'Beveridge Plan' indicates, increasingly the preoccupations of *Cruiskeen Lawn* were less those of the urbane man of letters than of the distracted civil servant.

In 1943, the year O'Nolan's political satire *Faustus Kelly* was produced in the Abbey, Myles first began to express the disgruntlement of his alter ego trapped in the Department of Local Government and Public Health.[90] Over the following years, the day job increasingly seemed to inform the literary work, as the column was punctuated by long and pedantic analyses of government documents, such as the 1944 Vocational Report.[91] Despite the restrictions governing the public utterances of civil servants, by April 1945 the tortuous prose of a Department of Finance memo on 'The Post-War Building Programme' was being subjected to a Mylesian decimation; that November, O'Nolan began his advance on the publications of his own department (or as it was termed: the 'Department of Yokel Government and Public Houses').[92] As early as 1946, this caused consternation in official quarters; that year the Department of Finance objected to his promotion, citing concern over his 'outside work'. But despite the offence Myles habitually caused to O'Nolan's political masters, he received a certain measure of protection from some, as a colleague testified:

> It was even whispered that a minister was tickled to have him in his retinue. Fair enough – if the mere servant were of such cultural calibre, the upper-class electoral imagination might be induced to boggle at the stature of the master.[93]

Cruiskeen Lawn would certainly be a useful ally in any public debate, given its self-professed reputation as the enemy of native humbug and cant, and especially considering that it was (quite literally) well-placed to undermine Smyllie's anti-Fianna Fáil commentary across the page. Understandably, on points of conflict Myles did not usually comment on matters directly relating to O'Nolan's own Minister or Department. In January 1942, for example, Seán MacEntee was pilloried in *The Irish Times* for his opposition to the provision of free hot lunches in Dublin schools, with Smyllie describing the Minister's letter to Dublin Corporation on the topic as 'a masterpiece of unctuous folly and platitude.'[94] MacEntee professed himself opposed to the scheme 'for moral and social reasons', arguing that providing meals in schools would undermine family life. While he was satirised by editor, correspondents and letter writers alike, there was not a whisper of the farce in *Cruiskeen Lawn*.[95]

As Curran points out, the confluence of the roles of writer and civil servant is illustrated most clearly in Myles's contribution to the debate over social planning which was conducted in *The Irish Press* after the publication of the Beveridge Plan in December 1942. Curran has tracked his extensive criticism of the Irish reports that followed in 1944 and which were rejected by the Fianna Fáil government, despite winning widespread support in the press – particularly from Smyllie's *Irish Times*. It was O'Nolan's department which dealt with such plans, and *Cruiskeen Lawn* produced a more trenchant criticism of the proposals for social insurance than appeared elsewhere in the media, at least in the case of their financial viability.[96] Up to this point, he had been reasonably careful to separate his two careers, not least because civil servants were not free to express their political preferences in public.[97] However, on this occasion, Myles's opinions fortuitously echoed those of MacEntee, who in January 1945 resoundingly rejected the social security plan proposed by Bishop Dignan.[98] His opposition to the proposals chimed with his criticism of the modern art exhibitions that had recently invaded Dublin: 'It is my considered view that Paud keeping step with world hysteria in the belief that he is being "modern" is a woeful spectacle . . . Eighty per cent of what has been put up before us is blatant imitation of what tremendous and strictly local revolutions have thrown up elsewhere and our "planners" have lacked the wit to dish up even some native sort of jargon'.[99] The flawed logic pointed to a cultural anxiety that arguably was allowed to outweigh the social merits of the plans.

It is at such points that Myles, or his various creators, betray his sympathy with the social conservatism of his generation. In 1942, Seán MacEntee had defended his objection to school meals with reference to a branch of Catholic social thinking that venerated the family unit and strictly defended its independence against state interference. Myles's response to the 1944 proposals on social security seem to follow a similar line. Much of his commentary on the plans was made in the guise of the efficient civil servant (leavened with a dash of Mylesian hyperbole), as he pointed out flaws in their design. But he also showed a large measure of resistance to the idea that the state – or a body not answerable to the state – should be allowed the degree of interference in the individual's life as would be required by the implementation (and funding) of a national health scheme.[100] While Smyllie pointed out that if Britain alone was equipped with social security this would only exacerbate emigration, he took the broader view:

> The growth . . . of mechanistic philosophies, pragmatical methodolo-
> gies, pathological ideologies and technological mysticism . . . had the
> net result of leaving men weak, wanton and witless – believing cre-
> ation to be remediable, believing 'life' to be a . . . a . . . fact . . .
> responsible persons who offer a plan to cover "all the hazards of life"
> are either not terribly serious or else believe that their commerce is
> with fools . . . is such a plan desirable, granted that the reversal of the
> eternal order is within human power?[101]

The philosophy may be tongue-in-cheek, but with a tart recognition of
the vast ambitions of many planners. Life, he later argued, was an
unceasing struggle which strengthened the soul; planners may 'inhabit
the earth by act of parliament with a vast fraternity of insured stooges, by
statute immune from "want," bedded, dressed, fed and supplied with
false teeth by mammoth intellectual stamp-vending ganglions . . . But do
not prate to me of "freedom from want". For that phrase connotes
repose, and repose is possible only in cemeteries.'[102] Cronin argues that
this scepticism towards the promise of a brave new world stemmed partly
from O'Nolan's gloomy Manicheanism, a sense that eternal (and earthly)
bliss was not the natural human condition.[103] But Myles betrayed a pragmatic edge that was shared by O'Nolan's minister; on reviewing the
schemes set forth in the 1944 Planning Exhibition, Myles dourly
reflected that given the depopulation of the Irish countryside, the planners might 'As well erect traffic lights in a grave-yard'.[104]

By 1944, the new wave of social planning and modernist art exhibitions were taking the place of O'Faoláin and *The Bell* as the butt of
Myles's attacks on liberal Ireland. Though *Cruiskeen Lawn* had launched
itself in 1940 with assaults on the anachronistic models of Irishness popularised by organisations like the Gaelic League, four years later Myles
was now targeting the forces of modernisation. There was certainly a
capricious element in *Cruiskeen Lawn*'s humour, a tendency to usurp any
burgeoning establishment, but the change of focus also pointed to a new
cultural orthodoxy. For Myles, the derivative nature of these enterprises
(like that of the revival impulse itself) only offered more evidence of the
Irishman's inferiority complex:

> . . . your problem is that you . . . become more and more Irish every
> day – that is, more 'anxious' about things that don't concern you (e.g.
> art), more voracious for alien social nostrums (e.g. 'planning', 'social
> security', 'vocationalism') . . . more saturated with the humble dog-like
> desire to please, to shine, to be regarded as 'advanced' . . .[105]

Cruiskeen Lawn instead cultivated a defensive individualism (and of
course the power to affront). Once the hostilities in Europe had ended,

he assured his readers that post-war planning had merely been a joke, and not something they need worry themselves about. The foolish debate had been started, he wrote, when the hapless Paud pressed his face to the window and wondered why the great bounty promised across the sea could not be found at home.[106] Now Ireland's self-imposed isolation was over, and Paud could take a closer look at the other side. Over the summer of 1945, Myles became less preoccupied with the Irishman's quarrel with himself, and instead turned his moral cynicism on the great powers overseas.

When press censorship was finally lifted in May 1945, Smyllie railed that it had been 'in some respects as Draconian and irrational as anything that ever was devised in the fertile brain of the late Josef Goebbels'.[107] Myles simply observed that no one had ever dared to censor *him*. In his own post-war speech, he adopted the patrician tone that the plain people might have associated with the editor of *The Irish Times* but which also bore the traces of their paternalistic rulers:

> Now, it has been borne in upon me – and this gave me of sadness – that some of you resented the effects of my censors. I say it with great humility but say it I must – that was terribly wrong of you. After all, when I now read the things you are writing without their help, I cannot help feeling you are trying to prove I was right . . .
>
> *I want to congratulate you, all of you – you have been very good* . . . I have no special message for you to-day, nothing that 'can be published now'. I have always spoken my mind. But I still have the old message: Hold fast to your humility, your poverty, your talent for suffering. These are the clean enduring things.[108]

Myles had always suffered from a regal delusion, now he was assuming the voice of de Valera himself; the following day he modestly took responsibility for Churchill's notorious radio address as well.[109] His grandiose persona had once been satisfied by the stewardship of the WAAMA League, but like the Brother, he was now comporting himself as an international statesman. In that last summer of war, when peace in Europe freed Myles from the busy pencil of a press censor, *Cruiskeen Lawn* could finally take account of the momentous events of the past few years. Jokes about the Research Bureau and the black bread on sale in neutral Dublin were replaced with more dour observations on the effects of the atomic bomb and the conduct of the victorious allied powers. The world, as the uncensored Myles now portrayed it, was a forbidding place, one which was more than equal to the febrile inventiveness of his black humour.

While Myles took his customary fortnight's holiday in August 1945, the atomic bomb was launched on Japan. On the day of Japan's surrender, Smyllie observed with grotesque equanimity that 'it may be that the immolation of the people of Hiroshima and Nagasaki has prevented, in the end, a greater slaughter'.[110] The immolation of the people of Hiroshima and Nagasaki was the first subject of *Cruiskeen Lawn* on its return, and it remained so for the better part of the week:

> Why should this outsize barbarity be visited on the Japanese? It cannot be because Japan was at war with America, since human rights remain intact even in war . . . No, it must be because the Japanese are considered unpleasant folk; few of them are Knights of Columbanus, Elks or Rotarians, they are not afraid of death, they respect authority and live frugally. And they have manners.[111]

The suspicion that a sublimated racism permitted the use of the atomic bomb in far-off Asia was not shared by Smyllie, and on 10 September, Myles began a week-long denunciation of his editor, seeing a contemptible cultural superiority in Smyllie's celebration of the British victory over Germany and Japan. Over the week, he compared the relative merits of Western and Eastern art, drama and philosophy, always to Europe's disadvantage:

> Western civilisation starts with man, his body and his foolish mind, and ends there . . . I must say to the Editor of *The Irish Times* (a brave albeit foolish man) – *go east, young man*, learn the value of contemplation, the glory of the spirit, the grandeur of nature and forget, for the nonce, your whole wardrobe of penicillins, panaceas, plurality of county councils, Home Rule, statutory hospitals for Cork fever, planning. The East, by the way, is slightly larger than Ireland . . .[112]

Cruiskeen Lawn promptly disappeared for the next week, possibly due to Smyllie's irritation at his columnist's incessant criticism.[113] In the first week of its return, there was a resurgence of the inoffensive adventures of Keats and Chapman. But Myles's humour was never without its bite and even Keats and Chapman could have their satiric purposes. Back in the first week of September, when he had returned from holidays to a post-atomic world, the duo had made one of their most ghoulish appearances. One night, as Myles told it, they were caught in an area where atomic bombs were being tested: 'The dread instrument produced a number of freak effects, the most noteworthy of which was to blow the backs off several humans, leaving them alive, conscious, and otherwise intact. Chapman arrived back from the nearest village to find Keats minus his entire back, lying face down on the wreckage of a bed and cursing loudly'.[114] The following morning, they came upon a heap of human backs neatly piled in a nearby field. Keats began to search among them, still cursing and vowing vengeance, despite Chapman's remonstrances: '"I'm going to get my own back," Keats said savagely, turning over nearby fleshes.' The atrocity story had now not only finally infiltrated the uncensored Irish press, but even the weird humour of *Cruiskeen Lawn*. The column was no longer a playground where Myles performed juggling tricks while tiptoeing about the main topics of the day. As for the problem presented by the bomb, in early October he came to a conclusion on how to handle this diabolical new creation – to gather together all the scientists who had any knowledge of it and simply shoot them: 'Or else, and maybe this is better, make a very big atomic bomb, say about 7/8", and just let it off and kill everyone. Sure you'd never be missed.'[115]

Throughout the rest of the autumn, Myles kept his eye on international affairs of state – as well as the conduct of Dublin Corporation, the state of Irish drama ('I still say there is a place in your Dublin for a play that does not take place in Thade's cabin . . .'),[116] Britain's new Labour government and the variety of Bores to be met with on the streets of Dublin. But the more acerbic political element of *Cruiskeen Lawn* continued with his commentary on the Nuremberg trials in late 1945. While criticising the bombing of Japan, he also noted that 'Copaleen's Law' (a Law of 'Unilateral Responsibility in War') had never been shown such respect as now, when it was being used to 'sanctify' the trials of war criminals.[117] This illegality of the proposed Nuremberg trials was to become a regular theme:

> . . . tamper thus with the sacred tabernacle of Justice, thus prostitute to a predetermined end the holy processes of the juridical ratio . . . [and] ye have procured an abomination that will, as if by atomic enheatment, sear all life from the planet.[118]

Myles later responded scabrously to readers who charged him with defending the accused: 'I defend nothing: I explain. I attack nothing: I merely annihilate what offends'.[119] The remark unwittingly captures some of the contradictions of the persona as it had developed over the previous five years. His affectation of a judicial impersonality (not defending, merely explaining) is undermined by his admission that he indeed annihilates 'what offends' him. Myles na gCopaleen, in the guise in which Brian O'Nolan had first created him, had maintained the ambiguity which characterised *At Swim*'s humour; the character's inflated authorial ego masked his creator in the same manner as the various parodic voices of *At Swim*. Even on his critical days, Myles was as often a pedant and a stylist, as he was a polemicist. However, by 1945 this ambiguity was dissipating and Myles often appeared a more dogmatic character. How much of this is attributable to the different personalities behind *Cruiskeen Lawn* is impossible to say. The treatment of Nuremberg was a world away from

Myles's delighted examination of the quaint jargon in *Cruiskeen Lawn*'s District Court. He could still bluster in December 1945 that '*The mock-juridical proceedings currently in train at Nuremberg have not from me obtained of sanction one hint or whisper. This I have stated and it is a fact*'.[120] A few days earlier, suddenly aghast, he queried why he did not have a seat in the Cabinet. And what had happened to the minority report of the na gCopaleen Commission?[121] But despite its layers of irony, over the war years *Cruiskeen Lawn* had acquired a considerable satirical bite; certainly more than its genial rival, *Dublin Opinion*.[122] By the end of 1945, Myles na gCopaleen was more often abandoning the indirect routes of comedy and the persona was coalescing into the self-appointed conscience of Irish political and aesthetic affairs.

Myles and the brother: the post-war *Cruiskeen Lawn*

In January 1946, Myles was looking dourly on the coming year; the prospect was dominated by more debates on 'various "planning" ramps', more inefficiency from CIE, the hanging of the Nuremberg 'criminals', and a ban on yet another book 'by distinguished son of Cork farmer'. It was all too predictable, even the inevitable fall-out from 'the crippling horror of war': 'catastrophe, rise in unemployment, murder, rapine and pestilence'.[123] But so was *Cruiskeen Lawn* itself, alternating over the next fortnight between shots at art critics and caustic reflections on post-war politics. If Ireland entered the United Nations, for example, it would flood the country with diplomats and impel the Irish person to get himself safely to jail where he would have no 'rights' but would be free from 'mendacious and vile propaganda, communism, fascism, effete democracy, etc, etc'.[124] The same scepticism coloured Myles's reflections on the trouble between General MacArthur and the cousin, Hir O'Hito, who had just renounced his divinity and Japan's right to rule the world: 'How very unique Japan must be . . . practising imperialism without believing that she is destined to rule the world? . . . Does one know of other imperial races who have lacked this comfortable sensation (i.e. that of being destined to r.t.w.)?'[125] This preoccupation with the iniquity of the new world order and the emerging superpowers would be more representative of Montgomery's later columns, though without surviving archival material for this period the attribution cannot be definite. Over the following weeks *Cruiskeen Lawn* generally shied away from this political tone, ranging instead over the inefficiency of the public services, the vagaries of pub talk, a new Abbey play, or the strange fate of Myles's honorary degree from Trinity College. While a reader could never foresee what Myles would be up to on any day, six years into its run the most unpredictable aspect of *Cruiskeen Lawn* was its fluctuation between a sometimes cantakerous satire and the more purely comic elements which had characterised the column since its beginning.

Yet these tendencies did not go unmarked by Myles himself. While Ireland held a conference on North Atlantic aviation in March 1946, he was busy predicting the next global war before 1950, this time with the country playing unwilling host to American military airships. But as he mounted the podium to address his readers, he also berated their slack-jawed credulity:

> Must we then today – back to folly? Discuss something 'important'? Something 'vital'? Discuss a 'burning question of the day'? . . . But of course – why not? Blind mouths as Milton called ye – *anything* will stuff that vacant opening. Is there anything comparable to it – this craving to be lectured and instructed? To be comforted? (What was Fianna Fáil invented for if not for that? Or those reverend pine ears, Cumann an Jail, who are now beginning to wonder whether their claim that they founded your Irish state is still a sound boast? . . .)[126]

Myles was long used to assuming an absurd position of vast and unassailable authority, one that variously exploited and subverted the unspoken influence of the newspaper columnist. Yet in deriding such seriousness he also exposed the contradictory strains in *Cruiskeen Lawn*. At times a more acerbic political sensibility is to the fore; at other points Myles can seem to lack any anchoring seriousness, and his ability to subject anything to his levelling irony produces sometimes brilliant and sometimes disquieting results. On the day following his prediction of war, his customary persecution of CIE continued with musings on their train conductors, a 'new Gestapo' who would strip and flog unticketed passengers, despatching them to a 'dread *Arbeitslager* . . . for the "correction" and "protective custody" of refractory passengers. CIE moans about the shortage of rubber. For what – truncheons?'.[127] The glib tone of a writer far removed from the realities of wartime Europe betrayed one effect of neutral Ireland's isolation. But *Cruiskeen Lawn* at the same time showed a recognition that the post-war climate allowed less indulgence of the Gael's insular self-obsession. When the president of the GAA warned against the danger of forgetting Ireland's 'individuality' in these uncertain times, Myles kindly seconded the notion: 'In the tragic aftermath of war, items such as pestilence and famine blind unthinking people to their duty in the matter of customs, games and dances. Probably at no time in the history of the world has there been such exigent need for sixteen-handed reels . . .'[128]

But conflicting though its treatment of politics could be, the view from *Cruiskeen Lawn* indicated a broader shift in Irish cultural perspectives. In the post-war world, the 'thoughtful Irish reader' must now be concerned with Ireland's ambiguous relationship to the Commonwealth and beyond: 'We simple cawn't gow on pretending that we're not part of the world . . .'[129] Yet even this bid to move beyond a repetitive national discourse was coloured by its old concerns, Myles's tone implying that this new internationalism was only a symptom of a more familiar cultural cringe, a concern for the opinion of London 'journalists': 'Sinn Fein officers with, with swords, old boy, I give you my word, plenty of clothes, one fellow I saw had two pairs of pants! No rationing . . . Streets with *houses* in them, *not a gunman in sight* . . .' But international relations were rapidly changing and Ireland was having to reconsider itself within a wider frame, dealing on the domestic front with a common post-war legacy of shortages and industrial unrest.[130] In some respects, little had changed in the world of *Cruiskeen Lawn*; Myles often simply offered relief from the daily tedium, as he had during the Emergency:

> Take this other nonsense known as 'better hours': would the Tirade Unions kindly inform my person what is wrong with the ordinary common or garden sixty-minute hour frequented by decent grandparents, housed by them in elegant repeaters, hunters, and . . . grandfather clocks, in the early days of . . . the movement?[131]

But at other times *Cruiskeen Lawn* exposed an uneasy rapprochement with post-war realities, and a sense of disconnection that was echoed by many of its readers. When the Nuremberg sentences were finally reported in October 1946, there was an unexplained three-day absence from Myles, but his response finally came a week later. Collapsing two political worlds on each other, he queried why 'the Nuremberg juridical canon' should be confined to international upheavals – why not, after a general election, put an outgoing Cabinet on trial?

> Can you picture the present Cabinet seated in a long dock wearing head-phones receiving justice from that revered and supernatural figure, an English judge – one, possibly, from Belfast? Hmmm? . . . If you defile the waters of true justice and law, you will find to your horror that they have common source and circulation and that they will in time poison yourself.[132]

This suspicion was not unrepresentative of Irish opinion. That same day, *The Irish Times* reported a meeting of Cashel Urban Council at which one member called for clemency for men who, after all, were 'the brains of Germany'. Others denied any sympathy for the accused but criticised the lack of neutral judges, or argued that countries responsible for the use of the atomic bomb were simply punishing the defeated for war crimes both had committed.[133] In this case, Myles might have sailed closer to the sympathies of the Plain People than to those of his editor, but if Irish public opinion was finally assuming the more international perspective advocated by *The Irish Times*, it is questionable with what understanding of the European experience. Despite Myles's mockery of the GAA's narrow response to a worldwide calamity, a sense of national paranoia sometimes invades even the post-war *Cruiskeen Lawn*. The Ireland it depicts is one under threat – whether from the realignment of international power (the Marshall Plan presented as a ploy to buy up European governments) or from the importation of foreign social and cultural models, like the burgeoning welfare state.

Reading the column day by day, the cumulative effect of such complaints is to make them seem increasingly superficial and automatic, as if Myles were simply acquiring a store of worn attitudes. Nuremberg was still turning up in May 1947, though now as a preamble to comments made in the Dáil: 'Progress, justice, decency, sin, socialism, murder – call it what you will (incidentally, all these words refer to the same thing) . . .'[134] Yet even at this stage, politics and nonsense were not always far apart. In December 1946, *Cruiskeen Lawn* reported the text of an agreement between 'Carlow sugar workers, the Institute of Motor Traders, the Azerbaijan government . . . General Franco, Mr. O. Flanagan (Ind.), Mr. Walt Disney and Mr. Myles na gCopaleen . . .', its anarchic terms including arrangements for regulation of 'the global zone' and a common standard of living 'for persons mostly'. In the true spirit of the post-war conference, one supremely important speech after another is reported, 'the substance of which has not been disclosed', while Myles variously thanks his people for their conduct during the Emergency, jeers at Ernest Bevin, declines British honours, and sees the king 'in a dream of unusual vividness'. In the following phantasmagoria, de Valera and the Provisional Government host talks with Gladstone in Dublin, Nelson's fleet floats threateningly off Dublin Bay and the anti-neutrality TD, James Dillon, addresses the Young Irelanders. Myles ends by protesting his friendship for the USSR against personal attacks from the Soviet press ('they're peasants too. We're all in this together'), attends an exhibition of 'Irish-assembled automobiles' in Herbert Park and is made (in parenthesis) a Knight of the Garter.[135] While delicately poised on the composed and informative (but largely meaningless) prose of official press releases, this is political reporting as filtered through *Ulysses*. The associative narrative might be read as a microcosm of *Cruiskeen Lawn* itself, or at least of one of its various moods. While Myles was acquiring a reputation as an aggrieved satirist, such fantasias lingered on to remind his readers of a more gently skewed way of looking at the world.

From May 1946, *Cruiskeen Lawn* was reduced to three columns a week. Later that year, Thomas Hogan's *Bell* profile would pay uncertain tribute to O'Nolan's current line of work as being 'brilliant but futile'. With the achievement of *At Swim-Two-Birds* noted to be 'far behind him', his intellectual obituary was already being written.[136] Though Hogan argued that Myles's fatal limitation was in being 'essentially destructive',[137] his own perceptive essay has something of the same failing. The critical, reactive element of *Cruiskeen Lawn* is undeniable, but it was also leavened by surreal invention.[138] And when shrewdly deployed, this destructive ability could itself be constructive, particularly in the public controversies that would increasingly contribute to Myles's popular reputation. A case in point was the censorship row which had erupted some months previously over the banning of Frank O'Connor's translation of *The Midnight Court*. Although Myles had previously complained of 'corduroys' using the censorship issue as a means of self-promotion (a grumble dangerously close to those of pro-censorship advocates), he waded in on the side of O'Connor. Since a hearing by the Censorship Appeals Board had been refused, Myles suggested exploiting a legal loophole by dramatising the text; if all those who opposed censorship attended its performance, it would pay the costs of a hearing in open court: 'Come on now lads – let's see who's prepared to *do* something and stop whingeing!'[139] But the wrangling in *The Irish Times* letters page over the merits of O'Connor's translation proved that talk was a more popular option. The debate between correspondents and the Censorship Board may have maintained the illusion of an intellectual freedom of speech (if not freedom for the plain reader), but Myles swiftly debunked that impression when the Board's chairman, Professor James Hogan, made comparisons between O'Connor's version and the original 'Mud in Hyde Court':

> . . . ah no now, Professor boy, you're not serious. (Beams, begins to pat Professor's head.) . . . Maybe taking only a couplet of Mr. Connors' works would be only a venial sin but you must remember that your Honour and your Honour's colleagues have confirmed the ban on *the whole* book and it is therefore illegal to buy or sell it and it is thus illegal for anyone to take any part of it or to try and ascertain whether everything you say is accurate or whether you are, as you suggest Mr. O'Connell may be, deficient in Gaelic scholarship . . . When we are all in Heaven, we will know which of them was right – Professor Condon or Mr. Frank Wogan. For the present, it is illegal and sinful to find out.[140]

As Myles later noted, it was not writers but *readers* who were outlawed by the censorship. In his most sorrowfully authoritarian mode, he admitted that in the 'dark years of national resurgence' he had been tolerant of literature, but 'alas for the waywardness of a people to whom learning is an acquired taste! Tolerance was mistaken for weakness, culture for degeneracy . . .' and he was forced to found the Censorship Board. Evidently, literature was useless as a human occupation:

> . . . if one is the well-bred wealthy person that nature intended one to be then the use of the intellect can be nothing but a very vile and sinful affectation and one which, if persisted in, may be expected ultimately to bring into contempt and misprision law, order, holy religion and the ordinary common or garden decencies. Mr. na gCopaleen wishes it to be clearly understood that neither he nor his Government in Ireland will countenance any such subversive activity.[141]

But Myles na gCopaleen had, in a sense, trumped this unpromising situation. Despite the commercial failure of *At Swim-Two-Birds*, Brian O'Nolan had long subsisted in a popular arena where most modernist authors would fear to tread.[142] The censorship débâcle might have proved that literature was impossible in a country 'of four million illiterates where education is illegal', but the success of *Cruiskeen Lawn* was one argument to the contrary. In a censorship climate in which much contemporary writing was effectively 'outlawed', the column's intellectual guerilla tactics were a fitting response. But Hogan was only the first of many critics to write off *Cruiskeen Lawn* in favour of the earlier novels; in 1946, O'Nolan's reputation was already suffering from his combination of the roles of imaginative writer and controversialist, of the destructive, critical force as much as the creative. As Alan Titley notes, the long-running O'Connor controversy became one of the 'very few examples of a lengthy discussion of the merits of a work of Irish literature carried out in the public domain of a newspaper'.[143] But as Myles pointed out, it was also a discussion between a privileged few, those with access to the censored text. In a broader sense, *Cruiskeen Lawn*'s fusion of fiction, criticism and controversy, of pedantic analysis and quixotic opinion, might stand as a challenge to the merits of 'literature' itself, at least as contemporaries such as Thomas Hogan understood it. The column had created a new genre of its own, one whose appeal encompassed both the broad readership of *The Irish Times* and the literary audience for a novel like *At Swim Two Birds* – and perhaps one that could only have been bred in the stringencies of 1940s Ireland.

In March 1947, another case exposed 'how Ireland treats her literary men' when *Cruiskeen Lawn* reported that *The Irish Times* had been brought to the District Court for cruelty towards Myles na gCopaleen. He was discovered unshod and in an unfit condition; a member of the editorial staff 'had him wedged into the wall near Webb's bookshop and was working him very hard, compelling him to write stuff on the backs of envelopes ... WITNESS: His little face was all blue.'[144] Of course, O'Nolan had long escaped such a predicament by using a substitute, but the surviving records of Montgomery's work only date from this year. While he was only a filler-in (when O'Nolan broke his leg that January the column was suspended for three months), his presence in the column is inescapable. For most of May 1947, for example, he was contributing one of the three articles published each week.[145] (By June, Myles was spinning out nearly two weeks of material from the Institute of Architecture's Yearbook.)[146] Over the next few years, Montgomery's pieces stand out most when O'Nolan goes through an arid phase of producing filler material – typically long extracts from newspaper articles interspersed with a few dry comments. At other points, the continuity between them can appear seamless. When M.J. McManus, the literary editor of *The Irish Press*, warned of a lack of work coming through from young writers, Myles sorrowfully contemplated the disparity between promise and achievement in his young protégés like Yeats and Wilde: 'What is there about this country that blights so many hopes?'. Though it was Montgomery who was writing the piece, Seán O'Faoláin's comments in '*The Bawl*' received the usual treatment:

> Clever article it's all about this new discovery his name is on the tip of my tongue wrote a Nest of Gentle Folk and it shows how people are foolish without consulting him. That's a thing I like to see a bit of self-confidence and devil. (Poor George Shaw!)[147]

But later in the month, a column responding to a complaint about the working conditions of Irish artists more clearly exposed the differences in their approaches.[148] The final version was an elaboration of Montgomery's scorn for the idea that the 'ordinary man' should worry about (much less subsidise) an artistic caste unfitted for the daily grind. In the published article, Myles, before pronouncing on the matter, sets out with a knowing grandiloquence his credentials as 'literary *Uachtarán*' (or President of the Irish Republic of Letters) – otherwise known as 'The Irish Disraeli, The Man in The Hat, The Gaelic Demosthenes ...' Wryly defusing any hint of self-importance, it is a suitable riposte to the earlier draft, which has much more of the political orator about it. There, the offending *Irish Times* article is only one irritation in a range of 'shocking proposals ... advanced in an issue of the Sinn Féin organ, *The Irish Times*', including the government's notion 'that fuel, food and houses are

Asiatic effeminacies which we must learn to do without if the full industrial programme is to be implemented', the prospect of foreign investment
('*if* the country is to be sold I will personally see to it that we get a decent
price for the thing (Not like last time)') and Ireland's involvement in the
International Civil Aviation Organisation: 'little neutral Erie [stet] is
down as airbase No. 1 in War No. 3, a fixture which the Americans
intend to play "Away" as usual'.[149] But few of Montgomery's columns were
so heavily rewritten, most being published with very minor changes. An
exception, which received the opposite treatment, was a piece on the
Marshall Plan, its published version underscoring the hint that European
governments had simply been 'purchased for military purposes'.[150]

Apart from their polemical character, Montgomery's columns also
tended to include more critical broadsides on art and literature. This
inclination produced the most striking instance of Mylesian doubletalk
in the form of an admonitory 'Open Letter' which Myles 'inadvertently'
wrote to himself in September 1948. In fact, it was written by
Montgomery over a year earlier and despite its ironic tone, the delay in
publication is unsurprising. The revised opening paragraph suggests that
its critical assessment of *Cruiskeen Lawn* in 1947 had hit its mark:

> . . . I meant to kill the thing but then decided that that would not be
> the BIG way. Besides, the strictures in my letter apply *a fortiori* to every
> other wretch who writes in newspapers . . .[151]

Much of what follows is fairly innocuous, scolding Myles for dealing with
serious subjects 'in colloquial or vulgar language', and ordering him to
be careful not to annoy 'Paddy Kavanagh'. Criticisms of his discursive-
ness and his failure to keep to a point might purposely miss the joke of
Cruiskeen Lawn, but as the letter progresses it strikes closer to home:

> . . . for goodness sake *try to make your stuff interesting!* All that philo-
> sophical stuff and the big words and the little private jokes you do be
> having to yourself – not only is it downright bad manners but it's –
> now don't take this amiss – it's . . . boring. (I'm sorry. You asked for
> it.) Attacks on CIE, ponderous stuff about world wars and the atom
> bomb, 'warnings' about the collapse of civilisation, schoolboy criti-
> cisms, attacks on other people's English style, tediously deliberate
> misprints – there y'are now, that's got your goat! – it'll all have to stop
> before someone else stops it . . . You will have to write soberly and
> properly or blooming well starve! . . . Mind you, it may not be easy –
> stringing your thoughts together into one coherent whole, knocking
> the thing into shape, giving it a bit of elegance, you *know. But* . . . the
> thing would be far less trouble to you if you had . . . a bit of . . . back-
> ground . . . do you ever read a book at all these days?

For O'Nolan, there was no escaping the echo of *At Swim*'s nagging uncle, and regular readers would have recognised all too well the sometimes tedious habits that Montgomery identified. If there was a hint to be taken, it was steadily ignored and *Cruiskeen Lawn* continued on in the same vein. But evidently it was Montgomery who was inclined to cast a more critical eye on the proceedings, bringing more definition to the persona of Myles na gCopaleen. It was he who provided the first biography of Myles – again written early in 1947 though published much later. As suggested by his birth in Montevideo in 1646, Myles's history is predictably fantastical, but is not without its suggestive moments:

> Sometimes one is tempted to see in him a Nietzche, denying, rejecting, joyless, obsessed with destruction. His work, one feels, is the *apologia* of despair, despair under its many forms – boredom, obsession with death, with evil, with many weird caprices.[152]

While Hogan's assessment of Myles, the destructive genius, might have fed into Montgomery's parodic biography, Brian O'Nolan was to receive similar treatment from later critics (and without the leavening irony). Indeed, bearing in mind his critical reception, it is tempting to see Montgomery mischievously conflating Myles with the author of *At Swim*: 'that great dolorous brother, whose published work led literature to a tragic blind alley most worthy of the new era'.[153] But Myles is also presented as the epitome of the modern writer, an 'ingenuous bohemian' who exploited the unconscious and remade a universe 'devoid of obvious order, apparently without formed phrases, with images and expressions born fortuitously in his over-stimulated brain'. He might loosely resemble the creator of *Finnegans Wake*, but he is also 'a Freeman of the town of Birr, a Burgess of Kilkenny . . . an honorary life member of the Yacht Club', European literary colossus and homegrown dignitary in one. The joke lies in the juxtaposition, but it is also strangely apt; *Cruiskeen Lawn* being one product of splicing European modernism with the nativist culture of the Plain People of Ireland.

But if the column gained yet another layer of self-awareness from the coded critical dialogue conducted between Montgomery and his alter ego, his critical instincts had more damaging repercussions on the separate reputation of Flann O'Brien. While O'Nolan's debts to Joyce are well noted, claims of a debilitating anxiety of influence have usually been buttressed by the resentful tone which creeps into Myles's references to Joyce in the later 1940s and 1950s. One throwaway quip, for example ('I do not think he used up much cunning in those days – if he had, it is possible that we might have had just a little more . . . silence from him')[154] has been noted to be 'one of the first real digs at Joyce to appear in *Cruiskeen Lawn*, an indication perhaps that the Joycean label . . . was wearing thin'.[155] But as earlier noted, most of the jokes at Joyce's expense which proliferate in the later *Cruiskeen Lawn* come from Montgomery's columns. It is the homegrown *Wake* scholar who sourly contemplates the prospect of Irish pubs in the summer months: 'I encounter nothing but a stream composed of your earnest, solemn Americans, with rimless glasses and thin lips, all armed to the teeth with notebooks, *all* doing James Joyce for their degree!'[156] And it is also Montgomery who delicately notes not only the stray apostrophe bedevilling the title of *Finnegan's Wake* (a regular offence to Myles), but also the 'fantastic accuracy' achieved by Joyce in withholding the comma that Irish journalists eagerly restored to Davy Byrne's comment: 'It ruined many a man the same horses'.[157] He was the first to suggest the existence of the 'celebrated Irish-American syndicate' (incorporating Myles, Beckett, Niall Sheridan, Father Prout and others) which wrote under the name of James Joyce – an idea later to find its way into *The Dalkey Archive*.[158] But if Myles's famed grudge against Joyce has been partly attributed to the wrong individual, the literary collaborators undoubtedly had plenty in common. A Montgomery article on an exhibition by Oskar Kokoschka effectively re-stated the underlying terms of O'Nolan's own fiction:

> Only a person wishing to appear . . . innocent will pretend to judge art by the imponderable and treacherous canons of verisimilitude . . . I am assuming of course the case where verisimilitude is related to the factitious real world which persons of our class must always treat with the contempt it deserves.[159]

In retrospect, the observation contains a salutary warning for Myles's critics. Not only does he not necessarily mean what he says, but back in 'the factitious real world' he is probably not even the person you think he is. (The alleged Joyce syndicate may have found some consolation in the idea that it takes one to know one.) The infection spread; Myles in turn claimed to be deputising for other Irish writers. According to himself, not only had he written various stories published in *The Bell*, but 'A Prominent Novelist' had contacted him to ask whether he would do next year's novel, two stories for *Harper's* and a clutch of reviews. Myles innocently wondered whether he really had to be angry, and about what: 'Oh . . . life, or . . . or Obscurantism, or Irish bourgeois society, or censorship, or the brutalisation of what a few of us, back in '22, went out gun in hand to ennoble . . .'[160] (He also claimed responsibility for *The Irish Times* crossword, provoking its author to retort that it was the other way round, *he* sometimes wrote Myles's stuff.)[161] The literary merry-go-round is comparable to the recursive parodies of *At Swim* and *An Béal Bocht*, but *Cruiskeen Lawn* was the literal transcription of the idea, one author hopping on where another hopped off. Myles might pose as the brilliant literary polymath who could turn his hand to anything, but the obverse of this image was a sense that all this literary matter was simply interchangeable. And it was not only O'Faoláin's editorialising which had become repetitive and ripe for caricature, like the ever-regurgitating revivalist culture which had originally fuelled the humour of *Cruiskeen Lawn*. At this stage, Myles himself had been proved to be interchangeable – his manner easily imitated, the impersonations often indistinguishable from the original. The parodist was being parodied, and in his own column.

Myles na gCopaleen crowned king of Ireland: the later *Cruiskeen Lawn*

By 1948, *Cruiskeen Lawn* was settling on a recurrent loop. Despite its superficial variety and discontinuity, inspiration was waning and the parodist was becoming parasitic – often, columns were now either trailing after current events or annotating extracts from other newspapers and magazines. It seemed that there was nothing new under the sun, and Myles was now firmly entrenched as the natural foil to an establishment caste of public servants and literary intellectuals. For the past few months, his ultimate image for this civil servants' republic (in all but name) had been the 'County Manager's Hat', the *Cruiskeen* symbol for all that was officious and self-important in the local bureaucracy. The first 'Order of the County Manager's Hat' appeared in his honours list that January, Patrick Kavanagh being among its recipients: 'For sustained literary terrorism in 1947, when I was personally too busy to look after such tasks . . .'[162] In deference to a different tradition of public service, he confessed that he had let his name go forward for the upcoming general election, which would ultimately break the sixteen-year rule of de Valera's government: 'Note please that when the name has gone as far forward as possible, my selves will be back here in the office leading a nameless life but all the time working, working, working for . . . for humanity, sanity, and Ireland.'[163] But whether due to this dissipation of his nameless selves or to O'Nolan's promotion within the Department of Local Government, more often in 1948 it seemed that Myles was simply not all there.[164] Towards the end of February, *Cruiskeen Lawn* was alternating between Montgomery's columns and the extracts racket, and old work was beginning to be re-published (though this would remain a fairly rare occurrence). The usual tricks were wearing thin, not to mention the usual targets – like O'Faoláin's essays in *The Bell*:

> ... if I quote a few bits out of it here fair enough it will look funny, self-conscious, pretentious, precious, 'literary' ... Yet, is such quotation fair? I mean, should one exhibit in a tuppenny family newspaper what looks well enough in place in an expensive monthly? How would a parakeet from Brazil look if caged in a small flat in darkest Dunshaughlin?[165]

Only a month later Myles was recording the demise of his longtime adversary, which had just lost its market in Britain due to a trade ban on Irish publications.[166] A literary era was passing on but *Cruiskeen Lawn* was still surviving; upon returning from a short bout of illness, Myles ominously remarked that another war was needed to inspire good writing.[167]

A new ploy was inviting readers to supply their own Keats and Chapman stories, as well as the recurring biographies of Myles na gCopaleen 'adapted' from the lives of famous men.[168] Old jokes were also re-worked; returning to an old Mylesian solution for unemployment, it was suggested that if Queen Victoria was removed from Leinster House she should be replaced with a living statue (de Valera would be too tall to replace her, though they might use a '*part* of Dev – signifying incompleteness, partition, mutilation').[169] Weeks later, when 'Dublin's irrepressible congregation of chauvins' were now calling for the removal of Nelson's Pillar, his suggestion was to send a Dublin Corporation worker up to take his place: 'Not all statues, remember, need be stone.'[170] The age of empire was coming to an end, as John A. Costello confirmed when he suddenly announced plans to declare Ireland a republic. The next day, Myles himself proclaimed the establishment of the Irish Transport Republic, or the Consolidated Irish Empire (CIE).[171] As always, his gripe was with the running of this vaunted republic, not with its symbolic political status. The pragmatism of the plain Dubliner had been expressed in a slightly more philosophical mode over a year earlier:

> It is fashionable nowadays to sneer at Descartes but let me say this, it comes ill from Irish cave-dwellers ... I ever bow before the grandeur of the French philosopher's great diagnostic enthymeme COGITO, ERGO SUM or, translated, 'I think, therefore I am an Irishman'. ('Ergo' is from the Greek *ergo* meaning closed up, hemmed in, confused on an island, an islandman, an Irishman, Cf. 'Eire'.) ... I think you Irishmen should pay more attention to his great discovery that a lot of problems arise from a preoccupation with words and definitions ... What you are 'politically' does not interest you at all, but whether

you call it 'republic' or 'commonwealth' – that is so critical a question that the effusion of blood is an essential rite in the ceremony of searching for an answer.[172]

Perhaps the focus of *Cruiskeen Lawn* was narrowing, but Myles's later pre-occupation with incompetence and failure in Irish public life might be read, for all its determined banality, as the most suitable riposte to the grand rhetoric of cultural nationalism. And on the evidence of *Cruiskeen Lawn*'s growing attention to the foreign press, the dominance of Anglo-American popular culture was now felt to be of greater relevance than the complexities of the old colonial relationship. By the late 1940s, the Irishman was as likely to feel 'hemmed in' by the opinions of the *Daily Mail*, or the Celtic fantasies of a Pan-Am brochure, as by the 'British music hall' Irishry of the GAA.[173]

While by the end of the column's first decade some of the old perennials remained – O'Faoláin and O'Connor, the iniquity of the British 'socialist universe', even the demagoguery of *Ailtirí na hAiséirí* – by now it had acquired a more combative style.[174] Myles had always respected certain limits, whether due to the vigilance of *The Irish Times* or to O'Nolan's own circumspection, and perhaps a certain weariness was showing in his more unguarded attacks on a 'national life that has been so long and so steadily disgracing itself'.[175] It was doing so with an unfailing monotony. 'Lynn C. Doyle' had long ago created a furore by resigning in frustration from the Censorship Board; in 1949 the controversy was replayed as another member departed, criticising the Board's failure to take into account the literary merit of books submitted to it. As if parodying its own timeless torpor, the response from the Board was to quote the Minister responsible for the 1929 legislation:

> There are books which are so blatantly indecent and known to be indecent, that it would be unnecessary for the members . . . to read every line of them. Should the members of the Board, for instance, be compelled to read every line of 'Ulysses', a book which has been universally condemned?[176]

On the evidence of the letters page of *The Irish Times*, the country was trapped in the debates (and judgements) of twenty years earlier. Myles reflected on the interesting suggestion that 'the written works of my old friend Mr. James Joyce were obscene and worthless. There was a day when I would laugh at that . . . I am now inclined to frown, look out of the window for long intervals, sometimes even have recourse to that ominous peregrination, the solitary walk. Poor Ireland!'[177] Trinity College had just refused a degree to a student who submitted a dissertation on Marx;

UCD had matched the gesture by banning a student debate on the *Communist Manifesto*. Months later, Myles was berating the students them-selves for not protesting a ban on selling the magazine *Comhar* on campus.[178] The new state's intellectual delinquency appeared to be growing, rather than abating, only aggravated by the onset of the Cold War. Yet the frustration with this expressed in *Cruiskeen Lawn* was hardly universal; when Maria Jolas complained of the Irish government's refusal to be officially represented at a Paris exhibition in memory of James Joyce, it provoked a vigorous (and sometimes abusive) letter controversy in *The Irish Times* which continued for weeks.[179]

Despite Myles's (or O'Nolan's) later notoriety as a fairly bitter cur-mudgeon, at this stage *Cruiskeen Lawn*'s satire could still be coolly underhand, particularly when expressing disdain for those who were apparently beyond criticism. A case in point was an episode in August 1949 which in a minor way foreshadowed the 1951 Mother and Child controversy. Galway Corporation had just rejected a school site proposed by the bishop, Dr Michael Brown; due to its location, as Myles reported, 'there was a danger that the chislers would be killed by traffic'. But they quickly retracted their selection of an alternative site when 'His Lordship of Galway' loudly declared the school site a spiritual matter, one involving the 'safeguarding of the Faith'. Not the safeguarding of the chil-dren, as Myles silently implied. Nevertheless, he quixotically declared himself on the side of the bishop – who had at least stood by his convic-tions – unlike the public representatives concerned:

> I offer them a tenner a skull to appear for one week at a certain Dublin variety theatre. In Dublin town, not particularly noted for moral courage, we would be awfully interested to have a look at them. And I have even the act arranged. When the curtain goes up, they are revealed at the top of tall ladders. Then they climb down.[180]

O'Nolan likely had little sympathy for Brown, previously the Chair of the Commission on Vocational Organisation whose report to the Department of Local Government had undergone a long and cruel decimation in *Cruiskeen Lawn*. But if Myles implied that the confusion of Church and State was less the fault of a pushy Catholic hierarchy than of a spineless public service, he was less inhibited in criticising other public figures. When the UCD President, Michael Tierney, intervened in a debate over the school-leaving age by suggesting the abolition of compulsory education (in effect, so that children could help on the family farm) Myles savaged the proposal. As he interpreted it, this was a call for a return to people knowing their place, to the homeliness of the cabin and self-sufficiency. Tierney, a former Cumman na nGaedheal TD, proponent of corporatism and Catholic social teaching, and head of the largest university in the State was a reasonably typical representative of the prevailing cultural and political orthodoxy; representative too of a stunted political imagination which would do nothing to improve the widespread poverty, unemployment and social inequality of the previous two decades. Myles seized on the intellectual bankruptcy of a professor in the National University advocating a policy to restrict education, casting his own institution as the 'nullest of all nullities', an 'intellectual slum' – the ultimate embodiment of all that was slowly and thoroughly disgracing Irish public life.[181] Yet it was this 'intellectual slum' which had once inspired the comedy of *At Swim-Two-Birds*; at the very least, the novel had drawn on the sceptical and creative undercurrents of an institution otherwise strongly identified with the cultural and political ethos of the new state. Ten years on, Myles's perspective on post-independence Ireland was a great deal more jaded.

In 1943 Myles na gCopaleen had crowned himself king of Ireland, *The Irish Times* dutifully recording his address to the sea-divided Gael from atop the Hill of Tara.[182] But it was only in later years that this self-proclaimed representative of the Irish nation was to become a figure of authority, a national scold, however double-edged this sense of authority was to remain. Yet by the end of its first decade, *Cruiskeen Lawn* was still something of a crazy jigsaw puzzle, even if the individual pieces did not stand so well apart. The column was now relying on its cumulative effect, on readers who were already intimate with its jokes and modes of operation. It was a unique literary enterprise: sprawling, unending, unauthored almost, insofar as the identity of Myles (both, or all of them) was a well-kept secret. And Myles na gCopaleen may have been purposely decked out in the livery of a literary gentleman, indulging in puns and meticulous turns of phrase, but where Joyce had purportedly set the scholars to work for a hundred years, *Cruiskeen Lawn* was designed to be thrown away by the following morning. In all this, arguably it broke with literary conventions more thoroughly than many of O'Nolan's modernist predecessors succeeded in doing. Myles's own assessment of the column was more modest; reviewing his year's work in 1949, he calculated that he had managed:

> ... 193,979 sneers at public institutions, 750,193 puns, 67,258 insulting references to public men, 926,838 Latin and Greek tags cogged out of the back of dictionaries, 34,866 similar tags or quotations from other languages, 1,977,343 jawbreakers, 700 Keats stories, and a mass of miscellaneous (or indescribable) matter.[183]

He also teasingly noted that he had been forced to lay off two ghosts, 'who had been with us for some years', for themselves employing deputy ghostwriters. A list of *Cruiskeen Lawn* shareholders follows which names Sheridan and Montgomery amid dozens of other eminent Dubliners, but that is the closest hint *Irish Times* readers would get of the varied provenance of Myles na gCopaleen. Later reflecting on the first decade of *Cruiskeen Lawn*, he asserted that as 'a long-term feat of denunciation and abuse, I do not think it has ever been equalled'.[184] Just as unique was the incredible omniscience of Myles, according to a later *Irish Times* profile: a man without enemies (because without equal), although he knew 'a countless congregation of nuisances, touchers and venal public scoundrels' whom he held in 'inexhaustible disdain'.[185] The development of *Cruiskeen Lawn* from an essentially witty and humorous piece of work to one which relied heavily on this sense of inexhaustible disdain casts an interesting light on O'Nolan's earlier career, exposing a sense of moral and intellectual authority that was almost refined out of existence in his self-reflexive novels. At the same time, the contribution of Niall Montgomery (and possibly others) in shaping this element of the column cannot be discounted; in that respect, it is telling that two of O'Nolan's contemporaries, Thomas Hogan and Anthony Cronin, depicted Myles na gCopaleen as an intellectual type, rather than an individual – as no more than the licensed jester of the Dublin intelligentsia. And certainly, Myles often played the respectable citizen; a harried everyman irritated by the petulant outbursts of liberal 'corduroys', by shrill revivalists in Abbey Street, or by the ineptitude of CIE. The sense of moral indignation which the column gradually acquired is similar to that which George Orwell identified in Myles's *Daily Express* rival:

> It is no accident that the best comic writers of our time – Belloc, Chesterton, 'Timothy Shy' and the recent 'Beachcomber' – have been Catholic apologists; that is, people with a serious purpose and a noticeable willingness to hit below the belt . . . all great humorous writers show a willingness to attack the beliefs and the virtues on which society necessarily rests . . .[186]

Elsewhere, Orwell would describe Beachcomber and Timothy Shy in less flattering terms as reactionary 'Catholic propagandists',[187] but his assumption of the essentially subversive quality of 'all great humorous writers' is interesting (if hardly unusual). If O'Nolan's humour had a serious purpose, it was not always simply allied with a subversive, critical perspective on 1940s Ireland. The moral certainties of the later, more satirical *Cruiskeen Lawn* also need to be read in light of the earlier work; the multivalent ironies of Myles na gCopaleen reflecting the complex (rather than capricious) nature of his humour. Myles was something of a conservative subversive, at ease neither with reactionary cultural nationalism and the paternalism of Irish politics, nor with those who were convinced of the backward nature of Irish culture and society. With his antipathy to the demagogue (of whatever political shade) and his suspicion of every degree of rhetoric, in O'Nolan's hands he tended to adopt a position self-consciously outside literary or political fraternities. As such, his relationship to the Plain People of Ireland (or the less than plain *Irish Times* reader) could be conducted on an equal footing reminiscent of the comic dialogues between writers and readers in *At Swim*. In the post-war phase of *Cruiskeen Lawn*, O'Nolan's long quarrel with the role of the Irish writer was only resolved as the more satirical Myles adopted not a position of superiority over his readership, but the role of the public servant, the satirist on their behalf. He may not have been a humorist who was ultimately willing to attack the beliefs and values of his society, as Orwell considered the task to be, but O'Nolan's comic writing was equally effective for providing a criticism from within. The humour of this licensed jester was inflected with all the biases and prejudices of his readers; as the variable nature of *Cruiskeen Lawn* demonstrated, this intimacy could be disabling, but it could also enable a lacerating self-interrogation.

6

'The Dublin Character':
plays and later work

By the early 1950s, Myles na gCopaleen was congealing into a parody of himself. Now repeatedly absent from *The Irish Times* due to O'Nolan's illnesses or disputes with management, the habitual manner which Myles had developed was that of the 'Dublin Character',[1] with all the limitations that might imply. Though still the erudite gentleman, the persona was also firmly established as a bullish and often cantankerous representative of the Plain People of Ireland, and the particular scourge of politicians and public servants. The scope of the column had narrowed until its image of Ireland resembled little more than that of a shabby office of public administration with Myles hectoring all aspects of mismanagement from the rear. O'Nolan himself was forcibly retired from the Department of Local Government in 1953 on grounds of ill-health, but evidently refused to stay away from public service; by 1957 he was standing for election to the Seanad, despite his long antipathy to politicians and ideologues of all kinds. It is debatable how seriously he took this political venture; neglecting to canvass, he polled (under his own name) only four hundred votes.[2] Of course, his natural constituency was the readership of *Cruiskeen Lawn*, but there was no real means of gauging the extent of his influence here. As the electoral farce showed, any writer could over-estimate the power of his own rhetoric. Ironically, it was O'Nolan who had dryly demonstrated that fact back in the 1940s, deftly undermining the earnest pronouncements of O'Faoláin and O'Connor on the state of Irish society. But in the end, it was Myles who was left talking on and on to a captive audience – sometimes six days a week, sometimes three – his brilliant inventiveness slowly sliding into fatuity.

The particular danger of O'Nolan's talent, as earlier noted in Frank Swinnerton's review of *At Swim*, was its facility; with his gift for eloquence and mimicry, it was all too easy to ignore the fact that he could end up saying nothing at all.[3] By the 1950s and 1960s it seemed that Myles had too much to say, a too tetchy readiness to flog his own personal hobbyhorses. But a certain reticence was useful in the 1940s when *Cruiskeen Lawn* was first established; after all, the 'Emergency' itself was a careful statement of what could not be said, eloquent in its own way without saying anything at all. In wartime Dublin it may not have been openly declared that loose talk costs lives, but it could certainly cost a civil service job, or at least provoke a censor to stop publication. In this strange atmosphere, suspended between the extremes of silent caution and the loud hysteria of 'self-appointed pedagogues',[4] *Cruiskeen Lawn* maintained an illusion of wayward freedom. In this regard, the two plays that O'Nolan had produced by the Abbey and Gate theatres in the spring of 1943 are revealing, though relatively neglected. On the one hand, they overtly anticipate the preoccupations of his later work, with their (reasonably gentle) satire of the petty weaknesses of Irish public life. But they are also curious companion pieces, *Faustus Kelly* being, in its most successful points, a study of eloquent fatuity, while O'Nolan's adaptation of Josef and Karel Capek's *Insect Play* unwittingly dramatises the predicament of the writer at war who is constrained from even acknowledging that fact. Donohue persuasively argues that the plays mark a point of transition in his career, poised between the experimentalism of the early novels and the more satirical and conventional modes of the later work.[5] It is telling that O'Nolan agreed to adapt the Capeks' political satire only after Hilton Edwards rejected his proposal to write a fantastic and unusual play for the Gate, one which sounds very like an adaptation of *The Third Policeman*.[6] Edwards's hint would be echoed in the critical reception of both plays, with Dublin's critics registering their disappointment that as a dramatist Myles strived for entertainment rather than for 'incisive satire on the New Ireland'.[7] Following on the commercial failure of *At Swim* and the rejection of *The Third Policeman*, in 1943 it might well have seemed to O'Nolan that there was greater demand for the acid tongue of Myles na gCopaleen than for the flights of fancy he shared with Flann O'Brien. When he eventually returned to fiction nearly twenty years later, it was with far more vocal and less subtle attacks on Ireland's sacred cows. But what was perhaps more obvious to the original audiences of *Faustus Kelly* and *The Insect Play* was the tension they enacted between a pointless garrulity and the silences of self-censorship.

At the time both were commercial failures, and what might have initially seemed a promising vein of work proved to be little more than a short diversion in his career.[8] As Myles wryly reported after his Abbey play closed, nobody recognised him as he strolled through Dublin: 'although I did hear one Cork accent mutter something about ex-playwrights as I passed'.[9] A diary entry for January 1943 was more tersely eloquent: '*Droch-léirmheastaí ar Faustus Kelly*. Fuck'.[10] The disappointment may have been all the greater since the prospect of Myles's first play had attracted a good deal of interest the previous summer; it was only on realising he had lost it to the Abbey that Hilton Edwards had secured O'Nolan to adapt *The Insect Play* instead. As a satire of political mendacity and greed, *Faustus Kelly* certainly had natural potential. Kelly, a local councillor who sells his soul to the devil in order to become a TD,[11] is adept at the pompous, self-serving rhetoric which *Cruiskeen Lawn* ridiculed in artists and politicians alike. But he is also mercifully free of all conviction, and while his meandering speeches show the Mylesian eye for rabble-rousing clichés, it is notable that this is a play about Irish political life which is nevertheless wholly devoid of politics. When it was revived for a provincial production in 1954, Myles made a typically self-aggrandising claim that in its first incarnation, Ernest Blythe had closed the play early due to political pressure.[12] However, he also betrayed a more credible element of self-doubt concerning its actual merits:

> Why did we all, including myself, think it so bad? In that now distant year, I thought I had gone too far, that the play (though straight farce) had hurt too many people, and that that sort of thing doesn't pay in this country. I also thought it exaggerated some notorious national failings. Re-reading it in this different age, I am convinced I was right, but that the work takes on a new importance by reason of life and facts catching up on it. It had an unsuspected oracular and prophetic content.[13]

If this 'straight farce' really seemed that scathing and incisive all those years ago, these qualities were universally overlooked by its critics. O'Nolan was re-creating his younger self in the image of the later, more virulent Myles; at the time, it was he who was wary of its 'political implications', given his position as a civil servant.[14] And even *The Irish Times* reviewer was disappointed with Myles's first production, admitting that Kelly himself was a good character but commenting that his fellow councillors 'tend to bring him down to the level of ordinary Abbey comedy, and to get laughs in the old-fashioned way'.[15] Admittedly, mocking local politics was a risky venture for a civil servant working in the very department which governed its activities, but *Faustus Kelly* conspicuously trades on a standard comic currency of political venality and rural buffoonery. Seán MacEntee, then O'Nolan's minister, was present at its first night and according to one account 'was obviously much entertained by his private secretary's shafts of humour'.[16]

Faustus Kelly tread in the footsteps of William Boyle's *The Eloquent Dempsy* (1906), a satire of local politicians which had given a name to a 'generation of flatulent carry-overs from a departed period of great political oratory'.[17] But if his own satire lacked all substance, then Myles was arguably in danger of acquiring some of the qualities of the eloquent Kelly himself. The bombast was at least familiar:

> I am determined to expose – to drag into the inexorable light of day – every knave, time-server, sycophant and party camp-follower. I will meet them all and fight them. I will declare war on the Masons and the Knights. I will challenge the cheat and the money-changer . . . (SP, 180–181).

But O'Nolan's gift for mimicry, the multiple voices which give a *Cruiskeen Lawn* column its peculiarly indefinable character, strangely worked to less effect in a dramatic context. Although *Faustus Kelly* is in part a play about political rhetoric, Kelly himself is little more than a political echo-chamber. Once the Faustian plot cranks into action the play loses the sense of inconsequential comedy built up in the first act through the rambling conversations in the council chamber. Lacking the creative friction produced by writing against type, the 'old-fashioned'[18] quality of *Faustus Kelly* is the most bewildering thing about it. O'Nolan remarked, perhaps consolingly, to Hilton Edwards that it was conceived as 'an Abbey play'[19] and certainly it did not disturb the Abbey's standard brand of rural comedy. Despite Myles's delight in targeting that theatre and its audiences in *Cruiskeen Lawn*, *Faustus Kelly* seems to deliberately pander to its conservatism. While the play depicts crooked electioneering, nepotism, and apathy on the part of public representatives (not to mention the Dáil candidate prepared to sell his soul for victory), its underlying cautiousness was typified in O'Nolan's compliance with Blythe's request to revise an instance where a senior clerical figure is induced by 'the Stranger' to vote for Kelly. The suggestion that he might instead blackmail 'the most respectable man in town'[20] was translated, in the final version, to a Fianna Fáil TD.

The result of such caution was that besides sacrificing O'Nolan's literary strengths to the laws of genre, *Faustus Kelly* also failed to exploit Myles's talent for vituperation. After all, it was not as if he was incapable of summoning a great deal of bile on the subject of local government. On one day in June 1943, for example, he was presumably having a very bad day at the office:

> England's dirtiest blow at our national self-respect was the Local Government Act of 1898, which was the scaffolding within which has risen our present unique edifice of gombeen bourgeoisie . . . you will go a long way before you will encounter anything as awful as Paddy whack after he has enveloped himself in some 'robe' and tangled himself up in a 'gold' chain made in Manchester . . . [21]

But his urban district councillors do at least play more cunning versions of the Plain People of Ireland, embodying the Dublin civil servant's distant impressions of the local politicians he serves. As if to acknowledge the slightly hackneyed quality of this band of comic rustics, Shawn Kilshaughraun echoes Boucicault's archetypal stage-Irishman: '*He is a thick, smug, oafish character . . . exudes a treacly good-humour, always wears an inane smile and talks with a thick western brogue upon which sea-weed could be hung*' (*SP*, 121–122). But it is Myles himself who is putting on the greatest act, struggling into the motley of the Abbey comedy. In *Faustus Kelly*, O'Nolan gave its audience what it was accustomed to expect, or rather, what he presumed it would expect. It was perhaps a pragmatic move, but not one to be expected of Flann O'Brien.

Overall, *Faustus Kelly*'s sharpest political satire lies in its windy futility. Kelly's banal flights of oratory marshal all the clichés O'Nolan had honed in *Cruiskeen Lawn*, with only occasionally a more pointed dart at Irish public life. When the Stranger faces losing his position as a rates collector since his appointment has not been sanctioned by 'the Department', the town clerk outlines in gleeful detail his inevitable social excommunication: 'Shure you might as well be dead, man' (*SP*, 188). The fate of the man who has slipped through the cracks of government bureaucracy might recall that of *The Third Policeman*'s narrator, who can easily be hanged because there would be 'no entry to be made in the death papers' (*TP*, 105), but O'Nolan now withholds from stretching his comic idea to its eerily logical end. And one of the play's bitterest denunciations of Irish politics is put into the mouth of one of its most stilted characters, Mrs Crockett:

> You talk about Christian charity . . . and decency . . . and reforming all the nasty things one sees today in this country. What are you, the whole lot of you, but vulgar despicable hypocrites, a gang of drunken louts, worrying all day and all night about your own delicate hides! (*SP*, 185)

Given the appeals to Christian charity and decency made by many in Irish politics – even in the contribution of O'Nolan's minister, Seán MacEntee, to the school dinners controversy the previous year – this is about the most trenchant point made in *Faustus Kelly*. Its lingering impression is one of all talk and no substance, though perhaps for that reason alone it could be defended as an astute political statire on 'the New Ireland'. Yet this is also a frustrating, and maybe a frustrated, play; O'Nolan's first impression of it in rehearsal was that it was 'petty, weak, half-baked'[22] and his own exasperation is most obvious in the final curtain. At this point the Stranger, who is left alone on the stage, recalls the author turned ventriloquist. Only the voices of the foolish politicians remain, each of which speaks through him in turn:

> Not for any favour . . . in heaven or earth or hell . . . would I take that Kelly and the others with me to where I live, to be in their company for ever . . . and ever . . . and ever . . . I WANT NOTHING MORE OF IRISH PUBLIC LIFE! (SP, 196–197)

O'Nolan was not to be so fortunate, he was to stay in their company for at least another decade.

The Insect Play at least offered an imaginative escape from this claus-trophobia. First performed in Czechoslovakia in 1922, it was a political fable very much of its time, with a First World War veteran providing a wry chorus to its anatomy of human society in the modern age. The ants who bring about its bloody climax are slaves to time and speed who are labouring for ever-increased efficiency; the futile war they wage is in the interests of state, industry, race, colonial power and a myriad of other empty enthusiasms. Arguably, the adaptation was a promising idea, an astute commission which played to O'Nolan's strengths. Provided with a ready-made dramatic structure, he would be free to exploit his lin-guistic fantasies rather than laboriously develop plot or character, and Edwards evidently anticipated that the author of Cruiskeen Lawn would have an especially acute understanding of how this fable might apply in an Irish context:

> I think very nice analogies might be made: the tramp and the Communist; the fraightfully refained upper middle class and the common people, etc, etc. What about the plain people of Ireland, or why not Miles [sic] himself?[23]

In the event, Myles remained behind the scenes, but the Plain People – from Dublin beetles to Cork crickets and Ulster ants – were all over this insect fable, now re-named Rhapsody in Stephen's Green. Most probably working from Paul Selver's translation, which was first performed and published in London in 1923, O'Nolan introduced a more local and topical element to his version.[24] At the same time, it is also more humorous and less didactic than the original English translation, with the Tramp providing far less commentary and direction than he did in Selver's hands. But it was this blunting of The Insect Play's satire which seems to have most frustrated Dublin's theatre critics, who generally con-curred in viewing the play as a lost opportunity. For some, the mockery of local grievances – particularly in the war between the Green Ants and the Orange Ants – was too pointed; for others, a serious satire on capitalism and war had been diluted to mere music hall comedy. In the spring of 1943, the decision to hibernicise the Capeks' political fable certainly had its pitfalls. In adapting it to a local perspective, the satire might cut closer to home, but O'Nolan also ran the risk of appearing to make too trivial, (or even provincial), a significant anti-war polemic which was being revived in the midst of another worldwide cataclysm.

The new context is forcibly presented in the prologue, with the tramp wistfully contemplating the social welfare proposals that were being widely debated in the Dublin press (and thoroughly derided in *Cruiskeen Lawn*):

> What a man like me wants is . . . family allowances, yeh know . . . family allowances . . . and plenty of free insurance, d'yeh undherstand me. (*He is becoming more and more maudlin.*) An' house-buildin' facilities for getting' married, d'yeh know. An' . . . wan more cow . . . wan more sow . . . an' wan . . . more . . . acre . . . undher th'plough. (*IP*, 25–26)[25]

The act which follows marks the most dramatic departure from Selver's text, which transformed the flappers of London high society into capricious social butterflies. A convincingly Irish version needed to find a more sober equivalent, though Edwards's polite response to an early draft was that he 'always thought it unfortunate that the play opened with those impossible creatures, but monkeys are not insects – does it matter?'.[26] O'Nolan dourly noted in his diary that it was Montgomery who had written most of the offending act.[27] In the final version, the Capeks' butterflies are replaced by morbidly existential worker bees who do no work, while the play's depiction of a post-war sexual freedom is savagely inverted – licentious female butterflies give way to frustrated bees who forego 'the sensuous delight of stinging' and remain 'chaste' in order to survive long enough to meet their queen (*IP*, 30–31). (This innovation outraged at least one reader of *The Standard*, who complained that the first act was 'blasphemous and most suggestive'.)[28] In contrast, the second act follows the original text fairly closely, albeit with acquisitive beetles reinvented as socially-aspirant civil servants from Cork. The most controversial transposition was saved for the final act's ant war, a debacle brewed by the loyal, industrious and 'hord-headed' Orange Ants (*IP*, 65), the Green Ants led by 'Deevil so-ond-so' (*IP*, 66), and the imperial Red Ants. Given O'Nolan's parody of political rhetoric in *Faustus Kelly*, it is unsurprising that these political fights are, at the root, language wars, whether centred in the Orange Ants' slogans ('The Awnt State will feight ond the Awnt State wull be reight!' (*IP*, 62)) or in the dispute over compulsory Latin which ends in civil war between the 'ants of the Gael and

ants of the Pale' (*IP*, 19). Naturally, the victorious *fáinne*-wearing Green
Ant, self-proclaimed emperor of the earth, ends by declaring that he will
allow only Irish to be spoken throughout the world. In a heady moment
of wish-fulfilment, O'Nolan's tramp squashes his uppity revivalist insect.
Yet despite transferring the focus of the ant war to partition and Ireland's
internal culture wars, there is an odd concession to the original text in
maintaining the tramp as a veteran of the First World War (albeit now of
the Royal Munster Fusiliers (*IP*, 76)). While Selver's translation explicitly
links the ant war to this conflict, O'Nolan's adaptation quietly depends
on a disconnection from these larger scenes of war – most obviously from
the war being conducted off-stage in Europe, Africa and Asia. Yet perhaps
that tactical silence made the pettiness of the ants' internal wars appear
all the keener to a contemporary audience. Certainly, some critics felt
that his comedy did not allow them the space to view the national passions with sufficient gravity. The *Irish Press* reviewer complained that the
Capeks 'wrote a serious satire on the cruelties of the world . . . They
would have been surprised to find their cornerstone being used . . . to
burlesque the divisions in this country to make a theatrical holiday'.[29]
Others were more generous on this point, but despite praising its
Swiftian satire, *The Irish Times* itself argued that Myles had taken away
much of the original play and made it 'rather more of an entertainment'.[30] Perhaps his ultimate achievement was to have reduced the scene
of war to the utterly ridiculous, allowing no room for portentous moral-
ising. But perhaps also what many contemporaries found so lacking in
O'Nolan's play ironically stemmed from the strength of his adaptation.
Though he had successfully wrested the play from its original European
context and turned its satire on contemporary Ireland, it was the Capeks'
work which now resonated all the more strongly – even to a neutral
Dublin audience – in the midst of another European war.

Watching this play in wartime, it was surely impossible to ignore its
original portent. By focusing the Capeks' satire on more provincial concerns, arguably O'Nolan's *Insect Play* exploited this unspoken,
ever-present backdrop to reduce the national obsessions to their proper
proportion. The frustration of many reviewers, and the play's failure to
attract audiences that could outlast a week's run, suggests that his contemporaries disagreed. Tellingly, Paul Vincent Carroll's *The Strings Are
False*, a play about the Glasgow blitz which contained an implicit interrogation of Irish neutrality, had managed a successful twelve-week run the
previous summer.[31] But it is debatable whether Myles na gCopaleen
would have enjoyed the same latitude from the censors as Carroll had,
particularly since he was closely identified with a newspaper that so continually provoked them. However, in responding to a typical complaint

that his adaptation was little more than music hall burlesque, complete with vulgar double entendres, O'Nolan asserted that the 'entire play is a salutary double entendre and may well present to the mentally adolescent the same sort of shock that was given by the Rouault picture'.[32] It might not be too great a leap of the imagination to look beyond the allegorical Irish insect war to the larger conflicts beyond it, but the charge that this adaptation was little more than literary vaudeville stuck. It would be an unfair criticism of even the early *Cruiskeen Lawn*, where an anatomy of Irish cultural rhetoric is always subordinate to the plain business of being funny. But by the time O'Nolan returned to writing novels in the 1960s, the column was showing no lack of opinionated satire – sometimes without the satire. In this later period, it is as if he was working against his own comic eloquence, his own facility, abandoning the technician's fondness for structural innovation in order to make it clear that he had something to say. The late Flann O'Brien is no longer writing against the grain, but against the natural courses of his own talent. O'Nolan's deteriorating health was the largest factor in this decline, but perhaps he had also grown too much into the habit of satisfying his readers' demands.

The return of Flann O'Brien: *The Hard Life*

The re-issue of *At Swim-Two-Birds* in 1960 effectively launched O'Nolan's career for a second time, but while the reviews were more lavish this time round, his own estimate of Flann O'Brien was proportionally more scathing. Even his contribution to negotiations on including *At Swim* in Penguin's paperback list was, as his agent dryly noted, 'not particularly helpful':[33] 'Although the original publication in 1939 was killed stone-dead at birth by Mr. Adolf Hitler, I was not particularly saddened or hurt at the time because I regarded the book as juvenile trash, written mostly for my own amusement; I did not foresee that it could have any wide appeal or sale.'[34] In his judgement, *The Hard Life* was a far better proposition for any publisher. Whether his estimate of the novels' relative value was made purely on commercial terms, it was nevertheless surely perverse. Even publishers and reviewers who welcomed the long-awaited appearance of a 'second' novel from Flann O'Brien found themselves regarding *The Hard Life* with some confusion. Besides its dramatic departure from the experimentalism of *At Swim*, by 1960 few had expected him to write another novel at all. Even Timothy O'Keeffe, the publisher responsible for *At Swim*'s revival, doubted a new work was possible when he secured an option for a second novel. Assuming, 'for all kinds of reasons', that O'Nolan would never write anything else, he had been hoping to publish 'the lost book' of Dublin lore, the typescript which had passed from hand to hand in the 1940s 'to the admiration and consternation of all!'.[35] But *The Third Policeman* never appeared. While O'Nolan professed bemusement and irritation at the enthusiastic reviews *At Swim* had received, its publication at least gave him sufficient impetus to begin work on *The Hard Life*, the book no one could have anticipated – for all kinds of reasons.

There had been stirrings of another novel as far back as 1950 when the American edition of *At Swim* was being prepared; according to Niall Montgomery, it was 'some fairly poisonous scheme that has been going through his head since early in the forties'.[36] In 1953, Myles was confiding to his readers that a new novel, *The Hard Life: A Study in Perfectionism*, would soon be published by 'Felix Kulpa'.[37] Though work only finally began in the autumn of 1960, by the following January the manuscript was already largely complete. The quick composition was reminiscent of *The Third Policeman*, and the novel itself has been similarly (and optimistically) described as 'a small masterpiece',[38] but they have little else in common. New readers who had only just encountered the idiosyncracies of *At Swim-Two-Birds* might have been excused for imagining that the pallid humour of this second novel was the work of an ineffectual ghostwriter. In a way, it was. Yet while structurally the least complex of all O'Nolan's novels, *The Hard Life* – like *At Swim* – might struggle to be considered a novel at all. Stray comic routines from *Cruiskeen Lawn* are re-worked into a hazy plot (Collopy and Fahrt's pedantic dialogues, the unlikely schemes of the brother), along with jokes from as far back as *Comhthrom Féinne* (the correspondence course to cure all ills). The extended gag which precariously connects these strands – Collopy's mysterious work on behalf of womankind – has all the tedious elaboration of a Keats and Chapman story. But despite its tendency to repeat old jokes, and the irony that its publication was only due to the success of *At Swim*, *The Hard Life* might be read as a late attempt to rewrite the literary character of Flann O'Brien. The haphazard comic performances which characterise his first novel are shoehorned here into a conventional linear narrative, which is restrained almost to the point of dullness. And where *At Swim*'s student coyly provoked the censors, it is telling that the later novel takes a far more blunt approach with 'Fr. Kurt Fahrt'. With this return to fiction, O'Nolan began the revision of his literary past that would lead to the cannibalism of *The Dalkey Archive* and end in a blatant play for popular success with his last planned work, *Slattery's Sago Saga*. This was designed as a broad political satire, an indictment of Irish-America (and more particularly, of the Kennedy clan) 'with no "literary" complication'.[39] The subject matter may have hearkened back to *Children of Destiny*, that cynical product of the 'ready-made'[40] school of fiction, just as its scornful disavowal of literary pretensions recalled the young author of *At Swim-Two-Birds*. But there was none of the irony of the earlier work here, and O'Nolan's response to his publisher's understandable wariness was simply to defend the novel as the basis for a more lucrative comic film.[41] It is worth bearing in mind, perhaps, that these late novels did not result from the spare-time activities of the civil servant, but were written under all the pressures of the professional writer. Tellingly, in the midst of a financial dispute in May 1965, O'Nolan blustered that he intended to replace the literary agency which had acted on his behalf since 1939: 'For me this change coincides with total change in style and intent so far as work is concerned, and (if only temporarily) Eng. Lit. is a thing of the past. We are now after money.'[42] While his threat was never carried out, the need for financial success was surely one of the factors anchoring these novels in the kind of bland but marketable comic realism that was quite alien to Flann O'Brien's earlier fantasies.

In any assessment of the late novels, it is difficult to ignore the circumstances in which they were written. The last decade of O'Nolan's life was not only dominated by his alcoholism, but also punctuated by financial difficulties, accidents and recurrent illnesses, a combination that had its most destructive effect on the rushed composition of *The Dalkey Archive*, a novel which in execution is almost unrecognisable from what was apparently intended. Even Myles na gCopaleen himself came under threat in the 1960s, as O'Nolan's relationship with *The Irish Times* grew increasingly fractious. At the time that work on *The Hard Life* was beginning, he was again complaining to friends that the newspaper was regularly not publishing his material, and so (more importantly) not paying for it.[43] Since at least 1956 he had been attempting to disengage from *Cruiskeen Lawn*, offering columns to the *Daily Express*, *The Spectator*, *The Evening Press*, and – under the name of Flann O'Brien – to *The Guardian*, in order to escape from 'very ignorant slobs who have no experience of editorial work or any aspect of productive writing'.[44] But *Cruiskeen Lawn* was to remain the one constant in O'Nolan's writing life, despite his intermittent attempts to break free from the column. His late novels tread a similarly wearying pattern. On the face of it, *The Hard Life* and *The Dalkey Archive* signalled a new style; the low sales of *At Swim-Two-Birds* in 1939, the rejection of *The Third Policeman* for being 'too fantastic',[45] were mistakes that could be avoided by the older and wiser professional. But their repetition of earlier comic material, and their lacklustre commitment to the novelistic conventions which his experimental novels had joyfully unpicked, betray a fairly crippled consistency. Yet even while O'Nolan continued to tread over old ground, the compulsive

parodist-cum-editor of At Swim-Two-Birds also turned his destructive critical talents on himself. His decision to pillage The Third Policeman for The
Dalkey Archive was not only his ultimate act of literary cannibalism, but
also his most brutal piece of literary revisionism. Arguably it is not Joyce
who is the true victim of The Dalkey Archive, but Flann O'Brien.

But this text was not O'Nolan's only salvage operation. The opening of
The Hard Life also re-visits the territory of The Third Policeman, as if consciously returning to the point where his career had left off nearly twenty
years earlier:

> It is not that I half knew my mother. I knew half of her: the lower half
> – her lap, legs, feet, her hands and wrists as she bent forward. Very
> dimly I seem to remember her voice. At the time, of course, I was very
> young. Then one day she did not seem to be there any more. (HL, 1)

This naïve narrator is also partly descended from Bónapárt Ó Cúnasa
(and Stephen Dedalus), but this novel is full of such echoes that never
seem to amount to the sum of their parts. Finbarr's innocence presages
none of the dark confusion which marks The Third Policeman; this time
the atmosphere of dim misunderstanding serves only to set up the
Collopy plot, an extended exercise on the double entendre. Again, there
is a deadpan narrative to set off the characters' comic idiosyncrasies, a
degree of narrative self-consciousness ('How long this situation – a sort of
interregnum, lacuna or hiatus – lasted I cannot say' (HL, 2)), and the odd
grand-standing descriptive awkwardness. But while in 1940, O'Nolan had
followed At Swim with a novel which he promised 'cannot be said to be a
lot of highbrow guff like the last book',[46] the rejection of The Third
Policeman seems to have produced a follow-up of even more ferociously
contained ambition. Its reception at the time was decidedly mixed, a
sense of disappointment usually being tempered by a desire not to dis-
courage future and better work. The private verdict of The Guardian's
literary editor, otherwise an enthusiastic supporter of O'Nolan's work,
was fairly typical:

> What a rum book that was. It cost me a lot of pains, as you may have
> guessed from that crabbed and creaking review . . . most of the other
> reviews were vague, stoopid, or even antagonistic. Do you know how
> he has taken it all, or doesn't he bother? I wonder if he'll ever do any-
> thing else.[47]

Later critics have viewed the text more generously, excavating the realist
surface of The Hard Life in search of a more subtle brand of Flann
O'Brien's intertextual, self-reflexive fiction.[48] However, this degree of

stealth and cunning on his part seems unlikely, given that those present at the time were mostly surprised that he had managed to finish a novel at all.[49] O'Nolan himself expressed 'awful doubts' about the manuscript, which had not progressed too far before he decided that the first draft would serve as the end-product.[50] On the one hand, he stoutly defended the perversity of this sequel to At Swim: 'The plot, episodically evolved, is sternly consecutive and conclusive and makes the book compact and short. Digression and expatiation would be easy but I feel would injure the book's spontaneity . . . A few people here . . . are really impressed, particularly by the Collopy-Father Fahrt dialogues, which are set down in absolutely accurate Dublinese.'[51] The rejection of his own tendency for easy digression and elaboration seems a deliberate rebuff to any who expected a re-run of At Swim, quite aside from the questionable 'Dublinese' of Collopy's 'thooleramawns' and 'pishrogues'. But defensiveness once the job is done is one thing; O'Nolan's tone when describing his work-in-progress was more queasily double-edged: 'I do think this is a very funny book, though no dog is a judge of his own vomit. It is old, elegant, nostalgic piss . . . ';[52] 'I believe The Hard Life is a very funny book but at this stage my belief can be disregarded, for it's a poor crow who isn't proud of its own dirt.'[53] So according to its author, The Hard Life is piss, excrement, vomit – perhaps fitting descriptions for a novel quite literally founded on 'toilet humour',[54] but given the degree of recycled waste material involved, the terms cut a little close to the bone.

Yet it is, of course, a novel which fully exploits the comedy of disgust and squalor: from Annie's greasy mince balls to Fahrt's psoriasis, Mrs Crotty's rotted mattress and the sickly sexuality typified by Manus's fascinated discourse on venereal disease. But perhaps it is not even this 'exegesis of squalor', but the novel's persistent regurgitation of old ideas which ultimately justifies its conclusion – a grotesque but apposite image of the re-run: 'everything inside me came up in a tidal surge of vomit' (HL, 149). The excerpt from the brother's correspondence course on tightrope walking, which reads as if culled from a medical dictionary, recalls similar passages in At Swim (though it lacks their disorienting function). Most clearly, his scheme regurgitates a central concept from that novel: 'You could regard the list in the margin as a manifesto, a statement of what we intend to do. We really aim at the mass-production of knowledge, human accomplishment and civilization' (HL, 94). Overall, The Hard Life's patchwork style – veering between an exaggeratedly squalid naturalism, the fantastic accomplishments of the brother, pedantic disputations of the Dublin man and the farcical trip to Rome – combines with the strange device of having the last chapters narrated by Manus's letters to beg comparison with At Swim's narrative instability. As Brooker argues, it is tempting to conclude that the 'central paradox of late Flann O'Brien is that what distinguished his debut anti-novel spoils his attempts to write plain novels.'[55] While the epigraph to *The Hard Life* seems to promise Flann O'Brien's characteristic topsy-turveydom ('All the persons in this book are real and none is fictitious even in part'), in this novel an inconsistent narrative is forced into a more conventional form and ultimately seems clumsily stitched together: 'I will tell all about that later but just now I wish to give an account of the sort of evening we had in our kitchen, not once but very many times, and the type of talk that went on' (*HL*, 23). Most damagingly, the playful self-reflexiveness of the earlier work repeatedly gives way to a hint of narrative recoil: 'Well, that was a long and rather turgid letter . . . ' (*HL*, 108), 'Our conversation, as may be seen, was trivial and pointless enough, and the rest of it was that kind' (*HL*, 102).[56] In a sense, the disgust and dissatisfaction which permeate this novel extend even to the narrative itself. Finbarr's bland invisibility may be a failure of the writing, but as in *The Third Policeman* and *The Dalkey Archive*, O'Nolan had originally planned his narrator to be the most unappealing character of all.[57]

There is a suggestive precursor for *The Hard Life*'s twinning of writing and disgust, its grotesque image of literary regurgitation, in the images which litter the 'Lestrygonians' episode of *Ulysses*: 'At Duke lane a ravenous terrier choked up a sick knuckly cud on the cobblestones and lapped it with new zest. Surfeit. Returned with thanks having fully digested the contents. First sweet then savoury' (*U* 8.1031–33). Unlike O'Nolan, Joyce's dog is evidently a more forgiving judge of its own vomit,[58] as well as being a microcosmic version of this episode's cyclical digestive images, which are writ large in Bloom's visions of civilisations rising and falling, the masses born and dying, and in the repetitive acts of writing and re-writing, metaphorically chewing the cud ('Never know whose thoughts you're chewing' (*U* 8.717–18)). Of course, parody – the most obvious means of chewing the literary cud – is a structuring principle in all of O'Nolan's early novels; one effect of its absence from *The Dalkey Archive* was a blatant act of cannibalism or self-plagiarism. But there are already echoes of Joyce's cannibal Lestrygonians in *The Hard Life* which suggest a degree of wry self-consciousness on O'Nolan's part about the plundering of his back catalogue. J.C.C. Mays has identified a possible source for the Collopy plot in this episode, as Bloom muses on passing the men's urinals under the Thomas Moore statue that there 'Ought to be places for women. Running into cakeshops. Settle my hat straight' (*U* 8.415–16).[59] In a more general way, Bloom's concern for women's welfare throughout this chapter – prompted by his meeting with Mrs Breen and his sympathy for Mina Purefoy's latest bout of labour in

Holles Street Hospital – anticipates Collopy's hushed anxiety on the same matter. However, the Joycean correspondences in the text are otherwise fairly loose, despite the best efforts of O'Nolan's reviewers.[60] The timeline of *The Hard Life* (1890–1910) may be similar to that of *A Portrait*, and its dreary restraint might recall the scrupulous meanness of *Dubliners*, but here the Joycean touches seem more casual than parodic (the love interest named 'Penelope', for example) as if merely to acknowledge their common territory.[61] For all the comparisons to be made between their work as studies of stunted lives in a priest-ridden Dublin squalor – and Fahrt is too comic to be a real adversary – the brashly offhand treatment of Joyce in *At Swim* is replaced here with a more convincing carelessness.

Yet the fact that 'Lestrygonians' was the first instalment of *Ulysses* to be stopped by the American censors points to one telling correspondence with *The Hard Life*. This episode's vivid moments of revulsion and disgust – provoking what is in some way the lowest point of Bloom's day ('Feel as if I have been eaten and spewed' (*U* 8. 495)) – not only sound behind the later novel's 'exegesis of squalor', they also provided a model for outraging noxious public guardians. The US Post Office authorities effectively launched Joyce's career of notoriety by stopping importation of the *Little Review* in January 1919, and it is this aspect of the Joycean reputation which *The Hard Life* most openly invokes.[62] As his own publication date approached, O'Nolan revealed to O'Keeffe the controversy which he fully expected the novel to create. In his mind, the Irish Censorship Board, 'composed exclusively of ignorant balloxes . . . [who] pursue their purpose with the single-mindedness of Gadarene swine', would be sure to have it banned, despite the fact that it did not offend on the statutory grounds: 'the mere name of Father Kurt Fahrt, S J will justify the thunderclap'.[63] His plan was to challenge the ban in the High Court and expose the illegality of the Board's decisions, collecting damages along the way. O'Nolan may well have been inspired by a more recent cause célèbre, since the *Lady Chatterley* case had just made D.H. Lawrence a figure of popular fascination in a far more sensational manner than the *Ulysses* trial had ever done for Joyce. But at the same time, he was conducting a strange kind of doublethink on the censorship issue. Though promising an embarrassing legal action against any ban, he stipulated that the novel's dustjacket should provide no gratuitous ammunition to 'those most reverend spivs'; in other words, no biographical material: 'the book in appearance should be utterly colourless, anonymous (pseudonymous), neutral . . . Our bread and butter depends on being one jump ahead of the other crowd.'[64] O'Keeffe wryly pointed out that if he was sure the book would be banned 'it looks a bit weak to bend over so far backwards', though the jacket copy was duly depersonalised and emasculated: 'I think it not altogether reasonable to be provocative *vis à vis* Irish susceptibilities (they're part of our heritage, after all . . .) but a book like *The Hard Life* laughs them away. Laugh hard enough and the censors will have to laugh with you . . . '[65]And the censors did. Again O'Nolan proved that he was perhaps the only Irish writer of note working in this period who could successfully negotiate the whims of the Irish censorship authorities.

Leaving aside the possibility that no censor would want to get caught up in a public controversy with the bilious Myles, it is an odd achievement for a writer who had a reputation (deserved or otherwise) for consistently being at odds with all authority. Of course, *At Swim* slyly smuggled in a wealth of material unpalatable to the puritan mind, even if the crucifixion of Dermot Trellis didn't quite make the final cut. But *The Hard Life* is far less sophisticated in its methods. Where the uglier aspects of *At Swim*'s comedy accumulate almost by stealth, the later novel openly wallows in the grotesque. Back in 1946, Thomas Hogan had appropriated H. G. Wells' infamous judgement on *Ulysses* to declare that Myles, too, betrayed 'the cloacal obsession of the Irish'.[66] Nearly two decades later *The Hard Life* obligingly fleshed out this critical caricature – perhaps as comment on the reputation of Joyce, or Myles, or both. Indeed, Wells's literary judgement is closely echoed by Collopy, who on hearing that Manus has gone into the book business, makes the kind of assumptions that would not embarrass the more excitable members of the Censorship Board: 'if those books are dirty books, lascivious peregrinations on the fringes of filthy indecency, cloacal spewings in the face of Providence, with pictures of prostitutes in their pelts, then out of this house they will go and their owner along with them' (*HL*, 58). But the treatment of Collopy throughout the novel is humorously indulgent rather than antagonistic, even taking into account his Trellis-like demise as a result of the brother's Gravid Water. Admittedly, *The Hard Life* is in many ways a gleefully 'dirty' book, maybe not managing dramatic re-enactments of 'cloacal spewings' but certainly spewings of other kinds, along with a dainty attention to skin ailments, venereal disease, prostitution, incontinence and a pervasive undertone of grimy ill-health, from Collopy's 'slack grey face' (*HL*, 7) to Synge Street's 'greasy Brother' (*HL*, 15) and the suspiciously livid complexions of Hanafin and Mrs Crotty. Nevertheless, the novel abides sufficiently by the rules to escape offending the sensibilities even of a Mr Collopy. While its scatological humour superficially allies it with the contemporary reputation enjoyed by Joyce's 'dirty books', it also neatly skirts his 'salacities'.[67] In an earlier review of Joyce criticism, Myles had dismissed the writer's 'noisy detachment of enemies' who assumed he spent 'what must have been a very uncomfortable life-time investing

the immemorial preoccupations of the *cloaca* with literary obscurities',
but he also criticised Joyce's 'exceptional lack of moral judgement' in
regard to sexual content, arguing that it simply 'repelled' many in Ireland
and lost him the domestic readership he deserved.[68] *The Hard Life*,
designed to play a cat-and-mouse game with the Censorship Board, carefully treads a line between the two.

This may point to an underlying orthodoxy, or simply pragmatism. As
noted earlier, *At Swim* and *An Béal Bocht* had undergone a degree of self-
censorship in response to publishers' demands, though in private
O'Nolan gave freer rein to his humour.[69] He was again instinctively cal-
culating his limits during discussions over Hugh Leonard's adaptation of
The Dalkey Archive for the Dublin stage. Where O'Nolan wanted to omit
the novel's biblical material, deeming it 'unsuitable for overt public presentation. We wouldn't want a "Playboy" sort of row',[70] Leonard resisted
his repeated demands to remove 'objectionable' material: 'The word in
quotes makes you sound like John Charles McQuaid . . . The moronic
bastards, as you call them, will find ammunition if they are looking for
ammunition, quite irrespective of what we take out or leave in.'[71] It is
debatable whether O'Nolan was pragmatically pre-empting the 'moronic
bastards' or instead internalising their standards; Fr Kurt Fahrt might
have been expected to create 'holy bloody ructions' in Ireland,[72] but the
novel itself could hardly give a case for obscenity. On the one hand this is
a canny response to contemporary mores; the loaded silences of
O'Nolan's texts are partly the calculated omissions of a writer finely-
tuned to the absurdities of Ireland's censorship culture. But *The Hard Life*
is also emblematic of the conservative nature of his comic subversion,
gently provoking the censors while in fact playing by their rules. Hopper
persuasively argues for relating a pattern of omissions and repressions in
his fiction – an absence of female figures, a sniggering attitude to sexuality, and the casual misogyny which invades even Collopy's advocacy of
women's rights – to its macabre humour of violence and sexual cruelty:

> In all of his work there is a painful awareness that a cloistered
> Catholic ethos has damaged Irish male attitudes to these issues. At
> times O'Brien gamely attempts to deconstruct certain cultural taboos
> within the restrictive parameters of an oppressive censorship code
> (itself a reflection of socio-sexual anxiety), but in the process loses
> track and reveals himself to be a participant as well as an observer . . .
> enshrining yet strangely subverting the patriarchal presumptions of
> the paradigm.[73]

As Collopy notes, the smell of piety 'is only the absence of the smell of
women' (*HL*, 13), and the rank dwellings of the Christian Brothers

('God's Disjointed' (*HL*, 87)) lend an almost physical repulsiveness to the clerical life. But this disgust extends equally to the female world; even the sketchily saintly Penelope can induce unhappy thoughts ('What was the meaning of this thing sex, what was the nature of sexual attraction? Was it all bad and dangerous?' (*HL*, 103)), quite apart from the image of Annie, a lank 'streel of a girl' (*HL*, 1) cavorting with pox-ridden suitors along the Grand Canal's red-light district. Finbarr may occupy the same dysfunctional sexual culture as the Stephen Dedalus of *A Portrait*, but in this case the lesson of sexual repulsion has been more successfully internalised.[74]

The *Hard Life* plays within and around Ireland's censorship mentality. For D.H. Lawrence, the contempt which confused sex with 'dirt' belied the attitude of the true pornographer: 'the sex flow and the excrement flow is the same thing to them . . . sex is dirt and dirt is sex . . . and any sign of sex in a woman becomes a show of her dirt.'[75] In this sense, the novel lays traps for over-eager censors and their unhealthy obsessions, primed to suspect sexual obscenity in all matters female. Collopy's devotion to 'women and their wants' (*HL*, 46) exposes the language of euphemism and modesty as the underside of the double entendre:

> — Tell me this, Father. Would you say it's *natural* for a woman to have children?
> — Provided she is married in a union blessed by the Church – yes . . .
> — Very good, Mr Collopy said warmly. Then tell me this. Is the other business natural?
> — Certainly. Our bodies are sacred temples. It is a function.
> — Very well. What name have you for the dirty ignoramuses who more or less ban that function? (*HL*, 26)

What 'the other business' refers to is satisfyingly ambiguous, though the theme of Collopy's rant is the Church-sanctioned suffering of child-bearing women who must continually endure husbands 'ablaze with the fires of lust!' (*HL*, 25).[76] It was a potentially neat trap if read as a marked passage taken out of context for the Board's consideration. O'Nolan's comedy makes literal the concept expressed by Lawrence; by confusing 'the sex flow and the excrement flow' – allowing one to stand for the other in the censor's mind – a clever defence could expose his accuser as the true pornographer. Yet ironically, the central joke of The *Hard Life* itself depends on Collopy's capacity for self-censorship, on what is deliberately not said. His modesty is as risible as his credentials as a campaigner for women's rights. While complaining that women have no presence in Irish public life because men 'have only two uses for women . . . either go to bed with them or else thrash the life out of them', he also assumes that the only woman who would deign to appear at a public meeting would be a prostitute (*HL*, 31). It is an attitude echoed by all the other (male) characters; the only role for a woman in this novel is that of a cartoon grotesque who harbours a threat of sexual degradation, if not outright disease. Finbarr immediately assumes even the grey-haired and feeble Mrs Crotty to be 'a kept-woman or resident prostitute' (*HL*, 10), while Manus's first impression of Rome is that it is 'full of brothels' (*HL*, 121) and his only female encounter in London is to remonstrate with a misused servant from Ireland: 'one of the thousands of ladies who flood the streets here' (*HL*, 94). As with the prurient Trellis – representative of campaigners against 'evil' literature and yet the only perpetrator of sexual assault in *At Swim* – *The Hard Life* caricatures those who are all too ready to cast sex (and women) as a cartoon obscenity, associated with disease, prostitution, 'dirty intentions' (*HL*, 103) and in the novel's central pun, excrement.

However, Collopy's point about the absence of women from Irish public life at the turn of the century had little to distinguish it from O'Nolan's own perception of 1960s Ireland. When challenged by a BBC interviewer on the lack of women in his fiction, his response was a masterpiece of passive misogyny:

> Well, women are not important in Ireland in any sense of the social determinance, if there's such a word . . . What I mean is they make our breakfast and they make our beds, but they are not really formative . . . [T]hey're not really a social force in this country . . . [Y]ou can't leave them out but you mustn't allow them to intrude too much. It would be a very artifical book that gave women a big role.[77]

The defence is a little too brazen, considering that O'Nolan himself did not write state-of-the-nation novels concerned with public life or social forces. Indeed, *The Hard Life* is resolutely domestic in its setting. But the world of Flann O'Brien is undoubtedly a male one, for better or worse. And the difficulty of determining to what extent the censorship mentality infiltrates this particular novel – with what degree of irony, for example, to take the implication that women are either 'industrious, well-built quiet' domestic slaveys or 'nearly all prostitutes' (*HL*, 148) – is partly a failure of the narrative itself. Its misogynistic, schoolboyish humour might be filtered satirically through the puritanical mind of the censor, but it might not. Yet by preventing discussion of abortion and contraception, the censorship legislation which O'Nolan undoubtedly disdained was effectively designed to remove women's sexual issues from view. So it is strangely fitting that a novel written with an eye on the matter opens with the disappearance of a series of women, from a faintly-remembered

mother to the mysterious sister, Teresa, who is only mentioned to repri-
mand Finbarr for making a 'coarse' remark about the sexually-confused
mare, Marius. Whether she was a momentary invention of Manus or
simply another loose thread in a very loose plot, Teresa is important only
for being of no importance. As such, she might well be O'Nolan's most
archetypal female character. In a characteristic move, on finishing the
novel he sent copies to a pair of readers 'deliberately chosen for what we
will call their incongruity of temperament and judgment':

> The first found it very, very funny – uproarious. The second (a lady)
> handed it back to me sadly. She said she did not understand me and
> now doubted whether she ever had. But of one thing I could be sure.
> Not one night would pass but she would say a Hail Mary for me.[78]

The tactic had been used before in dispatching copies of At Swim-Two-
Birds to James Joyce and Ethel Mannin, allowing its author the
satisfaction of proving that his work amused some and provoked others.
But it also betrayed his own habits of thought; for the second time round,
it was the woman who played the straight man.

Hell goes round and round: The Dalkey Archive

With The Hard Life, O'Nolan achieved a commercial success which had
eluded his earlier novels. Despite its mixed critical reception, there was
the odd review which would have pleased an author keen to dissociate
himself from his 'juvenilia':

> Because of its stories wrapped within stories within stories the earlier
> book [At Swim] gave an impression of depth which one can now
> realize was illusory. He now reveals himself as the late Wyndham
> Lewis's ideal of a satirist, a worker with surfaces whose characters are
> 'little monuments of logic'.[79]

It now seems strange to view the earlier work through the prism of The
Hard Life, but with The Dalkey Archive, O'Nolan continued his revisionist
take on his own career. Although ostensibly a more ambitious novel, not
only did it pillage the manuscript of The Third Policeman, but returned to
re-write its subversion of space and time in a new key. Planned as a
'farrago of geophysics, Einsteinian energy, theology, hagiography and
booze',[80] this last novel is at best a comic juggling trick when compared to
the eerily logical nonsense of its source text. Though it showed O'Nolan
embarking on a more complicated venture than the strictly linear narrative of The Hard Life, it nevertheless veers towards composition as

self-parody. Here, Pluck's Atomic Theory does not follow an unsettling pattern of perverse logic, but is a one-stop joke dragged into a fiction insufficiently rational to sustain it. Besides the obvious re-runs from *The Third Policeman* are also reprisals of the theological debates between Collopy and Fr Fahrt (continuing the attempt to snare the Irish censors), as if the text itself were caught in a kind of hellish repetition. A full year before the manuscript was complete, O'Nolan predicted that this would be a novel 'to which the word extraordinary would be considerable understatement, though it will be very readable indeed and in parts quite funny . . . '[81] Yet it never gives full flight to its own peculiar logic, instead toying with plausible (and not so plausible) sub-plots and laboured attempts at characterisation. The few who had read *The Third Policeman* might have been hopeful at his promise that 'time and the physical universe will get scant respect' in the new work, but *The Dalkey Archive* ends O'Nolan's career on a downward note, a rushed job in which his ambition was not matched by his powers of execution.

The contrast with the earlier work is underlined by the seemingly monumental effort it took to produce this last novel. Only a month after the publication of *The Hard Life*, Myles was already informing his readers that Joyce was not dead but living in Skerries, a topic on which he would write a book in 1962.[82] It was May before he again declared that he was 'about to start on a real book', to be finished by Christmas, but a full draft was completed only in October 1963.[83] Yet on Bloomsday 1962, Myles had alerted his readers that the first chapter of a new work was written, with Joyce and St Augustine as two of his characters, and all the other main concepts were in place fairly early on.[84] The actual writing of the book was the difficulty, despite an advance which was designed to release him from newspaper work – a benefit he didn't usually enjoy, but one which would eventually hang dourly over the whole enterprise. Whatever progress was initially made, in January 1963 O'Nolan announced a 'second launching' and at the same time imposed monthly progress reports on himself, as if doubtful of getting the job done any other way.[85] Ironically, the reports sent to his publisher over the following months only traced a tragicomic litany of mishaps: first a bad fall (necessitating dictation), then the distraction of writing television scripts for RTÉ, 'some Asian plague',[86] various other illnesses, a broken typewriter, and finally hospitalisation as the contractual deadline loomed. The evidence is that the job was finally rushed and that O'Nolan himself – as much as his publisher – was unhappy with the results. At the time, he freely accepted most of the criticism offered:

> All such defects arise from what used to be known in early broad-
> casting days as a technical hitch. I determined on a new method of

writing, comprising two stages: (a) Think out a worthwhile theme, then write or scribble BUT GET SOME DAMN THING DOWN ON PAPER; (b) type the raw stuff, creatively and finally.

That book *The Dalkey Archive* is now finished, as in the manner started. Steps so extreme as to be almost supernatural were taken to get the MS finished to meet the date-line . . . They can publish and be damned (so long as they pay me a certain sum thus clinched) but I can't by any means regard the MS as an end-product at all. The idea and base-material is far too good to be thus thrown away . . . [87]

But the typescript that O'Nolan found so unsatisfactory in November 1963 is not radically different from the final published text. The most dramatic revision was of the James Joyce section, otherwise the surviving manuscript drafts show only very minor alterations (in changing the narrative from first-person to third-person, he confined his effort to switching pronouns). 'In its final shape,' he wrote, 'I believe this will be an important and scalding book, and one that will not be ignored . . . The MS is all bleary for want of definition and emphasis but I regard the MS as something worthwhile to chew on'.[88] But these second thoughts were not acted on and besides the treatment of Joyce, there is not much in *The Dalkey Archive* to support his assertion in the same letter that it was 'not meant to be a novel or anything of the kind but a study in derision, various writers with their styles, and sundry modes, attitudes and cults being the rats in the cage.' His 'new method' signalled a desperation to get something, anything, down on paper, a lack of confidence in his ability to get the job done. But while acknowledging the weaknesses this created (effectively churning out a novel as if it were a disposable *Irish Times* column), *The Dalkey Archive* was dispatched with little extra polish.[89]

The result is a mediocre novel by O'Nolan's standards, even if read not as a novel at all but as 'an essay in extreme derision of literary attitudes and people'.[90] (Some have more generously assumed its failings to be a sign of its parody of a mediocre novel.)[91] His description of what he was doing seems more suited to his earlier work, as if unable to think imaginatively beyond that well-worn groove, despite the very different character of his later writing. Arguably, despite *The Dalkey Archive*'s much-touted revenge on Joyce, what is most interesting about this novel's treatment of 'various writers with their styles . . . attitudes and cults' is the manner in which it engages with his *own* literary reputation. Joyce, Mick declares, is 'Dublin's incomparable archivist' (*DA*, 124) but O'Nolan was of course a literary archivist too, one who was now busily sifting through his own back catalogue. Even the inclusion of Joyce, the only obvious literary target of this 'study in derision', is a self-conscious gesture to his overbearing influence on the reputation of Flann O'Brien.[92] Admittedly,

Mary asserts in the closing pages of the novel that 'One must write outside oneself. I'm fed up with writers who put a fictional gloss over their own squabbles and troubles. It's a form of conceit and usually it's very tedious' (*DA*, 191). Coming from a character who is at one point touted as a Joycean scholar, the reproof has some point. But with its stolen passages from *The Third Policeman* and its very personal revenge on Joyce, Flann O'Brien's self-referential habits reach their apotheosis in this novel. The tinge of self-consciousness in Mary's remark reveals one of *The Dalkey Archive*'s primary weaknesses; at this late stage of his career, O'Nolan's quarrel was no longer primarily with Joyce's achievements, but with his own obvious limitations.

This is a novel that has been described as an attack on illusions of mastery, albeit one which in its own narrative untidiness unwittingly proves its point.[93] But the characteristic impulse to undermine all authority and pretension assumes a very different aspect here. Where *At Swim* stands at the beginning of his career as a virtuoso embodiment of the work-in-progress, *The Dalkey Archive* provides a rather dismal mirror image from its final years. As Mick flounders to keep his plots in line, the narrative of this novel seems to inadvertently trace a slow process of decomposition. And at this stage, the preoccupation with mastery seems less the product of a strutting self-doubt than the result of soured aspiration. *The Dalkey Archive* opens with a descriptive passage which loosely mimics the estranged diction of *The Third Policeman*, but here the stilted prose remains just that. Its self-conscious theatricality soon gives way to a blandly realist narrative voice, yet it most immediately evokes the old idea of the satisfactory novel as a 'self-evident sham' (*ASTB*, 25): '[Dalkey] is an unlikely town, huddled, quiet, pretending to be asleep. Its streets are narrow, not quite self-evident as streets and with meetings which seem accidental' (*DA*, 7). Hinting at scenes that are 'unlikely', that are 'not quite self-evident' or may even be 'accidental', this opening itself would provide fair criticism of the novel which follows.[94] Its dramatics also betray all the habits of a self-conscious first-person narrator: 'Ascend a shaded, dull, lane-like way, *per iter*, as it were, *tenebricosum*, and see it burst upon you as if a curtain had been miraculously whisked away. Yes, the Vico Road. Good Lord!' (*DA*, 7). The affected voice builds to a farcical climax ('a wonder that is quite vert, verdant, vertical, verticillate, vertiginous, in the shade of branches even vespertine'), but implodes with an exclamation wholly alien to the fastidious cool of *At Swim*'s student: 'Heavens, has something escaped from the lexicon of Sergeant Fottrell?' (*DA*, 7). If this were *At Swim*, where one voice inevitably bleeds into another, this might be a reasonable expectation. But while the manner might nod to the upper-middle-class character of Dalkey village, still presided over by a monument to Queen Victoria, the self-consciously flamboyant opening sits uneasily with the blank character of the narrative as a whole.

Repeatedly in *The Dalkey Archive* there is this sense of things which don't quite knit together, and its slack pace and narrative looseness are only exacerbated by intrusive attempts to keep the multiple stories in line. A conversation with Mary is only one of the passages which trail off into bored synopsis (*DA*, 56), while the list of tasks which Mick concocts when he realises that 'Several tides seemed to be running simultaneously on the same shore' (*DA*, 110) reads as if O'Nolan was despairing of pulling his diverging plots into line. Of course such devices had worked before, notably the ploy of exposing the novel's skeleton by slipping working notes into *At Swim*. One of the curiosities of *The Dalkey Archive* is how closely it imitates such aspects of the earlier work – even to the point of repeating its pun on French letters (*DA*, 98-99)[95] – and yet how thoroughly it differs in execution. The brilliantly pointless conversations of Shanahan and friends have a frustrating counterpart in the pub-talk at the Colza Hotel; continually on the point of petering out, it never does so soon enough. And as Brooker notes, there are many points in the novel where O'Nolan himself seems conscious of its deficiencies.[96] At a particularly low point, Hackett's rhyme on the Trappists is presented almost apologetically, accompanied by the literary equivalent of canned laughter: 'Recite your composition, please, Mick ordered. The other did so, in a solemn voice, and Mick certainly laughed at the end of it. A little bawdy perhaps, but not dirty . . . Yes, funny' (*DA*, 156-157). The cautious bid for approval sounds the death knell of the comic writer.

O'Nolan's other narrators may tread the line between fiction and reality, they might take a hand in the writing of a novel or question the order of the world, but none had yet forgotten their place so far as to point to the humour itself (or even acknowledge its existence). Myles was the exception, but part of his effectiveness was in openly playing the role of court jester. Where O'Nolan once presented his work with a careful nonchalance, he now insistently draws attention to its comic value. Sergeant Fottrell, the descendant of Sergeant Pluck and keeper of 'the comic little police station' (*DA*, 45), is now no more than a harmless local character: 'what he said and how he said it was known throughout all south County Dublin' (*DA*, 46). The sergeant is a 'dacent lovable man!' (*DA*, 51) according to Pluck's namesake, himself a comic countryman direct from the pages of Somerville and Ross, and so of course humorously scandalised by the outrage perpetrated on the parish priest's garden. The association of de Selby's terrible invention with the Dublin Metropolitan Police is a similarly farcical touch, and as if further direction were needed on how to take this comic bobby, Mick laughs delightedly on hearing of Fottrell's (formerly MacCruiskeen's) light and sound machine, 'and at the whole wonderful idea. There had been, he seemed to remember, an organ that "played" light on a screen, enchanting patterns of mixes and colour' (*DA*, 74). As Mick observes (or O'Nolan reminds himself), Fottrell's 'fancies were usually amusing but not so good when they were meaningless' (*DA*, 75).[97] But the 'Mollycule Theory' itself is reduced to a comic fancy, there being no question here of the love between a man and his bicycle (outside the limits of Fottrell's story) and no underpinning of the notion by de Selbian physics. Indeed, the most successful import from *The Third Policeman* is also accompanied by the most glaring misplacement of an original passage, as the theory inexplicably leads Mick to muse on 'country places he had known in his earlier days', that bogland which had seemed to his predecessor also 'real and incontrovertible but at variance with the talk of the sergeant' (*DA*, 77; see *TP*, 89). It is at such moments that *The Third Policeman*'s narrator grasps for solid ground, and for very different reasons the reader of *The Dalkey Archive* might be inclined to do the same.

But if there are unflattering similarities with the earlier work, this novel is of course a deliberate re-writing of it as well. As if betraying a bad conscience, the action of revision and redress is itself mimicked throughout the text – most notoriously with Joyce attacking his own reputation by denying authorship of *Ulysses* and all knowledge of *Finnegans Wake*, though his religious counterpart, St Augustine, also debunks his spiritual autobiography: '*I invented obscene feats out of bravado, lest I be thought innocent or cowardly . . . Book Two of my Confessions is all shocking exaggeration*' (*DA*, 33–34). In the one case, authorship is exposed as a legal fiction; in the other, as an opportunity for shamanistic hoaxes. Obviously this is familiar Flann O'Brien territory; O'Nolan himself had long exploited the illusion of the shape-changing author, always ready to deny responsibility for his maverick texts. When *At Swim* was re-issued in 1960 and an unfamiliar humorist was exhumed from his past, Myles had greeted the interloper with affected suspicion:

> There's stories going around that Flann O'Brien and my good self are wan and the same pairson. I know my own know about that caper . . . nobody on or under this world knows what I have written or can declare on oath what I have not written . . . I absolutely deny that I ever wrote it. I am not the oney wan in the leaky boat. Longmans swear that they never published it.[98]

Though the joke is re-run in *The Dalkey Archive* with Joyce at the helm, the pathetic figure whom Mick assumes to have been unbalanced by the war is a disturbing echo of the writer who it was now difficult to identify with the brilliance of *At Swim-Two-Birds*. His pseudonyms had allowed him to indulge the notion of compartmentation of personality, an illusion of literary freedom, but somehow these discrepant entities had wandered too far apart. The author of *The Third Policeman* is only another of the literary figures being derailed in *The Dalkey Archive*, another whose reputation is being furiously scrubbed out. But while the novel treacherously denies its former incarnation, in its place it at least acquires some of the scabrous energy of the later *Cruiskeen Lawn*. This was a book which O'Nolan wished to be 'bitterly funny', to have all 'the beauty of jewelled ulcers'.[99] Now that de Selby had migrated from the lunatic fringe of its source text to play the more straightforward role of the mad scientist, this scorn is focused in the figures of Joyce and Augustine. And what is undeniably new in the late fiction, is that both characters allowed O'Nolan to display his mastery of 'the comic content of sanctity',[100] a quality that was surely all too visible to the Irish readership he had been addressing for over twenty years, but which until now had been strangely absent from the writing of the country's foremost satirist.

Until *The Hard Life*, O'Nolan's most public foray into ecclesiastical matters had been Myles's evisceration of Alfred O'Rahilly during the 1951 controversy over the Mother and Child Scheme. Even then, he had defended the Catholic bishops' 'perfectly legitimate intervention' (*FC*, 163) in scuppering Noel Browne's welfare proposal, though arguing that their objection to the plan should have been made openly.[101] But in contrast to this apparent tolerance for the influence of the Catholic Church in Irish public affairs, there is an almost physical distaste for Ireland's clerics in that novel, from the griminess of the Synge Street home of the Christian Brothers ('slaves to their own sadistic passions' (*HL*, 54)), to Collopy's litany of the brutal crimes of the Jesuit Order's 'sacerdotal politicians' (*HL*, 71). The Church-sanctioned creed of patient suffering voiced by Fahrt has a suitably demeaning comic foil in Collopy's campaign for women's public toilets. And the bathetic climax in the Vatican raises the comic mystery of why ecclesiastical authorities should interest themselves at all in women's 'private little affairs' (*HL*, 130). Cronin rightly points out that the humour of both these novels relies a good deal on their ability to shock, assuming a reader who feels implicated in O'Nolan's sense of mischievous transgression.[102] There is certainly a hint that any criticism of Ireland's clerics should not be taken too seriously, as Fahrt suspects: 'You are merely trying to annoy me. You don't believe in what you say at all ... At the back of it all, you are a pious Godfearing man, may the Lord be good to you' (*HL*, 75). But perhaps that too is a sign of Fahrt's unshakeable arrogance; there is more at work here than simply the juvenile humour typified in O'Nolan's bid to establish (to stage-directed gasps) whether St Augustine was '*a Nigger*' (*DA*, 40). It is clear that he, at least, considered the religious content of *The Dalkey Archive* to be genuinely provocative, as can be seen by his anxious letters on its dramatisation to Hugh Leonard. (He may have been right: unflattering remarks he made about the Jesuits were cut from the tape of a 1964 RTÉ interview. Strangely, the tape was otherwise unedited because it was never broadcast – he was drunk throughout the interview.)[103] In private, O'Nolan was happy to boast that the novel would be 'a fucking masterpiece, devoid of obscenity, and with all the laughs at the expense of Almighty God and his slobs, the saints'.[104] One of its targets is certainly an ignorant piety – Mrs Laverty names her hotel after the apocryphal Saint Colza (*DA*, 25) – and de Selby's underwater theological debates rely not just on the questionable humorous potential of haemorrhoids or 'rutting ceremonials' (*DA*, 33), but also on a comic frisson from a sense of forbidden intellectual fruit. In that sense, it is disappointing that the pious Joyce later agrees with Augustine's cautious observation that spiritual concepts are not apprehensible in words or by intellectual work: '*it is our final duty to believe, to have and to nourish faith*' (*DA*, 39). Rather than developing into a subversive theology of its own, the *pneuma* which loosely links the philosophies of de Selby, Fottrell and Joyce immediately expires, exposed as a vague gesture towards plot resolution.

It is O'Nolan who takes on the Joycean character here (as outlined in 'A Bash in the Tunnel') – not rebelling against the Catholic Church as such 'but against its near-schism Irish eccentricities, its pretence that there is only one Commandment, the vulgarity of its edifices, the shallowness and stupidity of many of its ministers'.[105] For all the novel's attempts to shock, *The Dalkey Archive* is more interesting as a comic exposure of 'the sin syndrome',[106] particularly in its Irish manifestation. By inverting the reputations of Augustine and Joyce, the reformed saint and the unrepentant sinner, it exposes the tenuous distinction between them. O'Nolan's Joyce, last seen as a 'truly fear-shaken Irish Catholic',[107] is now fully fleshed into a study of the archetypal 'holy Mary Ann' (*DA*, 128) despite his protests to the contrary. And the writer who once distantly directed his own critical reception now speaks in the tongues of the critics who damned 'Penelope' as 'Pornography and filth and literary vomit' (*DA*, 167). His saintly namesake, on the other hand, is caught out boasting of his exploits like a Dublin cornerboy, showing all the true puritan's fascination with the pornographic. When de Selby points out that after Augustine's rampaging youth, this 'hagiarchic senility' must have been 'a thunderous contrast, the ascent to piety sudden and even distressing' (*DA*, 33), the remark might be better addressed to the confused Joyce. (Stephen Dedalus, of course, had already mapped his travels in the opposite direction; O'Nolan completes his reversal of Stephen's adventures by bringing Joyce back face-to-face with an English Jesuit priest.) To complete the unholy trinity, Joyce's Damascene conversion is reflected in Mick's growing delusion that he is a redeemer of humanity, capable of saving the world from de Selby's nefarious plots. The little revision O'Nolan made of the first draft included making his protagonist a more reprehensibly puritan figure, replacing his stout with 'Vichy water' and introducing a more ambiguous attitude to Mary. The passages of worst condescension towards her come from the late effort to make this 'conceited prig' even 'more revolting':[108]

> Without swallowing whole all the warnings one could readily hear and read about the spiritual dangers of intellectual arrogance and literary freebooting, there was menace in the overpoise that high education and a rich way of living could confer on a young girl. Unknowingly, she could exceed her own strength . . . he would make Mary more of his own quiet kind, and down to earth. (DA, 53)

This wavers towards a priestly paternalism, though even at an early stage Mary's character concerned one reader, who found the tone of her scenes as 'hating rather than one of development'.[109] Yet the awkwardness with which she is handled is wholly characteristic of Mick himself, the original first-person narrator: 'Mary was not a simple girl, not an easy subject to write about nor Mick the one to write. He thought women in general were hopeless as a theme for discussion or discourse . . . The mutual compulsion is a mystery, not just a foible or biogenesis, and this sort of mystery, even if comprehensible to the two concerned, is at least absolutely private' (DA, 52). Admittedly, O'Nolan also declared women a hopeless theme for his fiction, which slightly undermines the suspicion that it is Mick's less flattering characteristics that are on show here. Yet for one of O'Nolan's female creations, Mary is uncharacteristically intelligent and independent. Tellingly, she puzzled a friend who saw the manuscript until, as O'Nolan recorded: 'in a blinding flash, he got the point. MARY was a surname, and the emergence of Mr Mary at the [end of the] book would have shown the story to have taken, unnoticed, a quite new direction . . . '[110] However, with Mick's 'virgin Mary' (DA, 111) ending the novel on an ambiguously non-virginal note, the novel's final twist exposes only the poverty of his fantasies of religious celibacy. (Tellingly, as his piety progresses, Mary predictably becomes in his mind a 'gilded trollop' (DA, 133), loosely associated with the 'base' character of Molly Bloom (DA, 132).) By the end, Mick's obedience of a sexual code casually ignored by Hackett (and the Fathers of the Church) has landed him in a dubious position. In retrospect, his comparison of de Selby's diffusion of the deadly DMP to the mission to spread Catholicism throughout the world carries some point (*DA*, 105).[111] The fact that de Selby's ultimate motive in destroying the world is to save it from its Churches (*DA*, 70) makes it all the more interesting that the threat of DMP is finally allowed to survive.

Something of the old Flann O'Brien resonates in de Selby's disillusioned suspicion that the battle in heaven did not go as popularly reported. For if this unhappy world were indeed the devil's work, 'who but Lucifer would be certain to put about the other and opposite story?' (*DA*, 21). *The Third Policeman* was a masterpiece created from such a minor shift in perspective, but it is one that the anxious humorist behind *The Dalkey Archive* is not brave enough to make. Instead, Mick's increasing sense of 'his own personal majesty' leads to a hint of Luciferian pride as his imagination expounds on his future plans: 'Was he not himself a god-figure of some sort? . . . Was it his long-term duty to overturn the whole Jesuit Order with all its clowns of the like of Father Cobble . . . or was it his duty to overturn the Holy Father himself?' (*DA*, 111). The fantasy is later downgraded to regarding himself as a kind of priest (*DA*, 134), or at least a prime minister (*DA*, 161), while his plot for the 'salvation' (*DA*, 140) of Jack Downes (and his watch) is cast as the compassionate act of the good Samaritan. But this growing arrogance is partly masked by the self-conscious nature of the narration – barely recast into the third person – which manifests itself in a series of small irritated checks and corrections. The effect is to give Mick the hubris of a nonentity supervising men of the calibre of Joyce and de Selby (however 'indeterminate' (*DA*, 134) he suspects that calibre to be). Suggestively, he is 'conscious of a pervasive ambiguity: sometimes he seemed to be dictating events with deific authority, at other times he saw himself the plaything of implacable forces' (*DA*, 162). Mick's dilemma is that of authorship, as much as anything else, but his meddling ultimately backfires as the de Selby plot is unaccountably resolved off-stage and his only contribution turns out to have been to save DMP from destruction. Wrong-footed by Hackett and Mary, incapable of moulding the world to his own design (despite his scheming), Mick's sin after all may not be his proud delusions of grandeur, but his inability to bridge the gap between a runaway imagination and his own ineffectiveness. In that sense he may indeed be, as Cronin argues, an inadvertent portrait of O'Nolan himself.[112] As he carefully notes, his relationship with Mary 'had not been sinful' (*DA*, 135), and if Mick finds sanctity in his own sins of omission then he is easily abandoned to the enclosed life, whatever form it takes. But in O'Nolan's last wishful act of revision, the promise (or threat) of captivity is instead transferred to his literary hero. While Mick's vocation is stopped in its tracks in the last, fairly perfunctory scene, it is not before he has sold out a distracted Joyce to the religious authorities. It is no surprise, in a novel with confused themes of salvation and redemption, that along the way Hackett makes a case for the rehabilitation of Judas Iscariot, and the novel's first draft further betrays the import of Mick's action: 'I was a benevolent warder, about to hand over a prisoner to more accomplished care. With no hint of Pilate's thought, I was about to wash my hands'.[113] Over a decade earlier, 'A Bash in the Tunnel' had also betrayed Joyce into the role of the fretful Catholic, despite his protests of *non serviam*: 'His revolt, noble in itself, carried him away . . . But I think he meant well. We all do anyway'.[114] In the midst of writing *The Dalkey Archive*, O'Nolan noted that he wanted to make a 'greater mess' of Joyce than he had yet achieved. He finally did it by dragging Joyce into his own world, incarcerating him in orthodoxy.

Although Joyce had been resurrected in *Cruiskeen Lawn* as early as 1951 ('What happened to that other fellow with the glasses and the nice tenor voice that used to sing BELIEVE ME IF ALL? . . . I seen him in the Bailey off Grafton street two days ago and I never seen him looking better in himself . . . '),[115] the reception of *The Hard Life* had soured the gimmick. However, O'Nolan's reputation for angry begrudgery has overshadowed the extent to which, in designing this revenge, he was also merely exploiting Joyce's fame. The Joycean connection was central to his ploy to market the book in America, even using his image on the American dust-jacket itself, a slightly misleading gesture resisted by the publisher.[116] The idea would not have been much helped if the Joyce material had been published – like the rest of the novel – more or less as it appeared in November 1963. Not only was it fairly inept (he was originally said to be posing as a Frenchman under the name of 'M. Barrass')[117] but it was also focused primarily on 'Stupid American commentators', their stupidity being demonstrated by their naïve adoption of his joke name for Nora: 'you cling so closely to me that I'll call you my barnacle'.[118] In this version, Joyce is clearly the hapless victim of international critics:

> 'Those terrible and ignorant bastards in the American universities nearly ruined me . . .'
> 'I quite agree. You must remember that you are yourself an American industry.'
> 'Yes – in the sense that brothels comprise an industry.'
> 'But I hope that your mind is too big to be worried by the snapping of jackals.'
> 'Ah, easy to say.'[119]

This aspect survived in more diluted form in the expanded final version: 'It was not the false imputations of authorship which drove Joyce askew but rather the lonely exertion of keeping pace with a contrived reputation . . . ' (DA, 177-178). On the contrary, it was not any ordinary illness which killed Joyce, Montgomery wrote to O'Nolan as he worked on the revisions, but his 'utter astonishment and desolation over the public failure to rave over F.W.'[120] The same could be said of Flann O'Brien and the reception of his own novels (with about as much merit). In any case, what this novel finally presents is James Joyce in the image of Brian O'Nolan. This is a world where, in imitation of his own literary collaborations, *Ulysses* is the work of many hands, a trick concocted by Sylvia Beach and friends; even *Dubliners* is produced in league with Oliver St John Gogarty and almost ruined by his 'Castle cavorting' (DA, 165). Here it is Joyce who does not sign his name to his work, who assumes pseudonyms, and who inexplicably denies all responsibility for his greatest novel. It is Joyce who ends up handling the Jesuits' dirty laundry, because in O'Nolan's punning imagination that is what he has always done. Or perhaps that is more true of Flann O'Brien, or Myles na gCopaleen, publicly scouring the nation in the pages of *The Irish Times*. Since O'Nolan began his career as a novelist in the image of James Joyce, it is strangely fitting that this is finally reversed in *The Dalkey Archive*. Joyce's judgement of his own work echoes O'Nolan's comments on *The Hard Life* – *Ulysses*, he says, is 'literary vomit' (DA, 167). Damning his masterpiece as the product of 'lascivious pornographic blackguards' (DA, 175), it is no wonder – if Joyce has accepted the judgement of the world on his work – that he has 'gone (as was supposed) queer in the head', or that he has become a nondescript individual who looks to the by-stander no more than 'a tired senior civil servant; certainly not a writer' (DA, 177). His particular talents are also those of his author, 'mimicry and mockery were usually among the skills of the intellectually gifted', but there is little comfort to be had in that: 'precision in playing a role ordained by morbid cerebral hypostasis is characteristic of most persons troubled in the mind' (DA, 177). Neither does he escape the usual fate of O'Nolan's protagonists, being led off to final internment in the Jesuit house, while Mick is condemned to the only other alternative, induction into a world of sodden respectability. If *The Dalkey Archive* has little else in common with *The Third Policeman*, it at least proves that creative hell goes round and round.

Afterword

It is undeniable that Brian O'Nolan's literary career ended on a downward note, and perhaps the only critical consensus on his eclectic body of work is that it all too quickly went into decline. This has often been attributed partly to the demands of *Cruiskeen Lawn*, which dominated his output after *The Third Policeman*. Whatever the truth of this, it is a measure of the long wait which the newspaper column had for critical acceptance that even the late novels have received far more attention, perhaps simply by virtue of their genre. Yet as a sprawling mass of comic writing that defies easy classification, *Cruiskeen Lawn* is unique in modern Irish writing and can have few parallels elsewhere. Its inevitable contradictions have cast Myles na gCopaleen as a comic chameleon, a ventriloquist of mid-century Ireland in all its guises. But they also reflect the continual complexity of O'Nolan's comedy – fuelled to some degree by a conservative instinct, but complicated by a disruptive critical intelligence. At its best, the column fully exploited his gifts as a literary magpie; it was an ideal vehicle for the comic dexterity which produced in *At Swim-Two-Birds* a medley of popular fiction, Gaelic scholarship and Joycean modernism. The early *Cruiskeen Lawn* juggled endless variations of nonsense, satire, parody, wordplay and wit, and its open-ended nature allows any number of narratives to be assembled from the column (loosely resembling the cut-and-paste nature of *At Swim* itself). But as politics slowly crept into the column – whether in debates on social welfare or in the post-war suspicion that one colonial master had simply been swapped for another – it became evident that *Cruiskeen Lawn* was taking on a very different character. Perhaps it was inevitable that its inventiveness could not be sustained over a long period of time, or perhaps this more political slant was partly the mark of Montgomery's influence. Nevertheless, the later *Cruiskeen Lawn* leaves a sometimes intriguing (sometimes exhausting) record of cultural and political debate in post-war Dublin which surely bears further analysis.

The discovery of the extent of Montgomery's involvement in *Cruiskeen Lawn* (and even in drafting the *Insect Play* adaptation) of course casts a new light on Myles's contradictory nature. It also reveals that O'Nolan's wry attitude to the notion of original authorship had a much more practical basis than has been recognised. In a very literal sense, the multi-authored *Cruiskeen Lawn* really *was* the product of the Dublin intelligentsia, as Anthony Cronin suggested, besides the fact that the column's habit of derision was far from peculiar to Myles na gCopaleen. A daily column inevitably becomes on intimate terms with its readership and their attitudes, and from its very beginning as the 'Gaelic cuckoo'[1] in *The Irish Times*, *Cruiskeen Lawn* was imbricated in the cultural conflicts of post-independence Ireland. It is worth noting that even Flann O'Brien, sometimes associated by critics with a peculiarly self-involved brand of metafiction, also made his debut courting controversy in the pages of a newspaper. From the outset, O'Nolan's brand of nonsensical, esoteric humour provided a counterpoint to Seán O'Faoláin's attempts to negotiate a role as a public intellectual. As a whole, his own literary career shows a varying tension between the temptations of Joycean inscrutability and the satisfactions of playing to the public gallery. Even *At Swim*'s humour is self-consciously performative, always directed to one internal audience or another (and very often to unappreciative audiences, their criticism adding a further layer of irony to the student's modernist ambitions). But this intimacy with a projected readership, an intimacy that would deepen throughout the 1940s as O'Nolan was increasingly confined to the pages of *The Irish Times*, could easily shade into claustrophobia. That mood was already thickening in *The Third Policeman*, its sinister world in one sense being a fantasia on the theme of entrapment. It would return in *An Béal Bocht*, another comically bleak tale of predestination.

Yet it is too easy to say that the daily column was his ruin, or to trace his decline – as some do – to a cultural stagnation in contemporary Ireland. The babel of *At Swim-Two-Birds* is itself a lively comic image of the competing strains in Dublin's intellectual life in the 1930s. That novel is not simply founded on literary parody, its humour is in a way parasitic on contemporary Irish culture. *At Swim*'s Stephen Dedalus is too wryly self-aware to imagine himself flying by any nets of nationality or religion. Similarly, it often seems that O'Nolan's comic sense is simply too knowing, too ironic, to allow him to settle into a consistently oppositional stance to de Valera's Ireland, the position adopted by so many of his contemporaries. When he does (or when Myles does, which is not entirely the same thing) a certain degree of sophistication has usually been lost in the writing. *At Swim*, on the other hand, hinges on comic ambivalence; there is nothing in the novel that is beyond parody, no solid foundation from which to mock its cowboys and Gaels, querulous uncles and precocious students. Myles's commentary on the Irish language is similarly agile, sometimes defending the language's virtues, while also mocking its political and cultural baggage. But the ironies of such a stance are not wholly within his control; O'Nolan's eventual turn to English could be read as a defiant gesture to the revival movement, but it was also a surrender to a society which notoriously paid lip-service to the Irish language and yet made no place for it in daily life. There is an obvious case to be made for Flann O'Brien and Myles na gCopaleen as subversive comics, relentlessly exposing the failings of their time. But the ironic perspective acknowledges that all humour is necessarily compromised. There were inevitably blind spots in O'Nolan's demystifying comic vision, besides the fact that he pragmatically adapted his work to take account of contemporary sensitivities. Of all people, it was the scabrous Myles na gCopaleen who carefully edited obvious signs of the 'mock-religious' from his first novel, a feature which would only re-emerge in his novels in the comparatively liberal 1960s and then only as a deliberate shock tactic. And as Hopper has argued, the absence of women or any open discussion of sexuality throughout his writing reflects a real constriction to the male world of pub and pulpit.[2] All of which is to make the fairly obvious point that these works, like any, are delimited by their time – not only subversive of contemporary Ireland's social and cultural mores, but also implicated in them.

For all of his career Brian O'Nolan wrote in Ireland, and after *The Third Policeman* was rejected he effectively wrote only for an Irish readership. In 2005, a hint that the novel might provide a clue to the mysteries of the ABC television series 'Lost' belatedly placed it on a bestseller list in America. The irony of turning to *The Third Policeman* to solve any mystery was surely not lost on the screenwriters who planted that information. It seems O'Nolan now occupies a peculiar position, somewhere between the international citizenship of James Joyce and the purely domestic readership of many of his Irish contemporaries. It is a position that reflects the scope of his own writing, responsive to the innovations of modernist writers yet wholly indebted to the oddities of contemporary Irish culture. Among these oddities was an ingrained disdain for the kind of social and cultural elitism which was fostered by some branches of modernism and revivalism. A native counterpart might be the sanctimonious superiority of the *fíor-Ghael*. O'Nolan's comic writing managed a sophisticated accommodation of this populist streak in Irish culture. Its humour spiralled from the erudite and the ordinary, scolding the Plain People of Ireland while very much remaining a part of their world. There is not much else like it.

Notes and references

Introduction

1 Oscar Wilde, 'The Decay of Lying', in Merlin Holland (ed.), *Essays and Letters* (London: Folio, 1993), p. 214.

2 James Joyce, *Ulysses*, Hans Walter Gabler (ed.) (London: The Bodley Head, 1922, 1986), p. 6. Future references are cited in the text by chapter and line number.

3 Letter to Grant Richards (23 June 1906) in Stuart Gilbert (ed.), *Letters of James Joyce*, 3 vols. (New York: Viking, 1957, 1966), vol. 1, p. 64.

4 Wilde, 'The Decay of Lying', p. 224.

5 CL (25 March 1942); reprinted in BM, p. 93.

1. THE CULT OF THE AUTHOR

1 The Flann O'Brien collection in the John J. Burns Library, Boston College includes Irish articles by a 'Seán Ó Longáin' (unlisted in any of O'Nolan's bibliographies) with the name 'Myles na Gopaleen' added in the margins.

2 Keith Hopper, *Flann O'Brien: A Portrait of the Artist as a Young Post-modernist* (Cork: Cork University Press, 1995), p. 18.

3 ibid., pp. 20-21.

4 There was only one study then published that might have fitted Hopper's description of the international criticism on O'Nolan: Thomas F. Shea, *Flann O'Brien's Exorbitant Novels* (Lewisburg: Bucknell University Press, 1992). A lack of critical acumen seems an unfair charge to level at Anthony Cronin's biography, *No Laughing Matter: The Life and Times of Flann O'Brien* (London: Grafton, 1989) or at J.C.C. Mays's long article, 'Brian O'Nolan: Literalist of the Imagination', in Timothy O'Keeffe (ed.), *Myles: Portraits of Brian O'Nolan* (London: Martin, Brien & O'Keeffe, 1973), pp. 77-119.

5 Hopper, *Flann O'Brien*, pp. 18-19.

6 See *Myles: Portraits of Brian O'Nolan*, edited by O'Nolan's publisher Timothy O'Keeffe, with contributions from his brother, Kevin O'Nolan, Niall Sheridan and colleagues John Garvin and Jack White.

7 See Breandán Ó Conaire, *Myles na Gaeilge* (Baile Átha Cliath: An Clóchomhar, 1986); Michael Cronin, 'The Imaginary Gaeilgeoir', *Graph* vol. 6, Summer 1989, pp. 16-18; Declan Kiberd, 'The Fall of the Stage-Irishman', in Ronald Schleifer (ed.), *The Genres of the Irish Literary Revival* (Dublin: Wolfhound, 1980), pp. 39-60; and Cathal Ó Háinle, 'Fionn and Suibhne in At *Swim-Two-Birds*', *Hermathena*, vol. 142, 1987, 13-49.

8   Hopper, *Flann O'Brien*, p. 21.

9   See José Lanters, *Unauthorized Versions: Irish Menippean Satire 1919–1952* (Washington: Catholic University of America Press, 2000), Keith Donohue, *The Irish Anatomist: A Study of Flann O'Brien* (Dublin, Oxford, Bethesda: Maunsel/Academica Press, 2002), M. Keith Booker, *Flann O'Brien, Bakthin and Menippean Satire* (Syracuse: SUP, 1995) and Joe Brooker, 'Estopped by Grand Playsaunce: Flann O'Brien's Postcolonial Lore', *Journal of Law and Society*, vol. 31, no. 1, March 2004, pp. 15–37.

10   Hugh Kenner, *A Colder Eye: The Modern Irish Writers* (Harmondsworth: Penguin, 1983), p. 321.

11   Stephen Young, 'Fact/Fiction: *Cruiskeen Lawn*, 1945–66', in Anne Clune and Tess Hurson (eds.), *Conjuring Complexities: Essays on Flann O'Brien* (Belfast: Institute of Irish Studies, 1997), p. 116.

12   Stephen Curran also makes this point: 'In his first novel, *At Swim-Two-Birds*, audiences already figure as an indispensable structuring motif, and the presence of an alert, responsive readership proved a pre-condition for the satirical program initiated in his journalism.' ' "No, this is not from *The Bell*": Brian O'Nolan's 1943 *Cruiskeen Lawn* Anthology', *Éire-Ireland*, vol. 32, no. 2–3, 1997, p. 80.

13   Jack White, 'Myles, Flann and Brian', in *Myles: Portraits of Brian O'Nolan*, p. 67.

14   Anthony Cronin, *No Laughing Matter*, p. vii.

15   This is the term O'Nolan used in a letter to Ethel Mannin (14 July 1939), Brian O'Nolan Collection, Southern Illinois University Carbondale. This collection is hereafter referred to as SIUC.

16   Arthur Kuhl, 'New Books', cutting dated 2 April 1951. SIUC.

17   In 1949, for example, he expressed the fond hope that all his books might be catalogued for posterity: 'Why, the horde of American *thullabawns* now infesting Dublin looking for the footprints of James Joyce might even do a thesis on them! (Or am I presumptuous in aspiring to such fame).' *CL* (28 August 1949), cited in Donohue, *The Irish Anatomist*, p. 148.

18   'If you write very obscure verse (and why shouldn't you, pray?) for which there is little or no market, you pretend that there is an enormous demand, and that the stuff has to be rationed . . . I beg to announce respectfully my coming volume of verse entitled 'Scorn for Taurus' . . . But look out for the catch. When the type has been set up, it will be instantly destroyed and NO COPY WHATEVER WILL BE PRINTED . . . The edition will be so utterly limited that a thousand pounds will not buy even one copy. This is my idea of being exclusive.' *CL* (7 January 1942); *BM*, p. 228.

19   Hopper, *Flann O'Brien*, p. 114.

20   'Omniscient omnipotent Myles/Writes a column in multiple styles,/While chastising the nation/He gets inspiration/From Odearest – a Buddha all smiles'. Peter Costello and Peter van de Kamp, *Flann O'Brien: An Illustrated Biography* (London: Bloomsbury, 1987), p. 95.

21   Myles na gCopaleen, 'De Me', *New Ireland*, March 1964, p. 41.

22   John Ryan, *Remembering How We Stood* (Dublin: Lilliput, 1975, 1987), p. 130.

23   Anthony Cronin, *Dead As Doornails* (Dublin: Lilliput, 1976, 1999), p. 114.

24   Costello and van de Kamp, *Flann O'Brien: An Illustrated Biography*, p. 15. This characterisation was reflected in the title of an RTÉ radio programme on Brian O'Nolan, a series of four interviews entitled 'Myles, Yer Only Man' (prod. Dave McHugh, 2004). Ironically, in their interviews both Mícheál Ó Nualláin and Anthony Cronin were at pains to dismiss the image of O'Nolan as the irascible character of Dublin legend.

25 The series ran from 15–21 December 1960 and 17–24 January 1961. Ann Clissmann, *Flann O'Brien: A Critical Introduction* (Dublin: Gill & Macmillan, 1975), p. 193.

26 A play on the title of the Irish transport company, Corais Iompar Éireann. Quidnunc [Renagh Holohan]. 'A holy show', *The Irish Times* (11 April 1998).

27 Dick Walsh, 'Magisterium of chancers for new millennium', ibid. (15 December 2001), p. 14.

28 Although arguably O'Nolan courted the reputation even in *At Swim-Two-Birds*, in which the student narrator has a particularly fluid lifestyle.

29 Costello and van de Kamp, *Flann O'Brien: An Illustrated Biography*, p. 85.

30 Donohue, *The Irish Anatomist*, p. 123.

31 Cronin, *No Laughing Matter*, p. 134.

32 Richard Watts Jr., 'Flann O'Brien, Man of Names and Talents', *New York Herald Tribune* (4 April 1943).

33 'Myles on the Front Page', *The Irish Times* (3 July 1943).

34 Watts, 'Flann O'Brien: Man of Names and Talents'.

35 *CL* (19 May 1943), cited in Donohue, *The Irish Anatomist*, p. 3.

36 This apocryphal marriage was investigated at length in Costello and van de Kamp, *Flann O'Brien: An Illustrated Biography*, pp. 48–49.

37 Anon. [Stanford Lee Cooper], 'Eire's Columnist', *Time* (23 August 1943), pp. 90–92.

38 'Thomas Hogan' [Thomas Woods], 'Myles na gCopaleen', *The Bell*, vol. 13, no. 2, November 1946, p. 140.

39 *CL* (16 June 1954).

40 On their relationship see Bernard Benstock, 'The Three Faces of Brian O'Nolan', *Éire-Ireland*, vol. 3, no. 3, Autumn 1968, pp. 51–65; Ivan Del Janik, 'Flann O'Brien: The Novelist as Critic', *Éire-Ireland*, vol. 4, no. 4, Winter 1964, pp. 64–72; J.C.C. Mays, 'Brian O'Nolan and Joyce on Art and on Life', *James Joyce Quarterly*, vol. 11, no. 3, Spring 1974, pp. 238–256; Joseph Browne, 'Flann O'Brien: "Post" Joyce or "Propter" Joyce?', *Éire-Ireland*, vol. 19, no. 4, 1984, 148–157; David Cohen, 'James Joyce and the Decline of Flann O'Brien', *Éire-Ireland*, vol. 22, no. 2, Summer 1987, pp. 153–160; William M. Chace, 'Joyce and Flann O'Brien', *Éire-Ireland*, vol. 22, no. 4, Winter 1987, pp. 140–152; Ronald L. Dotterer, 'Flann O'Brien, James Joyce and *The Dalkey Archive*', *New Hibernia Review*, vol. 8, no. 2, Summer 2004, pp. 54–63.

41 Among Niall Montgomery's papers in the National Library of Ireland are drafts of *Cruiskeen Lawn* columns dating mainly from mid-1947 to late-1949. Running at a rate of two volumes per year, with the first surviving file numbered volume fourteen, the collection indicates that he was contributing regularly to the column from an early stage. Of the eleven published pieces referring wholly or partly to Joyce in this period, seven were written by Montgomery.

42 Letter from Brian O'Nolan to Ethel Mannin (14 July 1939), SIUC.

43 Seán O'Faoláin, 'Irish Gasconade', *John O'London's Weekly* (24 March 1939), p. 970; cited in Cronin, *No Laughing Matter*, p. 92.

44 Niall Sheridan, 'The Joyce Country', *Ireland Today*, vol. 2, no. 11, November 1937, p. 88

45 See 'In Brathair Barnapas cct. Tri Filid in Domain Homer O Grecaip, Fergil O Latinnip ocus Parnabus O Gaedelaip', *The National Student/Comhthrom Féinne*, vol. 2, no. 3, June 1935, pp. 80, 83, and 'Pisa bec oc Parnabus. Extractum O Bhark I bPragrais le Briain O Nuallain', *Ireland Today*, vol. 3, February 1938, pp. 138, 165. One *Cruiskeen Lawn* column claims an attempt in 1951 to translate *Ulysses* into

Irish: 'If they won't read it in English, I said to myself, bedamn but we'll put them in the situation that they can boast they won't read it in Irish aither.' (*HD*, 135).

46 This emphasis was anticipated by Thomas MacGreevy in his insistence on the 'deep-rooted Catholicism' of *Ulysses*. 'The Catholic Element in *Work in Progress*' in *An Exagmination Round his Factification for Incamination of Work in Progress* (New York: New Directions, 1929, 1972), p. 121.

47 O'Nolan himself typified this tendency: 'It seems to me that Joyce emerges, through curtains of salacity and blasphemy, as a truly fear-shaken Irish Catholic, rebelling not so much against the Church but against its near-schism Irish eccentricities . . . His revolt, noble in itself, carried him away. He could not see the tree for the woods. But I think he meant well. We all do, anyway.' 'A Bash in the Tunnel', in John Ryan (ed.), *A Bash in the Tunnel: James Joyce by the Irish* (Brighton: Clifton Books, 1970), p. 19.

48 ibid., p. 19.

49 *CL* (6 June 1957), cited in David Powell, 'An Annotated Bibliography of Myles na Gopaleen's (Flann O'Brien's) "Cruiskeen Lawn" Commentaries on Joyce', *James Joyce Quarterly*, vol. 9, no. 1, Fall 1971, pp. 56–57.

50 Lanters, *Unauthorized Versions*, p. 7.

51 Brian Nolan, 'A Bash in the Tunnel', in *A Bash in the Tunnel*, p. 17.

52 ibid., p. 18.

53 Samuel Beckett, 'Recent Irish Poetry', *Disjecta* (London: John Calder, 1983), p. 70.

54 Niall Sheridan, 'Brian, Flann and Myles', in *Myles: Portraits of Brian O'Nolan*, p. 39.

55 Cronin, *No Laughing Matter*, p. 52.

56 Seon Givens (ed.), *James Joyce: Two Decades of Criticism* (New York: Vanguard Press, 1948), cited in *CL* (18 August 1948).

57 *CL* (18 August 1948). Original dated 5 August 1948, Cruiskeen Lawn File, Vol. 16, Niall Montgomery Papers, National Library of Ireland. These will hereafter be referred to as NM.

58 Myles na gCopaleen, 'Baudelaire and Kavanagh', *Envoy*, no. 3, 1950, p. 79.

59 *CL* (16 June 1954).

60 ibid.

61 *CL* (5 April 1944).

62 Myles remarked of Jack Yeats that 'Unlike Joyce he was not an abominable prig and expressed himself freely instead of taking refuge in Joyce's peculiar form of "silence".' *CL* (11 April 1957), cited in Powell, 'An Annotated Bibliography', p. 56.

63 Garvin was a colleague and friend of O'Nolan's in the Department of Local Government who supplied *At Swim-Two-Birds* with its Greek epigraph.

64 The ellipses are original. John Garvin, *James Joyce's Disunited Kingdom and the Irish Dimension* (Dublin: Gill & Macmillan, 1976), pp. 100–101.

65 James Joyce, 'The Day of the Rabblement', Kevin Barry (ed.), *Occasional, Critical, and Political Writing* (Oxford: OUP, 2000), p. 50.

66 John Eglinton, *Irish Literary Portraits* (London: Macmillan, 1935), p. 135.

67 ibid., pp. 142–143.

68 Stephen Gwynn, *Irish Literature and Drama* (New York: Nelson & Sons, 1936), p. 192.

69 ibid., p. 195.

70 Aodh de Blácam, *A First Book of Irish Literature*, (New York, London: Kennikat, 1934, 1970), p. 225. De Blácam was a favourite target of O'Nolan's: 'He invented a fabulous world of whangs (leather boot-laces), boxty, poundies, crubeens, sheelamagoorlas, fairy mounds, crassogues, patterns, the Mountains of Mourne, *mo phiopa goirid dom* – a frightening apparatus' (*HD*, 103).

71   De Blácam, *A First Book of Irish Literature*, p. 218.
72   Of O'Connor's early support for 'Work in Progress' see 'Joyce – The Third Period', *Irish Statesman* (12 April 1930); reprinted in Robert H. Deming (ed.), *James Joyce: The Critical Heritage*, 2 vols. (London: Routledge & Kegan Paul, 1970), vol. 2, p. 516.
73   See the 1922 revised edition of Ernest Boyd's *Ireland's Literary Renaissance*, where *Ulysses* is described as 'a masterpiece of realism, of documentation, and a most original dissection of the Irish mind', cited in Robert H. Deming (ed.), *James Joyce: The Critical Heritage*, 2 vols. (London: Routledge & Kegan Paul, 1970), vol. 1, p. 304.
74   Joseph Hone, 'A Letter from Ireland', *London Mercury* (January 1923); reprinted in *James Joyce: The Critical Heritage*, vol. 1, p. 298.
75   Seán O'Faoláin, 'Style and Limitations of Speech', *Criterion*, vol. 4, September 1928, p. 86.
76   Seán O'Faoláin, 'This Is Your Magazine', *The Bell*, vol. 1, no. 1, October 1940, p. 5.
77   Frank O'Connor, 'A Broadcast that was Cancelled: Lawrence and Joyce', *The Irish Times* (21 July 1937). This was written as a lecture for the 'Great Writers of Today' series on Radió Éireann, which was never broadcast.
78   Frank O'Connor, 'James Joyce – A Post-Mortem', *The Bell*, vol. 5, no. 5, February 1943, p. 371.
79   CL (16 June 1954). Yet it was O'Nolan and friends (Anthony Cronin, Patrick Kavanagh and others) who decided to mark the fortieth anniversary of Bloom's travels with the first literary pilgrimage around Dublin.
80   Brian Nolan, 'A Bash in the Tunnel', p. 15.
81   CL (6 June 1957); cited in Powell, 'An Annotated Bibliography', pp. 56–57.
82   Seán O'Faoláin, 'Don Quixote O'Flaherty', *London Mercury*, vol. 37, no. 218, December 1937, p. 175.
83   CL (21 March 1944); reprinted in *FW*, pp. 121–122.
84   Herbert Read, 'On Subjective Art', *The Bell*, vol.7, no. 5, February 1944, p. 425.
85   'Finnegans Wake by reason of language and image left a sort of Wake Island in the sea of literature, yet today it is regarded as a towering *chef d'oeuvre*, used by some people as a prayer book – and indeed I have heard its author referred to as St James'. CL (22 December 1964), cited in Powell, 'An Annotated Bibliography', pp. 61–62.
86   CL (18 March 1944); cited in ibid., p. 51.
87   CL (1 September 1944); reprinted in *BM*, p. 256.
88   CL (9 February 1956); cited in Powell, 'An Annotated Bibliography', p. 55.
89   CL (21 March 1944).
90   Cronin, *No Laughing Matter*, p. 52.
91   J.C.C. Mays, 'Brian O'Nolan and Joyce on Art and on Life', *James Joyce Quarterly*, vol. 11, no. 3, Spring 1974, p. 249.
92   ibid., p. 242.
93   Frank O'Connor, *The Irish Times* (3 October 1938) and Seán O'Faoláin, ibid. (12 October 1938).
94   Frank O'Connor, ibid. (12 October 1938).
95   Seán O'Faoláin, ibid. (15 October 1938).
96   Flann O'Brien, ibid. (15 October 1938).
97   Letter from Brian O'Nolan to James Montgomery (9 December 1938), NM.
98   Flann O'Brien, ibid. (8 November 1938). Ironically, O'Faoláin argued that writers should 'ignore such things as the censorship, which was merely the tool of vested

interests, and devote themselves to their own undisturbed vision of life'. 'Modern Novels Criticised', ibid. (5 November 1938). But Edward Garnett's introduction to his debut collection of stories, *Midsummer Night Madness,* in which he declared that the Irish were 'the most backward nation in Europe', the 'most indifferent to literature and art, and least aware of critical standards' no doubt stuck with O'Faoláin. (London: Macmillan, 1932), p. 11.

99 Hazel Ellis Warren, ibid. (10 November 1938). The point was echoed the following day by 'Mumbo-Jumbo', while another Hazel Ellis (whose play was being produced in the Gate that week) denied responsibility for the letter.

100 Flann O'Brien, ibid. (11 January 1939).

101 Frank O'Connor, ibid. (13 January 1939). O'Faoláin declined to reply to O'Brien, but he instead accused *The Irish Times* drama critic, David Sears, of playing the plain man: 'I'm only a plain reporter,/I'm only a simple guy,/I'd wear my hair much shorter/If my brow got any more high'. (13 January 1939).

102 Donohue, *The Irish Anatomist,* pp. 16–17.

103 Letter from Niall Montgomery to 'Thomas' (16 January 1939), NM.

104 Flann O'Brien appeared a week before O'Nolan's agents enquired about a pseudonym. A.M. Heath (19 October 1938), SIUC. 'Flann O'Brien' also denied authorship of the forthcoming *At Swim-Two-Birds* in *The Irish Press*: 'the supposed book is anti-clerical, blasphemous, and licentious and various lengthy extracts from it have been concocted to show the obscenity of the work'. Letter to *The Irish Press* (4 January 1939).

105 Letter to Longman's (15 January 1939), SIUC. On hearing that his publisher was to meet O'Faoláin, O'Nolan wrote: 'I believe O'Faoláin is a decent man but when he begins to write letters to the paper on the subject of Art he becomes the most unspeakable boob possible without a glimmer of humour ... I don't know whether O'Faoláin knows who I am but I would be glad if you would give him no information. He has already denounced me as a public sewer and a rapscallion and anything you say might be taken down in evidence ...' Letter to T.F. Burns, Longman's (6 February 1939), SIUC.

106 Seán O'Faoláin, 'Irish Gasconade', *John O'London's Weekly* (24 March 1939), p. 970.

107 Oscar Love, ibid. (10 January 1939).

108 Oscar Love, ibid. (12 January 1939). He returned later to the same theme: ibid. (18 October 1945) and (7 November 1945). O'Nolan's whereabouts in the early months of 1934 are notoriously vague, his biographers generally supposing him to be on an academic exchange in Germany from December 1933 to June 1934. Judging from his contributions to *Comhthrom Féinne,* Cronin finds this unlikely, arguing the trip likely lasted only a few weeks. *No Laughing Matter,* pp. 67–68.

109 Niall Sheridan, 'Brian, Flann and Myles', in *Myles: Portraits of Brian O'Nolan,* p. 49. Multiple authorship is asserted by Cronin, *No Laughing Matter,* p. 107 and Clissmann, *Flann O'Brien: A Critical Introduction,* p. 19. Donohue includes Niall Montgomery too, *The Irish Anatomist,* p. 15.

110 In the 1940s, a Lir O'Connor (a veteran of the letter controversies) contributed some articles to the *The Irish Times,* though their blandness leaves their attribution open to question. In the 1950s, O'Nolan also wrote as Jimmy Cunning for *The Irish Pictorial Times,* as George Knowall for *The Nationalist and Leinster Times (Carlow),* as John James Doe for *The Southern Star,* and as Matt Duffy for *The Sunday Review.*

111 In a diary entry on 11 January 1943 O'Nolan recorded that Edwards and MacLiammóir were still unhappy with the first act, most of which had been written by Niall Montgomery. 1943 diary, SIUC.

112 From January 1939 onwards he maintained a low level of nonsense correspondence. See Donohue, *The Irish Anatomist*, pp. 18–19. Another outing was prompted by a complaint that an exemplary production of *Three Sisters* was not receiving public support. Flann O'Brien agreed that 'overmuch Gaelic and Christianity', combined with the lure of 'exotic picture palaces' was taking its toll on theatre audiences. Flann O'Brien, *The Irish Times* (4 June 1940); reprinted in *MBM*, pp. 187–188. His mockery of the literary Dubliner launched a long correspondence on the dear dead days of the well-bred *litterateur*, involving anecdotes on Conrad, Lamb, Dostoyevsky (aka 'Flann Doyle, born and raised in Goatstown') and others. 'Whit Cassidy', ibid. (13 June 1940); reprinted in *MBM*, p. 196.

113 Patrick Kavanagh, *The Irish Times* (20 July 1940); *MBM*. p. 203.

114 F. O'Brien, ibid. (29 July 1940), *MBM*, p. 207.

115 Patrick Kavanagh, ibid. (7 August 1940); *MBM*, p. 225. The sewer gag originated with Seán O'Faoláin.

116 '. . . having all but exhausted, with the exercise of much ingenuity, the subject of Irish content and Irish style, will he not now sit down and try his hand at writing an Irish novel?' Anon. 'Nest of Novelists', *Times Literary Supplement* (18 March 1939). See also Frank Swinnerton, 'Right Proportions', *Observer* (19 March 1939).

117 Benstock, 'The Three Faces of Brian O'Nolan', p. 65.

118 O'Nolan's situation bears comparison to that of George Orwell, also author and journalist. He was, like Orwell, 'living . . . at a time and within a class in which the whole practice of writing was problematic. In the confident middle class, intent on its version of practicality, writing was thought of as an impractical secondary activity, an alternative to 'doing something real'. . . an escape route was allowed at that point where the impractical activity had practical effects: that is to say, made money.' Raymond Williams, *Orwell* (London: Fontana, 1971), pp. 30–31.

2. THE GENESIS OF *AT SWIM-TWO-BIRDS*

1 Jorge Luis Borges, 'When Fiction Lives in Fiction', in Eliot Weingberger (ed.), *The Total Library: Non-Fiction, 1922–1986* (London: Allen Lane, 2000), p. 162.

2 On correspondences to Stephen Dedalus see Clissmann, *Flann O'Brien*, pp. 106–110 and Ivan Del Janik, 'Flann O'Brien: The Novelist as Critic', *Eire-Ireland*, vol. 4, no. 4, Winter, 1969, 64–72.

3 See Terence Brown, 'The Counter-Revival: Provincialism and Censorship 1930–65', in Seamus Deane (ed.), *The Field Day Anthology of Irish Writing*, 3 vols. (Derry: Field Day, 1991), vol. 3, pp. 89–93. Interestingly, at the time of publication *The Irish Times* called *At Swim* 'a jeu d'esprit' which was written with 'verve' and 'gusto'. Anon. 'Irish Author's Experiment. Erudite Humour in Novel Form', *The Irish Times* (25 March 1939). It was not until its re-issue in 1960 that the novel was overlaid with the disappointments of Ireland's mid-century, as well as the disappointments of O'Nolan's later career. See John Jordan, 'The Saddest Book Ever to Come Out of Ireland', *Hibernia* (5 August 1960), p. 5.

4 See Ruth ap Roberts, '*At Swim-Two-Birds* and the Novel as Self-Evident Sham', *Éire-Ireland*, vol. 5, no. 2, Summer 1971, 76–97; David Cohen, 'An Atomy of the Novel: Flann O'Brien's *At Swim-Two-Birds*', *Twentieth-Century Literature*, vol. 39, no. 2, Summer 1993, 208–229; Monique Gallagher, 'Reflecting Mirrors in Flann

O'Brien's *At Swim-Two-Birds*', *The Journal of Narrative Technique*, vol. 22, no. 2, Spring 1992, 128–135; Keith Hopper, *Flann O'Brien: A Portrait of the Artist as a Young Post-modernist*.

5   Niall Sheridan, 'Brian, Flann and Myles' in *Myles: Portraits of Brian O'Nolan*, pp. 41–44. The title travesties the Fianna Fáil party, the 'Soldiers of Destiny'.

6   Even the central conceit of *At Swim* is not wholly O'Nolan's own. The Flann O'Brien collection in Boston College includes an undated notebook belonging to his father containing outlines for stories and plays; like his son's work, these sketches all hinge on a clever conceit or punchline, and many posit an unsteady boundary between fiction and reality. In 'Six Authors in Search of a Character', a man keeps a register of unused characters (from writers such as Shakespeare), for consultation by aspiring authors. In many other stories, acting, or playing games, transgresses into real life. One story has it that whatever a man imagines comes true; in another: 'A madman (not so very mad, though) collars all the lady novelists he can lay hands on – or all their characters . . .'.

7   Hugh Kenner, *Flaubert, Joyce and Beckett: The Stoic Comedians*. London: W.H. Allen, 1964, pp. 34–35.

8   Letter to A.M. Heath (3 October 1938), SIUC.

9   There are two surviving manuscripts of *At Swim-Two-Birds*, both undated, which are held in the Harry Ransom Research Center, University of Texas. The longer, earlier manuscript (MS1) appears to date from a late stage of composition, the second (MS2) largely corresponds to the published text. MS1, p. 206.

10 Frank Swinnerton, 'Right Proportions', *Observer* (19 March 1939).

11 Declan Kiberd, 'Gaelic Absurdism: *At Swim-Two-Birds*', *Irish Classics* (London: Granta, 2000), p. 507. Cathal Ó Háinle argues that the fact that the Sweeny poetry turns up amidst a haphazard collection of literary styles and registers gives it a bizarre quality of its own. 'Fionn and Suibhne in *At Swim-Two-Birds*', p. 42.

12 Most obvious are the novel's debts to the 'Cyclops' episode of *Ulysses*, with its parodies of revivalese, its frequent interpolations, the juxtaposition of mythic heroes with the reality of contemporary Dublin, and the constant alternation between the style of written and oral narratives. *At Swim*'s treatment of Finn MacCool in particular recalls Joyce's strategies, as O'Nolan elaborates the peculiar Victorianese which infected Standish Hayes O'Grady's translations of Fianna tales in *Silva Gadelica* (London: Williams & Norgate, 1892).

13 R.P. Lehmann, 'A Study of the *Buile Suibhne*', *Études Celt*, vol. 7, p. 136, cited in Pádraig Ó Riain, 'The Materials and Provenance of Buile Suibhne', *Éigse*, vol. 15, no. 3, Summer 1974, p. 187.

14 J.G. O'Keeffe, *Buile Suibhne* (London: Irish Texts Society, 1913), p. xxxiv.

15 Gerard Murphy, *The Ossianic Lore and Romantic Tales of Medieval Ireland* (Dublin: Three Candles, 1955), p. 25, cited in Ó Riain, 'The Materials and Provenance of Buile Suibhne', p. 173.

16 In his study of the manuscripts, Samuel Anderson argues that *At Swim* developed in two stages, its first incarnation being 'a long continuous story about the characters in the Narrator's novel', with the student's biographical reminiscences being added later. 'Pink Paper and the Composition of Flann O'Brien's *At Swim-Two-Birds*' (Louisiana State University, unpublished MA thesis, 2002), p. 28. *At Swim* might be as much the record of a brilliant piece of editing as anything else.

17 Letter from Niall Montgomery to 'Thomas' (16 January 1939), NM.

18 O'Keeffe, *Buile Suibhne*, p. xxxvi.

19 Naomi Mitchison, 'We're Writing a Book', *New Masses* (September 1936), cited in

Valentine Cunningham, *British Writers of the 1930s* (Oxford: Oxford University Press, 1988), p. 327.

20 See Joseph Brooker, *Flann O'Brien* (London: Northcote, 2005), p. 43.

21 Cunningham, *British Writers of the 1930s*, p. 334.

22 For revisionist accounts of the Irish cultural scene in the 1930s see Brian Fallon, *An Age of Innocence: Irish Culture 1930–1960* (Dublin: Gill & Macmillan, 1998) and Allan Gillis, *Irish Poetry of the 1930s* (Oxford: OUP, 2005).

23 Sheridan, 'Brian, Flann and Myles' in *Myles: Portraits of Brian O'Nolan*, p. 44.

24 In 1935, Niall Sheridan referred in *Comhthrom Féinne* to the novel O'Nolan had just begun. 'Literary Antecedents', *Comhthrom Féinne*, vol. 11, no. 3, June 1935, p. 63. However, in 'The Poultry Business', an unpublished article written on the 1960 re-issue of *At Swim*, O'Nolan referred to the novel being composed around 1937. BC.

25 Brian Ó Nualláin, *Tráchtas ar Nádúir-fhilíocht na Gaedhilge* (UCD, unpublished MA thesis, 1934). O'Nolan's contribution to a history of UCD effectively repeats the student's description of his college. See Brian O'Nolan, 'The Last of the Old Physics', in James Meenan (ed.), *A Centenary History of the Literary and Historical Society of University College Dublin, 1855–1955* (Tralee: Kerryman, 1956), p. 240, and *ASTB*, p. 33.

26 Niall Sheridan 'Literary Antecedents' (1935), p. 63.

27 Niall Sheridan, 'Ad Lesbiam', in Niall Sheridan, Donagh MacDonagh, *Twenty Poems* (Dublin, 1934), p. 7. See *ASTB*, p. 38.

28 Sheridan, Brian, Flann and Myles' in *Myles: Portraits of Brian O'Nolan*, p. 45. See *ASTB*, p. 37.

29 Clissmann, *Flann O'Brien*, p. 105.

30 Timothy Corcoran (ed.), *The National University Handbook 1908–1932* (Dublin: Sign of the Three Candles, 1932), p. 67.

31 At a Home Rule rally in March 1912, Hyde, Bergin, and Eoin MacNeill shared one of four official platforms as representatives of the Faculty of Celtic Studies. Brian Ó Cuív, 'Irish Language and Literature, 1845–1921' in W.E. Vaughan (ed.), *A New History of Ireland*, 9 vols. (Oxford: Clarendon, 1996), vol. 6, p. 410.

32 Cited in Tomás Ó Fiaich, 'The Great Controversy' in Seán Ó Tuama (ed.), *The Gaelic League Idea* (Cork: Mercier, 1972), p. 70.

33 Corcoran, *The National University Handbook 1908–1932*, p. 107.

34 See Cronin, *No Laughing Matter*, pp. 50–52. Indeed, many wholly supported it. The contentious 1935 Public Dance Halls Act was passionately defended in the college magazine, which disdainfully referred to the 'wanton orgies which we have eagerly borrowed from debased and bestial peoples.' Sean D. O Cahtlain, 'To Hell with the Devil's Rhythm!', *The National Student*, vol. 13, no. 2, November 1935, p. 38.

35 T.D. Williams, 'The College and the Nation', in Michael Tierney (ed.), *Struggle With Fortune* (Dublin: Browne & Nolan, 1954), p. 187.

36 O'Nolan's first contribution to *Comhthrom Féinne* was on this subject. Brian Ó Nualláin, 'Caoimhghín de Barra', *Comhthrom Féinne*, vol. 2, no. 1, 13 November 1931, p. 77. The Kevin Barry window was finally erected in 1936.

37 *Comhthrom Féinne*, vol. 9, no. 3, December 1934. See Donal McCartney, *UCD, A National Idea* (Dublin: Gill & Macmillan, 1999), pp. 165–166.

38 J.J. O'Connell, *The National Student* (May 1910); cited in McCartney, *UCD: A National Idea*, p. 58.

39 Prof. Robert Donovan, of UCD's English Department, was chairman of the 1926

Committee on Evil Literature which ushered in the 1929 Censorship Act. The subsequent Censorship Board had five members, with UCD academics featuring prominently. ibid., p. 174.

40   Anon. 'The Reincarnation of Brother Barnabas', *The Irish Times* (8 May 1939).

41   Niall Sheridan, 'Literary Antecedents', *Comhthrom Féinne*, vol. 11, no. 3, June 1935, p. 62.

42   A contributor who had clashed swords with O'Nolan over his irreverent contributions to L&H debates attacked the influence of his circle on the magazine: 'it seems to be our misfortune that the antics of this literary menagerie is taken for the attitude of all. Whereas, in fact, the menagerie in question does not represent any section of the students . . .' James T. Fitzpatrick, 'The College Magazine With the Lid off!', *The National Student*, vol. 13, no.1, October 1935, p. 11.

43   Niall Sheridan, 'Brian, Flann and Myles' in *Myles: Portraits of Brian O'Nolan*, p. 35.

44   Samuel Hall's first play starred Allen Bogg, his wife, and a bog-trotter. 'The Bog of Allen', *Comhthrom Féinne*, vol. 5, no. 3, March 1933; reprinted in *MBM*, p. 40. He also founded 'University College Ballybrack' and returned to drama by popular demand in a piece signed by Ciarán Ó Nualláin: 'The West's Awake', *Comhthrom Féinne*, vol. 5, no. 4, May 1933, pp. 66–67. The brothers worked the same vein of humour, later collaborating on *Blather*. Ciarán even anticipated *At Swim* in an interview with Finn MacCool, who was now living in a Rathmines boarding-house and had an ambition to open a sweetshop in Cabra (like *At Swim*'s 'villain', John Furriskey). 'The Return of Finn', *Comhthrom Féinne*, vol. 11, no. 1, April 1935, 8–9.

45   ibid., vol. 1, no. 2, 15 May 1931, 31–32.

46   ibid., vol. 11, no. 3, June 1935, 80, 83.

47   ibid., vol. 11, no. 2, May 1935, p. 25.

48   '. . . we made an effort to make the magazine the organ of student opinion and humour – not forgetting the former or over stressing the latter.' *The National Student*, vol. 13, no. 1, October 1935, p. 2.

49   Brother Barnabas, 'A Brass Hat in Bannow Strand', *Comhthrom Féinne*, vol. 7, no. 1, January 1934, pp. 12–13; reprinted in *MBM*, p. 74.

50   Charles Donnelly, 'Literature in Ireland', ibid., vol. 5, no. 4, May 1933, p. 65.

51   Daniel Corkery, *Synge and Anglo-Irish Literature* (Cork: Mercier, 1931, 1966), p. 16.

52   O'Nolan was named as editor of the February 1933 number and most editors continued in the post for three or four issues. Those published between February and October of that year certainly have a disproportionate amount of material that is obviously from his hand.

53   Donnelly, 'Literature in Ireland', p. 65.

54   *Comhthrom Féinne*, vol. 7, no. 1, January 1934, p. 1.

55   Donnelly, 'Literature in Ireland', p. 65.

56   'Bhíthear i gcomhnaidhe ag caoineadh Éireann ar a h-anbhroid agus ar a daoirse . . . Aon tagairt abhí do'n nádúir ins na h-aislingibh seo, sean-abairtí chríonna chaithte abhí ionnta, clichés a caitheadh isteach ar mhaithe le sean-nós litríochta, gan fuil gan fuinneamh gan míniú ionnta' ('They were always lamenting Ireland's bondage and oppression . . . Any allusions to nature in these *aisling* were made with old worn phrases, clichés thrown in for the sake of an old literary tradition, which had no passion or vigour or meaning.') Brian Ó Nualláin, '*Tráchtas ar Nádúir-Fhilíocht na Gaedhilge*', UCD, unpublished MA thesis, 1934, p. 16. My translation. According to O'Nolan, there was not much to be said for the verse of Eoin Rua Ó Súilleabháin as nature poetry, nor as poetry of any other kind.

57   University College Dublin, *Calendar 1931–32*, p. 193.

58 The contents page of one issue of *Blather* gives an indication of O'Nolan's opinion of de Blácam: 'The Night that Larry was Stretched, By Lord Longford. Whangs, Pishrogues and Banshees, By Aodh de Blacam. Paris with the Lid Off, By Blazes O'Blather. Cad Dheanaimis Feasta Gan Adhmad? By a Blueshirt. Banshees, Pishrogues and Whangs, By Aodh de Blacam. And Lots of Funny Pictures.' *Blather*, vol. 1, no. 5, January 1935, p. 85.

59 Aodh de Blácam, *Gaelic Literature Surveyed* (Dublin: Talbot, 1929, 1973), p. xi.

60 T.S. Eliot, 'Tradition and the Individual Talent', *Selected Essays* (London: Faber & Faber, 1934), p. 14.

61 The student cites the work of eighteenth-century poets, William Cowper and William Falconer, and borrows money from his uncle to buy Heine's *Die Harzreise*, another comic and ironic work, which was a set text for O'Nolan's BA course in German.

62 The Ringsend cowboys' tales are laced with Finn MacCool's coinages as well as the clichés of imperial adventure stories, see Clissmann, *Flann O'Brien*, p. 136. However, the true provenance of these latter-day heroes is more likely to be the Christian Brothers' paper *Our Boys* (which adapted the imperial *Boy's Own* for the Catholic schoolboy) than the Gaelic tradition. *Our Boys* was replete with cowboys with names like 'Sean and Donall, so the wild west could be transported to towns and villages in the Free State'. Elizabeth Russell, 'Holy Crosses, Guns and Roses: Themes in Popular Reading Material', in Joost Augusteijn (ed.), *Ireland in the 1930s* (Dublin: Four Courts Press, 1999), p. 25.

63 Kiberd, 'Gaelic Absurdism: *At Swim-Two-Birds*', p. 502.

64 '. . . Joyce spent a lifetime establishing himself as a character in fiction. Joyce created, in narcissus fascination, the ageless Stephen. Beginning with importing real characters into his books, he achieves the magnificent inversion of making them legendary and fictional . . .' Brian Nolan, 'A Bash in the Tunnel', p. 19.

65 James T. Fitzpatrick, 'The College Magazine With the Lid off!', *The National Student*, vol. 13, no. 1, October 1935, p. 10.

66 Donagh MacDonagh, 'The Cradle of Civilization', *Comhthrom Féinne*, vol. 6. no. 1, October 1933, p. 12.

67 Orlick deserves the criticism, but in the passage in question his pompous prose is reminiscent of the student: 'The refinements of physical agony . . . are limited by an ingenious arrangement of the cerebral mechanism and the sensory nerves which precludes from registration all emotions, sensations and perceptions abhorrent to the fastidious maintenance by Reason of its discipline and rule over the faculties and the functions of the body . . .' (*ASTB*, 168).

68 As Michael Adams reports, in the 1920s the Irish Vigilance Association directed its attention to the policing of newspaper and periodicals rather than books, because it was the 'mass mind' which it wished to protect, and the main threat was the cheap press. *Censorship: The Irish Experience* (Dublin: Scepter Books, 1968), p. 17. Part of the self-proclaimed remit of the Catholic Truth Society was to 'combat the pernicious influence of infidel and immoral publications by the circulation of *good, cheap and popular* Catholic literature', p. 19 (my italics).

69 F.R. Leavis, *Mass Civilisation and Minority Culture* (London: Arden, 1930, 1979), p. 12.

70 *CL* (20 December 1957); cited in David Powell, 'An Annotated Bibliography', p. 58.

71 Charles Duff, *James Joyce and the Plain Reader* (New York: Haskell House, 1932, 1971), p. 20.

72 Brian Ó Nualláin, 'What is Wrong With The L. and H.?', *Comhthrom Féinne*, vol. 10, no. 3, March 1935, 58–59. Frequent satire of literary pretension was a feature

of O'Nolan's humour from the earliest days of his career. A Brother Barnabas review of 'My Best Poems, by Donough Coffey' (an amalgam of the student poets Donagh MacDonagh and Brian Coffey) anticipates Myles na gCopaleen's treatment of *The Bell*: 'It is many years since we have seen anything so fine, so delicately wrought, so apparently aetherial yet actually substantial, so chaste and pure, so sympathetic, as the paper used in the printing of this book . . .' 'The Latest Books. Reviewed by Brother Barnabas', *Comhthrom Féinne*, vol. 2, no. 3, Christmas 1931, pp. 116–117.

73 Cronin, *No Laughing Matter*, p. 95.

74 By the autumn of 1940, *At Swim* had sold only 244 copies. ibid., p. 99.

75 Brian O'Nolan to Ethel Mannin (10 July 1939), SIUC.

76 Brian O'Nolan to Ethel Mannin (14 July 1939), SIUC. In 1955 O'Nolan approached the publishers of the Sexton Blake detective series offering his services and proposing to sketch an outline for a book, but there is no further correspondence on the matter. Brian O'Nolan to Mr Hale (16 October 1955), SIUC.

77 José Lanters argues that O'Nolan may have sent Mannin a copy because of her notoriety as a best-selling author banned in Ireland (Mannin herself declared that she had fought against the censorship of books such as *Ulysses*). *Unauthorized Versions*, pp. 196–197.

78 Original italics. Ethel Mannin in *The Bookworm's Turn*, cited in Q.D. Leavis, *Fiction and the Reading Public* (London: Chatto and Windus, 1932, 1965), pp. 24–25.

79 Niall Sheridan's description of the idea behind *Children of Destiny* makes this blatantly clear: 'A vast market was ready and waiting. Compulsory education had produced millions of semi-literates who were partial to 'a good read'. So it must be a big book, weighing at least two-and-a-half pounds. We must give them length without depth, splendour without style. Existing works would be plundered wholesale for material, and the ingredients of the saga would be mainly violence, patriotism, sex, religion, politics and the pursuit of money and power'. 'Brian, Flann and Myles', in *Myles: Portraits of Brian O'Nolan*, p. 42.

80 Lionel Johnson, 'Poetry and Patriotism', in *Poetry and Ireland: Essays by W.B. Yeats and Lionel Johnson* (Dublin: Cuala Press, 1908, 1970), p. 21.

81 Corkery, *Synge and Anglo-Irish Literature*, p. 16.

82 De Blácam, *Gaelic Literature Surveyed*, p. xii.

83 Letter from Brian O'Nolan to A.M. Heath (25 September 1938), SIUC.

84 Letter from Brian O'Nolan to Longman's (15 January 1939), SIUC.

85 Myles na gCopaleen, review of L.A.G. Strong, *The Sacred River: An Approach to James Joyce*, in *Irish Writing*, vol. 10, January 1950, p. 72.

86 Lanters, *Unauthorised Versions*, p. 190.

87 'The Poultry Business', BC.

88 *The Irish Press* (16 October 1940). Flann O'Brien had been invited to intervene in a letter controversy on the censorship issue, euphemistically billed as 'The Literary Conscience'.

89 'Academic Enterprise at Ballybrack', *Comhthrom Féinne*, vol. 5, no. 2, February 1933, pp. 28–29; reprinted in *MBM*, pp. 43–47. Donagh MacDonagh's contribution in this line was an Anti-Censor Ship, which, under the captaincy of Brian Ó Nualláin, peddled proscribed books and films off the Irish coast. Donagh MacDonagh, 'Legal Illegality: Amazing State of Affairs off Irish Coast', *Comhthrom Féinne*, vol. 6, no. 3, December 1933, 58–60.

90 Donohue, *The Irish Anatomist*, p. 38. Sheridan reports a similar outbreak when he requested O'Nolan to write a kind of Dublin *Decameron* for *Comhthrom Féinne* and

he did so, in Old Irish: 'I soon found myself summoned . . . on the rather unusual charge of publishing obscene matter, written in Old Irish, in the semi-official University organ'. 'Brian, Flann and Myles', *Myles: Portraits of Brian O'Nolan*, p. 37. However, there is no such article in *Comhthrom Féinne*.

91 Lanters provides a startling list of such topics turning up in *At Swim*: 'private acts' in lavatories, piss, excrement and vomit, male and female underwear . . . bodily functions and body parts (including buttocks, testicles and pubic hair), condoms, suicide, homosexuality, rape, incest, prostitution and abortion, artificial insemination, obscenities, expletives and dirty jokes, and graphic violence', *Unauthorized Versions*, p. 203.

92 Hopper, *Flann O'Brien*, p. 81.

93 MS2, p. 68. See *At Swim-Two-Birds*, p. 50.

94 Letter to A.M. Heath (25 September 1938), SIUC.

95 MS1, p. 82.

96 Anderson, 'Pink Paper and the Composition of Flann O'Brien's *At Swim-Two-Birds*', p. 38.

97 Letter to A.M. Heath (3 October 1938), SIUC.

98 'Immaculate conception' is mentioned four times in MS1. Anderson, 'Pink Paper and the Composition of Flann O'Brien's *At Swim-Two-Birds*', p. 25.

99 ibid., p. 60.

100 MS1, p. 24.

101 ibid., p. 22.

102 Myles Dillon, *Early Irish Literature* (Chicago: Chicago University Press, 1948), p. 40, cited in Eva Wappling, *Four Irish Legendary Figures in At Swim-Two-Birds* (Uppsala: Studia Anglistica Upsaliensis, 1984), p. 32.

103 O'Keeffe, *Buile Suibhne*, p. xxxiv.

104 MS1, p. 18.

105 ibid., p. 22.

106 ibid., p. 146.

107 ibid., p. 192.

108 ibid., p. 91.

109 O'Keeffe, *Buile Suibhne*, p. 35. See *ASTB*, p. 68.

110 Wappling, *Four Irish Legendary Figures in At Swim-Two-Birds*, p. 37.

111 MS1, n.p.

112 Judging by the range of titles O'Nolan offered them – 'Sweeny in the Trees', 'Sweet-Scented Manuscript', 'Truth is an Odd Number', 'Task-Master's Eye', 'Through an Angel's eye-lid' – the simple and irrelevant obscurity of 'At Swim-Two-Birds' may have been a large part of the attraction. Letter to A.M. Heath (3 October 1938), SIUC.

113 MS1, p. 228.

114 ibid., p. 232.

115 ibid., p. 233, p. 238.

116 The only other major excision was in the racist treatment of 'black skivvies' in Shanahan's cowboy story, including a reference to an 'inter-racial stud' designed to breed green men. MS1, p. 79.

117 'I had perceived (if the truth were told) that an analogy might be established by a cunning dialectician between my work and a certain other work to which I neglect to refer in detail . . .', ibid., pp. 67–68.

118 While an extract from a life of James Beatty provides a description of Trellis in the final text (*ASTB*, 30–31) there are many more in the earlier draft, all circulating around the theme of madness: a passage dealing with his wife's insanity (MS1, pp.

53–54), his son's 'nervous atrophy' and the calamitous effect of the shock of a second son's death (MS1, p. 62), as well as mention of Trellis's eccentric habit of securing nine seats at the theatre, where he would 'sit alone attired in a black cloak in the centre seat of his square, being at all times separated by at least the thickness of a seat from all others' MS1, p. 64.

119   ibid., p. 221. There is yet another reference to madness and literary composition in another excerpt from the Conspectus. ibid., p. 287.

120   O'Nolan's short stories are effectively extended gags, all supplied with a punchline, such as 'The Martyr's Crown', *Envoy*, vol. 1, no. 3, February 1950, pp. 57–62, on the man who was *born* for Ireland.

121   Luigi Pirandello, *On Humour*, Antonio Illiano and Daniel P. Testa (trans.) (Chapel Hill: University of North Carolina Press, 1974), p. 124. Charles Baudelaire expressed a similar theory: 'Laughter is the expression of a double, or contradictory, feeling . . .', 'On the Essence of Laughter', in Jonathan Mayne (ed.), *The Mirror of Art* (London: Phaidon, 1955), p. 143.

122   Pirandello, *On Humour*, p. 119.

123   See Linda Hutcheon, *A Theory of Parody: The Teachings of Twentieth-Century Art Forms* (New York and London: Methuen, 1985).

124   In O'Nolan's hands, O'Grady acquires shades of Myles: 'He seems to have had brushes with the staider servants of his day owing to his weakness for erudite multilingual puns and jokes, which were rarely construed in the manner intended by those to whom they were addressed.' Flann O'Brien, 'Standish Hayes O'Grady', *The Irish Times* (16 October 1940).

125   Linda Hutcheon identifies just such a duplicity at the heart of post-modern writing, where an inability to work free of a tradition in which the writer has little faith ends again and again in duplicitous parody. *The Politics of Postmodernism* (New York, London: Routledge, 1989), p. 8. On O'Nolan and post-modernism see Hopper, *Flann O'Brien* and also Kim McMullen, 'Culture as Colloquy – Flann O'Brien's Postmodern Dialogue with Irish Tradition', *Novel – A Forum on Fiction*, vol. 27, no. 1, 1993, pp. 62–84 and Joshua Esty, 'Flann O'Brien's At Swim-Two-Birds and the Post-Post Debate', *Ariel*, vol. 26, no. 4, October 1995, pp. 23–46.

126   Neil Corcoran, *After Yeats and Joyce* (Oxford: OUP, 1997), p. 23.

127   His introduction divides Irish nature poetry into two types – that which solely concerns the natural world, rather than the poet himself, and a later (inferior) poetry in which nature imagery is used to mirror the state of the poet's mind. On this topic, O'Nolan approvingly quotes Ruskin on Walter Scott: 'He conquers all tendencies to the 'pathetic fallacy' and instead of making Nature anywise subservient to himself, he makes himself subservient to Nature . . . and appears therefore at first shallower than other poets, being in reality wider and healthier.' *Modern Painters*, cited in Ó Nualláin, *Tráchtas ar Nádúir-fhilíocht na Gaedhilge*, p. 2.

128   See Lanters, *Unauthorized Versions*, Donohue, *The Irish Anatomist* and M. Keith Booker, *Flann O'Brien, Bakhtin and Menippean Satire*.

129   Gordon Henderson, 'An Interview With Mervyn Wall', *Journal of Irish Literature*, vol. 11, no. 1–2, January-May 1982, p. 7.

130   ibid.

3. 'NONSENSE IS A NEW SENSE'

1   Letter to Patience Ross of A.M. Heath (10 October 1939), SIUC.
2   Patience Ross to Brian O'Nolan (11 October 1939), SIUC.

3 Cronin, *No Laughing Matter*, p. 102. O'Nolan's stories were perhaps inspired by the fact that his American agents did lose their copy of the manuscript in early 1941. Letter from Harold Matson to Brian O'Nolan (27 March 1941), SIUC.

4 He possibly considered adapting the manuscript for a play in 1943, as William Saroyan earlier advised. Letter from Saroyan to O'Nolan (9 June 1940), BC. Mervyn Wall reports that O'Nolan dismissively showed the manuscript of *The Third Policeman* to some friends in 1959, but guesses that he 'apparently worked on it, disciplining and improving it beyond all measure' and that it was this revised version which was published in 1967. If that was the case, it is curious that O'Nolan did not attempt to have it published after the successful re-issue of *At Swim-Two-Birds* in 1960, and instead pillaged the manuscript for *The Dalkey Archive*. Mervyn Wall, 'A Nightmare of Humour and Horror', *Hibernia* (September 1967), p. 22, cited in Lanters, *Unauthorized Versions*, p. 206.

5 *CL* (20 August 1945); reprinted in *FW*, p. 172.

6 Letter from Patience Ross, A.M. Heath (11 March 1940), SIUC.

7 In *The Dalkey Archive*, the fantastic is contained within a reassuringly mundane universe, unlike *The Third Policeman*. Aside from this, it always maintains the possibility that these sojourns under the sea are the result of hallucinations – Mick in fact suspects that he has been drugged by de Selby. The airless cave in which de Selby conducts his supernatural meetings is evidently in Mick's thoughts as he imagines de Selby in a drunken state, 'clutched in the airless womb of liquor' (*DA*, 154).

8 Letter from Brian O'Nolan to William Saroyan (14 February 1940); reprinted in *TP*, p. 207.

9 Oscar Love, *The Irish Times* (18 October 1940).

10 ibid.

11 *CL* (15 March 1944); reprinted in *BM*, p. 248.

12 *CL* (8 May 1942); *BM*, p. 230. While it was banned in Ireland under the Emergency censorship, O'Nolan would have been able to view the film at a private club screening. The censor was similarly sensitive to the film's political satire, defending his decision to ban the film by asserting: 'If that picture had been shown in this country . . . it would have meant riots and bloodshed. I'm ab-sol-ute-ly convinced of that.' The Bellman, 'Meet Dr. Hayes: or The Genial Censor,' *The Bell*, vol. 3, no. 2, November 1941, p. 109.

13 *CL* (8 May 1942); *BM*, p. 231.

14 *The Hard Life* is unusual among these in being set in Dublin at the turn of the century, the period most associated with Joyce's fiction.

15 To Patience Ross, A.M. Heath (24 January 1940), SIUC. Once it was rejected by Longman's (who thought otherwise), he suggested they offer it to a publisher of mystery novels. To Patience Ross (16 March 1940), SIUC.

16 Oscar Love, *The Irish Times* (3 October 1940).

17 Letter to Patience Ross of A.M.Heath (10 October 1939), SIUC.

18 Lanters, *Unauthorized Versions*, p. 233.

19 Cronin, *No Laughing Matter*, p. 104.

20 Lanters, *Unauthorized Versions*, p. 233.

21 Hugh Kenner, 'The Fourth Policeman' in *Conjuring Complexities*, p. 66.

22 Author's note on *The Third Policeman* (*TP*, 20).

23 Hopper, *Flann O'Brien: A Portrait of the Artist as a Young Post-modernist*.

24 Brooker, *Flann O'Brien*, p. 59.

25 Kenner, 'The Fourth Policeman', p. 69.

26 José Lanters, '"Still Life" Versus Real Life: The English Writers of Brian O'Nolan', in Wim Tigges (ed.), *Explorations in the Field of Nonsense* (Amsterdam: Rodopi, 1989), p.162.

27 On nonsense and *The Third Policeman* see also Wim Tigges, 'Ireland in Wonderland: Flann O'Brien's *The Third Policeman* as a Nonsense Novel' in C.C. Barfoot and Theo d'Haen (eds.), *The Clash of Ireland* (Amsterdam: Rodopi, 1987), pp. 195–208.

28 Wim Tigges, *An Anatomy of Literary Nonsense* (Amsterdam: Rodopi, 1988), p. 55.

29 See Susan Stewart, *Nonsense: Aspects of Interetxtuality in Folklore and Literature* (Baltimore, London: John Hopkins, 1979).

30 The manuscript was returned to O'Nolan two weeks after *Cruiskeen Lawn* first appeared. Letter to Brian O'Nolan from Patience Ross (A.M.Heath), (1 November 1940), SIUC.

31 See Jean-Jacques Lecercle, *Philosophy of Nonsense: The Intuitions of Victorian Nonsense Writers* (London, New York: Routledge, 1994).

32 Interestingly, his brother Ciarán was at work on an Irish-language detective novel while O'Nolan was writing *At Swim*. *Oíche i nGleann na nGealt* was published by An Gúm in 1939.

33 Brooker, *Flann O'Brien*, p. 44.

34 J.C.C. Mays identifies de Selby with Huysman's aesthete, who feels that there is a correspondence between the sensual make-up of a person and the colour they respond to most strongly. 'Brian O'Nolan: Literalist of the Imagination', p. 92. On *Saltair na Rann* see Lanters, *Unauthorized Versions*, pp. 224–225. Swift records the theory of the Aeolists that '*man* brings with him into the world a peculiar portion or grain of wind, which may be called a *quinta essential* . . . This *quintessence* is of a catholic use upon all emergencies of life, is improveable into all arts and sciences, and may be wonderfully refined as well as enlarged, by certain methods in education.' *A Tale of a Tub* (Oxford: OUP, 1986), p. 73. Hence, his recommendation – as a matter of common courtesy – to break wind as often as possible.

35 Cited in J.H. Matthews, *Surrealism and the Novel* (Ann Arbor: University of Michigan Press, 1966), p. 3.

36 ibid., p. 4.

37 Jerry L. McGuire discusses the novel as a metafiction, 'Teasing After Death: Metatextuality in *The Third Policeman*', *Éire-Ireland*, vol.16, no. 2, Summer 1981, pp. 107–121, while Charles Kemnitz concocts a very involved allegory of contemporary physics, 'Beyond the Zone of Middle Dimensions: A Relativistic Reading of *The Third Policeman*', *Irish University Review*, vol. 15, no. 1, Spring 1985, pp. 56–72.

38 The novel was begun in August and delivered at the beginning of January: 'the whole thing has been done rather hastily. I have another copy which I will go over slowly and see what improvements can be made'. Letter to Patience Ross of A.M. Heath (24 January 1940), SIUC.

39 See author's note on *The Third Policeman* (*TP*, 207).

40 Susan Stewart points to the proliferation of legal trials in nonsense, citing both Lewis Carroll's *Alice's Adventures in Wonderland* and the closing trial of *At Swim-Two-Birds*: 'In nonsense the law becomes a procedure without content, the systematic and arbitrary application of rule without regard to context.' *Nonsense*, p. 192. On Myles's attraction to legal arcana, see Joseph Brooker, 'Estopped by Grand Playsaunce: Flann O'Brien's Post-colonial Lore', *Journal of Law and Society*, vol. 31 no. 1, March 2004, pp. 15–37.

41 Alice is also literally trapped at the end of her story, put on trial by the wonderland characters and left wholly at the mercy of the Queen of Hearts's wilfulness.

42 Theoretically, de Selby's experiment is sound, and according to Charles Kemnitz, it bears comparison with an experiment on the speed of light carried out with mirrors in the mid-1930s. Einstein hypothesized that if a man could stare in a mirror long enough for light to travel to the limit of the universe and back, he could watch the hair on the back of his head grow. 'Beyond the Zone of Middle Dimensions' (1985), p. 68.

43 Hopper, *Flann O'Brien*, p. 113.

44 Seamus Deane, *Strange Country: Modernity and Nationhood in Irish Writing Since 1790* (Oxford: Clarendon, 1997), p. 161.

45 Louis Aragon, 'Lewis Carroll. En 1931', *Le Surréalisme au service de la révolution* (1931), p. 25. The translation quoted here is Philip Thody's, from 'Lewis Carroll and the Surrealists', *Twentieth-Century*, May 1958, p. 429. André Breton also included Carroll in his *Anthologie de l'humour noir* (1939), while Aragon translated 'The Hunting of the Snark' in 1929. Michael Holquist, 'What is a Boojum? Nonsense and Modernism', *Yale French Studies*, no. 43, 1969, pp. 145–164.

46 Holquist, 'What is a Boojum? Nonsense and Modernism', p. 147.

47 However, quite apart from Aragon's claims for the political subversiveness of surrealism, there is an element of surrealist nightmare about *The Third Policeman*: the pump which Divney uses to kill Mathers undergoes a dream-like transformation, echoed in the policemen's obsession with bicycles. The narrator's state of mind at stressful points also evokes disturbingly surrealist images, like the oil lamp in Mathers's house which has 'a glass bowl with the wick dimly visible inside it, curling in convolutions like an intestine' (*TP*, 25) or the metamorphosis of Pluck's pipe when he proposes a hanging: 'when he stuck it in his face it looked like a great hatchet' (*TP*, 102).

48 Henkle, *Comedy and Culture. England 1820–1900*, p. 215.

49 ibid., p. 247.

50 Deane, *Strange Country*, p. 162.

51 Lecercle, *Philosophy of Nonsense*, pp. 195–196.

52 ibid., pp. 2–3. Admittedly, Lecercle's main point of reference in discussing Victorian nonsense is Lewis Carroll, whose clash between personality and literary persona perfectly exemplifies the theory.

53 ibid., p. 25.

54 Hopper, *Flann O'Brien*, p. 78. In contrast, Susan Stewart argues that nonsense manages 'an exposure of metonymic relationships as purely systematic, as having no context outside of their own conventions', *Nonsense*, p. 33.

55 Hopper, *Flann O'Brien*, p. 98. Andrea Bobotis turns this reading on its head, arguing that the *The Third Policeman*'s 'anti-teleological agenda challenges normative notions of gender and sexuality, and, in turn, the narrative's conspicuous misogyny.' 'Queering Knowledge in Flann O'Brien's *The Third Policeman*', *Irish University Review*, vol. 32, no. 2, Autumn/Winter 2002, p. 245. There is no good reason for assuming that Pluck's bicycle is female, it is just as likely to be a cross-dresser, p. 249.

56 Hopper, *Flann O'Brien*, p. 96.

57 Claire Wills, *That Neutral Island: A Cultural History of Ireland During the Second World War* (London: Faber & Faber, 2007), p. 265.

58 With music by Bell Helicopter, *Improbable Frequency* was produced by Rough Magic at the Abbey Theatre in 2005. Arthur Riordan, *Improbable Frequency* (London: Nick Hern, 2005).

59 For example, in Jerry L. McGuire, 'Teasing After Death: Metatextuality in *The Third Policeman*', *Eire-Ireland*, vol. 16, no. 2, Summer 1981, pp. 107-121; Hopper, *Flann O'Brien*; David Cohen, 'Arranged by Wise Hands: Flann O'Brien's Metafictions', in *Conjuring Complexities*, pp. 57-60.

60 Bergson writes that the comic is a reaction against automatism in human behaviour: 'The attitudes, gestures and movements of the human body are laughable in exact proportion as that body reminds us of a mere machine.' 'Laughter' (1911) in Wylie Sypher (ed.), *Comedy* (Baltimore, London: John Hopkins University Press, 1980), p. 79.

61 Seamus Deane finds a similar quality in *Cruiskeen Lawn* characters like Keats and Chapman and The Plain People of Ireland: 'It is the predictability and the strangeness of their discourse that make it both familiar and alienated. In the pervasive banality that suffuse all, the surreal lurks . . .' *Strange Country*, p. 160.

62 Having produced samples, O'Nolan solicited help from James Montgomery, the film censor, in approaching Stephens after he was first turned down by An Gúm – apparently because the author was reluctant to approve a translation: 'He is probably right as far as the usual Gaelic writers are concerned but I would like to have a shot at it.' (9 December 1938), NM.

63 'Hugh Maxton' [W.J. McCormack], postscript to Daniil Kharms, *The Plummeting Old Woman*, Neil Cornwell (trans.) (Dublin: Lilliput, 1989), pp. 95-96.

64 O'Nolan must have liked the joke since he retained it verbatim in *The Dalkey Archive* (*DA*, 75).

65 Kenner, 'The Fourth Policeman', p. 65.

66 *CL* (22 December 1950); cited in Donohue, *The Irish Anatomist*, p. 151.

67 Francis Doherty, '*Watt* in an Irish Frame', *Irish University Review*, vol. 21, no. 2, Autumn 1991, p. 187.

68 Sighle Kennedy has drawn attention to similarities between the comedy of Beckett and O'Nolan, hinting at a common Irish well of frustration. Citation in 'The Devil and Holy Water – Samuel Beckett's *Murphy* and Flann O'Brien's *At Swim-Two-Birds*', in Raymond A. Porter and James D. Brady (eds.), *Modern Irish Literature* (New York: Iona College Press, 1972), p. 251.

69 Cited in J.C.C. Mays, 'Brian O'Nolan: Literalist of the Imagination' in *Myles: Portraits of Brian O'Nolan*, p. 80.

70 Tigges, *An Anatomy of Literary Nonsense*, p. 128.

71 ibid., p. 130.

72 Hopper, *Flann O'Brien*, p. 264.

73 Hugh Kenner, *Samuel Beckett: A Critical Study* (London: John Calder, 1961), p. 37.

74 Samuel Beckett, *Watt* (London: John Calder, 1953, 1976), p. 47.

75 Niall Montgomery, 'No Symbols Where None Intended', in *New World Writing* (New York: New American Library of World Literature, 1954), p. 326.

76 See Lois Gordon, *The World of Samuel Beckett, 1906-1946* (New Haven and London: Yale University Press, 1996), p. 24.

77 Brian Nolan, 'A Bash in the Tunnel', p. 15.

78 ibid., p. 20.

79 Cronin, *No Laughing Matter*, pp. 104-105.

80 Roland Knox, *God and the Atom* (London: Sheed & Ward, 1945).

81 Clive Hart cites *The Serial Universe* in relation to the idea of serial regress in *Finnegans Wake*. *Structure and Motif in Finnegans Wake* (London: Faber & Faber, 1962), p. 93. On O'Nolan's use of Dunne see Mary O'Toole, 'The Theory of Serialism in *The Third Policeman*', *Irish University Review*, vol. 18, no. 2, Autumn

1988, 215-225. When planning *The Dalkey Archive*, O'Nolan wrote to the publisher Timothy O'Keeffe that 'You may remember Dunne's two books, "An Experiment With Time" and "The Serial Universe", also views of Einstein and others. The idea is that time is as a great flat motionless sea. Time does not pass; it is we who pass. With this concept as basic, fantastic but coherent situations can easily be devised, and in effect the whole universe torn up in a monstrous comic debauch.' (21 September 1962), SIUC. A sub-heading in one early *Cruiskeen Lawn* column on Irish matters was 'An Eicspéirimint Bhit Teidhm'. *CL* (22 May 1943).

82 J.W. Dunne, *The Serial Universe* (London: Faber & Faber, 1934), p. 18
83 ibid., p. 34.
84 ibid., p. 36.
85 William Shakespeare, *Julius Caesar*, Act V, scene i.
86 Donohue, *The Irish Anatomist*, p. 66.
87 Clissmann, *Flann O'Brien*, pp. 354-355.
88 Author's note, reprinted in *TP*, p. 207.
89 'At times the otherworld is conceptualized as coterminous with the world of experience, as existing parallel to the Ireland known to mortals, but in another plane; the two worlds are permeable at special locations and special times.' Maria Tymoczko, *The Irish Ulysses* (California: Berkeley, 1994), pp. 180-181. Keith Hopper particularly draws parallels between *The Third Policeman* and the medieval epic *Immran Maile Duin/ The Voyage of Maeldoon*. *Flann O'Brien*, p. 235. *The Voyage of Maeldoon* inspired the sequence in Hunger-stack mountain in *An Béal Bocht*.
90 This hellish otherworld is perhaps the only one in which de Selby's theories could be true; the cyclical eternity in which you may 'walk ahead to reach the same place here without coming back' (*TP*, 139) recalls his theory that life is a uni-directional journey around a sausage-shaped earth, death occuring in the alternate direction (*TP*, 97-98).
91 George O'Brien, 'Contemporary prose in English: 1940-2000' in Margaret Kelleher and Philip O'Leary (eds.), *The Cambridge History of Irish Literature*, 2 vols. (Cambridge: Cambridge University Press, 2006), vol. 2, p. 435.
92 Lanters, *Unauthorized Verions*, p. 226.
93 At one point O'Faoláin voiced a suspicion about the reality of 'Flann O'Brien' – Flann responded by wondering whether such a preposterous person as 'Mr Sean O'Faolain' existed at all. 'Apologia Pro Vita Sewer', *The Irish Times* (16 January 1939). Montgomery, around the same time, was writing in as 'Francis O'Connor'. Letter to 'Thomas' (16 December 1939), NM.
94 *CL* (10 April 1957), cited in Powell, 'An Annotated Bibliography', p. 56.

4. IRISH MYLES

1 Vivian Mercier, *The Irish Comic Tradition* (Oxford: OUP, 1962), p. ix.
2 Michael Cronin, 'The Imaginary Gaeilgeoir,' *Graph*, no. 6, Summer 1989, p. 16.
3 Reg Hindley, *The Death of the Irish Language: A Qualified Obituary* (London: Routledge, 1990), pp. 212-213.
4 Ó Ciosáin, *Buried Alive: A Reply to* The Death of the Irish Language. (Baile Átha Cliath: Dáil Uí Cadhain, 1991), p. 24.
5 Letter from Brian O'Nolan to Seán O'Casey (13 April 1942), SIUC.
6 *CL* (23 April 1940), cited in Ó Conaire, *Myles na Gaeilge*, p. 81.
7 Cronin, *No Laughing Matter*, p. 53.

8   See F.É. 'Gaelic Publications of Interest', *Irish Literary Bulletin*, vol. 3, no. 2, March/April 1942, p. 22.

9   The first appeared on 10 November 1931. Five of these articles are reproduced in translation in *MBM*.

10   In *'Díoltas ar Ghallaibh sa Bhliain 2032!'* (Revenge on an Englishman in 2032), *Irish Press* (18 January 1932), an English tourist of the future is left at the mercy of a vengeful translator in an Irish-speaking Ireland. The same joke appears in *'Madraí an Gaedealtachta'* (The dogs of the Gaeltacht), *Blather*, vol. 1, no. 4, Christmas 1934, p. 78, p. 83, in which English is said to have once been the common language of Ireland.

11   This was the only period in O'Nolan's career when he consistently signed his own name, although he made two contributions to *Envoy* in the 1950s as 'Brian Nolan'.

12   Brian *'Léigheannta'* Ó Nualláin, 'The Little Opinions of our Ancestors', *Irish Press* (29 September 1932), p. 4. Another correspondent, 'Anti-umbug', protests against the compulsory teaching of English to children, since everyone knows it will be of no use when they leave the country.

13   Brian Ó Nualláin, 'The Arrival and Departure of John Bull', *Irish Press* (13 June 1932). This story is referred to in *At Swim* as 'the Churl in the Puce Great-coat' (*ASTB*, 18), and derives from *Silva Gadelica*'s translation of 'The Adventure of the Carle of the Drab Coat'.

14   Cronin, *No Laughing Matter*, p. 5.

15   One of these, *'Glór an tSíoraíocht'* [The Glory of Eternity], also inverts the position of the languages, claiming that English was the ancient language of the Gaels. *Comhthrom Féinne*, vol. 5, no. 3, March 1933, p. 51.

16   Brian Ua Nualláin, *'Aistear Pheadair Dhuibh'* (Peadar Dubh's Journey), *Inisfáil*, vol. 1, no. 1, March 1933, pp. 63–64.

17   ibid., p. 64. All translations are mine unless otherwise specified. Given that Peadar was born in a small, white-washed house in the corner of the glen (like *An Béal Bocht*'s Bónapárt Ó Cúnasa), it is ironic that the cover of *Inisfáil* itself drew on the same hackneyed imagery, its illustration showing a deserted west of Ireland landscape with a small, white-washed cottage in the corner of a glen.

18   Published in London 'to maintain a sympathetic contact between Irishmen living abroad', *Inisfáil*'s title recalled a Conradh na Gaeilge monthly which was published for Irish emigrants from 1904 to 1910. Where this gave accounts of League lectures and notices of its meetings, 1933's *Inisfáil* was less concerned with organisation than with advertising the cultural health of the Irish Free State.

19   By the 1940s, the Gaelic League was long past its peak. In 1922 there were 819 branches nationwide. Two years later, after the chaos of the civil war, only 139 remained. Hindley attributes much of the decline to the institutionalisation of the language revival, making voluntary effort seem less necessary. *The Death of the Irish Language*, p. 40.

20   Breandán Ó Conaire, 'Flann O'Brien, *An Béal Bocht* and Other Irish Matters,' *Irish University Review*, vol. 3, no. 2, Autumn 1973, p. 123. See also Terence Brown, *Ireland: A Social and Cultural History 1922–2002* (London: Harper Perennial, 2004), pp. 176–180.

21   The habitual anxiety expressed in Irish journals about whether the government was really 'serious about the language' was a favourite cliché of O'Nolan's. One *Cruiskeen Lawn* took issue with the comical Irish in a Gaelic League notice: '*Ní dóigh liom go bhfuil Connradh na Gaedhilge dairíribh i dtaobh na Gaedhilge agus is eagal liom nach bhfuil an Ghaedhilg dairíribh i dtaobh an chonnartha. Ag magadh faoi n-a chéile*

atáid araon . . .'/'I doubt whether the Gaelic League is serious about the Irish language and I'm afraid that the Irish language is not serious about the League. They're making fun of each other . . .' *CL* (18 December 1940).

22 *The Irish Times* (28 September 1940).

23 Seán Ua Dhuibhne, ibid. (1 October 1940).

24 Oscar Love, ibid. (3 October 1940).

25 *CL* (4 October 1940). The hackneyed Irish phrases betray the revival's emphasis on classical bardic poetry and the folk Irish of proverbs and 'common speech' (lit. 'the speech of the people').

26 'Vinegar Eel', *The Standard* (8 November 1940). In a public debate on the motion that 'the Anglo-Saxon element in Eire is detrimental to its well-being', Myles again came under attack: 'S. MacCoclainn, who spoke in the affirmative, said that *The Irish Times* had constantly opposed the revival of the Irish language, and the articles that now appeared in its columns in Irish were even more injurious. They constituted a menace and an attack perhaps more sinister than any that had yet appeared. Written in Irish, they were designed to prove the unsuitability, the inadequacy and the impracticality of the Irish language for modern needs. The scurrilous style in which they were written left the reader in no doubt of what was the ultimate object of the writer of those articles'. *The Irish Times* (21 November 1940).

27 Éamon Ó Ciosáin notes that when Coiste Gnótha (a committee of the Gaelic League) learned in 1930 that *The Irish Press* was to be founded, it demanded that half the paper be published in Irish. De Valera promised one Irish issue per week, which never materialised, but it still published more Irish than any of the other dailies. *An t-Éireannach* (Baile Átha Cliath: An Clóchomhar Tta, 1993), p. 39.

28 Lir O'Connor, *The Irish Times* (22 October 1940).

29 ibid. (17 October 1940). See Ó Conaire, *Myles na Gaeilge*, p. 50.

30 Jack O'Neill, *The Irish Times* (18 October 1940).

31 'A West-Briton-Nationalist', ibid. (17 October 1940).

32 Alan Malone, ibid. (17 October 1940).

33 Donohue, *The Irish Anatomist*, p. 90.

34 An ambition which inspired the reflection that: '*Má chuirtear stop leis an nós so, beidh mo mhuc ar muin na muice . . .*'/If no one puts a stop to this, my pig will be on the pig's back. *CL* (28 December 1940).

35 *CL* (26 March 1942).

36 *CL* (15 March 1941). The gilt badges are awarded to fluent speakers of Irish.

37 *CL* (3 November 1940). An '*iarrthóir*' is a petitioner, and '*tuismitheoir*' a parent. The satiric dictionary obviously imitates Flaubert's *Dictionnaire des idées reçues*. On Dinneen see also *CL* (8 February 1944); reprinted in *BM*, pp. 276–278.

38 *CL* (29 December 1943).

39 *CL* (23 October 1940). The pedantic joke would be repeated in *An Béal Bocht*.

40 Ó Laoghaire was certainly one of the revival's most prolific authors. Brian Ó Cuív notes that between 1893 and 1920, he published fifty-two books and over 1,000 articles. 'Irish Language and Literature, 1895–1921', p. 419.

41 *CL* (7 June 1945).

42 *CL* (5 August 1941).

43 Rev. Peter O'Leary, 'The True Model', *Irish Prose Composition* (Dublin: Irish Book Co., 1907), p. 3.

44 ibid., p. 5. O'Nolan might have agreed with Ó Laoghaire on the decrepitude of modern English prose – he often dissected the work of his fellow journalists, with

unflattering results – but his judgement lacked any of the same xenophobia. It is a sobering fact that Ó Laoghaire was hailed by Osborn Bergin as '*an Gaedheal ba Ghaelaighe aigne in nÉirinn*'/'the Gael with the most Gaelic mind in Ireland'. *An Branar* (August 1920), cited in Ó Conaire, *Myles na Gaeilge*, p. 41.

45   O'Leary, 'The False Cry of "Corruptions"' in *Irish Prose Composition*, p. 12.

46   For example, responding to an observation that while an average English speaker got by on a fund of 400 words, the Irish speaker's was closer to 4,000, Myles opined that 400,000 was closer to the mark. Furthermore: 'There is scarcely a single word in the Irish (barring, possibly, *Sasanach*) that is simple and explicit. Apart from words with endless shades of cognate meaning, there are many with so complete a spectrum of graduated ambiguity that each of them can be made to express two directly contrary meanings . . .' *CL* (11 November 1941); *BM*, p. 278.

47   The sub-title of *An Béal Bocht* – omitted from its English translation – is '*An Milleánach*' (*ABB*, 3). The translation of '*An Milleánach*' is Breandán Ó Conaire's.

48   See for example *CL* (8 February 1941).

49   Tomás Ó Criomhthainn, *An tOileánach* (1929, trans. 1934); Peig Sayers, *Peig* (1936); Muiris Ó Súilleabháin, *Fiche Blian ag Fás* (1933, trans. 1933).

50   Breandán Ó Conaire claims that the style of the 'Tales from Corkadorky' is based on Éamon Ó Tuathail's *Sgéalta Mhuintir Luinigh* (Dublin: Irish Folklore Institute, 1933). *Myles na Gaeilge*, p. 122.

51   These were published respectively in *CL* (18 February 1941) and *CL* (1 March 1941).

52   *CL* (5 June 1941).

53   *CL* (29 October 1942). O'Nolan detected a large degree of phoney in all these endeavours to revive an 'authentic' Irish culture: 'I know of no civilisation to which anything so self-conscious could be indigenous. Why go to the trouble of proving that you are Irish? Who has questioned this notorious fact? If, after all, *you* are not Irish, who is?' *CL* (23 October 1944), cited in Ó Conaire, *Myles na Gaeilge*, p. 82.

54   'Fadó, Fadó', *CL* (14 November 1941). Seán Buí is speaking in English, transliterated in Irish (which, in the original, is printed in Gaelic type). The Gaels' last response does the reverse, in Roman type.

55   Myles-na-Coppaleen originated as a minor character in Gerald Griffin's *The Collegians* (1829) but came to fame as a lachrymose comedian in Dion Boucicault's *The Colleen Bawn* (1860).

56   One *Cruiskeen Lawn* took issue with a book Frank O'Connor had produced on his travels around Ireland, called *Irish Miles*. Myles was unimpressed by his attempts to 'draw out' the country people he met: 'He tries to suggest that his relationship with these people is that of a scientist examining his specimens. Personally I am by no means so persuaded. I think the specimens have analytic powers at least as good as Mr O'Connor's but functioning much more efficiently, since the specimens are at home in their own kitchen . . . quite at ease and with judgment unimpaired by superciliousness. *What was said after Mr O'Connor left?* . . . Having read the book, why cannot the reader read the Other Book?' *CL* (7 July 1947); *FC*, pp. 107–108.

57   '. . . Tomás Ó Criomhthain . . . wrote in Irish what I seriously say is among the most important life-stories of this century, mainly for its account of custom, isolation, the savagery of island life, the gallantry of the islanders, but, above all, for the astonishing precision and beauty of the Irish itself . . .' *CL* (26 November 1962); cited in Donohue, *The Irish Anatomist*, p. 72.

58   Edward Hirsch, 'The Imaginary Irish Peasant', *PMLA*, no. 106, 1991, p. 1130.

59   *CL* (28 August 1942); *BM*, p. 235.

60   The account of Bónapárt's beating in school, when he fails to recognise his English name as 'Jams O'Donnell', is from *Caisleáin Óir*. As 'Jams O'Donnell', Bónapárt is a sort of generic Gael to the outsider (all his peers in school are called 'Jams O'Donnell', as is the man he replaces in prison), but he has no more individuality among the Gaels. The mark of the Gaels is that they seem to do everything '*go cneasta*'/'meekly', and a heavy sense of fatality lies over the book. When a Gael is not submitting (*go cneasta*) to the vicissitudes of fate, he is patiently setting his face towards eternity or dimly cogitating the wonders of the world ('*ag meabhrú iontas an tsaoil*' (*ABB*, 57)).

61   The £2 grant allocated for each English-speaking child is the mirror image of the grant which Thomas Derrig, the Minister for Education, introduced in 1933 to encourage the use of Irish in the home. The inspector's weak English is a reminder that many inspectors purported to examine children whose Irish was far better than their own. Bónapárt politely calls the inspector 'sor', which Patrick Power notes is also the Irish for 'sow' (*PM*, 38).

62   Aodh de Blácam, 'The Age-Lasting Peasant,' *The Capuchin Annual*, 1935, p. 257.

63   The Seanduine Liath is another descendant of *Caisleáin Óir*.

64   J.J. Lee notes that this didn't prove too popular with the electorate. *Ireland 1912–1985: Politics and Society* (Cambridge: Cambridge University Press, 1989), p. 241.

65   Fr Gearóid Ó Nualláin, *Duine Beatha a Thoil* (1950), cited in Ó Conaire, *Myles na Gaeilge*, p. 22.

66   O'Nolan satirises those who fetishised the Gaeltacht's isolation and insularity. *An Béal Bocht* opens with a map of the world as it appears to the people of Corca Dorcha (this is omitted from the English edition). Ireland, dominated by Corca Dorcha, the western islands and Sligo jail, is sandwiched between '*de odar saighd*' (money order offices, George Bernard Shaw) and '*thar lear*' (money order offices, New York, Boston, the sea-divided Gael). All directions on the compass of the facing page point west, and the view from Ó Cúnasa's window similarly manages to encompass all of Ireland's Gaeltachts, but nothing else (*PM*, 21).

67   Donna L. Wong, 'Following the Law of the Letter: Myles na gCopaleen's *An Béal Bocht*', *New Hibernia Review*, vol. 4, no. 3, Autumn 2000, p. 105. 'The gentlemen had fluent English from birth but they never practised this noble tongue in the presence of the Gaels lest, it seemed, the Gaels might pick up an odd word of it as a protection against the difficulties of life' (*PM*, 48). Ironically (and ineffectively) the Corkadorkians often piously invoke the Irish language itself '*mar dhíon ar dheacractaí an tsaoil*'/'as a defence against the difficulties of life' (*ABB*, 25, 40).

68   Cited in Ó Conaire, *Myles na Gaeilge*, p. 21.

69   Letter from Brian O'Nolan to 'Peggy' in Browne & Nolan (16 April 1941), BC. He wrote that the book would now satisfy even the most 'puritanical objections', but it was ultimately rejected by them. Ironically, no book in Irish was ever censored. One difference between the 1941 and revised 1964 editions of *An Béal Bocht* is that only the latter contains exclamations such as 'God bless us!'

70   The first edition, edited by An Seabhac (Pádraig Ó Siochfhradha) in 1929, omits certain episodes and preserves less of Ó Criomhthainn's idiom than that edited by his grandson, Pádraig Ua Maoileoin, see Máire Cruise O'Brien, 'An tOileánach' in John Jordan (ed.), *The Pleasures of Gaelic Literature* (Cork: Mercier, 1977).

71   The brackets indicate a phrase which O'Nolan added to the 1964 edition. Arguably, the original line was more pointed.

72   On the very first page of the text, Myles helpfully footnotes Bónapárt's references to '*dibheairseans*' [diversions] and '*haidbhintiurs*' [adventures] with their Irish

translations: '*scléip*' and '*eachtraí*'. This joke is repeated a number of times throughout the 1941 edition, many of which are omitted from the 1964 text.

73 The *Irish Independent*'s reviewer queried the pig in the house: L.O.R., '*Leabhar Nua*' (17 February 1942), and the *Sunday Independent*'s reviewer found Ambrós's stench in bad taste: E. de B., 'An Béal Bocht' (14 December 1941).

74 S.O'F., 'A New and Quaint Departure in Irish Literature, *The Nationalist and Munster Advertiser* (7 January 1942).

75 P. O'S. *The Bell* (February 1942), pp. 405–406.

76 Anon. 'Current Affairs', *The Leader* (27 December 1941).

77 CL (4 October 1954), reprinted in *HD*, p. 102.

78 Ó Criomhthainn wryly tells how he would have to make time for the visiting scholars after his day's work was done. Robin Flower, trans. *The Islandman* (Oxford: OUP, 1937, 2000), p. 224, p. 238.

79 Despite *An Béal Bocht*'s war on 'the poor mouth', it does recognise the truth underlying these writers' accounts of hardship. The visiting *gaeilgeoirí* compete to see who can talk most gaelically about the Gaelic cause, while all around them the Gaels drop dead from hunger, cold and the exertion of the truly Gaelic *rince fada* (long dance). Admittedly the trials of the Corkadorkians are subject to the usual exaggeration: the *feis* is marked by incessant rain and myriad deaths from over-exertion, drink, dancing and starvation.

80 Patrick Power points to the similarity to the case of the Maamtrasna murders, for which Irish-speaking defendants were convicted, despite not understanding their English trial (*PM*, 128).

81 Power chose to translate the name as Osborne O'Loonassa. There is also a parody of Amergin's poetry in *At Swim-Two-Birds*, placed in the mouth of Finn MacCool: 'I am an Ulsterman, a Connachtman, a Greek . . ./I am Cuchulainn, I am Patrick/ . . . I am every hero from the crack of time' (*ASTB*, 19).

82 The episode recalls the medieval voyage tale *Immram curaig Mail Dúin*/ The Voyage of Maeldoon, but it also has a touch of H. Rider Haggard.

83 The Rosses is populated by a few stock figures: the two men who come courting; Mary, a young girl; the 'Gambler', a young man who is habitually off carousing in Scotland, and a wise old *seanachaí*.

84 *The Irish Times* (17 January 1942). A second edition was published in February 1942. The National Press wrote to O'Nolan on 15 September 1942 that there were only 300–400 copies left in stock, and by December 1943, there were only fifty (30 December 1943). In January 1944, O'Nolan proposed another print run of 500 but his publishers declined. Letter to P. Cannon, National Press (10 January 1944), BC.

85 Manus O'Neill, 'Live Irish', *The Standard* (2 January 1942).

86 Anon., 'Current Affairs', *The Leader* (27 December 1941).

87 F.É. 'Gaelic Publications of Interest,' *Irish Library Bulletin*, vol. 3, no. 2, March– April 1942, p. 22.

88 CL (25 October 1950); *HD*, p. 31. O'Nolan claimed that *An Béal Bocht* sold 12,000 copies, a feat unknown in Irish-language publishing. It certainly was unknown; the true figure was probably closer to 2,000, or the 3,000 he quoted in a letter to Timothy O'Keeffe. (27 February 1960), SIUC.

89 Browne & Nolan wrote to O'Nolan on 29 May 1941, inviting him to come in and talk about the manuscript. O'Nolan wrote on the letter that it was: 'To say that Foley "did not understand it" and would not advise publication.' BC.

90 This 'Summary of Observations of Persons to whom Book was sent by Browne and

Nolan' is held in Boston College. The points on which they objected were 'turning a dwelling house into a piggery', stealing, 'marital infidelity', the digression on Sitric, and a sly joke about the weight of a prominent female revivalist. The reader advised more material like the chapter on the Corca Dorcha *feis*.

91   Letter to Timothy O'Keeffe (27 February 1960), SIUC.

92   A virtually untranslatable example of this is O'Nolan's fantasia on the Irish phrase: '*Thit an lug ar an lag orm*'. At the end of the Corca Dorcha *feis*, O'Nolan stretches the phrase to depicit Bónapárt's misery as an endless avalanche of misfortunes (*ABB*, 52); the translation is in *PM*, pp. 60–61.

93   S.O'F. 'A New and Quaint Departure in Irish Literature', *The Nationalist and Munster Advertiser* (7 January 1942).

94   *Cruiskeen Lawn* was largely printed in Gaelic type, as was the first edition of *An Béal Bocht*. For its re-issue in 1964, the Dolmen Press developed a new form of Roman type, and O'Nolan modernised its spelling. This had been a point of contention with Sáirséal agus Dill, who had initially agreed to publish *An Béal Bocht* in 1956. Letter from Seán Ó hEigeartaigh, S&D to Brian O'Nolan (30 July 1957), BC.

95   *CL* (24 April 1944), cited in Ó Conaire, *Myles na Gaeilge*, p. 96.

96   *CL* (17 January 1955), cited in ibid., p. 120.

97   Myles na gCopaleen, 'Leabhair Nua', *The Irish Times* (22 February 1941).

98   *CL* (24 February 1942); *BM*, p. 268.

99   Ironically, *At Swim*, a novel which makes the reader highly conscious of its textuality, draws heavily on a tradition of oral storytelling. See Declan Kiberd, 'Gaelic Absurdism: *At Swim-Two-Birds*', p. 505. Similarly, anecdotal monologues (or monologues masked as dialogues) were a regular feature of *Cruiskeen Lawn*, as can be seen in the encounters with the Plain People of Ireland or the interminable tales about the Brother. But *An Béal Bocht* satirises the attempt to simply transpose oral narratives to the page, as in Ó Laoghaire's *Séadna*, which in its first serial publication was introduced each week as if it were a tale being recounted at the fireside. See editor's note, Peter O'Leary, *Séadna*, Cyril and Kit Ó Céirín (trans.) (Dublin: Glendale, 1989), p. 6.

100   These phrases can be translated as: 'that is another story and I'll write it down another day' and 'in the bottom of the house'.

101   This is the customary invocation of 'our forebears and our ancestors', and the proverb means: 'things are not as they seem'. Variations of '*slán mar a n-instear é agus i bhfad uainn an drochrud*' ('God save us from the likes of it and may evil be far from us') appear in *ABB*, pp. 9, 12, 21, 62. The Seanduine Liath's characteristic exclamation, '*m'anam ón riach*' ('my soul from the devil') is repeated on pp. 20, 23, 28, 32, 34, 78, 87, 102.

102   'It's a strange world that there is today,' *ABB*, pp. 23, 26, 29, 30, 57, 58, 68, 75, 102.

103   *CL* (13 August 1942). The first line reads: 'One day, maybe there will be some literary hack [lit: whore] trying to polish his foolish English with a smattering of Irish – a day not far from us, when Ireland will again belong to Cáit Ní Dhuibhir.' *Blas* – taste; *fága-bhealach* – leave-him-his-way; *thaidhbhsiúil* – spectral; *beagáinín* – a tiny, little bit; *mise is tusa is an bóthar go réidh faoi n-ár gcosa* – me and you and the road ready before us; *dána* – bold.

104   Neil Buttimer and Máire Ní Annrachán, 'Irish language and literature, 1921–84' in J.R. Hill (ed.), *A New History of Ireland*, vol. 7, p. 558. By 1935, one hundred dramas and twenty-four books of poetry had been published.

105 This was distinctive from other Irish publications since it was produced in the Gaeltacht and contained international news and new writing rather than the older Irish texts and folklore found in revival journals. It was also unusual in publishing humour, and writing for children. Ó Ciosáin compares its series of humorous letters from a character called 'Pilibín Ó Neachtain' [Pádraig Mac Fhionnghaile] (supposedly the owner of a students' lodging-house in Galway) to Myles na gCopaleen's columns. Ó Ciosáin, *An t-Éireannach*, p. 183.

106 Cronin, *Translating Ireland*, pp. 157–158.

107 Cited in ibid., p. 157.

108 León Ó Broin, 'Contemporary Gaelic Literature and Some of its Paradoxes,' *The Capuchin Annual*, 1935, pp. 126–127.

109 *CL* (25 January 1941). Ó Laoghaire published *Niamh* in 1907. The other works which O'Nolan refers to are Tomás Ó Máille's *An Béal Beo* (1936) and Patrick Pearse's *An Mháthair* (1916).

110 Ó Conaire attributes an intimidating range of references to the text: 'the Ó Grianna brothers, Seán Mac Maoláin, Pádraig Óg Ó Conaire, Niall Mac Giolla Bhríde, Fionn Mac Cumhaill, P. Pearse, Séamus Ó Searcaigh, Seán Mac Meanman, Aindrias Ó Baoill, Peader Mac Fhionnlaoich, Peig Sayers, Séamus Ó Dubhghaill, Muiris Ó Suilleabháin, Séamus Mac an Bháird and Aodh Ó Curnáin'. 'An *Béal Bocht* and Other Irish Matters', p. 137.

111 Ó Conaire, *Myles na Gaeilge*, p. 50. Jack White, a fellow *Irish Times* staff member, stated that the decline in Irish 'was not a matter of editorial policy; in fact, Smyllie was very keen to keep on teasing the Gaelic-Leaguers, and he tried to insist that Myles should produce his quota of Irish; but in practice Myles did as he pleased.' 'Myles, Flann and Brian', in *Myles: Portraits of Brian O'Nolan*, p. 67.

112 Donohue, *The Irish Anatomist*, p. 158. The decision to do so was O'Nolan's own.

113 Louis de Paor drew attention to the *Cruiskeen Lawn* commentaries on these groups in 'Twisting the Knife', *The Irish Times* (29 March 2002). Their titles are enlightening in themselves, Glun na Buaidhe meaning 'Generation of Victory', and Ailtirí na hAiseirí proclaiming themselves to be 'Architects of the Revolution'. (Although an alternative popular translation of Glun na Buaidhe was 'Cow's Knees').

114 ibid.

115 *CL* (21 November 1942).

116 *CL* (15 March 1943). The character described is likely to be Proinsias Mac an Bheatha, the Belfastman who founded Glun na Buaidhe.

117 Ailtirí na hAiséirí ran candidates in the 1943 and 1944 general elections, though to little effect. On its fascist leanings see Wills, *That Neutral Island*, pp. 364–367.

118 *CL* (13 December 1943).

119 *CL* (22 February 1943).

120 The manuscript of *An Scian* is held in Boston College and is dated 5 December 1944. De Paor notes that it formed part of the Gate Theatre's Christmas variety show that year. 'Twisting the Knife', *The Irish Times* (29 March 2002). Included in the Flann O'Brien collection in Boston College is a typescript of acts three and four of another Irish play (concerning a dragon, a princess and a marriage match), though this seems unlikely to be O'Nolan's work.

121 O'Nolan wrote a similar sketch in English, called 'The Handsome Carvers'. In this version, the argument is over the husband's alcoholism. After he stabs his wife, there is a flashback to the day he was presented with the wedding present by his colleagues. To mark the occasion, he had accepted his first glass of whiskey. SIUC.

122   Brian O'Nolan himself contributed to the paper throughout 1955. See Ó Conaire, *Myles na Gaeilge*, pp. 243–244.

123   The Bellman, 'Meet R. M. Smyllie', *The Bell*, vol. 3, no. 3, December 1941, p. 187.

124   Ironically, this echoed Smyllie's criticism of the language which had raised Myles's ire in the first *Cruiskeen Lawn*.

125   CL (11 October 1943); *BM*, pp. 283–284.

126   CL (9 December 1943). The gag was revived a few months later: 'Are they unaware that the stuff can't be got – that there hasn't been a word of Irish come into this country for near on three year?'. CL (20 May 1944).

127   CL (5 June 1944).

128   This unpublished manuscript is held in Boston College, and its existence has not hitherto been adverted to by any of O'Nolan's critics. Internal evidence suggests that it was written around 1947 – at one point, he adapts a remark made by Thomas Davis a hundred years ago to apply to that year. He also refers to the 1946 census, noting that its findings would not be made public for some years. The few notes he made for the book are in a notebook used at the 1943 tribunal on the Cavan orphanage fire.

129   CL (30 October 1946); *HD*, p. 8.

130   There is no reliable indication of the original order of the chapters. Preliminary notes indicate that O'Nolan considered an alternative structure for the book, under the following headings: 'The Cult of the Peasant, The Fate of the Gaeltacht, The Literary Background, The Language and Nationality, INTO – Education'. Language Revival Notebook, BC.

131   'The Pathology of Revivalism', p. 3. This is hereafter cited in the text as PR.

132   'What is the position of the Gaeltacht?', p. 5. This is hereafter cited in the text as WG.

133   *Coimisiún na Gaeltachta: Report* (Dublin: Stationery Office, 1926), article 129.

134   The government considered that it was not equitable to distinguish between Irish-speaking and non Irish-speaking families in redistribution of lands under the 1923 Land Act. Coimisiún na Gaeltachta, *Statement of Government Policy on Recommendations of the Commission* (Dublin: Stationery Office, 1928), p. 21.

135   Seán Ó Murthuile, Dublin (21 July 1925); cited in John Walsh, *Díchoimisiúnú Teanga: Coimisiún na Gaeltachta 1926* (Dublin: Cois Life, 2002), pp. 130–131.

136   Daniel Corkery was persisting with just such a notion in 1942: 'We do not lack Irishmen who, while they openly proclaim their interest in reviving the language, will not allow that it is advisable to put it instead of English as the language of the general purpose. For them its value is purely cultural. They do not seem to take the view that Irish nationality cannot do without it . . .' *What's this about the Gaelic League?* (Dublin: Connradh na Gaedhilge, 1942), p. 24.

137   Indeed the author claims that this was a policy adopted as early as 1366. Anon., *You May Revive the Gaelic Language . . .* (Dublin: Connradh na Gaedhilge, 1937), p. 12.

138   'There is no reason to suppose that the Protestant overlord minority were not all in favour of the Catholics speaking Irish, and that to retain such a situation was one of the main objects of prohibiting education. Even today, many people ignorant of Irish think it is barbarous. Nor must one assume that the British in a later day were entirely destitute of benevolent sentiments when they introduced the teaching of English in the national schools in the Gaeltacht . . . Not only the English, but the Irish themselves, came to associate the Irish language with degradation and servitude.' 'Decline and Revival', p. 3. Hereafter cited in the text as DR.

139   O'Nolan does allow himself the observation that the later Gaelic League, by 'often making itself ridiculous by intransigent and exaggerated attitudes, lost favour with the public, and today can claim to exist scarcely more than in name.' Ibid., p. 8.

140   'The Native Irish Speaker has a command of the beauties of language which is inculcated amongst English Speakers only by the laboured teaching of the Classics. There is no parallel in English for this refined popular culture, which is the highly wrought product of generations of Gaelic civilisation.' Comisiún na Gaeltachta (1926), article 79.

141   'The Pathology of Revivalism', p. 1. This is hereafter cited in the text as PR.

142   In a *Bell* editorial some years earlier, Seán O'Faoláin quoted from a Gaelic League pamphlet on film-making in Ireland which expressed similarly ominous motivations: 'We cannot permit film-making to remain in the hands of the Jews, the eternal enemies of Christianity, for Ireland's sake at any rate . . . Let us make Ireland the master of Europe in the twentieth century!' 'The Gaelic League', *The Bell*, vol. 4, no. 2, May 1942, pp. 84–85.

143   Séamus Ó Grianna and others anticipated O'Nolan's depiction of the revivalist, calling the Gaelic League 'something of a breeding-ground for cranks . . . [It] developed in many of its members a peculiar outlook which made them aggressive, narrow, and self-righteous. That had its advantages when the supporters of the language were in the wilderness. Nowadays freakishness is something which should be avoided.' 'Kilts and Jigs', *Star* (29 March 1930); cited in Philip O'Leary, *Gaelic Prose in the Irish Free State, 1922–1939* (Dublin: UCD Press, 2004), p. 50.

144   *The Irish Times* review picked up on this point: 'Even the Irish is somewhat new: the author has got to grips with the problem of evolving a clear unprovincial style, and shows up with skill the evocative, colourful and humorous content of certain Irish words and phrases.' F. O'R. 'Myles Takes off His Coat!' (13 December 1941).

5. NEWSPAPER WARS

1   Letter from Brian O'Nolan to the Department of Finance (13 November 1946), BC. Cronin identifies the substitutes as Niall Montgomery and Niall Sheridan, *No Laughing Matter*, p. 182, though Sheridan himself only privately noted that Montgomery 'worked closely with Brian in the later period of the Myles na gCopaleen column . . .' Letter to Timothy O'Keeffe (24 November 1971), Timothy O'Keeffe Collection, McFarlin Library, University of Tulsa. This collection is hereafter cited as TOK.

2   Terence de Vere White, 'Smyllie and his people', *The Irish Times* (14 June 1984).

3   He declined to contribute either to the first publication on O'Nolan, Timothy O'Keeffe's 1973 collection of biographical and critical essays, or to Anthony Cronin's 1989 biography. Letter to Anthony Cronin (11 August 1986), NM; letter to Timothy O'Keeffe (6 December 1971), TOK.

4   I am grateful to Christine O'Neill, cataloguer of Montgomery's papers, for bringing them to my attention.

5   Cronin, *No Laughing Matter*, p. vii.

6   Myles na Gopaleen. 'Two in One', *The Bell* 19:8 (July 1954), 30–34.

7   Brooker, *Flann O'Brien*, p. 90.

8   This week opened with the immaculately Irish heading of '*Cruiscín Lán*'. Myles reminded his readers the following day that '*Seo seachtain an Béarla. Má tá Béarla agat, labhair é. Cur síntiús chuig ciste na teangan, leabhar Béarla ar an nGuthán*' ('This

is English Week. If you know English, speak it. Make a donation to the language fund, speak English on the Telephone').

9   It is telling that on the occasions when Smyllie's editorials thundered against the government's language policy, Myles typically lept to its defence (in English), despite his own mockery of its premises.

10   There were intermittent breaks in the publication of *Cruiskeen Lawn* in the 1950s and 1960s, due to O'Nolan's ill-health. The column also disappeared for much of 1951, at a time when his relations with *The Irish Times* were soured by its suppression of potentially libellous pieces (and apologies for others). Cronin, *No Laughing Matter*, pp. 177–179.

11   When requesting a raise in 1942, O'Nolan pointed out the popularity which *Cruiskeen Lawn* had already achieved over the previous two years. Letter from Brian O'Nolan to *The Irish Times* (21 October 1942), BC. His case would have been supported by a report in *The Leinster Leader* on 16 May 1942 on the conviction of a newsboy for stealing copies of *The Irish Independent* and *The Irish Press*. When making his ruling, the judge observed that Myles would be distressed to know that *The Irish Times* was left behind.

12   See Donohue, *The Irish Anatomist*, p. 109.

13   Seán O'Faoláin, 'Silent Ireland', *The Bell*, vol. 6, no. 6, September 1943, p. 457–66.

14   On the 'ambiguous attitude to nationalism' betrayed in O'Faoláin's editorials see Frank Shovlin, *The Irish Literary Periodical 1923–1958* (Oxford: Clarendon Press, 2003), pp. 105–108.

15   Mercier argues that 'the writers who remained at home during the war did feel a sense of gratitude to their country for sheltering them and providing them with alternative sources of income . . . The Abbey Theatre devoted itself almost entirely to the production of new Irish plays, while the Gate, Gaiety, and Olympia theatres all produced more Irish work than before'. 'Literature in English, 1921–84', in *A New History of Ireland*, vol. 7, p. 503.

16   Wills, *That Neutral Island*, p. 263.

17   For O'Nolan's comments on the first Irish Exhibition of Living Art see *CL* (4 October 1943), and on the Subjective Art Exhibition mounted the following January see *CL* (10 January 1944).

18   Stephen Young, 'Fact/Fiction: Cruiskeen Lawn, 1945–66', in *Conjuring Complexities*, p. 118.

19   Stephen Curran discusses how O'Nolan's criticism of *The Bell* highlights 'the capacity of critics . . . to initiate debate that is itself fraudulent', whether overtaken by critical clichés or, in the case of O'Faoláin, a hidden nationalist bias. '"No-this-is-not-from-the-Bell": Brian O'Nolan's 1943 *Cruiskeen Lawn* Anthology', *Éire-Ireland*, vol. 34, no. 2–3, 1997, p. 86.

20   *CL* (20 October 1945).

21   *CL*, 24 May to 11 June 1948. The following week's columns were written by Niall Montgomery.

22   *CL* (7 May 1947).

23   'Thomas Hogan' [Thomas Woods], 'Myles na gCopaleen,' *The Bell*, vol. 13, no. 2, November 1946, p. 132.

24   ibid., p. 139.

25   Morton had been writing the Beachcomber column, 'By the Way', since 1924, when he had succeeded D.B. Wyndham-Lewis in the job.

26   Robert Allen, *Voice of Britain: The Inside Story of the Daily Express* (Cambridge: Patrick Stephens, 1983), p. 5.

27 The Bellman, 'Meet R. M. Smyllie', *The Bell*, vol. 3, no. 3, December 1941, p. 185. As Vivian Mercier recognised, the paper's contemporary readership little reflected its reputation as 'a dyed-in-the-wool, dry-as-dust, dead-in-the-last-ditch Ascendancy organ, the sworn enemy of the Irish people, for ever wailing whatever may be the Ballsbridge equivalent of "Wisha, God be with the good ould times" . . .' 'The Fourth Estate: The Times (Irish)', *The Bell*, vol. 9, no. 4, January 1945, p. 290-291.

28 Tony Gray, *Mr Smyllie, Sir* (Dublin: Gill & Macmillan, 1991), p. 169.

29 Ironically, paper shortages during the Emergency meant that *The Irish Times* eventually had to resort to requiring subscriptions from its readers.

30 'Donat O'Donnell' [Conor Cruise O'Brien], 'The Fourth Estate: The Irish Independent', *The Bell*, vol. 9, no. 5, February 1945, p. 393.

31 Donal Ó Drisceoil, *Censorship in Ireland 1939-1945: Neutrality, Politics and Society* (Cork: CUP, 1996), p. 188.

32 As early as January 1940, *The Irish Times* was severely punished by being ordered to submit to the censor in full before publication. On this occasion, the order was lifted after Smyllie appealed to de Valera, though with the condition that all his editorials would be submitted prior to publication – a requirement which Smyllie flouted as far as he could. After three such omissions, Aiken re-introduced the order in December 1942 and *The Irish Times* was compelled to submit each issue in full to the censor until May 1945. See ibid., pp. 162-164.

33 Nichevo, 'Irishman's Diary', *The Irish Times* (11 February 1941); cited in Ó Drisceoil, *Censorship in Ireland 1939-1945*, p. 164. Seán T. O'Kelly was still the Minister for Local Government and Public Health when O'Nolan joined the department in 1935, which makes the episode a little suspicious. This particular classical tag was also a favourite of Myles.

34 ibid., p. 260.

35 ibid., p. 261.

36 *CL* (6 October 1941).

37 Vivian Mercier, 'The Fourth Estate: The Times (Irish)', *The Bell*, p. 295.

38 This stance was another reason for *The Irish Times*'s difficult relationship with Fianna Fáil. On 30 September 1943 the front page gleefully reported de Valera's attack on the paper during his closing speech at the Fianna Fáil Ard Fheis. The Taoiseach had complained that the editor's habitual criticism of the government's language policy was detrimental to the revival movement.

39 *CL* (3 March 1943).

40 *CL* (24 July 1945).

41 Young, 'Fact/Fiction: Cruiskeen Lawn 1940-66', p. 118.

42 Donohue, *The Irish Anatomist*, p. 122.

43 *CL* (17 March 1947).

44 It was not just the press which underwent dissection by Myles – an anthology of essays on *Irish Art* provided a full week of column fodder in April 1944, while a tortuous fortnight on the constitutions of European nation states followed in April 1945.

45 *CL* (27 March 1942); *BM*, p. 202. It is only fair to acknowledge that he paid equally close attention to the banalities wheeled out at bus stop or barstool: 'And I'll tell you a man that went off very quickly, Mickie D., shure I seen him there at the last smoker, he was the size of your fist look, the poor fella couldn' stand straight but he wouldn't let the crowd down, he sang "In Cellar Cool" and do you know what I'm going to tell you, he never sang it better. Ahh he was real Dublin, the ould crowd are goin fast, sure there's poor little Rooney that's not lookin himself this two year, I wouldn't say he's long for this world, Ahh yes, Ahh but shure we'll all go

the one way, every man of us. And we'll all meet again. We'll all meet again. Aye . . .' *CL* (4 February 1942).

46 *CL* (1 May 1942); *BM*, p. 203.

47 *BM*, p. 227.

48 *CL* (2 October 1942); *BM*, p. 219.

49 O'Nolan's parody of journalistic conventions was continued in his 1943 *Cruiskeen Lawn* anthology. This maintains the layout of the newspaper, its cover mimicking an *Irish Times* front page. Inside, the pages are split into two columns, the left headed with an arrow pointing to: 'So-called English down below here/ *Annso síos an dranntán gallda neamh-Ghaedealach*' and its right-hand counterpart announcing: '*An teanga mhín mhathardha gidh mí-ghramadúil annso síos*/ Here the kingly and melodious Irish.' As if to exaggerate the dual character of his bilingual anthology, O'Nolan's titles do not exactly correspond. The lines in Irish read respectively: 'Here below the foreign, un-Gaelic growling,' and: 'The mothertongue, sweet but ungrammatical, here below'.

50 *CL* (1 March 1943).

51 Admittedly, Myles's criticism of his fellow journalists often had little to do with the perils of language itself – frequently, he merely adopted the attitude of an impatient schoolmaster. Dissecting one issue of *The Bell*, he complained that 'if these uppish highly trained writing savants who are sure they are worth more than five bob insist on dragging in foreign words by the scruff of the fair hair, why not do it accurately and thus show that the use of these words is perfectly natural and the result of long sojourns abroad?' *CL* (1 June 1942); *BM*, pp. 232–233.

52 *CL* (4 March 1958).

53 Curran, '"No-this-is-not-from-*The-Bell*": Brian O'Nolan's 1943 *Cruiskeen Lawn* Anthology', p. 80.

54 Jack White, 'Myles, Flann and Brian', p. 67.

55 ibid., p. 67.

56 *CL* (25 March 1942); *BM*, p. 93.

57 *CL* (5 September 1941); *BM*, pp. 15–16.

58 *CL* (23 January 1942); *BM*, p. 31.

59 *CL* (7 November 1941); *BM*, p. 19.

60 *CL* (17 November 1941); *BM*, p. 23.

61 *CL* (4 October 1954); *HD*, p. 103.

62 Seán O'Faoláin, 'This Is Your Magazine', *The Bell* vol. 1, no. 1, October 1940, p. 5. O'Faoláin's mission to seek out the 'real' Ireland, inviting readers' submissions on their own lives so that all could experience a part of 'the Ireland we are making' met a withering response in *Cruiskeen Lawn*. Myles answered that 'one can only point out (a) that it would be a queer business if it was a *medieval . . . China* we are making and anyhow, (b) that we are not making any Ireland. We just live here (the travel ban) – some of us even *work* here'. *CL* (26 August 1944); *BM*, p. 389.

63 Brown, *Ireland: A Social and Cultural History, 1922–2002*, p. 168.

64 To counteract the government's isolationist policy, Shovlin notes, O'Faoláin 'occasionally wrote a "One World" editorial focusing on international affairs and certain issues of the magazine were devoted solely to foreign matters of interest. Pieces by writers as diverse as Erwin Shroedinger, Cecil Day-Lewis, and Abdul Aziz of the Indian National Congress were featured.' *The Irish Literary Periodical 1923–1958*, p. 101.

65 James Joyce, *A Portrait of the Artist as a Young Man* (London: Flamingo, 1916, 1994), p. 219.

66   CL (7 July 1947); FC, pp. 106–107.

67   Frank O'Connor, 'The Future of Irish Literature', *Horizon*, vol. 5, no. 25, January 1942, p. 60.

68   The only exception was a short story published in America: Flann O'Brien, 'John Duffy's Brother', *Story* (1941). As noted, O'Nolan managed a profile in *Time* magazine in March 1943 (written by Stanford Lee Cooper, an American press attaché to Ireland), but never succeeded in publishing in America until *At Swim-Two-Birds* was issued by Pantheon in 1951.

69   CL (9 September 1944).

70   See CL (10 April 1942).

71   Roibéard Ó Faracháin, *The Irish Times* (21 February 1942).

72   Frank O'Connor, ibid., (25 February 1942).

73   CL (2 March 1942).

74   ibid.

75   ibid.

76   ibid. Considering O'Connor's virulent reaction to Ó Faracháin's review, his response to Myles was relatively mild. In a letter to *The Irish Times*, O'Connor claimed to be planning a biography of the late columnist which promised to provide a 'treasure-house of complexes' to continental psychologists. *The Irish Times* (3 March 1942).

77   CL (15 March 1944); BM, p. 248.

78   Letter from Flann O'Brien, *The Irish Times* (5 April 1941). Myles made a similar point during the Rouault controversy, when the National Gallery refused a loan of 'Christ and the Soldier' fearing that it would cause offence. In his view, the protestors on *both* sides would not allow the public to make up their own minds: 'inasmuch as the modern artist makes his own rules, the onlooker must also be permitted to fix his own standards of appraisal . . . Must we "like" whatever some individual or coterie has pronounced to be good?' CL (10 October 1942); BM, pp. 236–37.

79   Flann O'Brien, 'Going to the Dogs,' *The Bell*, vol. 1, no. 2, October 1940, pp. 19–24; 'The Trade in Dublin,' *The Bell*, vol. 1, no. 2, November 1940, pp. 6–16; 'The Dance Halls,' *The Bell*, vol. 1, no. 5, February 1941, pp. 44–52.

80   CL (5 January 1942).

81   'The Plain People of Ireland: How about those jokes. Myself: Well wait till I see. Would you say that the cousin of the French Pretender is the Duc de Guise? The Plain People of Ireland: Whaa? Myself: And I wonder would he be annything to the Wild Geese? The Plain People of Ireland: Dear knows some people are very smart, these County Council scholarships to the universities above in Dublin do more harm than good . . . You say you'd like a joke or two for a bit of crack and the finger of scorn is pointed at you. It's madness, the country's in a right state. Madness. There's no other word for it. Madness.' CL (25 March 1942); BM, p. 93.

82   Seán O'Faoláin, 'The Plain People of Ireland', *The Bell*, vol. 7, no. 1, October 1943, pp. 4–5. The Plain People's ubiquity may be gauged from a Seanad speech made by the Labour senator, Seán Campbell, during the 1945 review of the Censorship Act: 'the pseudo-intellectuals tell us that we must let up on censorship. They are making a mistake if they think that the plain people are going to stand for a reintroduction of the vicious type of literature which the original Act was largely successful in keeping out.' Adams, *Censorship: The Irish Experience*, pp. 106–107.

83   *Na Daoine Macánta* (1922).

84 Seán O'Faoláin, 'Attitudes', *The Bell*, vol. 2, no. 6, September 1941, p. 7. O'Faoláin spoils the effect of a merry aesthetic democracy by asserting further on that science and the arts rely on taste and special knowledge, though the populace should be deferred to in everything else.

85 *CL* (13 July 1943). See also *CL* (6 July 1943).

86 'The world will have heard that late to-day the Irish people were relieved at their own request of all rights of citizenship and have decided for the future to dissociate themselves permanently from all Irish situations, whether alcoholic, pugnacious or merely relevant to inchoate political formalisms. The resignations have been accepted with genuine regret. The Irish people leave at their own request to better themselves.' *CL* (6 September 1943). See also *CL* (16 May 1944).

87 See Donohue, *The Irish Anatomist*, p. 109. In late 1942 Myles was already showing signs of tedium: 'This seems reasonable enough until we bring (to bear) upon it our whole fatuous battery of professional paranoia, perversion and catachresis, rushing out with our precast vaudeville clown-routine of quotation, misinterpretation and drivelling comment. Does the result please anyone, bring the most faded polite laugh, the most tenuous giggle, the most bilious sneer?' *CL* (7 December 1942); *BM*, p. 330.

88 Curran, '"No-this-is-not-from-*The-Bell*": Brian O'Nolan's 1943 *Cruiskeen Lawn* Anthology', pp. 90–91.

89 *CL* (20 October 1944).

90 One day Myles received a visit from a shabby deputation: '" . . . are you civil servants of the Department of Home Affairs of the Free State Twenty Six Counties of Southern Ireland, Eire?" Yes; they were. Educated guess. What then could I do for them? One chap opens out. Scandal of the hours, service seething with unrest, talk of mutiny, thousands depressed below level of subsistence. Savings gone, no breakfast in second half of week, rickets, malnutrition, cost of living, vicious spiral, black market, expected to keep up appearances, tragedy of black-coated worker, scandal that cries to heaven, entire service on brink of strike action . . .', *CL* (22 November 1943). See also *CL* (15 May 1944).

91 The Report of the Commission on Vocational Organisation was published in August 1944, and thereafter thoroughly vilified in *Cruiskeen Lawn*. The first of the series on constitutions appeared on 5 April 1945 and ran for a week, after which it was resumed after a break.

92 *CL* (3 April 1945); *CL* (19 November 1945). O'Nolan's remarks increased in vituperation as the years passed. The civil service, he observed in 1953, was 'a secret society which holds its rites in the day-time behind closed doors and whose members are debarred under oath from adult employment.' *CL* (14 December 1953), cited in Donohue, p. 162.

93 Michael Phelan, 'Watcher in the Wings: A Lingering Look at Myles na gCopaleen', *Administration*, vol. 24, no. 1, Spring 1976, p. 99.

94 *The Irish Times* (20 January 1942).

95 O'Nolan's considerations also restricted Montgomery's columns. In 1948 he accused O'Nolan of not using a piece on public housing for fear it would offend the Minister. Letter to Brian O'Nolan (16 June 1948), NM. The original column, dated 23 May 1948, was finally published on 18 June.

96 Curran, '"Could Paddy leave off from copying just for five minutes": Brian O'Nolan and Eire's Beveridge Plan', *Irish University Review*, vol. 31, no. 2, Autumn/Winter 2001, p. 360. In particular, Curran discusses the report produced in October 1944 by Bishop Dignan, Chairman of the Committee of Management

of the National Health Society: *Social Security: Outlines of a Scheme of National Health Insurance.*

97 Though any kind of obfuscation was prime fodder for Myles, O'Nolan made no mention of a classic case from the period – the tribunal report on the Cavan orphanage fire, which was published in September 1943. As secretary to the tribunal, O'Nolan was present for the entire hearing in April of that year, but his Mylesian alter ego occupied the time with stories for steam men and debates with the Plain People of Ireland.

98 Curran, 'Brian O'Nolan and Eire's Beveridge Plan', p. 358.

99 *CL* (10 May 1944).

100 Curran points out that 'O'Nolan uses the language of propaganda – 'jack-booted secret police', 'neo-fascism', 'regimentation' – to associate the scheme with totalitarianism and the atmosphere of the fascist state'. 'Brian O'Nolan and Eire's Beveridge Plan', p. 368.

101 *CL* (3 October 1944).

102 *CL* (10 November 1944). At the end of the war, Myles disdained talk of human rights and freedoms as fashionable clichés and resumed his more familiar theme of human *conceit*: 'I do not see at all how one can being human at the same time be . . . free. Free to do what? And human rights – what on earth are these dowdy liberal artefacts? . . . Finally might I be permitted to ask: Who made the world?' *CL* (6 June 1945).

103 Cronin, *No Laughing Matter*, pp. 157–158.

104 *CL* (10 May 1944). On MacEntee, see Curran 'Brian O'Nolan and Eire's Beveridge Plan', p. 373.

105 *CL* (21 April 1945).

106 *CL* (14 May 1945).

107 *The Irish Times* (12 May 1945).

108 *CL* (17 May 1945).

109 See *CL* (18 May 1945). Obviously Churchill's speech rankled, as Myles returned to the topic on a number of occasions, for example, on 31 July 1943 and – most cuttingly – on 23 June: 'What, My Excellency inquires, is the difference between war and peace? Well, one difference is that when the world is at peace, horror camps are not photographed. When Dachau was already a household word with all peoples, the Foreign Office of a benign neighbour was benignly conducted by one Vansittart, while a distinguished Northern Ireland statesman wined and most royally fed the Rev. Joachim von Ribbentrop – indeed, frolicked with the last-named. Tastes change, you see . . .'

110 *The Irish Times* (11 August 1945).

111 *CL* (20 August 1945); *FW*, p. 172. The following day, Myles continued in an even darker fashion, arguing that the security of the world was now not merely dependent on the good behaviour of the nations in control of the bomb, but could also be at the mercy of their disgruntled scientists.

112 *CL* (14 September 1945).

113 Donohue, *The Irish Anatomist*, p. 122.

114 *CL* (1 September 1945); *FW*, p. 174.

115 *CL* (11 October 1945).

116 *CL* (12 October 1945).

117 *CL* (25 August 1945).

118 *CL* (7 September 1945).

119 *CL* (11 December 1945).

120 CL (11 December 1945).
121 CL (6 December 1945).
122 In fact, O'Nolan complained to his superiors that though *Dublin Opinion*'s C.E. Kelly was also a civil servant, Kelly's political satire was regarded with far less suspicion than his own work. Letter to the Dept of Finance (13 November 1946), BC.
123 CL (7 January 1946).
124 CL (14 January 1946).
125 CL (15 January 1946).
126 CL (19 March 1946).
127 CL (20 March 1946).
128 CL (26 April 1946).
129 CL (27 May 1946).
130 Given the international situation, Myles wondered whether he was more needed elsewhere – then he would open an Irish newspaper 'and I know Phil Weill that if I withdraw it'll oney be the same thing all over again the thribes at one another's throats birds in the trees those dying generations at their song, gang wars with the Tong Bo Cuailgne crowd in the ascendant, ambushes, 'stunts', pakistan, and all sorts of devilment . . .' ibid.
131 CL (23 August 1946).
132 CL (11 October 1946); FC, p. 139.
133 See letters from Robert Greacen (23 October 1946) and Frank Sutton (5 November 1946). This last letter was one of many responses to *The Irish Times*' publication on 31 October (over four full pages) of John Hersey's seminal report from Hiroshima for *The New Yorker*.
134 CL (14 May 1947).
135 CL (11 December 1946).
136 Thomas Hogan [Woods], 'Myles na gCopaleen', p. 140.
137 ibid., p. 139.
138 Myles recognised his own tendencies, declaring that 'I have devised a very frightening counter-measure (or half one), namely: *Some day soon I am going to point the finger of . . . praise! (SENSATION!)*. CL (16 September 1946).
139 CL (19 June 1946).
140 CL (2 August 1946).
141 CL (14 August 1946).
142 He had recently quoted the remarks of a Dáil deputy during a debate on Irish radio: '"We do not want any highbrow stuff here. We want to cater for our own people who have simple tastes and possibly right tastes because they are simple . . ." There you have what is really rather an aspiration than a fact; I doubt very much whether your own people in fact *have* simple tastes and I am unsure as to the unsimplicity of bad tastes . . .' CL (17 May 1946).
143 Alan Titley, 'The Interpretation of Tradition', in Hilary Lennon (ed.), *Frank O'Connor: Critical Essays* (Dublin: Four Courts, 2007), p. 230.
144 CL (12 March 1947); FC, p. 62.
145 CL 9 May, 19 May, 30 May 1947. Also 11 June, 13 June (FC, p. 99), 4 July, 18 July, 30 July, 1 August 1947 and so on.
146 CL, 23 June to 2 July 1947.
147 See M.J. McManus, 'A Critic's View of Irish Writing', *The Irish Times* (3 May 1947). CL (9 May 1947). Original dated 4 May 1947, Cruiskeen Lawn File Vol. 14. NM. While O'Faoláin writes on creating the conditions for literature at home, Myles (or Montgomery) knowingly agrees that 'the home-made job is the job in the long run

and, sure, look at it this way won't it keep you out of the pubs? Another act is to break your leg but I wouldn't advise it much . . .' On a similarly characteristic treatment of Frank O'Connor see *CL* (17 December 1948). Original dated 11 December 1948, Cruiskeen Lawn File, Vol. 16, NM.

148 Robert Greacen, 'Is the Artist Really Necessary?', *The Irish Times* (24 May 1947). *CL* (30 May 1947).

149 25 May 1947, Cruiskeen Lawn File, Vol. 14, NM. The theme returns in *CL* (14 January 1948), original 12 January 1948, Cruiskeen Lawn File, Vol. 16, NM.

150 *CL* (11 June 1947). Original dated 6 June 1947, Cruiskeen Lawn File, Vol. 15, NM.

151 *CL* (17 September 1948). Original dated 11 May 1947, marked 'rewrite' 17 August 1948. Cruiskeen Lawn File, Vol. 14, NM.

152 *CL* (25 February 1948). Original dated 10 January 1947, Cruiskeen Lawn File, Vol. 14, NM.

153 '. . . *At Swim-Two-Birds* had established a position from which he could neither advance nore decently withdraw. It had been a brilliantly conceived undertaking; but as far as the writing of novels was concerned, it was also brilliantly and deliberately nihilistic.' Cronin, *No Laughing Matter*, pp. 164–165.

154 *CL* (30 May 1947). Original dated 25 May 1947, Cruiskeen Lawn File, Vol. 14, NM.

155 Donohue, *The Irish Anatomist*, p. 138. See also a column for which O'Nolan has been charged with a characteristic misogyny: *CL* (13 June 1947), *FC*, p. 99. Original dated 8 June 1947, Cruiskeen Lawn File, Vol. 15, NM.

156 *CL* (1 June 1949). Original (a slightly altered version) dated 29 May 1949, Cruiskeen Lawn File, Vol. 17, NM.

157 *CL* (21 November 1949). Original dated 16 November 1949, Cruiskeen Lawn File, Vol. 17, NM. The point recurs in a Montgomery essay on Joyce: 'Joyeux Quicum Ulysse . . . Swissairis Dubellay Gadelice', in *A Bash in the Tunnel*, p. 68.

158 Tellingly, Myles appears twice in the distinguished list. *CL* (7 July 1950). Original dated 27 June 1950, Cruiskeen Lawn File, Vol. 18, NM. For other Montgomery columns on Joyce see 9 May 1947 (NM, 4 May); 21 January 1948 (NM, 16 January); 18 August 1948 (NM, 5 August); 12 September 1949 (NM, 8 September).

159 *CL* (16 June 1950). Original dated 11 June 1950, Cruiskeen Lawn File, Vol. 18, NM.

160 Arland Ussher asked a favour: '. . . would I mind shooting Sean O'Faolain? Felt tempted to send the terribly obvious reply "I'll be hanged if I do", but . . . do know, it's funny – laugh at me if you will – but . . . I'm considering it!' *CL* (28 March 1947).

161 Letter from 'Crosaire', *The Irish Times* (31 March 1947).

162 *CL* (5 January 1948).

163 *CL* (7 January 1948). Original dated 4 January 1948, Cruiskeen Lawn File, Vol. 16, NM.

164 In 1948 John Garvin was made Secretary of the Department and O'Nolan was appointed head of the Planning Section. Cronin, *No Laughing Matter*, p. 179.

165 *CL* (8 March 1948).

166 *CL* (9 April 1948).

167 *CL* (28 April 1948).

168 For readers' Keats and Chapman stories see *CL* 27 September, 1 October, 18 October, 15 November 1948. On 9 November 1949 Myles provided his own critique of these efforts, complaining they were too 'literary' and 'usually omit the

essential boredom of the build-up'. The first of these biographies was by Montgomery *CL* (25 October 1948), original dated 29 September 1948, Cruiskeen Lawn File, Vol. 16, NM.

169   *CL* (9 July 1948). The original idea was to regain agricultural land from ditches and boost employment by using human fencing, *CL* (21 January 1946). One of Myles's rare comments on partition was to note the biblical parallel: 'except the litigants in *that* case managed to see the joke and *didn't* cut the baby in two.' *CL* (25 March 1946).

170   *CL* (16 August 1948).

171   *CL* (10 September 1948).

172   *CL* (26 May 1947). Considering proposals for the new title of the state, he noted that the original *res publica* was shortened to *res* in Cicero, or 're' in English. This title, rather than 'Eire', 'would be a permanent reminder that the country, like the word, was partitioned.' *CL* (19 November 1948).

173   See *CL* (18 February 1949). The *Mail* announced that 'Ireland Puts the Clock Back Twenty Years' when the government refused to enter NATO because of partition. According to Myles, the piece was accompanied with a picture of a shillelagh. On the Pan-Am guide to Ireland see *CL* (25 March 1949) and on the GAA, *CL* (29 September 1948).

174   See respectively comments on O'Faoláin's article in *Poetry Ireland*: 'Translating from the Irish', *CL* (21 January 1949); on the British National Health Service, *CL* (28 November 1949), on the paper *Aiséirghe*, *CL* (4 February 1949).

175   *CL* (5 October 1949).

176   Dáil Debates, Vol. 28, Cols. 495-496, cited in letter from the Board's secretary, B. MacMahon, *The Irish Times* (14 July 1949).

177   *CL* (18 July 1949).

178   *CL* (7 December 1949).

179   Letter from Maria Jolas, *The Irish Times* (22 November 1949).

180   *CL* (7 September 1949).

181   *CL* (5 October 1949). A student charged Myles with being a mental serf to Britain while playing at being 'more Irish than the Irish themselves'. Letter from 'National Student' to *The Irish Times* (11 October 1949). Reprising the argument of the revival manuscript, Myles countered that the object in founding the NUI and Maynooth had been 'to perpetuate the provincialism of Ireland . . . to deny Irish people access to continental thought and experience . . .'. *CL* (14 October 1949).

182   This was a headline on the cover of his 1943 *Cruiskeen Lawn* anthology.

183   *CL* (23 December 1949).

184   *CL* (23 October 1950). In the same column, he interestingly notes that 'Keats must have sprung from an appalling pun made by the late and much-lamented Jimmy Montgomery', Niall Montgomery's father.

185   'Portrait Gallery: Myles na Gopaleen', *The Irish Times* (30–31 March 1956).

186   George Orwell, 'Funny, But Not Vulgar', in Sonia Orwell and Ian Angus (eds.), *The Collected Essays, Journalism and Letters of George Orwell*, 4 vols. (Harmondsworth: Penguin, 1970), vol. 3, p. 326. This article was first published in *The Leader* on 28 July 1945. D.B. Wyndham-Lewis wrote as 'Timothy Shy' for the *News Chronicle*.

187   This is from a 1944 article cited in Richard Ingrams's introduction to *Beachcomber: The Works of J. B. Morton* (London: Frederick Muller, 1974), p. 21.

6. 'THE DUBLIN CHARACTER'

1 As earler noted the popular image stuck, becoming a chapter title in one biography. Costello and van de Kamp, *Flann O'Brien: An Illustrated Biography*, p. 15.

2 O'Nolan stood for the NUI constituency, which had a total poll of nine thousand votes. Cronin writes that he regarded his candidature seriously and 'seemed to assume that the readership of his column would vote for him almost en bloc, so he might even top the poll.' *No Laughing Matter*, p. 192.

3 Frank Swinnerton, 'Right Properties', *The Observer* (19 March 1939).

4 *CL* (15 March 1944); reprinted in *BM*, p. 248.

5 See Donohue, *The Irish Anatomist*, pp. 105, 108. Mays sees the contrast dramatised in the structure of *Faustus Kelly* itself: 'the first act, which has all the charm and inconsequence of scenes in *The Third Policeman*'s barracks, is succeeded by two acts in which the moral implications come increasingly to determine how we react to the humour and in fact usurp it.' 'Brian O'Nolan: Literalist of the Imagination', in *Myles: Portrait of Brian O'Nolan*, p. 101.

6 Letter from Brian O'Nolan to Hilton Edwards (20 June 1942), SIUC. He was earlier encouraged by William Saroyan to adapt *The Third Policeman*: 'please make a play of it and don't worry about how it goes or how incredible or whatever it may be it seems to be.' (9 June 1940), SIUC.

7 R.M.F. 'Round the Theatres', *The Evening Mail* (26 January 1943).

8 *Faustus Kelly* opened in the Abbey on 25 January 1943 and ran for a fortnight. *The Insect Play* opened in the Gaiety on 22 March and closed after seven performances.

9 *Cruiskeen Lawn* (22 February 1943); cited in Donohue, *The Irish Anatomist*, p. 105. Though the plays were written as Myles na gCopaleen, there is no explicit reference to either play in the column.

10 'Bad reviews of Faustus Kelly'. Entry made on 26 January in a 1943 diary, SIUC.

11 *Teachta Dála* – a member of the Irish lower house of parliament.

12 Blythe wrote to O'Nolan that the takings were so low the play would have to close at the end of its second week. (4 February 1943), SIUC. However, the *Evening Mail* did report in the first week that audiences were enthusiastic, with *Faustus Kelly* playing to full houses. Man about Town, 'Jottings', *The Evening Mail* (1 February 1943).

13 *Cruiskeen Lawn* (3 April 1954); cited in Cronin, *No Laughing Matter*, p. 135.

14 Letter to Ernest Blythe (12 June 1942), SIUC.

15 Anon. 'Faustus Kelly', *The Irish Times* (26 January 1943).

16 Desmond Roche, *Local Government in Ireland* (Dublin: Institute of Public Administration, 1982), p. 347.

17 ibid., p. 344.

18 Anon. 'Faustus Kelly', *The Irish Times* (26 January 1943).

19 Letter to Hilton Edwards (20 June 1942), SIUC.

20 Letter from Ernest Blythe to Brian O'Nolan (4 July 1942), SIUC.

21 *CL* (25 June 1943).

22 '. . . *suar lag leathbruichte*'. Diary entry (11 January 1943), SIUC.

23 Hilton Edwards to Brian O'Nolan (24 July 1942), SIUC.

24 The first English production of *The Insect Play* was in 1922 in New York, with a translation by Owen Davis, *The World We Live In*. Paul Selver's translation (adapted by Nigel Playfair and Clifford Bax) – *And so ad infinitum* – was produced at the Regent Theatre in London, opening on 5 May 1923 (*IP*, 7).

25 Robert Tracy notes that the slogan is that of P.J. Hogan, a previous Minister for Agriculture.

26 Letter to Brian O'Nolan (21 October 1942), SIUC.
27 'Ní thaitheann leo an chéad mhír (a scríobh Montgomery nach mór an t-iomlán). D'iarradh orm mír nua ar fad a scríobhadh taobh istigh de seachtain. Gheallag go ndéan-fainn aimhlaidh air gan an t-am agam chuige.' 'They didn't like the first act (which was mostly written by Montgomery). They asked me to write a whole new act within the week. I promised I would do it without actually having the time for it.' Diary entry (11 January 1943), SIUC.
28 'References to the "Queen" up in the sky and "keeping pure till we meet her" made me squirm and the language and use of the Holy Name, along with the "mater-nity" act in the second part, was vile'. Letter from S.M. Dunn, *The Standard* (2 April 1943). On the same day, the paper published a retort from Myles to a scathing review from Gabriel Fallon. Robert Tracy thus suggests that 'S.M. Dunn' may be O'Nolan himself (*IP*, 15).
29 T.W. 'The Insect Play at the Gaiety', *The Irish Press* (23 March 1943).
30 'The Insect Play', *The Irish Times* (23 March 1943). See also D.S. 'The Insect Play. An Enjoyable Satire', *The Irish Independent* (23 March 1943).
31 Wills, *That Neutral Island*, pp. 217–218.
32 'There is no reference to sex as such anywhere; it is true that there are male and female characters, but very few people nowadays consider that alone an indelicacy.' Letter from Myles na gCopaleen. *The Standard* (2 April 1943). See Gabriel Fallon, 'Red, Red Roses!', *The Standard* (26 March 1943).
33 Michael Hamilton (A.M. Heath) to Timothy O'Keeffe (6 December 1961), TOK.
34 ibid, letter enclosed from Brian O'Nolan to Michael Hamilton (6 December 1961).
35 Timothy O'Keeffe to Gerald Gross (Pantheon), 4 September 1959, TOK. When *At Swim* was being prepared for its first American publication in 1951, editors were already wistfully speaking of *The Third Policeman* by name, which makes it doubly strange that the novel remained unpublished. Letter from Helen Wolff (Pantheon) to James Johnson Sweeney (12 October 1950), NM.
36 Niall Montgomery to James Johnson Sweeney (18 December 1950), NM.
37 'I was writing a novel, but I'm halfway through the title page alone. That's as much as the millions who read newspaper reviews and advertisements will ever see.' *CL* (10 February 1953).
38 Cronin, *No Laughing Matter*, p. 213.
39 Letter to Timothy O'Keeffe (29 October 1964), SIUC.
40 Niall Sheridan, 'Brian, Flann and Myles', p. 44.
41 O'Nolan boasted that he had excited Cyril Cusack with a promise of a good part, only then remarking that the book of the film wasn't written yet. Letter to Timothy O'Keeffe (11 January 1965), TOK. When Cecil Scott wrote that the novel would be a 'hopeless gamble' for the American market, he similarly bluffed that it would be 'no gamble at all; its US rights will be eagerly sought and it [will] almost certainly be made into a film, very likely by my pal John Huston'. (9 March 1965), SIUC.
42 Letter to Timothy O'Keeffe (28 May 1965), SIUC.
43 Letter to Brian Inglis (17 August 1960), SIUC. 'The I.T. is continually suppressing my stuff, which means I'll get next to nothing from them in a few weeks.' Letter to Niall Montgomery (6 August 1960), SIUC.
44 Letter to John Rosselli, Features Editor, *The Guardian* (6 April 1964), SIUC. O'Nolan proposed writing clandestinely for *The Evening Press*, with payment to be made to a third party. Letter to 'Pat' (24 August 1962), SIUC. See also letter from T. Hewart, *The Daily Express* (9 September 1956), SIUC. In late 1955, O'Nolan was attempting to set up his own paper, *The Dublin Man*. He reported at one stage that

he had promises of contributions from Oliver St John Gogarty, Seán O'Faoláin, Liam O'Flaherty, Patrick Kavanagh and Maurice Walsh. Letter to 'Billy' (17 October 1955), BC.

45 Letter from Patience Ross (A.M. Heath) to Brian O'Nolan (11 March 1940), SIUC.
46 Letter to Patience Ross (24 January 1940), SIUC.
47 W.L. Webb (*Guardian*) to Timothy O'Keeffe (7 December 1961), TOK.
48 See Thomas F. Shea, *Flann O'Brien's Exorbitant Novels* and M. Keith Booker, *Flann O'Brien, Bakhtin and Menippean Satire*.
49 Letter from Gerald Gross (Pantheon) to Timothy O'Keeffe (10 January 1961), TOK.
50 Letter from Brian O'Nolan to Timothy O'Keeffe (30 January 1961), TOK. He expressed similar sentiments on sending the manuscript to Mark Hamilton of A.M. Heath (27 January 1961), SIUC.
51 Letter to Mark Hamilton (20 February 1961), SIUC.
52 Letter to Mark Hamilton (n.d., December 1960?), SIUC.
53 Letter to Timothy O'Keeffe (16 December 1960). He also later argued to O'Keeffe that its importance would be confirmed by sales: 'Its apparently pedestrian style is delusive.' (7 June 1961), TOK.
54 Brooker, *Flann O'Brien*, p. 75.
55 ibid., p. 75.
56 ibid., p. 76.
57 'The "I" narrator or interlocutor, is himself a complete ass.' Letter to Mark Hamilton (20 February 1961), SIUC.
58 See letter to Mark Hamilton (n.d., December 1960?), SIUC.
59 Mays, 'Brian O'Nolan and Joyce on Art and on Life', p. 245.
60 '[A] Joycean and often very funny portrait of the novel's narrator as a young Dubliner', Paul Dehn, 'A Riot of Irishry', *The Sunday Telegraph* (12 November 1961). 'I was reminded more than once of Ellmann's account of the Joyce family life, especially by the relationship of bold brother Manus with his queer schemes for glory, and the cautious brother, Finbarr.' W.L. Webb, 'Flann O'Brien's Misterpiece', *The Manchester Guardian* (17 November 1961).
61 For an argument to the contrary see Booker, *Flann O'Brien, Bakhtin and Menippean Satire*, p. 86.
62 Paul Vanderham, *James Joyce and Censorship: The Trials of Ulysses* (New York: New York University Press, 1998), p. 28.
63 Letter to Timothy O'Keeffe (1 September 1961), TOK.
64 ibid.
65 Timothy O'Keeffe to Brian O'Nolan (5 September 1961), TOK.
66 Thomas Hogan, 'Myles na gCopaleen', p. 135.
67 Myles na gCopaleen, 'Joyce Re-Approached', *Irish Writing*, no. 10, January 1950, p. 72.
68 ibid. D.H. Lawrence also dismissed 'Penelope' as 'the dirtiest, most indecent, obscene thing ever written', cited in Paul Vanderham, *James Joyce and Censorship*, p. 27.
69 He wrote to Niall Montgomery, for example, that he was impatient to finish *The Dalkey Archive* 'so that I can write uproariously funny and obscene little book in Silva Gadelica Irish, poetry and all, with various familiar names . . . Naem moc in taei will bugger a small boy on the slopes of Slemish, afterwards asserting his innocence on the gods that Patrick is a myth, like his Master.' (18 January 1964), SIUC.
70 Letter to Hugh Leonard (27 October 1964), SIUC.
71 Hugh Leonard to Brian O'Nolan (17 August 1965), SIUC.

72 Letter to Timothy O'Keeffe (6 November 1961), SIUC.

73 Hopper, *Flann O'Brien*, p. 104.

74 Arguably, the ending is the final inscription of the sexual disgust which runs throughout the novel (Finbarr's vomiting follows the proposal that he 'settle down' with Annie). See ibid., pp. 70–71.

75 D.H. Lawrence, *Pornography and Obscenity* (London: Faber & Faber, 1929), p.15.

76 Booker argues that the underlying theme is contraception. *Flann O'Brien, Bakhtin and Menippean Satire*, p. 86.

77 Interview with Peter Duval-Smith, BBC (7 March 1962), cited in Asbee, *Flann O'Brien*, p. 107.

78 Letter to Timothy O'Keeffe (6 November 1961), SIUC.

79 'New Fiction', *The Times* (16 November 1961).

80 Letter to Mark Hamilton, A.M. Heath (10 March 1963), SIUC.

81 Letter to Gerald Gross, Pantheon (10 September 1962), SIUC.

82 CL (23 December 1961).

83 Letter to Timothy O'Keeffe (28 May 1962), TOK.

84 CL (16 June 1962).

85 Letter to Timothy O'Keeffe (10 January 1963), TOK.

86 Letter to Timothy O'Keeffe (30 April 1963), TOK.

87 Letter to Timothy O'Keeffe (15 November 1963), TOK.

88 ibid. The first typescript is dated October 1963 and held in the McFarlin Library, University of Tulsa. The final revised typescript is held in the Harry Ransom Center, University of Texas at Austin; although this replicates the dated title page of the earlier typescript (October 1963), it was only submitted to O'Nolan's London agents on 11 February 1964.

89 O'Nolan admitted that the final quarter of the manuscript was 'a farrago of mis-writing, slop, mistypes, repetition, with many passages quite meaningless'. However, it was transposed to the third person, 'pitilessly excoriated for verbal weeds, [and] bad sloppy writing', and dispatched in all of six weeks. Letter to Timothy O'Keeffe (22 January 1964), SIUC.

90 Letter to Mark Hamilton, A.M. Heath (28 November 1963), SIUC.

91 See Shea, *Flann O'Brien's Exorbitant Novels*, pp. 166–167 and for a complementary reading of *The Hard Life* see Donohue, *The Irish Anatomist*, pp. 182–184.

92 'Ignorant reviewers have messed me up with another man, to my intense embarrassment and disgust, and he will be another character. I mean James Joyce. I'm going to get my own back on that bugger.' Letter to Gerald Gross, Pantheon (10 September 1962), SIUC.

93 Booker, *Flann O'Brien, Bakhtin and Menippean Satire*, p. 105.

94 Shea highlights these qualities in the passage but interprets it as O'Nolan's comment on the nature of fiction, with a narrator who 'toys with our semiwilling suspension of disbelief'. *Flann O'Brien's Exorbitant Novels*, p. 154. In his reading, this narrator has a 'deliberately designed clumsiness', p. 161.

95 O'Nolan also re-hashed the old *Cruiskeen Lawn* joke that a scholar in the Institute of Advanced Studies had discovered there were two Saint Patricks but no God (DA, 35).

96 After a wholly superfluous conversation on income tax, the narrator remains sufficiently alert to note that his 'talk was arid and useless' – yet not sufficiently alert to cut it out (DA, 122). See Brooker, *Flann O'Brien*, pp. 85–86.

97 O'Nolan himself reminded Hugh Leonard to observe the principle in his adaptation of *The Dalkey Archive*: 'You must remember that the most crackpot invention must be subject to its own stern logic.' (14 November 1964), SIUC.

98 Anon. 'An Irishman's Diary', *The Irish Times* (23 July 1960). Before *At Swim* was re-published, O'Nolan confessed to his new publisher that '. . . I have personally no faith whatever in the book but I realise that its true worth is quite irrelevant.' Letter to Timothy O'Keeffe (1 September 1959), SIUC.

99 Letter to Timothy O'Keeffe (27 November 1963), SIUC.

100 Letter to Timothy O'Keeffe (30 April 1963), TOK.

101 For Myles's responses to O'Rahilly's diatribe in *The Standard* against *The Irish Times* editorial on the issue see *FC* pp. 158–173. He lambasted 'the absurdity of his idea that the Catholic Church in this country is in danger and in need of his protection, and that this protection must be afforded by something next-door to foul-mouthedness. The Church would not be the first institution or person to be embarrassed by the solicitous concern of friends' (*FC*, 159).

102 See *No Laughing Matter*, pp. 216–217. 'I enclose *curriculum mensis* of *The Dalkey Archive*. God forgive me but I find the material, so far, funny and sometimes shocking.' Letter to Timothy O'Keeffe (1 April 1963), TOK.

103 Interview with Tim Pat Coogan (RTÉ, 1964).

104 Letter to Leslie Daiken (19 April 1963), Leslie Daiken Papers, National Library of Ireland.

105 Brian Nolan, 'A Bash in the Tunnel', p. 19.

106 Letter to Timothy O'Keeffe (30 April 1963), TOK. 'If there was an attempt at defence, the hearing might put the Lady Chatterley case in the ha'penny class'. Letter to Timothy O'Keeffe (27 November 1963), TOK.

107 Brian Nolan, 'A Bash in the Tunnel', p. 19.

108 Letter to Cecil Scott (11 December 1963), quoted in Asbee, *Flann O'Brien*, p. 105.

109 Letter to Brian O'Nolan from Timothy O'Keeffe (22 October 1963), SIUC.

110 Letter to Cecil Scott (6 January 1964), SIUC.

111 On this point see Booker, *Flann O'Brien, Bakhtin and Menippean Satire*, p. 108.

112 Cronin, *No Laughing Matter*, p. 227. Though 'John Hackett' was a pseudonym O'Nolan had proposed as an alternative to Flann O'Brien. Letter to Longman's (15 January 1939), SIUC.

113 Tulsa manuscript, p. 202. *The Hard Life* also presents the religious life as captivity; when Manus compares the Christian Brothers' house to prison, Collopy protests that it 'may be a jail of a kind but the chains are of purest eighteen-carat finest gold which the holy brothers like to kiss on their bended knees' (*HL*, 13–14).

114 Brian Nolan, 'A Bash in the Tunnel', p. 19.

115 *CL* (6 October 1951).

116 Letter from Brian O'Nolan to Gerald Gross (13 August 1964), SIUC.

117 Tulsa manuscript, p. 111.

118 ibid., p. 147. When revising the draft, he rejected Montgomery's suggestion that he should target these critics. Few enough had even heard of Joyce, and 'the fraction who have read any of the exegetic bullshit or are aware of its absurdities is too tiny to be expressed.' (9 January 1964), SIUC.

119 Tulsa manuscript, p. 150.

120 Niall Montgomery to Brian O'Nolan (6 January 1964), SIUC.

7 AFTERWORD

1 'Vinegar Eel', *The Standard* (8 November 1940).

2 Hopper, *Flann O'Brien*, p. 60.

Bibliography

BOOKS

Flann O'Brien. *At Swim-Two-Birds*. London: Penguin, 1939, 2000.

Myles na gCopaleen. *An Béal Bocht*. Cork: Mercier, 1941, 1999.

—. *Cruiskeen Lawn*. Dublin: Cahill & Co., 1943.

Flann O'Brien. *The Hard Life*. London: Scribner, 1961, 2003.

—. *The Dalkey Archive*. London: Flamingo, 1964, 1993.

—. *The Third Policeman*. London: Flamingo, 1967, 1993.

Myles na Gopaleen (Flann O'Brien). *The Best of Myles*, Kevin O'Nolan (ed.). London: Picador, 1968, 1977.

Flann O'Brien. *The Poor Mouth*, Patrick C. Power (trans.). Illinois: Dalkey Archive, 1973, 1996.

—. *Stories and Plays*. London: Hart-Davis, MacGibbon, 1973.

—. *Further Cuttings from Cruiskeen Lawn*, Kevin O'Nolan (ed.). Illinois: Dalkey Archive, 1976, 2000.

—. *The Various Lives of Keats and Chapman and The Brother*, Benedict Kiely (ed.). London: Hart-Davis, MacGibbon, 1976.

Flann O'Brien (Myles na Gopaleen). *The Hair of the Dogma*, Kevin O'Nolan (ed.). London: Hart-Davis, MacGibbon, 1977.

—. *A Flann O'Brien Reader*, Stephen Jones (ed.). New York: Viking, 1978.

Myles na Gopaleen (Flann O'Brien). *Myles Away From Dublin*, Martin Green (ed.). London: Granada, 1985.

Flann O'Brien (Myles na Gopaleen). *Myles Before Myles*, John Wyse Jackson (ed.). London: Grafton, 1988.

—. *Rhapsody in Stephen's Green: The Insect Play*, Robert Tracy (ed.). Dublin: Lilliput, 1994.

Flann O'Brien. *Flann O'Brien at War: Myles na gCopaleen 1940–1945*, John Wyse Jackson (ed.). London: Duckworth, 1999.

UNPUBLISHED MATERIAL

Brian Ó Nualláin. 'Tráchtas ar Nádúir-fhilíocht na Gaedhilge', unpublished MA thesis, UCD, 1934.

SERIAL JOURNALISM

Brother Barnabas, et al. *Comhthrom Féinne/The National Student*. vol. 1, no. 2 – vol. 13, no. 3, 15 May 1931 – Christmas 1935.

Count O'Blather, et al. *Blather*. vol. 1, no. 4 – vol. 1, no. 5, August 1934 – January 1935.

Myles na gCopaleen. 'Cruiskeen Lawn', *The Irish Times*. (4 October 1940–1 April 1966).

OCCASIONAL ARTICLES AND STORIES

Brian Ua Nualláin. 'Seán Mac hÉil – Laoch gan Eagla', *The Irish Press*. (10 November 1931).

—. 'Mná Borba na Romha', *The Irish Press*. (2 January 1932).

—. 'Dioghaltais ar Ghallaibh 'sa Bhliain 2032!', *The Irish Press*. (18 January 1932).

—. 'Teacht agus Imtheacht Sheáin Bhuidhe', *The Irish Press*. (13 June 1932).

—. 'Scéal Beag gan Ghruaim', *The Evening Press*. (17 June 1932).

—. 'Carneraí na hÉireann', *The Evening Press*. (22 June 1932).

—. 'Gaedhealtacht na Lae Indiu: Breoiteacht gan Ainm', *The Evening Press*. (29 June 1932).

—. 'Siúbhlóid', *The Irish Press*. (4 July 1932).

—. 'Ní Mhaireann an Sógh acht Seal', *The Evening Press*. (7 July 1932).

—. 'Amuigh i mBáid', *The Evening Press*. (16 July 1932).

—. 'Reidhteach na Ceiste', *The Evening Telegraph and Evening Press*. (21 July 1932).

—. 'Rath agus Mío-Rath', *The Evening Telegraph and Evening Press*. (29 July 1932).

—. 'Cuaird Lae i gConamara', *The Evening Telegraph and Evening Press*. (16 August 1932).

—. 'Eachtra an Fhir Olta: !Ceol!', *The Irish Press*. (24 August 1932).

—. 'Tús na hoibre', *The Evening Telegraph and Evening Press*. (29 August 1932).

—. 'Míon-Tuairimí ár Sinnsir', *The Irish Press*. (29 September 1932).

—. 'Seoidín Fánach: Focal Fiuntach', *The Evening Telegraph and Evening Press*. (3 October 1932).

—. 'Mairg a bhíos i nGrádh', *The Evening Telegraph and Evening Press*. (13 October 1932).

—. 'Uaisle an Bhealaigh Mhóir', *The Irish Press*. (21 November 1932).

—. 'Ceist gan Reiteach', *The Irish Press*. (Christmas 1932?), reprinted in Breandán Ó Conaire (ed.), *Nua-Aois*. Áth Cliath: Coláiste na hOllscoile, 1970, 44–46.

—. 'Aistear Pheadair Dhuibh', *Inisfail*, vol. 1, no. 1, March 1933, 63–64.

—. 'Pisa bec oc Parnabus', *Ireland Today*, vol. 3, no. 2, February 1938, 138, 165.

Flann O'Brien. 'Standish Hayes O'Grady', *The Irish Times*. (16 October 1940).

—. 'Going to the Dogs!', *The Bell*, vol. 1, no. 1, October 1940, 19–24.

—. 'The Trade in Dublin', *The Bell*, vol. 1, no. 2, November 1940, 6–15.

—. 'The Dance Halls', *The Bell*, vol. 1, no. 5 , February 1941, 44–52.

—. 'John Duffy's Brother', *Story*, vol. 19, no. 90, July–August 1941, 65–68.

Lir O'Connor. 'The Beauty from Limerick', *The Irish Digest*. (August 1941), 101–104.

—. 'How to Behave in High Society', *The Irish Digest*. (March 1942), 38–41.

Flann O'Brien. 'When I Met William of Orange', *The Irish Digest*. (April 1942), 20–23.

Lir O'Connor. 'Let Me Choose Your Christmas Card', *The Irish Digest*. (December 1942), 27–29.

—. 'I'm Telling You No Lie!', *The Irish Digest*. (July 1943), 15–18.

Myles na gCopaleen. 'Drink and Time in Dublin', *Irish Writing*, no. 1, 1946, 71–77.

—. 'Forward' in Tom Merry (ed.), *Where to Drink: Well-Known Irish Bars and Lounges*. Tralee: The Kerryman, 1949.

Brian Nolan. 'The Martyr's Crown', *Envoy*, vol. 1, no. 3, February 1950, 57–62.

Myles na gCopaleen. 'Baudelaire and Kavanagh', *Envoy*, vol. 3, November 1950, 78–81.

Brian Nolan. 'A Bash in the Tunnel', *Envoy*, vol. 5, no. 17, April 1951, 5–11.

Myles na gCopaleen. 'I Don't Know', *Kavanagh's Weekly*, vol. 1, no. 3, 26 April 1952, 3–4.

—. 'The Sensational New "Phoenix"', *Kavanagh's Weekly*, vol. 1, no. 4, 3 May 1952, 4.

—. 'How Are You Off For Tostals?', *Kavanagh's Weekly*, vol. 1, no. 5, 10 May 1952, 4.

—. 'Motor Economics', *Kavanagh's Weekly*, vol. 1, no. 7, 24 May 1952, 6.

Myles na gCopaleen. 'Donabate', *Irish Writing*, no. 20–21, November 1952, 41–42.

Myles na Gopaleen. 'Two in One', *The Bell*, vol. 19, no. 8, July 1954, 30–34.

Myles na gCopaleen. 'Front-Of-The-House Man', in *RIAI Year Book* (1957), reprinted in John Graby (ed.) *150 Years of Architecture in Ireland*. Dublin: RIAI, 1989, 75.

Flann O'Brien. 'Words', *Development*, no. 9 Spring Show 1959, 63.

—. 'National Gallery: Sean O'Sullivan', *Development*, no. 16 December 1959, 10.

'Quidnunc'. 'An Irishman's Diary', *The Irish Times*. (23 July 1960).

Myles na Gopaleen. 'On Public Taste and Decorum', *Hibernia*, no. 24, 9 September 1960, 3.

—. 'Christmas Time at Santry', *The Harp*, vol. 3, no. 6, November–December 1960, 8.

—. 'Notes on 1961', *The Harp*, Winter 1961, 18.

Flann O'Brien. 'Enigma', *The Irish Times*. (16 June 1962).

Myles na Gopaleen. 'The Fausticity of Kelly', *RTV Guide*. (23 January 1963), 12–13.

—. 'Pots and Pains', *The Irish Housewife*, no. 14, 1963–64, 70–71.

Flann O'Brien. 'Behan, Master of Language', *The Sunday Telegraph*. (22 March 1964).

Myles na Gopaleen. 'De Me', *New Ireland*, March 1964, 41–42.

Flann O'Brien. 'Gael Days', *The Manchester Guardian*. (6 May 1964).

—. 'St Augustine Strikes Back: De scribendi periculo', *Bookmark*. (1964), 2.

Myles na Gopaleen. 'A Pint of Plain', *The Harp*, vol. 8, no. 2, Summer 1965, 27.

Flann O'Brien. 'The Saint and I', *The Manchester Guardian*. (19 January 1966).

Myles na gCopaleen. 'A Christmas Garland', *The Harp*, Christmas 1966, 19.

Brian O'Nolan. 'After Hours', *Threshold*, no. 21, Summer 1967, 15–18.

TRANSLATION

Myles na gCopaleen. 'The Tired Scribe', *Poetry Ireland*, no. 4, January 1949, 12.

Brian Ó Nualláin. *Mairéad Gillan*. Dublin: Stationery Office, 1953.

Myles na Gopaleen. 'Three Poems from the Irish', *Lace Curtain*, no. 4, Summer 1971, 46–47.

REVIEWS

Myles na gCopaleen, 'Leabhair Nua', *The Irish Times*. (8 February 1941).

—. 'Leabhair Nua', *The Irish Times*. (22 February 1941).

Anon. 'Two Irishmen. James Joyce and John McCormack', *The Irish Times*. (22 March 1941).

Myles na gCopaleen. 'The Presidential Office'. *The Irish Times*. (9 June 1945).

—. 'Joyce Re-approached', *Irish Writing*, no. 10, January 1950, 71–72.

—. 'A Glass of Punch', *Irish Writing*, no. 11, May 1950, 73.
—. 'Book Reviews', *Envoy*, vol. 3, no. 12, November 1950, 88–89.
—. 'Book Reviews', *Envoy*, vol. 4, no. 15, February 1951, 76–77.
Brian Nolan. 'Small Men and Black Dogs', *The Manchester Guardian*. (14 October 1960).
M. na G. 'Something New', *The Irish Times*. (20–1 April 1962).
Flann O'Brien. 'George Bernard Shaw on Language', *The Irish Times*. (23 January 1965).
—. 'At the Crossroads', *The Irish Times*. (20 February 1965).
—. 'The Cud of Memory', *The Manchester Guardian*. (15 October 1965).

CRITICAL BIBLIOGRAPHY

The following manuscript collections have been consulted:

Brian O'Nolan Papers, Morris Library, Southern Illinois University Carbondale.
Flann O'Brien Collection, John J. Burns Library, Boston College.
Flann O'Brien Collection, Harry Ransom Research Center, University of Texas at Austin.
Niall Montgomery Collection, National Library of Ireland
Timothy O'Keeffe Collection, McFarlin Library, University of Tulsa.

Adams, Michael. *Censorship: The Irish Experience*. Dublin: Scepter Books, 1968.
Alexander, James D. 'Frank O'Connor's Joyce Criticism', *The Journal of Irish Literature*, vol. 21, no. 1, May 1992, 40–53.
Allen, Robert. *Voice of Britain: The Inside Story of the Daily Express*. Cambridge: Patrick Stephens, 1983.
Almqvist, Bo. 'The Irish Folklore Commission: Achievement and Legacy', *Béaloideas*, no. 45–7, 1977–9, 6–26.
'An Púcan Meidhreach'. 'Reviews', *The National Student*, no. 81, December 1941, 14.
An Rialtas. *Gaeltacht Commission Report*. Dublin: Stationery Office, 1926.
—. *Statement of Government Policy on Recommendations of the Commission*. Dublin: Stationery Office, 1928.
Anderson, Samuel. 'Pink Paper and the Composition of Flann O'Brien's *At Swim-Two-Birds*', unpublished MA thesis, Louisiana State University, 2002.
Anon. *You May Revive the Gaelic Language* . . . Áth Cliath: Connradh na Gaedhilge, 1937.
—. 'Nest of Novelists', *Times Literary Supplement*. (18 March 1939).
—. 'Irish Author's Experiment. Erudite Humour in Novel Form', *The Irish Times*. (25 March 1939).
—. 'Surrealist Sandwich. The Ireland of Fact, Fiction and the Pooka', *Glasgow Herald*. (30 March 1939).
—. 'The Reincarnation of Brother Barnabas', *The Irish Times*. (8 May 1939).
—. 'Current Affairs', *The Leader*. (27 December 1941).
—. 'Myles na gCopaleen', *The Leader*. (27 December 1941).
—. 'Book Review: *An Béal Bocht*', *TCD – A College Miscellany*. (5 February 1942), 62.
—. 'Faustus Kelly', *The Irish Times*. (26 January 1943).
—. 'The Insect Play', *The Irish Times*. (23 March 1943).
—. [Stanford Lee Cooper]. 'Eire's Columnist', *Time*. (23 August 1943), 90–92.

—. 'Portrait Gallery: Myles na Gopaleen', *The Irish Times*. (30–31 March 1956).

—. 'New Fiction', *The Times*. (16 November 1961).

—. 'Mylestones', *Times Literary Supplement*. (19 September 1968).

Ap Roberts, Ruth. 'At *Swim-Two-Birds* and the Novel as Self-Evident Sham', *Éire-Ireland*, vol. 5, no. 2, Summer 1971, 76–97.

Aragon, Louis. 'Lewis Carroll. En 1931', *Le Surréalisme au service de la révolution*. (1931), 25–26.

Asbee, Sue. *Flann O'Brien*. Boston: Twayne, 1991.

Atherton, James S. 'Lewis Carroll: The Unforeseen Precursor', in *The Books At The Wake*. London: Faber & Faber, 1959, 124–136.

Augusteijn, Joost (ed.). *Ireland in the 1930s*. Dublin: Four Courts, 1999.

Baudelaire, Charles. 'On the Essence of Laughter', in Jonathan Mayne (ed. and trans.), *The Mirror of Art*. London: Phaidon, 1955, 131–153.

Beattie, James. 'An Essay on Laughter and Ludicrous Composition', in *Essays: On Poetry and Music*. London: Routledge/ Thoemmes Press, 1996, 295–450.

Beckett, Samuel. *Disjecta*. London: John Calder, 1983.

—. *Watt*. London: John Calder, 1953, 1976.

The Bellman. 'Meet Dr. Hayes: or The Genial Censor', *The Bell*, vol. 3, no. 2, November 1941, 106–114.

—. 'Meet R.M. Smyllie', *The Bell*, vol. 3, no. 3, December 1941, 180–188.

Benstock, Bernard. 'The Three Faces of Brian O'Nolan', *Éire-Ireland*, vol. 3, no. 3, Autumn 1968, 51–65.

Bergson, Henri. *Laughter*, Cloudesley Brereton and Fred Rothwell (trans.). London: Macmillan, 1911, 1921.

Bobotis, Andrea. 'Queering Knowledge in Flann O'Brien's *The Third Policeman*', *Irish University Review*, vol. 32, no. 2, Autumn/ Winter 2002, 242–258.

Booker, M. Keith. '*The Dalkey Archive*: Flann O'Brien's Critique of Mastery', *Irish University Review*, Autumn/ Winter 1993, 269–285.

—. *Flann O'Brien, Bakhtin and Menippean Satire*. Syracuse: Syracuse University Press, 1995.

Borges, Jorge Luis. 'When Fiction lives in Fiction', in Eliot Weinberger (ed.), *The Total Library: Non-Fiction 1922–1986*. London: Allen Lane, 2000, 160–162.

Boyd, Ernest. *Ireland's Literary Renaissance*. Dublin: Maunsel, 1922.

Boyle, William. *The Eloquent Dempsy*. Dublin and Waterford: M.H. Gill, n. d.

Brooker, Joseph. 'Estopped by Grand Playsaunce: Flann O'Brien's Post-colonial Lore', *Journal of Law and Society*, vol. 31, no. 1, March 2004, 15–37.

—. *Flann O'Brien*. London: Northcote, 2005.

—. 'Children of Destiny: Brian O'Nolan and the Irish Ready-Made School', http://eprints.bbk.ac.uk/archive/00000172/

Brown, Terence. *Ireland: A Social and Cultural History 1922–2002*. London: Harper Perennial, rev. ed. 2004.

—. 'The Counter-Revival: Provincialism and Censorship 1930-65', in Seamus Deane (ed.), *The Field Day Anthology of Irish Writing*, 3 vols. Derry: Field Day, 1991, vol. 3, 89–93.

Browne, Joseph. 'Flann O'Brien: 'Post' Joyce or 'Propter' Joyce?', *Éire-Ireland*, vol. 19, no. 4, 1984, 148–157.

Buttimer, Neil and Máire Ní Annracháin, 'Irish language and literature, 1921-84', in J.R. Hill (ed.), *A New History of Ireland*, 9 vols. Oxford: Oxford University Press, 2003, vol. 7, 538–386.

Capek, Josef and Karel. *R. U. R. and The Insect Play*. Oxford: Oxford University Press, 1923, 1961.

Carroll, Lewis. *Alice's Adventures in Wonderland*. London: Penguin, 1998.

Chace, William M. 'Joyce and Flann O'Brien', *Éire-Ireland*, vol. 22, no. 4, Winter 1987, 140–152.

Christian Brothers. *The Higher Literary Reader*. Dublin: M.H. Gill & Son, 1925.

Clissmann, Anne and David Powell (eds.). 'A Flann O'Brien/Myles na gCopaleen Number', *The Journal of Irish Literature*, vol. 3, no. 1, January 1974.

Clissmann, Anne. *Flann O'Brien: A Critical Introduction*. Dublin: Gill & Macmillan, 1975.

Clune, Anne. 'Mythologizing Sweeny', *Irish University Review*, vol. 26, no. 1, Spring/Summer 1996, 48–60.

— and Tess Hurson (eds.). *Conjuring Complexities*. Belfast: Institute of Irish Studies, 1997.

Cohen, David. 'James Joyce and the Decline of Flann O'Brien', *Éire-Ireland*, vol. 22, no. 2, Summer 1987, 153–160.

—. 'An Atomy of the Novel: Flann O'Brien's At *Swim-Two-Birds*', *Twentieth-Century Literature*, vol. 39, no. 2, Summer 1993, 208–229.

Colebrook, Claire. *Irony*. London and New York: Routledge, 2004.

Connolly, Cyril. *Enemies of Promise*. London: André Deutsch, 1938, 1988.

Coogan, Tim Pat. Interview with Brian O'Nolan. RTÉ archive, 1964.

Corcoran, Neil. *After Yeats and Joyce: Reading Modern Irish Literature*. Oxford: Oxford University Press, 1997.

Corkery, Daniel. *The Hidden Ireland*. Dublin and Melbourne: Gill, 1924, 1967.

—. *Synge and Anglo-Irish Literature*. Cork: Mercier, 1931, 1966.

—. *What's This About the Gaelic League?* Áth Cliath: Connradh na Gaedhilge, 1942.

—. *The Philosophy of the Gaelic League*. Áth Cliath: Connradh na Gaedhilge, 1948.

Cornwell, Neil. *The Literary Fantastic: from Gothic to postmodernism*. London: Harvester Wheatsheaf, 1990.

Costello, Peter and Peter Van de Kamp. *Flann O'Brien: An Illustrated Biography*. London: Bloomsbury, 1987.

Coughlan, Patricia and Alex Davis (eds.). *Modernism and Ireland: The Poetry of the 1930s*. Cork: Cork University Press, 1995.

Cronin, Anthony. *Dead As Doornails*. Dublin: Lilliput, 1976, 1999.

—. *Heritage Now*. Dingle: Brandon, 1982.

—. *No Laughing Matter: The Life and Times of Flann O'Brien*. London: Grafton, 1989.

Cronin, Michael. 'The Imaginary Gaeilgeoir,' *Graph*, no. 6, Summer 1989, 16–18.

Cunningham, Valentine. *British Writers of the 1930s*. Oxford: Oxford University Press, 1988.

Curran, Stephen. '"No-this-is-not-from-the-Bell": Brian O'Nolan's 1943 *Cruiskeen Lawn* Anthology', *Éire-Ireland*, vol. 34, no. 2–3, 1997, 78–92.

—. '"Could Paddy leave off from copying just for five minutes": Brian O'Nolan and Éire's Beveridge Plan', *Irish University Review*, vol. 31, no. 2, Autumn/Winter 2001, 353–375.

D. Ó C. 'An Béal Bocht', *Connacht Tribune*. (20 December 1941).

D.S. 'Witty Dialogues in Abbey Play', *The Irish Independent*. (26 January 1943).

—. '"The Insect Play". An Enjoyable Satire', *The Irish Independent*. (23 March 1943).

De Blácam, Aodh. *Gaelic Literature Surveyed*. Dublin: Talbot, 1929, 1973.

—. *A First Book of Irish Literature*. Dublin: Talbot, 1934.

—. 'The Age-Lasting Peasant', *The Capuchin Annual*, 1935, 251–257.

De Paor, Louis. 'Twisting the Knife', *The Irish Times*. (29 March 2002).

De Vere White, Terence. 'Smyllie and his people', *The Irish Times*. (14 June 1984).

Deane, Seamus. *Strange Country: Modernity and Nationhood in Irish Writing since 1790*. Oxford: Clarendon, 1997.

Dehn, Paul. 'A Riot of Irishry', *The Sunday Telegraph*. (12 November 1961).

Deming, Robert H. (ed.). *James Joyce: The Critical Heritage*. Vol. 1 1902–27, Vol. II 1928–41. London: Routledge & Kegan Paul, 1970.

Devlin, Joseph. 'The Politics of Comedy in At *Swim-Two-Birds*', *Éire-Ireland*, vol. 27, no. 4, Winter 1992, 91–105.

Doherty, Francis. '*Watt* in an Irish Frame', *Irish University Review*, vol. 21, no. 2, Autumn 1991, 187–203.

Donohue, Keith. *The Irish Anatomist: A Study of Flann O'Brien*. Dublin, Oxford, Bethesda: Maunsel/Academica Press 2002.

Dotterer, Ronald L. 'Flann O'Brien, James Joyce and *The Dalkey Archive*', *New Hibernia Review*, vol. 8, no. 2, Summer 2004, 54–63.

Downum, Denell. 'Citation and Spectrality in Flann O'Brien's At *Swim-Two-Birds*', *Irish University Review*, vol. 36, no. 2, Autumn/Winter 2006, 304–320.

Duff, Charles. *James Joyce and the Plain Reader*. New York: Haskell House, 1932, 1971.

Dunn, Douglas (ed.). *Two Decades of Irish Writing: A Critical Survey*. Chester Springs: Dufour, 1975.

Dunne, J.W. *An Experiment With Time*. London: Papermac, 1927, 1981.

—. *The Serial Universe*. London: Faber & Faber, 1934.

Duszenko, Andrzej. 'The Joyce of Science: Quantum Physics in *Finnegans Wake*', *Irish University Review*, Autumn/Winter 1994, 272–282.

E. de B. 'An Béal Bocht', *Sunday Independent*. (14 December 1941).

Eglinton, John. *Irish Literary Portraits*. London: Macmillan, 1935.

Eliot, T.S. *Selected Essays*. London: Faber & Faber, 1934.

Esty, Joshua D. 'Flann O'Brien's At *Swim-Two-Birds* and the Post-Post Debate', *Ariel*, vol. 26, no. 4, October 1995, 23–46.

Evans, Eibhlín. '"A Lacuna in the Palimpsest": A Reading of Flann O'Brien's At *Swim-Two-Birds*', *Critical Survey*, vol. 15, no. 1, January 2003, 91–107.

F. É. 'Gaelic Publications of Interest', *Irish Library Bulletin*, vol. 3, no. 2, March/April 1942, 22.

F. O'R. 'Myles Takes off His Coat!', *The Irish Times*. (13 December 1941).

Fallon, Brian. *An Age of Innocence: Irish Culture 1930–1960*. Dublin: Gill & Macmillan, 1998.

Fallon, Gabriel. 'Copaleen O'Brien', *The Standard*. (5 February 1943).

—. 'Red, Red Roses!', *The Standard*. (26 March 1943).

Fennell, Desmond. 'The Irish Language Movement: its Achievements and Failures', *Twentieth-Century Studies*, November 1970, 64–87.

Flaubert, Gustave. *Correspondance. Troisième Série (1852–1854)*. Paris: Louis Conard, Libraire-Éditeur, 1902.

—. *The Dictionary of Accepted Ideas*, Jacques Barzun (trans.). New York: New Directions, 1968.

Foley, Michael. 'The Comedy of Flann O'Brien', *The Honest Ulsterman*, vol. 19, no. 1, November 1969, 7–11.

Foster, Hal (ed.). *Postmodernism*. London: Pluto, 1985.

Foster, John Wilson (ed.). *The Cambridge Companion to the Irish Novel*. Cambridge: Cambridge University Press, 2006.

Foster, Thomas C. (ed.). *A Casebook on Flann O'Brien's At Swim-Two-Birds*. Dalkey Archive Press.

http://www.dalkeyarchive.com/casebooks/casebook_swim/introduction_swim.html

Freud, Sigmund. *Jokes and Their Relation to the Unconscious*, James Strachey (trans.), Angela Richards (ed.). London: Penguin, 1991.

Frye, Northrop. *Anatomy of Criticism*. Princeton: Princeton University Press, 1957.

Gallagher, Monique. 'The Poor Mouth: Flann O'Brien and the Gaeltacht', *Studies*. vol. lxxii, no. 287, Autumn 1983, 231–241.

—. 'Reflecting Mirrors in Flann O'Brien's *At Swim-Two-Birds*', *Journal of Narrative Technique*, vol. 22, no. 2, Spring 1992, 128–135.

Garvin, John. *James Joyce's Disunited Kingdom and the Irish Dimension*. Dublin: Gill & Macmillan, 1976.

Gibson, Andrew. *James Joyce*. London: Reaktion, 2006.

Giebus, Jay. 'Flann O'Brien's *At Swim-Two-Birds*', *Studies*, vol. 80, no. 317, Spring 1991, 65–75.

Gillis, Alan. *Irish Poetry of the 1930s*. Oxford: Oxford University Press, 2005.

Girvin, Alan Kevin. 'At the Limits of Cultural Nationalism: Language, Culture and Politics in the Earlier Writings of Brian O'Nolan/ Flann O'Brien/ Myles na Gopaleen'. Unpublished PhD thesis, Southampton, 1996.

Gordon, Lois. *The World of Samuel Beckett, 1906–1946*. New Haven and London: Yale University Press, 1996.

Gray, Donald J. 'The Uses of Victorian Laughter', *Victorian Studies*, vol. 10, no. 2, December 1966, 145–176.

Gray, Tony. *Mr Smyllie, Sir*. Dublin: Gill & Macmillan, 1991.

—. *The Lost Years: The Emergency in Ireland 1939–45*. London: Little, Brown, 1997.

Greacen, Robert. 'Is the Artist Really Necessary?', *The Irish Times*. (24 May 1947).

Gurewitch, Morton. *Comedy: The Irrational Vision*. Ithaca and London: Cornell University Press, 1975.

Gwynn, Stephen. *Irish Literature and Drama in the English Language: A Short History*. London, New York: T. Nelson, 1936.

Hart, Clive. *Structure and Motif in Finnegans Wake*. London: Faber & Faber, 1962.

Hassett, Joseph. 'Flann O'Brien and the Idea of the City', in Maurice Harmon (ed.). *The Irish Writer and the City*. Gerrards Cross: Smythe, 1984, 115–124.

Henderson, Gordon. 'An Interview With Mervyn Wall', *Journal of Irish Literature*, vol. 11, no. 1–2, January–May 1982, 3–18.

Henkle, Roger. *Comedy and Culture: England 1820–1900*. Princeton: Princeton University Press, 1980.

Henry, P.L. 'The Structure of Flann O'Brien's *At Swim-Two-Birds*', *Irish University Review*, vol. 20, no. 1, Spring 1990, 35–40.

Higgins, Aidan, prod. 'Discords of Good Humour: A Portrait of Brian O'Nolan', BBC Radio 3. (17 March 1982).

Hindley, Reg. *The Death of the Irish Language: A Qualified Obituary*. London, New York: Routledge, 1990.

Hirsch, Edward. 'The Imaginary Irish Peasant', *PMLA*, no. 106, 1991, 1116–1133.

Hogan, Thomas [Thomas Woods]. 'Myles na gCopaleen', *The Bell*, vol. 13, no. 2, November 1946, 129–140.

Holloway, Joseph. *Joseph Holloway's Irish Theatre* Vol. 3 (1938-1944), Robert Hogan and Michael J. O'Neill (eds). Dixon, California: Proscenium Press, 1970.

Holquist, Michael. 'What is a Boojum? Nonsense and Modernism', *Yale French Studies*, no. 43, 1969, 145-164.

Hopper, Keith. *Flann O'Brien: A Portrait of the Artist as a Young Post-modernist.* Cork: Cork University Press, 1995.

Horgan, John. 'Saving Us From Ourselves: Contraception, Censorship and the "Evil Literature" Controversy of 1926', *Irish Communications Review*, no. 5, 1995, 61-67.

Huber, Werner. 'Flann O'Brien and the Language of the Grotesque', in Birgit Bramsback and Martin Cohen (eds.). *Anglo-Irish and Irish Literature: Aspects of Language and Culture.* Uppsala: UUP, 1988, 123-130.

Hunt, Roy L. 'Hell Goes Round and Round: Flann O'Brien', *Canadian Journal of Irish Studies*, vol. 14, no. 2, January 1989, 60-73.

Hutchinson, John. *The Dynamics of Cultural Nationalism.* London: Allen & Unwin, 1987.

Hutcheon, Linda. *A Theory of Parody: The Teachings of Twentieth-Century Art Forms.* London, New York: Methuen, 1985.

—. *The Politics of Postmodernism.* London, New York: Routledge, 1989.

Huysmans, Joris-Karl. *Against Nature*, Margaret Mauldon (trans.). Oxford: Oxford University Press, 1998.

Huyssen, Andreas. *After the Great Divide: Modernism, Mass Culture, Postmodernism.* London & Basingstoke: Macmillan, 1988.

Imhof, Rudiger (ed.). *Alive Alive O!: Flann O'Brien's At Swim-Two-Birds.* Dublin and New Jersey: Wolfhound, 1985.

Janik, Ivan Del. 'Flann O'Brien: The Novelist as Critic', *Éire-Ireland*, vol. 4, no. 4, Winter 1969, 64-72.

Johnson, Lionel. 'Poetry and Patriotism', in *Poetry and Ireland: Essays by W.B.Yeats and Lionel Johnson.* Dublin: Cuala Press, 1908, 1970, 21-54.

Johnson, Nuala C. 'Building a nation: an examination of the Irish Gaeltacht Commission Report of 1926', *Journal of Historical Geography*, vol. 19, no. 2, 1993, 157-168.

—. 'Making Space: Gaeltacht Policy and the Politics of Identity', in Brian Graham (ed.). *In Search of Ireland: A Cultural Geography.* London: Routledge, 1997, 174-191.

Jordan, Heather Bryant. 'A Particular Flair, A Hound's Nose, A Keen Scent: Seán O'Faolain's Editorship of The Bell', *Éire-Ireland*, vol. 29, no. 4, 1997, 149-160.

Jordan, John. 'The Saddest Book Ever to Come out of Ireland', *Hibernia* (5 August 1960).

— (ed.). *The Pleasures of Gaelic Literature.* Cork: Mercier Press, 1977.

Joyce, James. *Dubliners.* London: Everyman, 1914, 1991.

—. *A Portrait of the Artist as a Young Man.* London: Flamingo, 1916, 1994.

—. *Ulysses*, Hans Walter Gabler (ed.). London: The Bodley Head, 1922, 1986.

—. *Letters of James Joyce.* vol. 1, Stuart Gilbert (ed.). New York: Viking, 1957, 1966.

—. *Occasional, Critical, and Political Writing*, Kevin Barry (ed.). Oxford: Oxford University Press, 2000.

Kearney, Richard. 'A Crisis of Imagination: An Analysis of a Counter-Tradition in the Irish Novel', *The Crane Bag*, vol. 3, no. 1, 1979, 58-70.

—. *Transitions: Narratives in Modern Irish Culture.* Manchester: Manchester University Press, 1988.

Kelleher, Margaret and Philip O'Leary (eds.). *The Cambridge History of Irish Literature*, 2 vols. Cambridge: Cambridge University Press, 2006.

Kemnitz, Charles. 'Beyond the Zone of Middle Dimensions: A Relativistic Reading of *The Third Policeman*', *Irish University Review*, vol. 15, no. 1, Spring 1985, 56–72.

Kennedy, Sighle. 'The Devil or Holy Water – Samuel Beckett's *Murphy* and Flann O'Brien's *At Swim-Two-Birds*', in Raymond Porter and James D. Brady (eds.). *Modern Irish Literature*. New York: Iona College Press, 1972, 251–260.

Kenner, Hugh. *Samuel Beckett: A Critical Study*. London: John Calder, 1961.

—. *Flaubert, Joyce and Beckett: The Stoic Comedians*. London: W.H. Allen, 1964.

Kharms, Daniil. *The Plummeting Old Woman*, Neil Cornwell (trans.). Dublin: Lilliput, 1989.

Kiberd, Declan. 'Writers in Quarantine? The Case for Irish Studies', *The Crane Bag*, vol. 3, no. 1, 1979, 9–21.

—. 'The Fall of the Stage Irishman', in Roland Schleifer (ed.). *The Genres of the Irish Literary Revival*. Dublin: Wolfhound, 1980, 39–60.

—. An *Béal Bocht* agus an Béarla', in *Idir Dhá Chúltur*. Baile Átha Cliath: Coiscéim, 1993, 202–27.

—. *Inventing Ireland*. London: Vintage, 1996.

—. *Irish Classics*. London: Granta, 2000.

Kiely, Benedict. 'Getting the Point', *The Irish Times*. (17 November 1973).

Kilroy, Tom. 'Mervyn Wall: The Demands of Satire', *Studies*, vol. 47, Spring 1958, 83–89.

Kinsella, Thomas. *The Dual Tradition*. Manchester: Carcanet, 1995.

Knox, Ronald. *God and the Atom*. London: Sheed & Ward, 1945.

Lanters, José. '"Still Life" Versus Real Life: The English Writings of Brian O'Nolan', in Wim Tigges (ed.). *Explorations in the Field of Nonsense*. Amsterdam: Rodopi, 1987, 161–181.

—. *Unauthorized Versions: Irish Menippean Satire, 1919–1952*. Washington: Catholic University of America Press, 2000.

L. B. 'Book Reviews', *Irish Rosary*. (February 1942).

L. O'R. 'Leabhair Nua', *Irish Independent*. (17 February 1942).

Lawrence, D.H. *Pornography and Obscenity*. London: Faber & Faber, 1929.

Leavis, F.R., *Mass Civilisation and Minority Culture*. London: Arden, 1930, 1979.

Leavis, Q.D. *Fiction and the Reading Public*. London: Chatto & Windus, 1932, 1965.

Lecercle, Jacques. *Philosophy of Nonsense: The Intuitions of Victorian Nonsense Literature*. London, New York: Routledge, 1994.

Lee, J.J. *Ireland 1912–1985*. Cambridge: Cambridge University Press, 1989.

Lee, L.L. 'The Dublin Cowboys of Flann O'Brien', *Western American Literature*, vol. 4, no. 3, Fall 1969, 219–225.

Lyons, F.S.L. 'The Battle of Two Civilisations', in *Ireland Since the Famine*. London: Weidenfeld & Nicolson, 1971, 219–242.

—. *Culture and Anarchy in Ireland, 1890–1939*. Oxford: Oxford University Press, 1979.

MacGill, Patrick. *Children of the Dead End*. Edinburgh: Canongate, 1914, 1999.

MacGreevy, Thomas. 'Homage to James Joyce', *transition*, no. 21, March 1932, 254–255.

McKibben, Sarah E. 'Born to Die . . . and to Live On: Terminal Metaphors in the Life of Irish', *The Irish Review*, vol. 26, Autumn 2000, 89–99.

MacKillop, James. *Fionn MacCumhail: Celtic Myth in English Literature*. Syracuse: Syracuse University Press, 1986.

MacMahon, Barbara. 'The Effects of Word Substitution in Slips of the Tongue: *Finnegans Wake* and *The Third Policeman*', *English Studies*, vol. 82, no. 3, 2001, 231–246.

MacManus, Francis (ed.). *The Years of the Great Test*. Cork: Mercier, 1967.

Mac Póilín, Aodán. '"Spiritual Beyond the Ways of Men" – Images of the Gael', *The Irish Review*, no. 16, 1994, 1–22.

Matthews, J.H. *Surrealism and the Novel*. Ann Arbor: University of Michigan Press, 1966.

Maume, David. *'Life That is Exile': Daniel Corkery and the Search for Irish Ireland*. Belfast: Institute of Irish Studies, 1993.

Mays J.C.C. 'Brian O'Nolan and Joyce on Art and on Life', *James Joyce Quarterly*, vol. 11, no. 3, Spring 1974, 238–256.

Mazzullo, Concetta. 'Flann O'Brien's Hellish Otherworld, from "Buile Suibhne" to *The Third Policeman*', *Irish University Review*, vol. 25, no. 2, Autumn/Winter 1995, 318–327.

McCartney, Donal. *UCD, A National Idea: The History of University College, Dublin*. Dublin: Gill & Macmillan, 1999.

McGuire, Jerry L. 'Teasing After Death: Metatextuality in *The Third Policeman*', *Éire-Ireland*, vol. 26, no. 2, Summer 1981, 107–121.

McHugh, Dave, prod. 'Myles, Yer Only Man'. RTÉ Radio 1 (17 February–9 March 2004).

McLoughlin, Timothy O. 'Brian O'Nolan/ Flann O'Brien/ Myles: Playing/ Spoiling', *Cycnos*, vol. 10, no. 2, 1993, 85–96.

McMullen, Kim. 'Culture as Colloquy – Flann O'Brien's Postmodern Dialogue with Irish Tradition', *Novel – A Forum on Fiction*, vol. 27, no. 1, 1993, 62–84.

Man About Town, 'Jottings', *The Evening Mail*. (1 February 1943).

Meenan, James (ed.). *A Centenary History of the Literary and Historical Society of University College Dublin, 1855–1955*. Tralee: Kerryman, 1956.

Mercier, Vivian. 'The Fourth Estate', *The Bell*, vol. 9, no. 4, January 1945, 290–297.

—. 'At Swim-Two-Birds', *Commonweal*, vol. 54, no. 3, 27 April 1951, 68–69.

—. *The Irish Comic Tradition*. Oxford: Oxford University Press, 1962.

—. 'Literature in English, 1921–84' in J.R.Hill (ed.). *A New History of Ireland, Vol. VII, Ireland, 1921–84*. Oxford: Oxford University Press, 2003, 487–537.

Merritt, Henry. 'Games, Ending and Dying in Flann O'Brien's *At Swim-Two-Birds*', *Irish University Review*, vol. 25, no. 2, Autumn/Winter 1995, 308–317.

Milner, G.B. 'Homo Ridens: Towards a Semiotic Theory of Humour and Laughter', *Semiotica*, vol. 5, 1972, 1–30.

Monro, D.H. *Argument of Laughter*. Carlton: Melbourne University Press, 1951.

Montgomery, Niall. 'The Pervigilium Phoenicis'. *New Mexico Quarterly*, vol. 23, no. 4, Winter 1953, 437–472.

—. 'No Symbols Where None Intended', in *New World Writing*. New York: New American Library of World Literature, 1954, 324–337.

—. 'Proust and Joyce. A Lecture', *The Dubliner*, no. 4, July–August 1962, 11–22.

Moran, D.P. *The Philosophy of Irish Ireland*. Dublin: James Duffy, 1905.

Morton, J.B. *The Best of Beachcomber*, Michael Frayn (ed.). London: Heinemann, 1963.

—. *The Bumper Beachcomber*, Richard Ingrams (ed.). London: Bloomsbury, 1974, 1991.

Moses, Michael Valdez. 'The Sadly Rejoycing Slave: Beckett, Joyce and Destructive Parody', *Modern Fiction Studies*, vol. 31, 1985, 659-674.

N. Ó M. 'An Béal Bocht" úd', *An Síol*. (1943-44).

Nowlan, Kevin B. and T. Desmond Williams (eds.). *Ireland in the War Years and After, 1939-51*. Dublin: Gill & Macmillan, 1969.

O'Brien, Conor Cruise. 'Our Wits About Us', in *Writers and Politics*. London: Chatto & Windus, 1965, 101-105.

O'Brien, George. 'Flann O'Brien', *Cambridge Quarterly*, vol. 7, no. 1, 1976, 85-92.

O'Brien, Kate. 'Fiction', *The Spectator*. (14 April 1939).

Ó Broin, León. 'Contemporary Gaelic Literature and Some of its Paradoxes', *The Capuchin Annual*, 1935, 121-134.

Ó Cadhain, Máirtín. 'Leabhar atá as Aora Móra Phróis na Gaeilge', *Feasta*, April 1965, 25-26.

Ó Ciosáin, Éamon. *Buried Alive: A Reply to* The Death of the Irish Language. Baile Átha Cliath: Dáil Uí Cadhain, 1991.

—. *An t-Éireannach 1934-1937: Páipéar Sóisialach Gaeltachta*. Baile Átha Cliath: An Clóchomhar Tta, 1993.

Ó Conaire, Breandán. 'Flann O'Brien, *An Béal Bocht* and Other Irish Matters', *Irish University Review*, vol. 3, no. 2, Autumn 1973, 121-140.

—. *Myles na Gaeilge*. Baile Átha Cliath: An Clóchomhar Tta, 1986.

O'Connor, Frank. 'Joyce - The Third Period', *The Irish Statesman*, 12 April 1930, 114-116.

—. 'A Broadcast that was Cancelled: D.H.Lawrence and Joyce', *The Irish Times*. (21 July 1937).

—. 'The Future of Irish Literature', *Horizon*, vol. 5, no. 25, January 1942, 53-63.

—. 'James Joyce: A Post-Mortem', *The Bell*, vol. 5, no. 5, February 1943, 363-375.

—. *Towards an Appreciation of Literature*. Dublin: Metropolitan Publishing Co., 1945.

—. *Irish Miles*. London: Hogarth Press, 1947, 1988.

—. *The Mirror in the Roadway*. New York: Knopf, 1956.

—. *The Backward Look*. London: Macmillan, 1967.

O'Crohan, Tomás. *The Islandman*, Robin Flower (trans.). Oxford: Oxford University Press, 1937, 2000.

Ó Cuív, Brian (ed.). *A View of the Irish Language*. Dublin: Stationery Office, 1969.

—. 'Irish Language and Literature, 1845-1921,' in W.E.Vaughan (ed.). *A New History of Ireland*, vol. 6. Oxford: Clarendon Press, 1996, 385-435.

'O'Donnell, Donat' [Conor Cruise O'Brien]. 'The Fourth Estate: The Irish Independent', *The Bell*, vol. 9, no. 5, February 1945, 386-394.

O'Donoghue, Bernard. 'Irish Humour and Verbal Logic', *Critical Quarterly*, vol. 24, no. 1, Spring 1982, 33-40.

Ó Drisceoil, Donal. *Censorship in Ireland 1939-1945*. Cork: Cork University Press, 1996.

O'Faoláin, Seán. 'Style and the Limitations of Speech', *Criterion*, vol. 4, September 1928, 67-87.

—. 'Anna Livia Plurabelle', *The Irish Statesman*, 5 January 1929, 354-355.

—. *Midsummer Night Madness*. London: Macmillan, 1932.

—. 'James Joyce and the New Fiction', *The American Mercury*, vol. 35, no. 140, August 1935, 433-437.

—. 'Daniel Corkery', *Dublin Magazine*, vol. 11, no. 2, April-June 1936, 49-61.

—. 'The Priests and the People', *Ireland Today*, no. 11, July 1937, 31-38.

–. 'Don Quixote O'Flaherty', *London Mercury*, vol. 37, no. 218, December 1937, 170–175.
–. 'This is Your Magazine', *The Bell*, vol. 1, no. 1, October 1940, 1–9.
–. '1916–1941: Tradition and Creation', *The Bell*, vol. 2, no. 1, April 1941, 5–12.
–. 'Provincialism', *The Bell*, vol. 2, no. 2, May 1941, 5–8.
–. 'Standards and Tastes', *The Bell*, vol. 2, no. 3, June 1941, 5–11.
–. 'Attitudes', *The Bell*, vol. 2, no. 6, September 1941, 5–12.
–. 'Yeats and the Younger Generation', *Horizon*, vol. 5, no. 25, January 1942, 43–54.
–. 'Fifty Years of Irish Literature', *The Bell*, vol. 3, no. 5, February 1942, 327–334.
–. 'The Gaelic League', *The Bell*, vol. 4, no. 2, May 1942, 77–86.
–. 'Gaelic – The Truth,' *The Bell*, vol. 5, no. 5, February 1943, 335–340.
–. 'Silent Ireland', *The Bell*, vol. 6, no. 6, September 1943, 457–466.
–. 'The Plain People of Ireland', *The Bell*, vol. 7, no. 1, October 1943, 1–7.
–. 'The Gaelic Cult', *The Bell*, vol. 9, no. 3, December 1944, 185–196.
Ó Giolláin, Diarmuid. *Locating Irish Folklore: Tradition, Modernity, Culture*. Cork: Cork University Press, 2000.
O'Grady, Thomas B. 'At *Swim-Two-Birds* and the Bardic Schools', *Éire-Ireland*, vol. 24, no. 3, Fall 1989, 65–77.
O'Grady, Standish Hayes (ed. and trans). *Silva Gadelica: A Collection of Tales in Irish*. Vol. 2. London: Williams & Norgate, 1892.
Ó Grianna, Seamus. *Caisleán Óir*. Cork: Mercier Press, 1924, 1999.
Ó Háinle, Cathal. 'Fionn and Suibhne in At *Swim-Two-Birds*', *Hermathena* vol. 142, 1987, 13–49.
O'Hara, Patricia. 'Finn MacCool and the Bard's Lament in Flann O'Brien's At *Swim-Two-Birds*', *Journal of Irish Literature*, vol. 15, no. 1, January 1986, 55–61.
O'Keeffe, J.G. (ed. and trans.). *Buile Suibhne*. London: The Irish Texts Society, 1913.
O'Keeffe, Timothy (ed.). *Myles: Portraits of Brian O'Nolan*. London: Martin, Brien & O'Keeffe, 1973.
O'Leary, Peter. *Irish Prose Composition*. Dublin: Irish Book Co., 1907.
–. *Papers on Irish Idiom*, Thomas F. O'Rahilly (ed.). Dublin: Browne & Nolan, 2nd ed., 1929.
–. *My Story*, Cyril O Céirín (trans.). Oxford: Oxford University Press, 1970, 1987.
–. *Séadna*, Cyril and Kit Ó Céirín (trans.). Dublin: Glendale Press, 1989.
O'Leary, Philip. *The Prose Literature of the Gaelic Revival, 1881–1921*. Pennsylvania: Pennsylvania University Press, 1994.
–. *Gaelic Prose in the Irish Free State, 1922–1939*. Dublin: UCD Press, 2004.
Ó Muircheartaigh, Tomás. '"There Are Lumps in it" – Myles', *An Glór*. (14 March 1942).
–. 'Ó Slán le Myles', *An Glór*. (25 April 1942).
O'Neill, Manus. 'Live Irish', *The Standard*. (2 January 1942).
Ó Nualláin, Ciarán. *The Early Years of Brian O'Nolan/ Flann O'Brien/ Myles na gCopaleen*, Róisín Ó Nualláin (trans.), Niall O'Nolan (ed.). Dublin: Lilliput, 1998.
Ó Riain, Pádraig. 'The Materials and Provenance of "Buile Shuibhne"', *Éigse*, vol. 15, no. 3, Samhradh 1974, 173–188.
O'Toole, Mary A. 'The Theory of Serialism in *The Third Policeman*', *Irish University Review*, vol. 18, no. 2, Autumn 1988, 215–225.

Ó Tuama, Seán, ed. *The Gaelic League Idea*. Cork: Mercier Press, 1972.

'Observer'. 'Scith', *Galway Observer*. (9 May 1942).

Oram, Hugh. *The Newspaper Book: A History of Newspapers in Ireland, 1649–1983*. Dublin: MO Books, 1983.

Orvell, Miles and D. Powell. 'Myles na Gopaleen: Mystic, Horse-doctor, Hackney Journalist and Ideological Catalyst', *Éire-Ireland*, vol. 10, no. 2, Summer 1975, 44–72.

Orwell, George, 'Funny, But Not Vulgar' in Sonia Orwell and Ian Angus (eds.). *The Collected Essays, Journalism and Letters of George Orwelll, Vol. 3 As I Please 1943–1945*. London: Penguin, 1970, 324–29.

P.E. MacFh. 'Leabhra Nua. *An Béal Bocht*', *Ar Aghaidh*. (January 1942).

Peterson, R.F. 'Visionary Gleam: Corkery and the O'Connor Generation', *New Hibernia Review*, vol. 1, no. 3, Autumn 1997, 121–133.

Phelan, Michael. 'Watcher in the Wings: A Lingering Look at Myles na gCopaleen', *Administration*, vol. 24, no. 1, Spring 1976, 96–106.

Phillips, Robert, ed. *Aspects of Alice: Lewis Carroll's Dream-Child as seen through the Critics' Looking-Glasses, 1865–1971*. London: Gollancz, 1972.

Pilkington, Lionel. *Theatre and the State in Twentieth-Century Ireland*. London, New York: Routledge, 2001.

Pinsker, Sanford. 'Flann O'Brien's Uncles and Orphans', *Éire-Ireland*, vol. 20, no. 2, Summer 1985, 133–138.

Pirandello, Luigi. *On Humour*, Antonio Illiano and Daniel P. Testa (trans.). Chapel Hill: University of North Carolina, 1974.

—. *Six Characters in Search of an Author*, John Linstrum (trans.). London: Eyre Methuen, 1979.

Platt, Len. *James Joyce and the Anglo-Irish*. Amsterdam: Rodopi, 1998.

Polhemus, Robert H. *Comic Faith: The Great Tradition from Austen to Joyce*. Chicago, London: University of Chicago Press, 1980.

'Popshiúil Mairneálach'. 'Gaels in the Pillory. "An Béal Bocht"', *Dublin Evening Mail*. (24 December 1941).

Powell, David. 'An Annotated Bibliography of Myles na Gopaleen's (Flann O'Brien's) "Cruiskeen Lawn" Commentaries on Joyce', *James Joyce Quarterly*, vol. 9, no. 1, Fall 1971, 50–62.

Power, Mary. 'Flann O'Brien and Classical Satire: An Exegesis of *The Hard Life*', *Éire-Ireland*, vol. 13, no. 1, Spring 1978, 87–102.

—. 'The Figure of the Magician in *The Third Policeman* and *The Hard Life*', *Canadian Journal of Irish Studies*, vol. 8, no. 1, June 1982, 55–63.

Pritchard, William H. *Seeing Through Everything: English Writers 1918–1940*. London: Faber & Faber, 1977.

'Quidnunc' [Renagh Holohan]. 'A Holy Show', *The Irish Times*. (11 April 1998).

R.M.F. 'Round the Theatres', *The Evening Mail*. (26 January 1943).

—. 'Round the Theatres', *The Evening Mail*. (23 March 1943).

Read, Herbert (ed.). *Surrealism*. London: Faber & Faber, 1936, 1971.

—. 'On Subjective Art', *The Bell*, vol. 7, no. 5, February 1944, 424–429.

Riordan, Arthur. *Improbable Frequency*. London: Nick Hern, 2005.

Roche, Desmond. *Local Government in Ireland*. Dublin: Institute of Public Administration, 1982.

'Ruairí Beag'. 'Cúinne na Léirmheas: *An Béal Bocht*', *An Glór*. (17 January 1942).

Ryan, John (ed.). *A Bash in the Tunnel: James Joyce by the Irish*. Brighton: Clifton Books, 1970.

—. *Remembering How We Stood: Bohemian Dublin in the 1930s*. Dublin: Lilliput, 1975, 1997.

S.O'F. 'A New and Quaint Departure in Irish Literature', *The Nationalist and Munster Advertiser*. (7 January 1942).

Sewell, Elizabeth. *The Field of Nonsense*. London: Chatto & Windus, 1952.

Share, Bernard. *The Emergency: Neutral Ireland 1939–45*. Dublin: Gill & Macmillan, 1978.

Shea, Thomas F. 'Flann O'Brien and John Keats: "John Duffy's Brother" and Train Allusions', *Éire-Ireland*, vol. 24, no. 2, Summer 1989, 109–120.

—. *Flann O'Brien's Exorbitant Novels*. Lewisburg: Bucknell University Press, 1992.

Sheridan, Niall, Donagh MacDonagh. *Twenty Poems*. Dublin, 1934.

—. 'The Joyce Country', *Ireland To-day*, vol. 2, no. 11, November 1937, 88.

Shovlin, Frank. *The Irish Literary Periodical 1923–1958*. Oxford: Clarendon Press, 2003.

Silverthorne, J.M. 'Time, Literature and Failure: Flann O'Brien's *At Swim-Two-Birds* and *The Third Policeman*', *Éire-Ireland*, vol. 6, no. 4, Winter 1976, 66–83.

Smyth, Gerry. *Decolonisation and Criticism: The Construction of Irish Literature*. London: Pluto, 1998.

Smyth, Michael. '*Michael Smith* asks *Mervyn Wall* Some Questions About the Thirties', *The Lace Curtain*, no. 4, 1971, 77–86.

Spencer, Andrew. 'Many Worlds: The New Physics in Flann O'Brien's *The Third Policeman*', *Éire-Ireland*, vol. 30, no. 1, Spring 1995, 145–158.

Stewart, Susan. *Nonsense: Aspects of Intertextuality in Folklore and Art*. Baltimore, London: John Hopkins University Press, 1979.

Swift, Jonathan. *A Tale of a Tub and Other Works*, Angus Ross and David Woolley (eds). Oxford: Oxford University Press, 1986.

Swinnerton, Frank. 'Right Proportions', *The Observer*. (19 March 1939).

Sypher, Wylie (ed.). *Comedy*. London, Baltimore: John Hopkins University Press, 1980.

T. W. 'The Insect Play at the Gaiety', *The Irish Press*. (23 March 1943).

Thody, Philip. 'Lewis Carroll and the Surrealists', *Twentieth Century*, vol. 163, no. 975, May 1958, 427–434.

Thomson, Philip. *The Grotesque*. London: Methuen, 1972.

Throne, Marilyn. 'The Provocative Bicycle of *The Third Policeman*', *Éire-Ireland*, vol. 21, no. 4, Winter 1986, 36–44.

Tierney, Michael (ed.). *Struggle With Fortune*. Dublin: Browne & Nolan, 1954.

Tigges, Wim (ed.). *Explorations in the Field of Nonsense*. Amsterdam: Rodopi, 1987.

—. *An Anatomy of Literary Nonsense*. Amsterdam: Rodopi, 1988.

—. 'Ireland in Wonderland: Flann O'Brien's *The Third Policeman* as a Nonsense Novel', in C.C. Barfoot and Theo D'Haen (eds.). *The Clash of Ireland: Literary Contrasts and Connections*. Amsterdam: Rodopi, 1989, 195–208.

Titley, Alan. 'The Interpretation of Tradition', in Hilary Lennon (ed.), *Frank O'Connor: Critical Essays*. Dublin: Four Courts, 2007, 218–232.

Todorov, Tzvetan. *The Fantastic: A Structural Approach to a Literary Genre*, Richard Howard (trans.). Ithaca, New York: Cornell University Press, 1975.

Tymoczko, Maria. *The Irish Ulysses*. Berkeley: University of California Press, 1994.

Ua Cróinín, Seán. 'Myles na gCopaleen ar Seachran', *An Glór*. (29 April 1944).

University College Dublin. *Calendar 1931–1932*.

Vanderham, Paul. *James Joyce and Censorship: The Trials of Ulysses*. New York: New York University Press, 1998.

Voelker, Joseph C. '"Doublends Jined": The Fiction of Flann O'Brien', *Journal of Irish Literature*, vol.12, no. 1, January 1983, 87–95.

Wain, John. '"To Write for My Own Race": The Fiction of Flann O'Brien', *Encounter*, vol. 29, no. 1, July 1967, 71–85.

—. 'Flann and Myles', *Observer Review*. (8 September 1968).

Walsh, Dick. 'Magisterium of Chancers for the new Millenium', *The Irish Times*. (15 December 2001).

Walsh, John. *Díchoimisiúnú Teanga: Coimisiún na Gaeltachta 1926*. Dublin: Cois Life, 2002.

Wappling, Eva. *Four Irish Legendary Figures in At Swim-Two-Birds: A Study of Flann O'Brien's Use of Finn, Suibhne, the Pooka and the Good Fairy*. Uppsala: Studia Anglistica Upsaliensis, 1984.

Watts Jr, Richard. 'Guest Critic', *The Bell*, vol. 5, no. 6, March 1943, 482–487.

—. 'Flann O'Brien, Man of Names and Talents', *New York Herald Tribune*. (4 April 1943).

Waugh, Patricia. *Metafiction*. New York, London: Methuen, 1984.

Webb, W.L. 'Flann O'Brien's Misterpiece', *The Manchester Guardian*. (17 November 1961).

West, Anthony. 'New Novels', *The New Statesman and Nation*. (17 June 1939).

Wilde, Oscar. *Essays and Letters*, Merlin Holland (ed.). London: Folio, 1993.

Williams, Raymond. *Orwell*. London: Fontana, 1971.

Williams, Virginia Parrott. *Surrealism, Quantum Philosophy and World War One*. New York, London: Garland, 1987.

Wills, Claire. *That Neutral Island: A Cultural History of Ireland During the Second World War*. London: Faber & Faber, 2007.

Wong, Donna L. 'Following the Law of the Letter: Myles na gCopaleen's *An Béal Bocht*', *New Hibernia Review*, vol. 4, no. 3, Autumn 2000, 93–106.

Y.O. [George Russell]. 'Literature and Life: New Languages', *The Irish Statesman*. (25 August 1928), 493.

Index

This index covers the main body of the text, but not the notes and bibliography. The abbreviation BON refers to Brian O'Nolan, and Myles refers to Myles na gCopaleen. Titles of works are displayed in italics.